The Construction of Communalism
in Colonial North India

The Construction of Communalism in Colonial North India

Second Edition

Gyanendra Pandey

OXFORD
UNIVERSITY PRESS

OXFORD
UNIVERSITY PRESS

YMCA Library Building, Jai Singh Road, New Delhi 110001

Oxford University Press is a department of the University of Oxford.
It furthers the University's objective of excellence in research, scholarship,
and education by publishing worldwide in

Oxford New York
Auckland   Cape Town   Dar es Salaam   Hong Kong   Karachi
Kuala Lumpur   Madrid   Melbourne   Mexico City   Nairobi
New Delhi   Shanghai   Taipei   Toronto

With offices in
Argentina Austria Brazil Chile Czech Republic France Greece
Guatemala Hungary Italy Japan Poland Portugal Singapore
South Korea Switzerland Thailand Turkey Ukraine Vietnam

Oxford is a registered trade mark of Oxford University Press
in the UK and in certain other countries

Published in India
by Oxford University Press, New Delhi

© Oxford University Press 2006

ISBN-13: 978-0-19-568364-6
ISBN-10: 0-19-568364-1

Printed in India at Rashtriya Printers, Delhi 110 032
Published by Manzar Khan, Oxford University Press
YMCA Library Building, Jai Singh Road, New Delhi 110 001

Contents

Preface to the Second Edition

The appearance of the second edition of a study published fifteen years ago raises questions about how much one should change in the work. There is some advantage in revising and updating the text to take account of subsequent political developments and writings. Yet what this often requires is a new book, very different from the original. If there was something of value in the original work, or in the context of its production, there is something to be said for retaining its particular positionality and perspective. Following the advice of my publisher and close academic friends, who believe that there is still a demand for this book in the form in which it first appeared, I have left the text unchanged except for the correction of a few typographical errors. What I have done instead is to write a new Preface and an Afterword that may meet some of the expectations of revision in the light of subsequent developments.

Although I am well aware that authorial intentions are far from being alone or even primary in shaping the way in which a text is received, this preface seeks, through a consideration of some of the criticisms of the first edition of this work, to clarify a few of the arguments I attempted to put forward in it. The Afterword seeks to carry the discussion further through an analysis of the uses of the category of communalism in a postcolonial world in which contradictory trends are plainly evident and the divergence between academic and popular political discourses is once again marked. On the one hand, then, in the academic domain, the idea of the 'naturalness' and sanctity of the national community is extensively questioned. On the other, in a wider political arena, assumptions regarding the national interest, and the need for all other communities to conform to the national project, are still taken for granted. Far from being eroded, the sanctity of the nation has—in Marx's compelling phrase—acquired the fixity of a popular prejudice.

When it first appeared in 1990, this book was swimming against the tide of historiographical orthodoxy. In some ways, I suspect, it still does. Some critics of the study jumped on its title and concluded that in my hands 'communalism', or 'communalisms' as some of them prefer to have it (meaning thereby distinct entities called 'Hindu communalism' and 'Muslim communalism'), were ultimately attributable to colonial discourses, 'the product of Western, colonial power–knowledge and its classificatory strategies.'[1] The suggestion is that my interpretation had somehow reduced 'real' happenings on the ground, real differences and real conflicts, to a matter of conceptualization, and made communalism—like caste in the hands of some other postcolonial scholars—into a phantom product of discourse, and above all of colonial discourse and its classificatory strategies.

Reading such responses, I have sometimes wondered whether the critics had bothered to read beyond the title of the book. How else could they fail to notice that when I described communalism as 'a form of colonialist knowledge', I added immediately that anti-colonialist nationalists were in the forefront of those who promoted its use (p. 6). How could they overlook that my object of enquiry was the category itself—notice the reference to 'colonialist *knowledge*' in the above statement—as much as the politics it was supposed to describe, and the edge that the acceptance of such a category gave to this kind of politics? Or forget that I had stressed the adjacency of nationalism and communalism, and argued that politics described in these terms overlapped and fed on one another?

The critics in question would be the last to suggest that anti-colonial nationalism was the gift of colonialism, even if the fact of colonial domination was its necessary ground. It is not clear to me why the contention that the colonialist intervention was crucial to the emergence of communalist categories, communalist organization, and the category of communalism itself, reduces communalist politics to the handiwork of colonialism. My point about communalism as a colonial mode

---

[1] See, for example, Sumit Sarkar, *Writing Social History* (Delhi, 1997), pp. 44, 98, 361; also Pradip Kumar Datta, *Carving Blocs: Communal Ideology in Early Twentieth Century Bengal* (Delhi, 1999), p. 17 and *passim*.

of thought or representation is that it was the product of a colonial interpretation of history in which religious assemblages (especially 'Hindus' and 'Muslims') existed as sharply differentiated and always already constituted and antagonistic communities, whose history consisted in periodic bouts of bloodletting.

I argued that nationalists stayed with the proposition of separatism, antagonism, and violence as the constitutive elements of communalism. They attributed the growth of these elements to the machinations of the colonial power, although sometimes, in some hands, deeper and longer-lasting memories and perceptions were also seen to be at work. More to the point, the nationalists stereotyped this kind of (communalist) political tendency as a discrete and substantive entity, which was the other of nationalism (another substance). They failed thereby to fully appreciate its force, its tentativeness or its complexity. Secular nationalist historiography in India has by and large adhered to this position, treating communalism as an isolated entity, a distinct phenomenon (or two distinct phenomena—'Hindu communalism' and 'Muslim communalism'),[2] lurking out there, in the field, on the streets and perhaps in people's heads, awaiting the attention of the historian, the ethnographer, the journalist, and the political activist.

What this view neglects too easily are the processes and articulations by which these political positions arose, the historical contexts that made them possible, and the conflicting and often ambiguous traits that characterized them and served to make them what they were. Rather than seeing communalism in this way as a thing-like creature, sharply distinguished from nationalism and other transformative struggles of the colonial period, what I had suggested was that these were contradictory yet related ways of conceptualizing the political world, thinking political futures and fighting for particular political arrangements.[3] 'The investigation of communalism must ... be part of a larger exercise,' as I wrote, 'aimed at understanding the construction of Indian society and politics in recent times.' It must take account

[2] Why not, one might ask, Sikh, Christian, Parsi, Brahmin, non-Brahmin, and other 'communalisms' too?

[3] I revisit these propositions and elaborate them further in the Afterword.

not only of sectarian mobilization and demands made on the basis of putative differences between people adhering loosely to diverse religious denominations, but of class and caste antagonisms, colonialist and nationalist perceptions and interventions, and more (p. 5 and *passim*).

Since 1990, there has been a flurry of publications on the history of inter-communal relations and religious/sectarian (or communalist) strife, ranging from Hindu and Muslim organization and mobilization in the later nineteenth and early twentieth centuries, to the violence of Partition, to the emergence of a powerful and aggressive new Hindu movement in India in the 1980s and 1990s. It is not my purpose to survey this literature here. The reader will get some sense of the debates, and a guide to further reading, from a reference to some of the more general works.

On the later nineteenth and early twentieth centuries, see Peter van der Veer, *Religious Nationalism: Hindus and Muslims in India* (Berkeley, 1994), and Tanika Sarkar, *Hindu Wife, Hindu Nation: Community, Religion, and Cultural Nationalism* (Delhi, 2001). I should also mention two important monographic studies: Pradip Kumar Datta's *Carving Blocs: Communal Ideology in Early Twentieth Century Bengal* (Delhi, 1999) and Anshu Malhotra's *Gender, Caste and Religious Identities: Restructuring Class in Colonial Punjab* (Delhi, 2002). For the plethora of new writings on Partition, the bibliographies contained in Mushirul Hasan's two edited volumes, *India's Partition: Process, Strategy and Mobilization* (Delhi, 1993) and *Inventing Boundaries: Gender, Politics and the Partition of India* (Delhi, 2000); and in my *Remembering Partition: Violence, Nationalism and History in India* (Cambridge, 2001) provide a useful starting point.

On the most recent phase of communalist mobilization and conflict, there is a good deal more. Tanika Sarkar and Urvashi Butalia, eds, *Women and the Hindu Right* (Delhi, 1995); Kaushik Basu and Sanjay Subrahmanyam, eds, *Unravelling the Nation: Sectarian Conflict and India's Secular Identity* (Delhi, 1996); David Ludden, ed., *Contesting the Nation: Religion, Community and the Politics of Democracy in India* (Delhi, 1996); Thomas Blom Hansen, *Saffron Wave: Democracy and Hindu Nationalism in Modern India* (Princeton, 1999); Amrita Basu and Atul Kohli, eds, *Community*

Conflicts and the State in India (Delhi, 2000); Ashutosh Varshney, *Ethnic Conflict and Civic Life: Hindus and Muslims in India* (New Haven, 2002); Sumit Sarkar, *Beyond Nationalist Frames: Postmodernism, Hindu Fundamentalism, History* (Delhi, 2002); and Paul Brass and Achin Vanaik, eds, *Competing Nationalisms in South Asia: Essays for Asghar Ali Engineer* (Delhi, 2002) are just a few examples.

There is in this new literature a far greater recognition than ever before of the need to study communalism and its history not in isolation from other political trends of the colonial and postcolonial period, but as part of a complex of caste, class, community, and nationalist mobilizations; and gender has emerged as a significant category of analysis. Scholars have emphasized, to take one important area of investigation, that existing studies of communalism fail to adequately differentiate between different castes involved in these events, or notice that the lower castes were at times the targets of attack, or (alternatively) that the lower castes were sometimes mobilized against upper-caste and upper-class (and occasionally also lower-caste) others by a variety of means. In some writings dealing with the Hindu–Muslim violence and the caste politics of the 1990s,[4] it is even suggested that caste is the *real* contradiction in Indian society, and that it is the violence of upper castes against lower castes (and, presumably, vice versa) that is often deflected into communalist, inter-religious strife.

Yet, the fact of the matter is that the violence of inter-caste oppression hardly cancels out that of inter-communal oppression and conflict. What we require is close attention to both, and to other cognate areas of conflict and strife, in order to produce richly textured studies of these multiple frames and multiple truth-claims. What is perhaps not very well understood even now is the necessity of examining the particular discourses and interventions that helped to establish the salience and power

[4]Mandir vs Mandal, as it has been dubbed, in reference to the right-wing Hindu campaign to destroy a 16th century mosque and build a new temple at the claimed site of the birth of Lord Ram in Ayodhya, as against the politics of the lower castes (especially those belonging to the Other Backward Classes) who were given new state support through the implementation at the centre of the Mandal Commission's recommendations for an extension of the advantages of reservations to these castes.

of these different constituencies: caste, class, community, and nation. Serious students of communalism still need to investigate the rise of the concept, the vocabulary and the discourse of communalism, along with—and as part of—its politics. As I have argued in this book, the discourse is as much part of the politics as any notion of real, lived experience. The two cannot be separated. And this applies to caste and its politics as much as to Hindu–Muslim, Muslim–Sikh, or Hindu–Sikh conflict and violence.

One other feature of recent left-wing and secular writings on sectarian (inter-communal) strife calls for some comment; and that is its crushing presentism. The 'big why' issue for the historiography of communalism has changed from the question 'Why Partition?' to 'Why Hindutva?' Scholars have focused overwhelmingly on the contemporary—Mandir vs. Mandal, Hindutva, the Sangh Parivar, the recurrent rounds of large-scale violence since the 1980s—and sought to read these developments back into history, just as they once did with Partition. There is a strange short-sightedness, and a peculiar inattention to history, in the effort to draw a straight line between the arrogant Hindu movement of today and the Hindu politics of Tilak, Aurobindo, *et al*, in the late nineteenth century, or various developments in western and central India in the early twentieth (with the writing of Savarkar's *Hindutva* during the First World War and the foundation of the RSS in 1925).[5]

I had noted with regard to earlier writings which suggested that the structure of 'communalism' might already be observed in northern India as early as the eighteenth century, that they lacked any real sense of context (p. 15). Exactly the same point might be made in relation to much of the historical writing that has appeared in the wake of the ascendancy of an aggressive right-

---

[5]As Sanjay Sharma notes in a review of Charu Gupta's *Sexuality, Obscenity, Community: Women, Muslims, and the Hindu Public in Colonial India* (Delhi, 2001), 'So anxious ... is the author about the present rise of Hindutva politics ... that for her the past seems relevant only as a backward extension of the present;' *Indian Economic and Social History Review* (*IESHR*), 42, 1 (2005), p. 133. Cf. also Gyan Prakash's review of Sumit Sarkar's *Beyond Nationalist Frames: Postmodernism, Hindu Fundamentalism, History* (Delhi, 2002) in *IESHR*, 41, 3 (2004), pp. 339–41.

wing Hindu movement in the 1980s and 90s. There is little place for historical complexity or contradictory trends in this kind of history, far less an appreciation of the fact that the results we see, the precipitations of past conflicts and contradictions, the new social, political, and intellectual formations, are not already contained in the 'causes'.[6]

It is striking to me that, in spite of all the talk of history and the battle over the nation's past, we have had so little in the way of detailed historical monographs examining inter-communal relations on the ground, in different places, among different classes, during the nineteenth and twentieth centuries, let alone for an earlier period. Given this absence of sustained historical inquiry, and consequent lack of historical depth, many of the questions raised in the first edition of *The Construction of Communalism in Colonial North India* remain to be investigated further. If this second edition of the book serves to re-open these questions, and to carry forward the debate on the political violence of our times, the targeting of minorities, and the status of history in all of this, it will have served its purpose.

Gyanendra Pandey
September 2005

[6]For an elaboration of this point, see my *Remembering Partition: Violence, Nationalism and History in India* (Cambridge, 2001), ch. 3.

Preface to the First Edition

Two words of explanation are perhaps necessary at the beginning of this book. One about why I continue to use the term 'communalism', with or without inverted commas, in spite of my argument (in chapter 1) that it is loaded and obfuscating. The answer is that the needs of communication, and of a convenient shorthand, have dictated this. The term has passed into the political and historiographical vocabulary in India: and while we can, and in my opinion must, question its use, finding other ways of talking about the experiences and ideas sometimes described as 'communalism' is not very easy. I have spoken in this book of 'sectarian politics' and 'sectarian strife', but it would have seemed precious to use 'sectarianism' for 'communalism' as a description of those sectarian and exclusivist trends that have been so evident, and dangerous, a feature of recent Indian history. What I would emphasize, however, is that the use of the term 'communalism' remains an heuristic device; that both the term and the politics and attitudes that it seeks to encapsulate have a history which can be charted; and that the boundaries separating these attitudes and politics from others existing at the same time are not as clear as has generally been supposed.

A second question that may be raised is what prompted the choice of the area and the period—the Bhojpuri-speaking tract of eastern UP and western Bihar from the early nineteenth to the early twentieth centuries—from which this study draws its evidence. Is the choice entirely arbitrary? Would another area or period have done as well? For dates, I see no real alternative—since it is the later nineteenth and early twentieth centuries that saw the development of 'modern' politics in India, including both nationalism and communalism. I have stretched back into the early nineteenth century to examine the record of Hindu-Muslim relations at an earlier stage, and how this was written about; and I have stretched forward into the 1930s and even 1940s where this helped to show

how the character of 'nationalism' and 'communalism' has changed in the subcontinent—at times dramatically.

The choice of area is a different matter. The Bhojpur region is one with which I already had some acquaintance, and one that I had studied to some extent before research specifically related to this book began. It is likely that other areas would have served equally well for a study of this kind. But the choice of this particular tract has certain advantages. It is part of that north Indian belt where separate 'Hindu' and 'Muslim' politics first developed. Colonial observers from an early date paid special attention to Banaras, a focal point of this area—for Banaras was, to them, the Mecca of the East, the Holy City of the Hindus, the quintessence of India. The central place of the city in the rise of the Hindi movement, the demand for a Hindu university, and the conservative culture of the entire region standing paradoxically against its militant participation in nationalist (and, later, socialist) politics lend a special interest to its study.

The specificities of the region, however, need to be carefully borne in mind. Neither Banaras, nor Bhojpur, is representative—or typical—of India. If the historical record is somewhat fuller here than it might be in many other places, it is also subject to very great distortion. I should note, too, that the UP/Bihar bias of this study has led to certain emphases which a Bengal or Maharashtra or Andhra bias is unlikely to have produced. I have written, for example, in chapters 6 and 7 of how the early nationalists saw India as a composite of Hindu + Muslim + Parsi + Christian, etc. I think, on reflection, that a different kind of emphasis would have arisen had I been studying some other region.

The underlining of the composite character of Indian culture, and Indian nationalism, is likely to have been greater in the Urdu/Hindi speaking belt of northern India where a sophisticated Indo-Muslim court culture had developed, where Hindus and Muslims (elite and non-elite) shared a good deal at the level of their quotidian social existence and cultural practice, and where (as I have already noted) competition between 'Hindu' and 'Muslim' arose rather earlier than it did elsewhere. In Bengal, for example, with its predominantly Hindu elite, there was not quite the same need to articulate nationalism in terms of Hindu *plus* Muslim until a some-what later date. Thus for Bankimchandra Chattopadhyaya, and even for Rabindranath Tagore until we come to *Gora*, Indian nationalism could quite unproblematically be a Hindu nationalism. The search for a 'higher' nationalism which historians have talked of, and which I mention at the end of chapter 6, becomes in Bengal the search for a nationalism that goes beyond the 'pre-existing' (Hindu) community, rather than beyond a coalition of existing communities—which is what it had to be over much of UP and Bihar.

Readers will observe that I have far more to say in the following pages about the 'Hindu' politics of the later nineteenth and early twentieth centuries than about the 'Muslim'. In part this is the product of a geographical and chronological quirk; for in the domain of institutionalized politics, the Bhojpuri region at the turn of the century was richer in 'Hindu' associations and movements than in 'Muslim' ones. In part it is the product of a historiographical accident—that 'Hindu' politics in the late nineteenth and early twentieth centuries had been far less throughly investigated than the 'Muslim' politics of the same period, a circumstance that has changed to some extent since this study was begun several years ago.

Since I shall nevertheless almost inevitably invite the charge of having been especially hard on Hindu politicians and publicists, while letting their Muslim counterparts off lightly, I must state categorically at this point that the act of balancing 'Hindu communalism' against 'Muslim communalism', one 'Hindu' atrocity against one 'Muslim' atrocity (with an example of 'Sikh' atrocity perhaps thrown in for good measure), which is a favourite recipe of liberalism in our day, is no part of the present exercise. A single experience of 'communalist' politics, looked at closely, may after all tell us a good deal about the construction of the category, and about its uses and abuses. Which is not to say that we do not need a much wider range of detailed studies of 'Hindu', 'Muslim', 'Sikh' and other politics. Obviously, the exact opposite is the case.

Finally I should state that this book is concerned not only with what is commonly taken to be the 'actual' historical experience of the people—that is, the social, economic and political struggles in which they were involved and which relate to the question of 'Hindu' or 'Muslim' politics. I am at least equally concerned with another aspect of their 'actual' historical experience, which has been relatively neglected in studies of nationalism and communalism. What I have tried to do is to investigate the meanings that different participants in the sectarian politics of the period—local Hindus and Muslims, nationalist spokesmen, colonial officials— attached to these politics. Indeed I do not believe that the two exercises can be separated. To put it in other words, my concern is not only with social, economic and political 'facts', if somehow we could isolate them, but also with how historians, administrators, politicians (and, for that matter, the 'people' about whom we know least of all) have isolated 'facts' and served them up as 'history'.

I must acknowledge my considerable debt to friends, colleagues, and 'local informants' who have contributed so greatly to the making of this book. Numerous people in Banaras, Azamgarh and Arrah gave generously of their time and knowledge. Without them this study could not have been undertaken. I must mention with special gratitude again for his learning, sympathy, and great hospitality, Qazi Atahar Mubarakpuri.

My colleagues in the editorial team of *Subaltern Studies*—Shahid Amin, David Arnold, Gautam Bhadra, Dipesh Chakrabarty, Partha Chatterji, David Hardiman, Ranajit Guha, Sumit Sarkar— have watched this book grow almost as closely as I have. Many of their ideas will have entered here, and I can only hope that I have not done them great injustice. My debt to the entire team is immense.

Colleagues at the Centre for Studies in Social Sciences, Calcutta, generously discussed many of the early formulations that have, in modified form, gone into this study. I remember with particular gratitude the criticism and encouragement of Javed Alam, Amiya Bagchi, Barun De, Partha Chatterji, Amalendu Guha, Saugata Mukherji, Asok Sen, and the late Indrani Ray and Hitesranjan Sanyal, whose untimely deaths have been a severe loss to Indian history.

Other friends and colleagues—Sudhir Chandra, Veena Das, Friedhelm Hardy, Sudipto Kaviraj, Kumkum Sangari—have read and commented most helpfully on the manuscript. My debt to other scholars who have worked and written on related questions will be evident from the footnotes, but I should like to mention particularly Chris Bayly, Sandria Frietag and Anand Yang for their help with criticism and information. My students at the University of Delhi over the last three years might not realize how much they have contributed as the first 'readers' of this book: I am most grateful to them.

I owe special thanks to Anu, Jayanti and Gitanjali for much gentle criticism and unfailing support; to my parents and to my brother and his family for all they have done.

I wish to acknowledge also the kindness of the librarians, archivists and other staff at the National Archives of India, the Nehru Memorial Museum and Library, the India Office Library, the West Bengal State Archives, UP State Archives at Lucknow, the UP Regional Archives at Allahabad, and the Commissioner's Record Room in Gorakhpur. Finally, the staff of OUP New Delhi have made the process of producing this book a pleasure, at least for its author.

Delhi, March 1990   GYANENDRA PANDEY

Abbreviations

BSCRO	Bihar State Central Records Office, Patna
CSSH	*Comparative Studies in Society and History*
CWMG	*Collected Works of Mahatma Gandhi*
IESHR	*Indian Economic and Social History Review*
IOL	India Office Library and Records, London
JAS	*Journal of Asian Studies*
MAS	*Modern Asian Studies*
NAI	National Archives of India, New Delhi
NWP & O	North-Western Provinces and Oudh (later known as the United Provinces)
RNP	Report on Native Newspapers (also called 'Selections from Vernacular Newspapers' for certain periods)
SWJN	*Selected Works of Jawaharlal Nehru*
UP	Uttar Pradesh (earlier known as the United Provinces of Agra and Awadh)
UPSA	Uttar Pradesh State Archives, Lucknow

Glossary

amil	government appointed revenue official: hence *amaldari*, official position
ashraf	plural of *sharif* (q.v.)
balwa	riot
begar	forced, unpaid labour
bhakta	worshipper, follower, often used to refer to the poets and saints associated with the so-called Bhakti movement
bigha	measure of land, in UP generally 5/8 of an acre
biradari	lit. 'brotherhood'; clan or kinship network
chaudhri	leader, headman
chutki	a system of contributions used in the Cow-Protection movement, and in later political movements, whereby porters set aside one *chutki* (or pinch) of grain daily for the cause
daroga	local-level police official, in-charge of a police station (cf. *thanedar*, q.v.)
dharma	religion; duty enjoined by one's position
dharmapatri	lit. 'religious circular', note or message enjoining particular actions in the name of religion
dharna	sit-down strike
farman	injunction, order, edict
fatwa	ruling given by a Muslim judge or theologian (*mufti*)
gaushala	home for cattle
hartal	strike, suspension of all business
jati	caste or sub-caste; at the turn of the century, also sometimes used for nation (rather like *qaum*, q.v.)
kaliyuga	in Hindu mythology the fourth and most degenerate age of human history

karkhana	workshop
lathi	a bamboo staff: hence *lathial*, person employed for protection or enlargement of a patron's interests
mahajan	wealthy trader or moneylender
mahtar/mahto	leader or headman
malik	owner, landowner
marsia	poetic composition relating the story of the martyrdom of Imams Hasan and Husain at the Karbala
mauza	village, revenue-paying unit
mazar	grave, tomb of a Muslim saint or revered person
minnat	prayer, accompanied by promise of a specified offering if the prayer is fulfilled
mleccha	non-Hindu, untouchable
mohalla	locality, ward of a town
mukhtar	legal agent not possessing the right to plead in a district or higher court
namaz	canonical prayer, enjoined on Muslims five times a day
naukri	service; usually refers to salaried employment away from one's home, village or town
panchayat	court of arbitrators, usually consisting of a community's elders; traditionally, their number was supposed to be fire (*panch*—hence *panchayat*)
patia (patra)	leaflet, letter; used here for circular or 'snowball' letters
phatakbandi	shutting of the entrance gate; a system of security used in Banaras and other towns for securing the property and people of a *mohalla* (q.v.) at night and other times of danger
pir	Sufi saint or religious leader able to guide disciples on the mystical way
qasba	small town
qaum	people, nation, also used for community

qurbani	sacrifice, here used for the ritual killing of cows at the Baqr Id
rais	notable
raiyat	subject, tenant (pl. *riyaya*)
razil	labouring ('lowly') people
sajjada nashin	person in-charge of a Muslim shrine or 'seat of prayer' (from *sajjada*, seat from where the *namaz*, q.v., is read, the seat of a Muslim saint or *pir*, q.v.)
sangathan	organization; here used for Hindu organization in defence of 'Hindu' interests
shankh	conch-shell, sounded by Hindus at prayer-time
shivalaya	small temple dedicated to Shiva
shuddhi	purification; Hindu movement in the later nineteenth and twentieth centuries to reclaim those who had converted from Hinduism to other religions
tabligh	a movement seeking conversions to Islam
tahsil	revenue sub-division of a district, in the charge of a *tahsildar*
taluqa	estate
tanzim	call for Muslim organization to promote education and unity among Muslims
tazia	model of the tombs of Imam Hasan and Imam Husain carried in procession on the occasion of Muharram
thakurdwara	small temple
thana	police station: hence *thanedar*—officer in-charge of a police station
thekedar	contractor; temporary manager or agent
varna	lit. 'colour'; the four major divisions of Hindu society into Brahmans, Kshatriyas, Vaishyas and Sudras (the 'untouchables' constitute a fifth category, which was outside the pale of classical Hindu society)
waqea	event, occurrence, incident
zamindar	landowner, individually or jointly engaged to pay land revenue and receive rent

Chapter One

Introduction

History is the self-consciousness of a nation
—Friedrich von Schlegel

All histories written over the last century or so have been national histories. It is not surprising, therefore, that the national movement should have dominated the historiography of modern India. If the history of communalism has sometimes seemed to occupy an equally important place, the reason for this too lies in the idea of nationalism entertained by historians of India. Communalism acquires its remarkable prominence in a certain kind of historical writing, beginning with the work of conservative colonialist writers at the turn of the century, because it is seen as being a subcontinental version of nationalism—the nearest thing to the genuine article that the South Asian region could produce. As Louis Dumont puts it, 'Communalism . . . gets the edge of its meaning through the parallelism with the other term: it is something like nationalism',[1] without of course being the same thing.

For the generality of colonialist writers, nationalism, nationness, was a Western attribute, unlikely to be found or easily replicated in the East.[2] In its developed form this perspective was established fairly late, only towards the end of the nineteenth century, when nationalism had emerged clearly as the discourse

---

[1] L. Dumont, 'Nationalism and Communalism' in *Religion/Politics and History in India* (Paris, 1970), p. 90.

[2] Conservative theorists of nationalism would appear to hold this view until today: see esp. E. Kedourie, *Nationalism* (London, 1969); also his edited *Nationalism in Asia and Africa* (New York, 1970), introduction. For a discussion of 'good' and 'bad' nationalism, as found in the work of such theorists, see Partha Chatterjee, *Nationalist Thought in the Colonial World: A Derivative Discourse?* (London and Delhi, 1986), chpt. 1.

of the age and strong nationalist stirrings against colonialism were beginning to be felt in India. Before then, interestingly enough, terms like 'race', 'nation', 'nationality' and 'class' (more commonly in the plural form) were regularly used by colonial writers and administrators in the subcontinent to describe groups as diverse as Rajputs, Sikhs, Muslims and Bhils. As late as the 1890s, the various groups of labourers recruited for the tea plantations in Assam were being described as belonging to different nationalities—Bhojpuri, Chota Nagpuri, Bengali, and so on. The comparatively bland term 'community' came to be far more commonly used after this, although it did not replace the notion of races, tribes and nationalities altogether. One reason for this choice appears to have been the fact that, in the Darwinian age, 'race' acquired a more specifically biological usage and 'nation' came to be appropriated for exclusive use by the new nation-states of Europe—and hence was consciously denied to the people or peoples of India.[3]

When, under the pressure of political events at a later stage, the 'national' quality was conceded as having some applicability to India, it was conceded grudgingly and in apparent recognition of what might be termed an Eastern form of nationalism. Theodore Morison spoke for a wide range of colonialist opinion when he wrote in 1932:

It is useless to enumerate the grounds of difference between Hindu and Muslim; the only thing that matters is that they do in fact feel and think of themselves as separate peoples. In all disquisitions on nationality this is the only test which is found to cover all cases.... Judged by this standard the Muslims of India are a nation. Communal differences, as they are called, are really national jealousies.[4]

Communalism, in this view, was nationalism.

For Indian nationalists, on the other hand, communalism was (and is) important precisely because it was *not* nationalism. Communalism was, in common with colonialism, the Other of nationalism, its opposite, its chief adversary, and hence a necessary

---

[3] I owe this point to David Arnold. For different European uses of the word 'nation' up to the nineteenth century, see Friedrich Meinecke, *Cosmopolitanism and the National State* (1907, tr. Princeton, 1963), pp. 23–4.

[4] Theodore Morison, 'Muhammedan Movements', in J. Cumming, ed., *Political India* (London, 1932).

part of the story of nation-building in India. Communalism was a blight on the body politic; for nationalists in India, like nationalists the world over in the later-nineteenth and early-twentieth centuries, saw nation-ness as *natural*, the heritage of every people, given by birth: '*Swaraj* is my birth-right', in Tilak's categorical phrase. For both colonialists and nationalists in India at the turn of the century, then, the quality of nation-ness was not only supreme but also concrete, identifiable and fixed. Both, it may be suggested, suffered from an insufficient appreciation of the historical struggles that had gone to produce specific nationalisms and nations, from a belief in some pure model of nationhood, deviations from which were by definition unacceptable. The problem remains, however: how is one to characterize the specificities of Indian nationalism, or of Indian politics in the age of nationalism?

Everywhere in the world the formation of modern nationalism has been propelled by contradictory forces. Yet these contradictions seem to stand out far more in India than in parallel European cases (Italy or Germany, for example), a consequence that is attributable to the size and diversity of the country and the particular historical circumstances in, and against, which Indian nationalism arose. Colonial India saw the persistence of many pre-capitalist economic forms and the attendant social diversities. It contained a vast range of regional conditions, cultures and interests. And its people now experienced a peculiar combination of 'modern' (colonial) and 'medieval' (colonial as well as pre-colonial) modes of domination and exploitation. In this context, a new cohesion developed around existing foci of loyalty, such as caste, language and religious community, even as a new national consciousness arose. This is where the concept of communalism came into play.

We may return to Dumont's sophisticated essay on 'Nationalism and Communalism' to appreciate the extent to which the intellectual problem has appeared to be the same to all varieties of historians and social scientists over a very long period. 'In communalism', writes Dumont, 'elements of both worlds [political entities of the traditional kind, on the one hand, and the modern nation, on the other] are mixed . . . [though] the main trend is perhaps modern.' Communalism appears as a 'hybrid, or intermediary, perhaps a transitory phenomenon'. But communalism is fundamentally 'ambiguous': 'It can finally appear either as a genuine transition to the nation, or as an attempt on the part of religion to oppose the transformation by allowing for the external appearances of a modern state.'[5]

An important aspect of the modern nation or state, according to Dumont, is the differentiation between population and territory. Territory here becomes 'a necessary attribute of the people, part of the cognitive and normative aspect of the system'; a necessary factor of the 'individuation' which is 'part of the very essence of the system'. With the replacement of the king as sovereign, 'Dharma is . . . replaced by the People as a collective individual mirroring itself in a territory.'[6] After making this theoretical proposition, Dumont appears to slide into an essentialism which is surprising. It would appear, from the last part of his essay, that the capacity for 'individuation' of religion, politics and social life, and for differentiation between people and territory, is inborn—among some nations. Dumont describes the notion of territoriality as being foreign to Indians, citing as evidence the ancient Hindu kingdoms, yet taking no account of Bharatvarsha, Jambudwipa, Hindustan and other such conceptions of a people's territory that the historical and anthropological record in India is full of. Then, even more surprisingly, he suggests that the notion of territoriality was suddenly brought into play at the end of the 1930s, presented to and, rather miraculously, accepted by the 'Muslims of India' as the appropriate form for the realization of their ideals as a community.[7] All this is based, of course, on the recognition—one might say assumption—of the 'duality' of India and the 'separateness' of the Hindus and the Muslims. 'The transition [from traditional to modern political forms]', Dumont concludes, 'is difficult, and has given rise to intermediary forms.'[8]

Thus Dumont returns, in the end, to the *given*, the *pure* form of the 'modern'—nationalism and the modern nation-state. What

---

[5] Dumont, *Religion/Politics and History*, pp. 93–4.

[6] Ibid., pp. 106–9.

[7] Ibid., p. 109. The point to note is that if the notion of territoriality was foreign to Indians, it was presumably doubly foreign to the Muslims of India for whom the sphere of Islam was surely coextensive with the world. Dumont himself notes, in passing, the opposition of Islamic tradition to the 'territorial state', ibid.

[8] Ibid., p. 110.

the focus on communalism does, even in his subtle analysis, is to typify the subcontinent as essentially different. What it tends to do much more obviously in other cases is to *reduce Indian history to a deviation from the model.* The specificities of the Indian experience have little chance of being explored thoroughly in, such a strait-jacket. The struggles of peoples all over the subcontinent, at every level of society, to make sense of a world radically altered by colonialism, to redefine their place in this world, and to forge new visions of 'the ideal kingdom', are reduced to the play of a predetermined nationalism and communalism. In the historical writings on South Asia, colonialist and nationalist, and in most of their modern versions as well, nationalism and the nation, and communalism too, emerge (at whatever stage they emerge) fully blown and even unalterable. They are not seen, or at least not treated adequately, as forces and conceptions that are the outcome of historical processes, arising over time, out of the diverse struggles of diverse peoples, in historical circumstances that were exceptional and yet, for all their uniqueness, pregnant with many possibilities.

Since this is the historiographical record, it seems necessary to stress, first, that it will not do to look at the question of communalism in isolation. Communalism in India is another characteristic and paradoxical product of the age of Reason (and of Capital) which also gave us colonialism and nationalism. It derives its meaning precisely from the political discourse which arises in that particular age, in this particular colonial country. 'Communalism' has appeared in this discourse as perhaps the central problem to be overcome in the development of a self-governing, national and democratic polity in India. The investigation of communalism must therefore be part of a larger exercise aimed at understanding the construction of Indian society and politics in recent times.

It is for this reason that the present study of communalism stretches into a consideration of many different aspects of this society and its politics, some more and some less obviously related to the central object of analysis: class relations in the towns and countryside, caste-uplift movements, the methods of mobilization in many different kinds of popular movements, the colonialist and nationalist outlook on the world—and especially the world of the lower classes. From a variety of starting points, this book seeks to examine the conditions, the character and (to a lesser extent) the consequences of what has been called 'communal' conflict in nineteenth and early-twentieth-century India. At the same time, it seeks to analyse a particular construction of knowledge about Indian society—the construction of a sociology and a history that is fairly well summed up in the term 'communalism'.

In other words, I hope to explore the history of the 'problem' of communalism through an examination of the discourse that gave it meaning. What follows, therefore, is by no means a comprehensive history of Hindu–Muslim (or Hindu–Sikh/Muslim–Sikh) relations in colonial north India, nor even in the region and period from where the study draws most of its evidence, namely the Bhojpuri-speaking districts of eastern Uttar Pradesh (U.P.) and western Bihar from the early-nineteenth to the early-twentieth centuries. It is rather an attempt to examine what we accomplish when we apply the term 'communalism' to this history, what remains hidden behind the term and what, if anything, it illuminates.

II

'Communalism', I would like to suggest, is a form of colonialist knowledge. The concept stands for the puerile and the primitive—all that colonialism, in its own reckoning, was not. The paradox is that the nationalists have done more than anyone else to propagate its use.

In its common Indian usage the word 'communalism' refers to a condition of suspicion, fear and hostility between members of different religious communities. In academic investigations, more often than not, the term is applied to organized political movements based on the proclaimed interests of a religious community, usually in response to a real or imagined threat from another religious community (or communities). It denotes movements that make sectional demands on state policy for a given share in jobs, education and legislative positions, leading on in some instances to demands for the creation of new provinces and states.

'The opposition to each other of religious communities is commonly designated as communalism', Dumont tells us in his essay on 'Nationalism and Communalism'. He goes on immediately, however, in the very next sentence, to define the term more cautiously in words first used by W. C. Smith in the early 1940s, as 'that ideology which emphasized as the social, political, and economic unit the group of adherents of each religion; and emphasizes the distinction, even the antagonism, between such groups.'[9] Bipan Chandra has reproduced this definition for us recently: 'Communalism is the belief that because a group of people follow a particular religion they have, as a result, common social, political and economic interests.'[10]

Let us note straightaway that the term 'communalism' is never applied in this sense to feudal Europe or other pre-capitalist societies where religiosity was no narrower and strife between members of different religious persuasions not rare; nor for that matter to the bloody conflict between Protestants and Catholics in Northern Ireland which persists to this day. The Indian meaning of the term has a certain noteworthy flexibility. 'Communalism' can refer to Hindu–Muslim or Hindu–Sikh conflict in northern India, Brahman–non-Brahman conflict in southern and western India, Sinhala–Tamil conflict in Sri Lanka, conflicts between Malays, Chinese and Indians in Malaysia, and between black, brown and white races in the West Indies. But it is reserved for the analysis of social and political conflicts in the 'backward' parts of the colonial and post-colonial world, and then read back by some analysts as a quality that must have existed in these societies long before the colonial intervention.

The *Oxford English Dictionary*, volume II (1933 edition) defines the words 'communal' and 'communalism' in the following way:

Communal: '1. Of or belonging to a commune. (b) Of or pertaining to the Paris Commune and its adherents. 2. Of or pertaining to a (or the) community. 3. Of or pertaining to the commonality or body of citizens of a burgh.'

Communalism: 'The principle of the communal organization of society: a theory of government which advocates the widest extension of

[9] Ibid., p. 89.

[10] Bipan Chandra, *Communalism in Modern India* (Delhi, 1984), p. 1. Sandria Frietag offers a slightly different definition: 'a position in which politicized religious identity claimed primary loyalty'; 'Religious Rites and Riots: From Community Identity to Communalism in North India, 1870–1940' (University of California, Berkeley, Ph.D. thesis, 1980), p. 2.

local autonomy for each locally definable community. Hence *Communalist*, a supporter of this system or an adherent of the Commune of Paris of 1871.'

The *Supplement to the Oxford English Dictionary*, published in 1972, adds only that a *communal kitchen* means 'a public kitchen under official management' and *communal land(s)* 'land held by a community'. But *The Shorter Oxford English Dictionary*, in its third revised edition of 1959, refers to the peculiar meaning of the term in India:

Communal: '1. Of or belonging to a Commune; of or pertaining to the Paris Commune 1871. 2. Of or pertaining to a (or the) community; especially, in India, of any of the racial [*sic*] or religious communities.'

What the dictionary indicates here is the unique meaning that many familiar concepts acquired in Orientalist usage in order to capture the Otherness of life—and politics—in the 'East'. That uniqueness of meaning is part of the intellectual baggage that has been inherited from the colonial experience. What is particularly striking, however, is how quickly Indian nationalists accepted the use of the term 'communalism' in this quite exceptional sense.

It would perhaps be an interesting exercise to try and locate the first instance in which the term was used in its Indian sense in a public statement or published piece on the subcontinent, but for our purposes it is unnecessary. What is clear beyond doubt is that this special usage developed fairly late—far later, in fact, than is generally supposed. Participants in the debates surrounding the Morley-Minto and the Montagu-Chelmsford reform frequently referred to 'communal feeling', 'communal representation' and the 'communal principle' of representation, pointing in the main to the putative needs and claims of the different religious 'communities'. But it was left to the nationalists in the 1920s and 1930s to mould the concept, through repeated use, into its fully developed Indian form.

In 1924 a Minority Report by four Indian members of the Reforms Enquiry Committee—Tej Bahadur Sapru, P. S. Sivaswami Aiyer, M. A. Jinnah and R. P. Paranjpye—included a section on 'Communal Tension and Tendencies'. Under this heading the authors wrote: 'We are fully aware that the unfortunate tension between the two principle communities Hindu and Muhammedan which has recently manifested itself in riots in some towns is held to be a serious warning against any . . . early move towards responsible Government.'[11] 'Communal' was on its way to becoming an adjective derived not from 'community' but from 'tension between the [religious] communities'.

By the time of the Nehru Report, 1928, this journey had ended. The Report included two chapters entitled 'The Communal Aspect' and declared that 'The communal problem of India is primarily the Hindu–Muslim problem.'[12] By the mid-1930s, when Jawaharlal Nehru wrote his *Autobiography* and Pattabhi Sitaramayya published his official history of the Congress, the nationalists were using phrases like the 'communal question' and 'communalism' freely to describe the problem of antagonism between Hindus and Muslims and the politics built up to protect their allegedly separate interests.[13]

For the nationalists, locked as they were in the 1920s and 1930s in bitter struggle to overthrow the colonial regime, communalism appeared as a great political threat, the most obvious source of danger for the advancing cause of nationalism. This threat had to be countered; and one way of countering it was to expose the narrowness, the opportunism, the backward-looking character, the 'illegitimacy' as it were, of communalist politics, which is why communalism had to be talked and written about.

III

As anyone can see, the nationalist approach to communalism was a far cry from the colonialist perception of the same tendencies and forces. Communalism in the colonialist perception served

[11] *Report of the Reforms Enquiry Committee 1924* (Calcutta, 1925), p. 176.

[12] *All Parties Conference 1928. Report of the Committee appointed by the Conference to determine the Principles of the Constitution for India* (AICC, Allahabad, 1928), p. 27.

[13] It is interesting to note that in popular, and academic, usage the term has sometimes been narrowed even further to refer only to 'the Muslims' and their politics. For an unexpected illustration, see R. Suntharalingam, *Politics and Nationalist Awakening in South India, 1852–91* (Arizona, 1974), sections entitled 'The Search for Communal Support', pp. 250ff., and 'Alienation of Communal Support', pp. 272ff., both of which are concerned exclusively with the question of Muslim support for the nationalists.

to designate a pathological condition. It was, like the term 'tribalism'—which has been widely employed in writings on African politics and history,[14] and indeed 'factionalism' which has been popular in western political science commentary on India since the 1960s—a statement on the *nature* of particular, 'primitive' societies.

Communalism captured for the colonialists what they had conceptualized as a basic feature of Indian society—its religious bigotry and its fundamentally irrational character—long before the term actually came to be used in its Indian sense. Like tribalism and factionalism, communalism is given, endemic, inborn. Like them, it denies consciousness and agency to the subjected peoples of the colonized world. 'History' happens to these people; it can hardly be a process in which they play a conscious and significant part.

However, while this approach to Indian society was widely applied by colonialist observers and writers to interpret the way in which people in the villages and towns all over the subcontinent related to one another in their quotidian existence, their secret thoughts and their public celebrations, it was not quite so readily used to explain the 'communalist' politics that developed among certain groups of Hindus, Muslims and Sikhs, usually in opposition to the Congress, after the First World War. There were liberal colonialists like Irwin who sometimes spoke about these new political developments in a language indistinguishable from that of the nationalists. Thus wrote Irwin in 1926: 'I appeal in the name of national life because communal tension is eating into it as a canker.'[15] But the generality of colonialist spokesmen, and even Irwin himself at other times, were more reluctant to use the term 'communalism' as a negative sign to designate the mutually hostile

---

[14] See P. H. Gulliver, ed., *Tradition and Transition in East Africa* (London, 1969), especially 'Introduction' and chapters by W. J. Argyle and P. H. Gulliver; and Max Gluckman, 'Tribalism, Ruralism and Urbanism in South and Central Africa' in V. Turner, ed., *Colonialism in Africa, 1870–1960, vol. 3, Profiles of Change* (Cambridge, 1971). Cf. R. Melson and H. Wolpe, eds., *Nigeria: Modernization and the Politics of Communalism* (Michigan, 1971), chpt. 17 and *passim*.

[15] Irwin's speech at the Chelmsford Club, Simla, 17 July 1926, cited in *Report of the Indian Statutory Commission, vol. 1, Survey* (London, 1930), p. 27.

politics of the 'religious communities' that grew rapidly from the mid-1920s.

It would follow from the above that there are fundamental differences between the nationalist and the colonialist interpretations of communalism. This is the nationalist view of the debate on the issue as it has been conducted from colonial times to today, and it is commonly accepted in the literature on the subject. The view, however, requires some re-examination; for there remains a significant overlap between the nationalists' and the colonialists' very acceptance and use of the term 'communalism' in its exceptional Indian sense.

The nationalist account of the differences between the colonialist and the nationalist interpretations may be summed up very briefly as follows: In the colonialist view the phenomenon of communalism in India is age-old; it flows from the essential character of the peoples of India; and it affects more or less the whole population, with only a few enlightened, liberal, western-educated men and women being truly free from the communal spirit. The nationalists, by contrast, recognize communalism as a problem of recent origins, as the outcome basically of economic and political inequality and conflict, and as the handiwork of a handful of self-interested elite-groups (colonial and native), with the mass of the people remaining largely unaffected.

On the face of it, the differences between these two positions are indeed fundamental. But my summary, and the nationalist discourse, glosses over a number of interesting variations. Colonialist interpretations of communalism in fact cover the range from the 'racist–essentialist' to the 'liberal–rationalist'; and elements of the essentialist may be found in nationalist explanations too. There were not a few colonial commentators in the nineteenth and twentieth centuries who explained Hindu–Muslim strife and the organization of a separate Muslim or Hindu political platform in terms of economic and political competition and losses.[16] On the

[16] For the classic nineteenth-century colonial statement on the reasons for the rise of extremist movements (like the Wahabi) among Muslims, see W. W. Hunter, *The Indian Musalmans* (3rd ed., London, 1876; reprinted Delhi, 1969). For evidence from the twentieth century, see, for example, Tanika Sarkar, 'Communal Riots in Bengal', in Mushirul Hasan, ed.,

other hand, there were nationalists like Bishan Narayan Dar,
Mohandas Karamchand Gandhi and Ganesh Shankar Vidyarthi,
to name only three, who spoke at crucial moments of the 'meekness' and 'natural cowardice' of the Hindu, the 'bullying nature'
of the Muslim, and the need to overcome these.[17] In other words,
the colonialist and the nationalist readings of communalism make
unexpected appearances in each other's discourses and cannot be
separated in quite the way suggested by the nationalists.

Even if we take the racist–essentialist view of Indian politics as
being the more characteristic of the colonialist discourse, as it surely
was, and the liberal–rationalist as the more characteristic of the
nationalist, it will be seen that the two share an important area of
common ground. What is perhaps still more surprising is that while
the nationalist version of the debate on communalism between
nationalists and colonialists has been widely accepted as accurate,
it is the colonialists who appear to have laid down the terms of the
debate itself.

As historiographical traditions, the nationalist and the colonialist
are both centrally concerned with causes. This is of course the
point on which they appear to differ most radically in their reading
of communalism. The colonialist view of communalism as reflecting the 'natural' condition of India would have to be described, as
I have suggested, as *essentialist*. The nationalist interpretation of it
as a distorted reflection of economic (and, building upon that,
political) conflict could be termed *economistic*. But the underlying
search for the causes of communalism points to a prior unity of
perception.

Both nationalist and colonialist accept the givenness of 'com-

---

Communal and Pan-Islamic Trends in Colonial India (Delhi, 1981); Sugata Bose,
'The Roots of Communal Violence in Rural Bengal: A Study of the Kishore-
ganj Riots, 1930', *Modern Asian Studies*, 16, 3 (July 1982); and Partha Chatterjee,
Bengal 1920–47: The Land Question (Calcutta, 1984), pp. 135ff.

[17] Cf. B. N. Dar, *An Appeal to the English Public on behalf of the Hindus of the
N.W.P. and Oudh* (Lucknow, 1983), p. 28, M. K. Gandhi, 'Hindu–Muslim
Tension: Its Cause and Cure', *Young India*, 29–5–24, in *Collected Works of
Mahatma Gandhi, vol. 24* (Ahmedabad, 1967), p. 142; Radhakrishna Awasthi,
ed., *Kranti ka Udghosh. Ganesh Shankar Vidyarthi ki kalam se*, pt. II (Kanpur,
1978), pp. 588, 811.

munalism' as a more or less tangible phenomenon whose causes can be readily identified, and of its Other—rationalism or liberalism, secularism or nationalism, however one chooses to put it. Both see the need of Indian society in the later colonial period, or at any rate of its 'backward' sections, as one of moving from 'communalism' to its Other, by means of education, political struggle, economic growth, whatever. Hence Irwin's 1926 appeal: 'I appeal in the name of national life because communal tension is eating into it as a canker.' In other words, both nationalist and colonialist positions derive from the same liberal ideology in which 'rationalism' and 'secularism' operate as adjacent elements of thought.

IV

The writing on communalism has of course advanced in many ways since the colonial period; and in academic accounts, at least, the elements of the liberal-rationalist position would appear to have largely supplanted those of the racist–essentialist one. Research done since the 1960s has considerably deepened our knowledge of the history of sectarian strife and sectarian politics by challenging the Orientalist vision of India as a world that was utterly, even irretrievably, different from the 'modern', 'scientific', 'rational' West.

Liberal nationalist, Marxist and even neo-colonialist historians have contributed to breaking down the false totalities of ready-made religious communities—'Hindu', 'Muslim', 'Sikh', and so on—by pointing to the immense differences in language, occupation, economic interest and even religious practice among the Hindus, Muslims, Sikhs, etc., of different regions, castes and classes. Many have underlined the fact that communalism as we know it is a new phenomenon: far from being of hoary origins, or even of very long standing, it is a development of the late colonial period, arising concurrently with nationalism if not being brought forward as a counterweight to it.[18] Social scientists and historians

[18] Romila Thapar, Harbans Mukhia, Bipan Chandra, *Communalism and the Writing of Indian History* (Delhi, 1969) was something of a landmark in this regard. Bipan Chandra's *Communalism in Modern India* is a more emphatic and detailed statement which follows the same lines. M. Mujeeb, *The Indian*

have also begun to look much more closely at the economic and political interests underlying sectional politics and sectarian strife, and many of them have focused attention on the economic circumstances and grievances of the masses of ordinary men and women who came to be involved in these struggles on different sides.[19]

Nevertheless, many traces of older positions remain. An old liberal-nationalist, and liberal-colonialist, view survives in the proposition—still among the most popular on the subject in India— that communalism was nationalism gone awry.[20] The attempted reduction of all South Asian politics—communalist, nationalist or other—to the play of self-interest and faction also has a long

---

Muslims (London, 1967); F. Robinson, *Separatism among Indian Muslims: The Politics of the United Provinces' Muslims, 1860–1923* (Cambridge, 1974), and Rafiuddin Ahmed, *The Bengal Muslims 1871–1906. A Quest for Identity* (Delhi, 1981), are important examples of works challenging the simple notions of a unified Muslim community.

[19] See, e.g., Sumit Sarkar, *The Swadeshi Movement in Bengal, 1903–8* (Delhi, 1973), chpt. 8, Section III; Ahmed, *Bengal Muslims 1871–1906*; Tanika Sarkar, Communal Riots in Bengal'; Sugata Bose, 'The Roots of Communal Violence in Rural Bengal'; and for northern India in the late nineteenth century, Anand Yang, 'Sacred Symbol and Sacred Space in Rural India: Community Mobilization in the "Anti-Cow Killing" Riot of 1893' and and Sandria Frietag, 'Sacred Symbol as Mobilizing Ideology: The North Indian Search for a "Hindu" Community', both in *Comparative Studies in Society and History*, 22, 4 (Oct. 1980); John McLane, *Indian Nationalism and the Early Congress* (Princeton, 1977), esp. chpt. 10; P. G. Robb, 'Officials and Non-officials as Leaders in Popular Agitations: Shahabad 1917 and Other Conspiracies', in B. N. Pandey, ed., *Leadership in South Asia* (Delhi, 1977); and G. Pandey, 'Rallying Round the Cow: Sectarian Strife in the Bhojpuri Region, *c.* 1888–1917' in R. Guha, ed., *Subaltern Studies II* (Delhi, 1983). For some important new perspectives on the local community and its struggles, see Dipesh Chakrabarty, 'Communal Riots and Labour: Bengal's Jute Mill-Hands in the 1890s', *Past and Present*, no. 91 (May 1981); Chatterjee, *Bengal, 1920–47. The Land Question*; and Majid Siddiqi, 'History and Society in a Popular Rebellion: Mewat, 1920–33', *Comparative Studies in Society and History*, 28, 3 (July 1986).

[20] See Bipan Chandra, 'Indian National Movement and the Communal Problem' in his *Nationalism and Colonialism in Modern India* (Delhi, 1979), p. 260, and his *Communalism in Modern India*, pp. 125–7 and *passim*.

history.[21] And the central thrust of an older, colonialist position has been reinforced by another recent historiographical trend which places a renewed emphasis on 'continuities' in Indian history. In effect the argument here is that much, if not nearly all, that happened in colonial India had its beginnings in the centuries before the coming of the British, and (logically) that the colonial intervention did not mark the break in Indian history that it has for so long been represented as marking.

The following example of a recent intervention in the debate on communalism should suffice to indicate the overall tendency of the 'continuity' argument. In a significant statement entitled 'The Pre-History of "Communalism"? Religious Conflict in India, 1700–1860', Christopher Bayly draws attention to 'the incidence of communal conflict in India over the period 1700 to 1860'. He goes on to suggest that many of these early conflicts 'bear a very close resemblance to the riots of the later colonial period': 'The "land wars" of the eighteenth century which saw the rise of agrarian Sikh and Hindu peasantry against Muslim rural gentry were apparently no more or less "communal" than the riots in eastern U.P. in the 1920s or eastern Bengal in the 1930s and 1940s [*sic*].'[22]

There is really no sense of context here, not a hint that human beings and their actions, the events of history, derive their meaning from the political, economic, social and intellectual circumstances in which they are placed—from the discourse of the age, or the whole historical epoch (as Gramsci would have called it). This is all the more surprising since an evident purpose of Bayly's intervention is to reopen the question of meaning. Like many others, he argues that what is described as communal is not really what is generally understood as communal. But, the argument goes, what

[21] Most prominently represented in the 'Cambridge School': see esp. J. Gallagher *et al.*, eds., *Locality, Province and Nation* (Cambridge, 1973); and C. J. Baker and D. A. Washbrook, *South India: Political Institutions and Political Change* (Delhi, 1975). For a useful critique of this kind of history, see D. Hardiman, 'The Indian Faction: A Political Theory Examined', in R. Guha, ed., *Subaltern Studies I* (Delhi, 1982).

[22] C. A. Bayly, 'The Pre-history of "Communalism?" Religious Conflict in India, 1700–1860', *Modern Asian Studies*, 19, 2 (April 1985).

appears to be communal in the eighteenth century is exactly the same—in appearance and 'reality'—two hundred years later. The context disappears.

It is perhaps enough to refer to only two aspects of the change in context between the eighteenth and the twentieth centuries. Let us note, first, the absence of any powerful sense of an '*all-India* Hindu community' or an '*all-India* Muslim community' at the former date, by contrast with its insistent presence at the latter, which so clearly overdetermined 'land wars', local quarrels, nationalist struggles and the lot. This is so obvious a point that it needs no elaboration. To take another obvious point, the significance of which is often lost, one may note the radically altered nature of the state—and not just of policies, or even of politics as a whole—under colonialism. This state is not only far more modern, powerful, centralized and interventionist than any state that had existed before in the subcontinent. It is also far more self-consciously 'neutral'—standing *above* society, and not really part of it—than any previous state, a position that no previous state had especially claimed or desired. For a long time, moreover, the claim to 'neutrality' formed a large part of the argument for the perpetuation of colonial government.[23] It is a claim that the post-colonial regime has continued to put forward with greater vehemence, and perhaps for a while in India and Sri Lanka with somewhat greater success.

Moreover, this claim of the colonial and post-colonial states has long been accepted by a very considerable body of academic opinion. This acceptance sometimes flows from the belief that the state was indeed unaligned ('above' it all) or that it could not, in its own interests, tolerate the more serious outrages that accompanied sectarian strife. Even when such a naïvely optimistic view of the state is not uncritically adopted, an element of it lives on in the repeatedly expressed hope that the state would intervene—that 'all necessary steps would be taken,' as the jargon has it—to put an end to sectarian propaganda and violence. It is only very recently that this view of the state has come to be seriously challenged. This has happened in the wake of the anti-Tamil pogrom in Colombo in 1983, the massacre of Sikhs in Delhi in 1984, the Hindu-Muslim

[23] See, e.g., the colonial argument discussed in chpt. 2 below.

riots in Bhiwandi and Bombay, Meerut and Moradabad, Delhi and elsewhere through this decade, in all of which the coercive arm of the state played an infamous role.[24]

To return to the issue of historical writings on communalism, the persistence of earlier colonialist and nationalist positions points to the survival of earlier questions and of long-established common ground. Behind the flurry of research activity since the 1960s, one still finds a continuous search for 'causes' and for 'rationality'. Indeed, since 'causes' and (bourgeois) 'rationality' have come to be linked together in recent historical work more perhaps than ever before, the arena of causality appears to have shrunk in most cases to one defined by tangible political and economic interests. Indeed, there would appear to be a consensus among historians now on the question of the hard-headed, economic 'rationality' that allegedly lay behind sectarian politics and strife. Recent work that stresses such motivation, especially in the analysis of mass involvement in communal riots, is not strikingly original, as a comparison with the nationalist and Marxist writings of the 1930s and 1940s—the works of Jawaharlal Nehru, R. P. Dutt and W. C. Smith, for instance—will readily show. What is new is the sophistication and detail in research and the fact that the current search for 'rational' economic and political motives has drawn in conservative, liberal and leftist scholars alike.

The following academic judgements on a variety of sectarian outbreaks and n.ovements will help to make the point clearer.

[24] For some important critical statements, see S. J. Tambiah, *Sri Lanka: Ethnic Fratricide and the Dismantling of Democracy* (London, 1986); Veena Das, ed., *Communities, Riots, Survivors: The South Asian Experience* (forthcoming); Asghar Ali Engineer, ed., *Communal Riots in Post-Independence India* (Hyderabad, 1984), and his *Bhiwandi-Bombay Riots: Analysis and Documentation* (Bombay, 1984) as well as his numerous articles in *Economic and Political Weekly*; Uma Chakravarti and Nandita Haksar, *The Delhi Riots: Three Days in the Life of a Nation* (Delhi, 1987); and numerous reports by Civil Liberties groups and Citizens' Enquiry Committees, such as the pamphlets: *Who are the Guilty? Report of a Joint Inquiry into the Causes and Impacts of the Riots in Delhi from 31 October to 10 November* (People's Union for Democratic Rights & People's Union for Civil Liberties, Delhi, 1984), and *Walled City Riots: A Report on the Police and Communal Violence in Delhi, 19–24 May 1987* (People's Union for Democratic Rights, Delhi, 1987).

Certain Hindu–Muslim riots in 1930–1 were 'isolated instances of class struggle fought in communal guise' or 'fundamentally agrarian jacqueries or the fury of the urban poor'. Sectarian antagonism was probably 'a surrogate . . . for several general [i.e. economic] grievances'. Rioting may be explained in terms of the 'displacement of leaders associated with fluctuating prices [*sic*]'. Or, again, 'It was the economic emphasis of the (Cow-Protection) Sabha's activities which accounted for the wide-spread support given to the (Cow-Protection) movement. . . . .'[25] A glance at the footnotes will indicate just how difficult it is to guess the political persuasion of the writer or the date of the writing from the content of his or her remarks.

What one might say, then, is that the parameters of the debate on communalism, at least as this debate is conducted in academic circles, have been considerably reduced. Within these narrower confines, the historian is still free to choose his or her own 'modern', 'secular' heroes and his or her own 'primitive', 'communal' villains. Two examples should suffice to illustrate this point. W. C. Smith spoke for a large body of liberal and left-wing opinion, then and now, when he wrote in the early 1940s, amidst the growing campaign for 'Pakistan', that in the preceding years 'communalism has expanded to involve *also* the lower classes.... The reactionaries... have managed to divert *even* the mass of the people (as they had diverted the middle classes) from a united nationalist front.'[26] The 'mass of the people', 'secular' in their pristine state, and also the 'middle classes', are here 'diverted' into communalism by the 'reactionary' upper classes, British and Indian.

John McLane represents a very different kind of liberal (developmentalist?) opinion. Writing in America in the 1970s, geographically and temporally far from the heat of the battle, he paints for us a very different picture of Indian society. It is not, in his view, the common man or woman of this society but the western educated elite that is 'rational'. He suggests that it was the 'ignorant and illiterate masses' who were responsible for earlier Hindu–Muslim riots. But, by the end of the nineteenth century, high-status Indians

---

[25] Tanika Sarkar, 'Communal Riots in Bengal'; Robb, 'Officials and Nonofficials as Leaders in Popular Agitations'; McLane, *Indian Nationalism*, p. 287.

[26] W. C. Smith, *Modern Islam in India* (London, 1946), p. 220 (emphasis added).

were identifying themselves with the lower-status members of their religious denominations and being drawn into such strife.

'Undoubtedly', he writes in partial explanation of this development, in a passage on the Gaurakshini Sabhas (or Cow-Protection Societies) of the 1880s and 1890s that I have already quoted, 'it was the economic emphasis of the Nagpur Sabha which accounted for the widespread support given to the movement in the Central Provinces by Maratha Brahmin pleaders and other prominent persons.'[27]

One or two other points may be made about the recent historiography of communalism. One feature common to many of the current explanations of sectarian strife in colonial India, including the two cited in the preceding paragraphs, is the drawing of a sharp line between elite and mass mentalities, manners and politics. On the face of it this may appear to be an acknowledgement of the structural split in the domain of Indian politics that contributors to *Subaltern Studies* have emphasized in recent years.[28] Where it differs from the latter, however, is not only in its rigid, *empirical* separation of the world of elite politics from that of mass politics, but also in its easy assumptions about the 'rationality' or 'irrationality' of 'the people' and in its refusal to investigate in any detail the specific features of popular politics in any particular instance: and in these respects it is no different from an earlier colonialist or nationalist historiography.

Thus, to take only one example, Francis Robinson, in his important and detailed study of the emergence of a 'separatist' Muslim political position in U.P., relegates to a single footnote what he calls 'the most severe communal outbreaks of the (nineteenth) century', namely the riots of 1893 in eastern U.P., on the curious ground that these, like the serious clashes in Faizabad in 1912–13, 'were rural not urban affairs'. This is of course not even an apology for an explanation: it is simply a refusal to take on board an important part of the historical experience which does not fit into his elitist framework of analysis and the conclusion that flows from it—that communalism arose earlier and was more rampant in western U.P., whereas eastern U.P. and Awadh

27 McLane, *Indian Nationalism*, pp. 278, 285, 287.
28 R. Guha, ed., *Subaltern Studies*, vols. I–VI (Delhi, 1982–89).

remained an area of relative communal harmony into the twentieth century. Another example of this refusal to consider the historical experience, conditions and concerns of the lower classes seriously is provided by Robinson's discussion of the Màcchlibazar mosque affair in Kanpur in 1913. Here, a major part of the explanation for the violence that occurred is provided in terms of the 'influx' of Muslim weavers or Julahas who were, in a phrase borrowed from the colonial administrators and ethnographers, 'renowned for their bigotry'.[29]

When all is said and done, moreover, most historians betray a deep-rooted faith in the primacy of the elite in determining the character of all political articulation and the course of all political change. This is revealed not only by Robinson's lack of interest in 'rural affairs' and Muslim weavers. It is implicit also in W. C. Smith's and John McLane's respective accounts of the development of the movement for Pakistan and the Cow-Protection agitation. For both it is the 'rational', i.e. mainly economic, interest of elite classes that accounts for the growth of these powerful movements.

The shortcomings of such an approach to the question of communalism are evident. For one thing, the approach is unsatisfactory because it sets aside a false, Orientalist 'irrationality of the East' and puts in its place an equally false, universal bourgeois rationality—the pursuit of the economic self-interest of the individual above all else—as the explanation of all strife in Indian society. One ahistorical assumption replaces another, and no attempt is made to study the qualities of a specific historical consciousness in this specific time and place—the units of solidarity, the requirements of status, the understanding of honour and shame, in a word the competing and conflicting meanings of 'rationality' in an old, highly developed non-capitalist society colonized by an advanced capitalist power.

The economistic explanation of sectarian movements and conflict is deficient in another sense as well. The substitution of 'class' or 'economic' struggle (and the two terms are often used interchangeably) for sectarian strife is, after all, a little too facile.

[29] Robinson, *Separatism among Indian Muslims*, pp. 78–9 and n. 27 and 213.

Historians writing in the 1960s and 1970s, under the shadow of science of economics, appear not to have been seriously bothered by the question of how 'class' struggles so readily took on a 'communal guise' or adopted a 'communal facade', or why 'communal antagonism' could become a 'surrogate' for general economic grievances. It is true that the lurking hand of elite manipulation can always be invoked. Yet it is hard to escape the feeling that the economistic interpretation of communalism remains, at bottom, essentialist. For while in particular instances the overlap between religion and class (Muslim peasants *vs.* Hindu landlords, etc.) may explain the rechanelling of class conflict into communal conflict, in a longer term and somewhat broader perspective the excessive religiosity (and stupidity) of the people can be the only explanation for the ease with which masses of ordinary peasants and workers, unemployed youth and petty bourgeois elements generally are diverted from what, we are assured, are their primary concerns.

Above all, perhaps, it needs to be said that all the historiographical advances noted above have left untouched one basic proposition that was developed originally by the colonialists and accepted by the nationalists, i.e. the fixity and finality of the category of communalism, as well as the value attached to it. The problem with the colonialist interpretation of Indian politics, powered as it is by an essentialist view of the society, is that it takes the history (if not the politics) out of the movements variously designated 'communalism', 'nationalism', and so on. In a very real sense that is precisely the problem with the nationalist enterprise as well, for large areas of the experience of the Indian people are simply wished away.

It is probably fair to say, too, that although subsequent scholarship has moved some way from the classical colonialist approach to communalism, it has nevertheless remained confined within a liberal–colonialist problematic. In this the failure of the Indian experience to conform to the European model of the nation–state constitutes the central problem for investigation, and the dyad 'communalism'/'nationalism' or 'communalism'/'secularism' a large part of the scholar's analytical apparatus. It is the growing awareness of the poverty of this formulation that has led to the repeated demand in recent years that students of Indian politics break out of this inherited problematic, challenge the imperialism of categories (as one scholar has called it),[30] and question the givenness of 'communalism', 'secularism', and for that matter 'nationalism'.

At the end of this Introduction, it may be well to underscore the *historical* character of 'communalism'. In his book on nationalism, Benedict Anderson has reminded us that all communities—from the 'little community' of the village, to the dialect community spanning a wide region, to the community called the nation—are 'imagined', 'made'.[31] Categories of thought and movements of people—'communalism', 'nationalism'—are also *made* in this sense and made, we should add, out of shared as well as contested experiences and common as well as mutually contradictory visions and struggles. There is a sense also in which such quests for the political community of the future are never quite finished, for new contests, new visions and new perceptions of earlier visions arise even before the older versions are fully played out.

In this respect, the quest for the 'imagined community' is a little bit like the historical investigation of which this book forms a part: a task which will necessarily always remain unfinished. If this study raises new questions before old ones have been answered, it will have served the purpose of contributing to an ongoing debate which, in India at any rate, has always had a political as well as a historiographical dimension.

[30] Ashis Nandy, 'An Anti-Secularist Manifesto', *Seminar*, no. 314, and 'The Politics of Secularism and the Recovery of Religious Tolerance' in Veena Das, ed., *Communities, Riots, Survivors*. For other recent statements challenging the givenness of 'communalism', 'secularism', 'nationalism' and so on, see T. N. Madan, 'Secularism in its Place', *Journal of Asian Studies*, 46, 4 (1987); Chatterjee, *Bengal 1920–47*, Preface; and Dipesh Chakrabarty, 'Invitation to a Dialogue' in Guha, ed., *Subaltern Studies IV* (Delhi, 1985).

[31] B. Anderson, *Imagined Communities. Reflections on the Origin and Spread of Nationalism* (London, 1983).

Chapter Two

The Colonial Construction of the Indian Past

Twenty-five centuries ago before Babylon was struggling with Nineveh for supremacy, before Rome was founded by Romulus, or Tyre was planting her colonies; before Greece had contended with Persia, or Cyrus had added lustre to the Persian Monarchy, Bénares had risen to greatness, if not to glory. And even now when most or all of these cities are obliterated by the ravages of time or sunk in the dust of ages, her temples and stately shrines remain, and it would be little less than a shame to Britain if those ancient relics should fall by the ruthless hand of the modern vandal and utilitarian.

—An American correspondent in a Chicago paper, June 1891[1]

The *historical* character of communalism (or nationalism) must come after the *historical* character of the past has been established. The past is historical not only in the obvious sense that the past makes up history. It is historical also in the sense that 'history' itself—the 'past' recalled—is *constructed*. The modern history of India, in this sense, was first written in colonial times and by colonialists. It was colonialist writers who established the pattern of the Indian past pretty much as we know it today. And in that pattern, sectarian strife was an important motif.

By the end of the nineteenth century, the dominant strand in colonialist historiography was representing religious bigotry and conflict between people of different religious persuasions as one of the more distinctive features of Indian society, past and present—a mark of the Indian section of the 'Orient'. This particular reading of Indian history was distinguished not only by its periodization in terms of the European experience ('ancient', 'medieval', 'modern'), nor simply by its use of communal—more specifically, religious—categories to differentiate these periods of Indian history (or, at least,

---

[1] Cited in *Navayuga*, 18 June 1891, in *Report on Native Newspapers* (hereafter RNP), Bengal 1891, week ending 27 June 1891, p. 674.

the first two of them: the 'Hindu' and the 'Muslim'). The historical reconstruction was characterized also by an emptying out of all history—in terms of the specific variations of time, place, class, issue—from the political experience of the people, and the identification of religion, or the religious community, as the moving force of all Indian politics. The communal riot narrative served to substantiate this reading of history.

Towards the end of the 1920s the Government of India drew up elaborate lists of Hindu–Muslim riots that had occurred in the country in the recent past. From one of these, we learn that there were 112 serious 'disturbances' between 1923 and 1927 which left approximately 450 people dead and 5000 more wounded. The year 1929 produced a carnage in Bombay, 1931 one more in Kanpur. Official statistics put the number of casualties in Bombay at 184 killed and 948 wounded. In Kanpur several hundreds were killed (for a casualty list of the same order, a government memorandum observed, one had to go back to the 'grave Benares riots' of 1809) and about 80,000 people are said to have left the city by rail alone on the first day of a conflagration that raged for three days.[2] The record of Hindu–Muslim strife was also extended further back, to the beginnings of colonial rule, as one can see from Table 2:1.

It is not difficult to add to these official lists. For the period 1800 to 1920 alone, a recent study speaks of 'riots and communal conflicts in many North Indian cities in the 1830s and again in the 1850s' and refers to Hindu–Muslim strife in Lucknow, for instance, in 1843, 1853, and 1856.[3] There are records of clashes between Hindus and Muslims in Bareilly in 1837 (in addition to the riots of 1871–2 mentioned in Table 2:1); in Faizabad-Ayodhya in 1855; and, to take the two most important cloth-producing centres of Azamgarh district as another example, in Mubarakpur in 1813, 1834, 1842, and 1904, and in Maunath Bhanjan (or Mau) in 1806 as well as on several occasions from the 1860s onwards.

Again, the bloodshed at the Baqr'Id in 1893 in Azamgarh and

---

[2] India Office Library and Records; hereafter IOL: L/P and J/7/132, 'Communal Disorders' (Memorandum prepared by the Government of India for the Indian Statutory Commission, 1928), and 'Notes' of 19–20 May 1931.

[3] C. A. Bayly, 'The Pre-History of "Communalism"?'

Table 2:1. Government Statement of
Major Hindu–Muslim Riots, 1800–1920

Year	Place	Observation by Officials
1809	Banaras	'Grave Benares riots'; several hundred persons killed, some 50 mosques destroyed
1871–2	Bareilly	'Serious riots'.
1885	Lahore & Karnal	
1886	Delhi	'The great riots'.
1889	Dera Ghazi Khan	
1891	Palakod	
1893	Azamgarh	'Grave outbreaks over a large area of country'.
	Bombay	'Very serious Muharram riots'; 80 persons killed.
1910	Peshawar	
1912	Ayodhya-Faizabad	
1913	Agra	
1917	Shahabad	'Baqr' Id disturbances which recalled the Azamgarh disturbances of 1893 and which are among the most serious which have occurred at any time since the British connection with the country'.
1918	Katarpur village (Saharanpur district)	30 Muslims killed, 60 or more injured; all Muslim houses in the village burnt.

SOURCE: L/P&J/7/132; *Report of the Indian Statutory Commission, volume* IV (1930), pp. 96–7.

other districts of eastern U.P. and western Bihar led to violent conflict between groups of Muslims in Bombay, Junagadh and Rangoon as well.[4] Bombay was witness to another round of fighting between Hindus and Muslims at the Muharram of 1911, and

[4] Burma was administered by the Government of India until 1935: hence

there was a serious riot in Calcutta in 1918—partly it appears in retaliation for the Hindu attacks on Muslims in Shahabad district the year before.[5]

If this is the sometimes neglected history of Hindu–Muslim strife before the 1920s, evidence of Hindu–Muslim 'riots' can also be found for the pre-colonial period. Scholars have written of riots in Gujarat in the seventeenth and eighteenth centuries, and again of 'sporadic' local conflict in Banaras, for example, from the 1750s.[6] Indeed the list of Hindu–Muslim riots in colonial and pre-colonial India lengthens all the time with lengthening research—as indeed it must if 'riots' are what one is looking for.

It is possible for the researcher, however, to do more than just look for riots or simply delineate their differing contexts (though colonialist historiography was not particularly guilty of the latter crime). It is possible, and necessary, also to ask how reports of sectarian strife were received by contemporary and subsequent observers, what meanings were derived from them, what place they were assigned in different representations of the changing colonial world. How did colonialist observers 'read' the history of Hindu–Muslim strife that they dug up in the course of their attempts to come to grips with Indian society? This is the question that I take up in this chapter through a close examination of the evidence relating to the 'grave' Banaras riots of 1809, which figure prominently in colonial diagnoses of the social and political condition of India in the nineteenth and twentieth centuries.

---

reports of riots in Rangoon appear together with the reports of riots in different parts of India.

[5] J. McLane, *Indian Nationalism and the Early Congress*, pp. 320–1; J. Masselos, 'Power in the Bombay "Moholla", 1904–5', *South Asia*, 6 (December 1976); K. Macpherson, *The Muslim Microcosm: Calcutta, 1918–35* (Wiesbaden, 1974), pp. 37, 40.

[6] S. A. A. Rizvi, *Shah Wali-allah and His Times* (Canberra, 1980), p. 197; L. Subramanian, 'Capital and Crowd in a Declining Asian Port City: The Anglo-Bania Order and the Surat Riots of 1795', *Modern Asian Studies*, 19, 2 (1985); Bayly, 'Pre-History of "Communalism",' p. 197. In regard to Banaras, however, it is worth pointing out that officials making detailed enquiries after the 1809 outbreak reported that there had been no notable outbreak of violence between Hindus and Muslims in the city for the previous hundred years.

II

The colonialist choice of Banaras as representative of India is scarcely surprising. Along with maharajas, tiger-skins and snake-charmers, 'Suttee', 'Thugee' and female infanticide, 'Banaras' has loomed large in the westerner's picture of India from a time predating the colonial era. Banaras was the Mecca of the subcontinent, repository of the unfathomable secrets of the Hindus. The place that Aligarh was to occupy in the attempted reckoning of Muslim politics in the first half of the twentieth century was already, before that period, occupied by Banaras in the attempt to reckon with the great, ancient and chaotic Hindu civilization that was said to be India. As the Rev. M. A. Sherring put it in 1868 with reference to the history of Banaras which was, in his view, 'to a great extent the history of India': 'While its career has been of long duration, it has not been of a character to awaken much enthusiasm or admiration. It cannot be said that either the moral, or the social, or even the intellectual, condition of the people residing here is a whit better than it was upwards of two thousand years ago. . . .'[7]

One vitally important part of the history of Banaras was captured, in the colonialist account, by the Hindu–Muslim riots that broke out in that city in October 1809. The *District Gazetteer* of Banaras compiled in 1907 introduces the 1809 riots as follows:

The only disturbance of the public peace [in Banaras during the first half of the nineteenth century] occurred in 1809 and the following year, when the city experienced one of those convulsions which had so frequently occurred in the past owing to the religious antagonism of the Hindu and Musalman sections of the population.

This comment is followed by a one-and-a-half-page description of the events of 1809, after which the compiler of the *Gazetteer* remarks:

A curious sequel of the riots was a feud that sprang up between the military and the police. This originated, no doubt, in religious differences, but these appear to have been dropped in the course of time and a long succession of affrays ensued, with Hindus and Musalmans indiscriminately mingled on either side.

[7] Rev. M. A. Sherring, *Benares: The Sacred City of the Hindus* (1868, reprinted Delhi, 1975), pp. 342–4.

The entry goes on as follows:

The trouble subsided with a partial reorganization of the city police in October 1810; but before peace had been restored fresh riots arose with the introduction of the house-tax under Regulation XV of 1810, and it was again found necessary to station troops throughout the city to repress the popular disorder till the withdrawal of the obnoxious measure in the ensuing year.[8]

This was the distilled account, as it were, of the history of Banaras in the troubled days before the soothing influence of British rule and their sense of fair play had 'civilized' the city. It was an account that was carried into the assessment of the constitutional and political condition of India in the 1920s and 1930s, and it has found its way into the history books.[9] Thus, a memorandum drawn up for submission to the Indian Statutory Commission of 1928 pointed to the 'grave Benares riots' of 1809 as evidence of the usual state of Hindu–Muslim coexistence, describing them as 'one of those convulsions which had frequently occurred in the past owing to the religious antagonism of the Hindu and Moslem sections of the population'.[10]

This particular description is of course lifted straight from the account contained in the Banaras *Gazetteer* of 1907, quoted above. Notice that scarcely a word is altered in the text: and yet the change of context completely transforms the statement. What applied to a *particular* city—the experience of 'convulsions' in the past and the 'religious antagonism' of the local Hindus and Muslims—now applies to the country as a whole. Banaras becomes the essence of India, the history of Banaras the history of India.

What makes Banaras stand in for India in this instance is more

[8] H. R. Nevill, *Benares: A Gazetteer, being vol. XXVI of the District Gazetteers of the United Provinces of Agra and Oudh* (Lucknow, 1929; Preface dated December 1907), pp. 207–9.

[9] Cf. M. McPherson 'The Origin and Growth of Communal Antagonism, especially between Hindus and Muhammadans, and the Communal Award' in J. Cummings, ed., *Political India* (London, 1932); R. Coupland, *The Constitutional Problem in India* (London, 1944), pt. I, p. 29; A. S. Altekar, *History of Benares from Pre-historic Times to the Present Day* (Banaras 1937), pp. 67–8; K. N. Shukul, *Varanasi Down the Ages* (Patna, 1974), pp. 281–2.

[10] L/P&J/7/132, 'Communal Disorders'.

than the 'typical' character of Banaras as a habitation, or the 'representative' character of the strife of 1809 (if 'typical' and 'representative' have any meaning in this context). It is the magnitude of the riots of 1809—the 'grave Benares riots', paralleled, we are told only after a century and a quarter, in the Kanpur outbreak of 1931—and the fact that they are among the first to be recorded in the colonial period, i.e. most nearly contiguous to pre-colonial times. This is a point to which we shall return.

It is necessary first to examine how the Hindu–Muslim strife of 1809—that significant 'fragment' of the history of India—was reconstructed in some of the earliest accounts of the Banaras riots of 1809. One can construct an interesting table by putting together the information regarding some of the basic features of the 1809 riots as these are presented in the contemporary reports of colonial officials and the major published accounts up to the *Gazetteer* of 1907 (see Table 2:2).

Plainly, there is not a great deal of agreement here even about the bare 'facts' of the incident, although every one of these accounts (barring the first, which is in a special category) was authenticated by the claim that it was based on the original government records or information supplied by officials who were in Banaras at the time. Heber notes that he obtained his information from the Acting Magistrate, W. W. Bird himself, who gave Heber 'a far more formidable idea of the tumult than I had previously formed'.[11] Mill's *History* refers to his use of 'personal information and ms. records'.[12] William Buyers' description of the 'War of the Lat', as he calls it, is based largely on Heber's account which, he writes, 'is *no doubt* more authentic than the common native reports of it... as he had the *facts* from Mr Bird, and other gentlemen, who were at that time in office at Benares, and had, themselves, the difficult task of quelling the tumult'.[13]

However, the purpose of the comparisons presented in Table 2:2

[11] R. Heber, *Narrative of a Journey through the Upper Provinces of India, from Calcutta to Bombay, 1824–25, vol. I* (London, 1828), p. 323.

[12] J. Mill (and H. H. Wilson), *The History of British India* (in ten volumes), vol. VII (London, 1858), p. 335.

[13] W. Buyers, *Recollections of Northern India* (London, 1848) p. 273 (emphasis added).

Table 2:2. Some 'Facts' Regarding the Hindu–Muslim Conflict in Banaras, October 1809

Source	Date of Outbreak	Site of the Initial Outbreak	Immediate Cause	Casualties	Role of Police & Military	Special Features of Protest
1 Ms. Colonial Government records (1809–10)	20–24 Oct 1809	Lat Bhairava	Pollution of Lat Bhairava following dispute over attempted conversion of a Hanuman shrine at the site from mud into stone.	28–29 killed; 70 wounded	Connivance and 'highly criminal', of the Hindus fast at riverside from evening 20 Oct. Persuaded to abandon fast on 23rd.–24th morning, Gosains assemble in protest at Ghats.
2 Heber (1824)	?	Lat Bhairava	Breaking down of the Lat	—	Temper of the sepoys was 'extremely doubtful' but they held true	Fasting at the riverside by 'all the Brahmins in the city, amounting to many thousands' for 2–3 days after the 'tumult' was quelled.
3 Prinsep (1825–30)	1805	Lat Bhairava	Frenzy excited by Muharram lamentations	About 20 Muslims killed; 70 people wounded	—	—
4 Mill (1845)	21–23 Oct 1809	Lat Bhairava and the Imambarah in close proximity to it	Altercation between Hindu and Muslim worshippers, leading to injury to the Imambarah and demolition of a makeshift		'The Sipahis, although of both persuasions, discharged their duties with perfect impartiality and military steadiness: the police, equally	'The Brahmans and principal inhabitants' fasted at the riverside 'night and day', during the continuance of the disorder'; persuaded with some difficulty

	Date	Place	Event	Deaths			
						mixed, had early taken part in the conflict according to their respective creeds.'	to abandon this on 23 Oct.
5 Buyers (1848)	—	Lat Bhairava	Clash between Holi 'procession' of Hindus and Muharram procession of Muslims	—	'Difficult . . . to trust the native soldiers; but, they did their duty well'		'After the riot had been suppressed, the worst difficulty still remained': 'all the Brahmans in the city, many thousands in number', fasted for 2–3 days.
6 Gazetteer (1907)	Oct 1809	Aurangzeb mosque on the site of the old Vishwanath temple	Friction over the mosque leads to a 'sudden' outbreak	Several hundred killed	Nothing worthy of special note during the 'riots'. But 'a curious sequel' was a feud between the military and the police, which 'originated, no doubt, in religious differences'.		

SOURCES: India Office Library and Records, London, Bengal Criminal Judicial Proceedings for 1809 and 1810; R. Heber, *Narrative of a Journey through the Upper Provinces of India, from Calcutta to Bombay, 1824–25*, vol. I (London, 1828); J. Prinsep, *Benares Illustrated (3 series of drawings)* (London, 1831, 1832, 1834); J. Mill (and H. H. Wilson), *The History of British India* (in ten volumes), vol. VII (London, 1858); W. Buyers, *Recollections of Northern India* (London, 1848); H. R. Nevill, *Benares: A Gazetteer, being vol. XXVI of the District Gazetteers of the United Provinces of Agra and Oudh* (Lucknow, 1922; Preface dated Dec 1907). Among other major colonial writings of the period, the Rev. M. A. Sherring, *Benares, the Sacred City of the Hindus* (1868; reprinted Delhi, 1975) and E. B. Havell, *Benares: The Sacred City* (London, 1905) agree in almost every particular with Buyer's account of 1848.

is not simply to point out the discrepancies to be found in the earliest and most 'authoritative' accounts of the 1809 outbreak, although these are striking enough. It is to suggest that even the 'bare facts' of the situation were *constructed*—and constructed out of the prejudices, biases and 'common sense' of the writers.

The rest of this chapter is devoted to an examination of the principal features of this construction. I shall try, first, to trace the steps whereby differences on major points of fact may have crept into the colonial accounts of the Banaras events of 1809. How did *figures* of 28 or 29 people killed and 70 wounded, which Mill put at about 20 Muslims killed and 70 wounded,[14] get inflated so dramatically in the *Gazetteer* of 1907 and the Government memorandum of 1928 to 'several hundred' killed? How did the *site* of the initial outbreak shift from the Lat Bhairava, in the open area a mile outside the limits of the city, to the Bisheshwar (or Vishwanath) temple in the very heart of it? What accounts for the displacement of the '*cause*' of the conflict from the pollution and breaking down of the Lat Bhairava, to the 'frenzy' excited by Muharram lamentations, to a clash between Holi and Muharram processions, to 'friction' over the mosque built by Aurangzeb at the Gyanvapi, the site of the Vishwanath temple?

Secondly, I shall argue that the reconstruction of the Banaras riots in colonialist discourse, in its successive recensions spread over a hundred years or so, amounts to the making of a narrative form of strategic importance for the analysis of Indian politics. This is a form of representation of communal riots which assumes, over time, the importance of a master narrative and acts as a sort of model for all descriptions, and hence evaluations, of communal riots in official (and, I might add, nationalist) prose. In the colonial case, this communal riot narrative, as we have called it, is simultaneously and necessarily a statement on the Indian 'past'.

III

In order to examine the basic features of this narrative, we may analyse the colonial accounts of the 1809 Banaras riots under three broad headings: (1) the question of 'origins' or 'causes'; (2) the

---

[14] Mill apparently took note only of the casualties reported during the worst phase of the violence on 22 October 1809.

identification of rival crowds and the description of collective actions; (3) the reduction of these actions to a law-and-order problem, a part of the history of colonial administration. The concern with 'origins' is evident from some of the earliest reports on the Banaras riots. This is how the matter is dealt with in a detailed letter written by the local Magistrate, W. W. Bird, to the government less than a week after the suppression of the violence.

At the site of the Lat Bhairava where, according to this report, a mosque and Imambarah[15] had been erected in the days of Aurangzeb, there was also a mud construction which housed an image of Hanuman. A Nagar Brahman tried to convert this shrine into one of stone in fulfilment of a vow. This was resisted by Muslim weavers who worshipped there, on the ground that the stone construction would be an encroachment on 'the *masjid* which surrounds the Laut'. The Hindus and Muslims involved in the dispute agreed to wait until after the Dasehra holidays, which ended on 19 October 1809, and to then refer the matter to the court. However, on the evening of 20 October, 'the Joolahirs [Julahas, Muslim weavers], instead of referring, assembled suddenly at the Laut to decide their differences in person' and committed 'those indignities' (i.e. the pollution of the Lat Bhairava) that led to the riots of 21 October.

Early on the morning of the 21st, the report goes on to say, large numbers of Hindus 'of all cast[e]s, especially Nagirs, Goshaieens, and Rajepoots' gathered and, after some hesitation, did some damage to the Imambarah that stood adjacent to the Lat. Upon this, Muslim weavers from the vicinity marched to the Lat and upset some of the images erected round about it. Tempers rose and the local police, both Hindus and Muslims, 'partook of the infection'. The Kotwal, a Muslim, succeeded through his personal exertions in holding off both the Muslim and the Hindu party for a while. However, 'at length the Joolahirs collecting in considerable numbers armed with swords and clubs, hoisted a standard, and exclaiming Imam Hoosein and beating their breasts, marched towards the city.' 'They were reported to be heading for the Bisheshwar or Vishwanath temple, 'the principal place of Hindoo

---

[15] Other reports speak of a mosque that extended into an Idgah, and that is what exists at the site today.

worship in the city'. But they were defeated on the way in a battle at Gai Ghat where a very large crowd of Hindus had assembled: two or three Muslim Julahas were killed or wounded in this encounter. Upon this, the assembled Julahas 'with great precipitation' retraced their steps and threw down and broke the Lat Bhairava. 'The effects of this outrage on the minds of the Hindus will be readily conceived'.[16]

This account, which we need pursue no further for the moment, perhaps provides a few clues as to where the later colonial writers got their ideas about the origins of the 1809 outbreak. Heber's view that the breaking down of the Lat was the immediate provocation for the riots comes naturally enough, for this was perhaps the moment of maximum fissility when things might have gone in any direction: after this, what was a fairly localized clash became a general fight over large parts of the city, and this moment may well have stood out in Bird's recollections when he talked to Heber fifteen years after these events.

Prinsep seems to have been the originator of the view that Muslim lamentations at the Muharram were responsible for the tension that led to the outbreak (see Table 2:2). It is possible that he obtained this idea from the report that, on 21 October 1809, a large body of Julahas marched towards the Vishwanath temple 'armed with swords and clubs, [carrying] a standard. . . exclaiming Imam Hoosein and beating their breasts'.[17]

'Muharram' refers to the ten-day period of mourning in the eponymous first month of the Muslim year which Muslims, especially Shias, observe in memory of the martyrs Imam Hasan and Imam Husain who lost their lives in battle at the Karbala. While orthodox Sunnis are supposed to take no part in this ritual, in the past Muslims of all persuasions, and indeed large numbers of Hindus too, in villages and small towns all over India joined in the processions of *tazias* (replicas of the tombs of the martyrs) and participated in the recitations of the story of their sacrifice. This public statement of community grief reaches its height on the last

---

[16] (IOL), Board's Collections, vol. 365 (F/4/365), no. 9093, W. W. Bird, Acting Magistrate, Benares—Dowdeswell, Secretary to the Government, Judicial Department, 30 October 1809 (Consultn. no. 23 of 5 December 1809).

[17] Ibid., para 4.

two or three days of the mourning period, when the processions become larger, the competition between different groups (each presenting their own laments and recitations) sharper, and the exhibition of sorrow takes on an extreme physical dimension. 'One of the most impressive religious spectacles in India', Crooke wrote in the 1890s, 'is . . . the long procession of Tazias and flags which streams along the streets, with a vast crowd of mourners, who scream out their lamentations and beat their breasts till the blood flows, or . . . sink fainting in an ecstacy of sorrow'.[18]

Prinsep described these same proceedings from what he had seen of the 'Procession of the Tazeeas' in Banaras in the late 1820s. For ten days in Muharram, Muslims clad in green and black, 'their trappings of woe', commemorate the martyrdom of Hasan and Husain, he observed. 'The piteous tale is chaunted [*sic*] in the current language by people hired, apparently, for their strength of lungs, who work themselves and their audience by degrees into a phrenzy of grief; tearing their hair, beating their breasts, and crying "Hoosyn, Hoosyn", until quite exhausted'.[19] This was not unlike the Banaras Magistrate's description of the Julahas' march towards the Vishwanath temple on 21 October 1809, 'armed with swords and clubs, [carrying] a standard . . . exclaiming Imam Hoosein and beating their breasts'.

It was perhaps this superficial resemblance that led Prinsep to conclude: 'It was under such a state of excited zeal [owing to Muharram lamentations] that a congregation at the Lat'h Imambareh, in 1805 [*sic*], was urged by some fanatic preacher to overthrow and defile the pillar and images of Hindoo worship at that place'.[20] In any event, we have no other evidence of a Muharram procession having been taken out at this time. A 'Muharram' procession, in any case, there could not have been, for Muharram on this occasion happened to come three-and-a-half months later, in early February 1810.

Here, in Prinsep's hands, 'Muharram' becomes a metaphor for the representation of the Other. This public exhibition of grief,

[18] W. Crooke, *The North-Western Provinces of India* (1897; Karachi, 1972), pp. 263–4.

[19] J. Prinsep, *Benares Illustrated* (3 series of drawings) (London, 1831, 1832, 1834), Note on 'Procession of the Tazeeas'.

[20] Ibid.

like its obverse the carnivalesque celebration of joy, is the kind of dramatized and ritualized behaviour that stands for the primitive— once found in the West, still widespread in the Orient. It is that aspect of Oriental life that is furthest removed from the restrained, privatized, 'civilized' life of modern Europe. It is volatile as well: insurgency and violence lurk just beneath the surface here; it is all too easy for the primitive to get out of control. As Crooke put it,

One of the most difficult duties of the Indian Magistrate is to regulate these [Muharram] processions and decide the precedence of its members. The air rings with the cries of these ardent fanatics, and their zeal often urges them to violence directed against Hindus or rival sectaries. But the English Gallio is no judge of such matters, and his anxieties do not end until he has steered without conflict or disturbance the howling crowd of devotees through the stifling city lanes into the open fields beyond, where the mimic sepulchres of the martyrs are supposed to be flung into a tank or buried.[21]

Or the Rev. C. P. Cape:

The annual celebration of the death of Husain undoubtedly helps in some Indian cities to accentuate the differences between the Shiahs and the Sunnis; and the Deputy Commissioner congratulates himself [again the singular form, testimony to the universality of the statement] if Muharram has passed off peacefully. In Bombay, British artillery and infantry have been requisitioned [when? every year?] to keep the excited crowds in order and to patrol the streets at night. . . . When this festival occurs at the same time as the Holi, the authorities in certain towns know that, unless great care is taken, there may be serious disturbance.[22]

Thus: Muharram (Muharram/Holi)→Excitement→Violence. Since these are the steps, an outbreak of violence such as that in Banaras in 1809, makes the colonial observer look for 'Muharram' as the 'cause'—and find it! Prinsep finds 'Muharram' in his search for the origins of the riot, Mill and Buyers the compound 'Holi-and-Muharram'.

---

[21] Crooke, *The North-Western Provinces*, p. 264.

[22] Rev. C. P. Cape, *Benares: The Stronghold of Hinduism* (London, n.d.), pp. 109–10. Cf. J. Masselos, 'Change and Custom in the Format of the Bombay Mohurrum during the 19th and 20th Centuries', *South Asia*, new series, v, 2 (December 1982), who notes (p. 48) that nineteenth-century colonialist observers looked at Muharram as 'a grand spectacle of religious passion'.

A similar metaphorical function is performed by the religious sites of the Hindus and Muslims. All the nineteenth-century accounts of the Banaras events of 1809 point to the significance of such sites and the 'irrational' attachment of the 'natives' to them (as to idols, cows, rivers, trees, what have you). Heber's account of the *dharna* that followed, or in some versions accompanied, the riots of October 1809, provides adequate illustration:

The holy city had been profaned; the blood of a cow had been mixed with the purest water of Gunga, and salvation was to be obtained at Benares no longer. All the brahmins in the city, amounting to many thousands, went down in melancholy procession, with ashes on their heads, naked and fasting, to the principal ghats leading to the river, and sate [sic] there with their hands folded, their heads hanging down, to all appearance inconsolable, and refusing to enter a house or to taste food. . . .[23]

In the same way, the colonial accounts dwell on the double sanctity—to Hindus and to Muslims—of the sites over which the disputes of October 1809 are supposed to have arisen. The Kapal Mochan ground, where the Lat Bhairava stood, was one of several places in the city where buildings sacred to the Hindus and the Muslims respectively stood adjacent to one another. Aurangzeb, they tell us, had ordered the demolition of a number of temples and the construction of mosques 'with the same materials and upon the same foundations', in Prinsep's words, 'leaving portions of the ancient walls exposed here and there as evidences of the indignity to which the Hindoo religion had been subjected'.[24]

Among these constructions, perhaps the most widely talked about was the Gyanvapi mosque built under Aurangzeb's instructions at the site of the old Vishwanath temple. Colonial observers in the nineteenth century were agreed that this spot was 'the chief source of friction' between the Hindus and Muslims of the city; 'a constant source of heart-burnings and feuds both to Hindus and Mohammedans'; 'a monuments of Moslem pride and intolerance and of Hindu humiliation in former times'.[25] The extraordinary sanctity accorded to the Vishwanath temple was testified

[23] Heber, *Narrative, vol. I*, p. 325.

[24] Prinsep, *Benares Illustrated*, p. 11 of chapter entitled 'Benares 1830'.

[25] *Benares Gazetteer*, p. 207; Sherring, *Benares: The Sacred City*, p. 52; Buyers, *Recollections*, p. 256 respectively.

to by the interesting observation in the Magistrate's report of 21 November 1809 that the rumour of an intended Muslim attack on the Vishwanath 'was at first not credited. It was too extravagant for belief'.[26]

These assessments regarding the destruction of temples and the construction of mosques in their vicinity at several places in Banaras, the resulting bitterness and friction, and the special sanctity attached by the Hindus to the principal temple of Vishwanath, perhaps help to explain both the shifting of the initial site of the 1809 outbreak in some of the later colonial writings and the *Gazetteer*'s exceptional account of its proximate cause. Mill, who obliquely suggested some link between the violence of October 1809 and the coincidence of the 'moveable feasts' of the Hindus and Muslims, went on further to write of friction at the sites where Muslim religious buildings had been erected near old temples as the context for the conflict in 1809.[27] The semantic field from which one may draw for an explanation of Indian politics ('riots') has been laid out. It is up to the individual writer to pick out the mixture of elements that best fits a particular case.

The Rev. C. P. Cape, a less careful historian than Mill, referred to the clash of the Muharram and Holi 'festivals', and then proceeded to write with such vagueness about the site of the outbreak that it becomes impossible to tell the exact location of even the buildings he specifically names; indeed it becomes clear that in his reckoning one place was as good as any other as an excuse for the violence. The Muslims were defeated in 'some street fighting' that broke out owing to the alleged clash of Holi and Muharram processions, Cape wrote. They then 'revenged themselves by retreating into a courtyard of Aurangzeb's mosque and broke down the Lat of Shiva, which the Hindus held in high esteem. The Hindus pulled down a mosque, and then the military intervened'.[28]

There is no way of knowing from this account whether 'Aurangzeb's mosque' refers to the mosque built adjacent to the Lat Bhairav (which no one referred to by this name), or whether Cape believed that the Lat was in fact located in the great mosque built at the

---

[26] F/4/365, E. Watson, Magistrate-Government, 21 November 1809.
[27] Mill, *History, vol. VII*, pp. 336–7.
[28] Cape, *Benares: The Stronghold*, p. 110.

Madhavrai ghat with its minarets towering over the city (which is still called the Alamgiri masjid) or in the Gyanvapi mosque built by Aurangzeb at the site of the Vishwanath temple (which was in fact the mosque attacked and partly demolished by Hindu rioters on 22 October after the felling of the Lat Bhairav on the day before). But the point is that, for Cape's purpose, it really does not matter. Processions clash: street-fighting follows: the defeated party retreats and despoils a sacred structure: the other party pulls down a mosque: the military intervenes. This is the structure of a tale. Evil clashes with evil. Good intervenes. Order is restored.

It is not very difficult to see, in this light, why the compiler of the Banaras *District Gazetteer*, writing around the same time as Cape, and more directly concerned to make a general statement regarding the benefits of British rule, should suppose that the worst instance of Hindu-Muslim strife in Banaras in the nineteenth century must have originated at the site of their most obvious quarrel, i.e. the spot where the Vishwanath temple and the Gyanvapi masjid stood cheek by jowl; or again why he should assume that such an instance of fighting over such a sensitive spot amongst such a fanatical people must, inevitably, have claimed 'several hundreds' of lives.[29]

What the colonial accounts sought to do was to give the violence of 1809 a cause and the cause a name (fanaticism, irrationality), thus emptying it of all other significance, including, as we shall see, its dangers for the colonial state. For the point of the exercise was a deeper one: it was to describe the 'native' character, establish the perverse nature of the population and the fundamental antagonism between 'Hindus' and 'Muslims'. This may be inferred from a glance at certain other features that recur over and over again in colonial writings on the Banaras events of the early nineteenth century: the emphasis on ethnic and doctrinal signs for the identification of rival crowds; the construction of a diachrony into which

[29] Since then, this colonial account, considerably amplified, has been widely accepted. K. N. Shukul, *Varanasi Down the Ages*, p. 281, speaks of major riots both in 1805 and 1809, accepting the dates given in both Prinsep and the *Benares Gazetteer*; Diana Eck, *Banaras: City of Light* (London, 1983), p. 197, attributes the 1809 riots to the attempted construction of a shrine between the Gyanvapi mosque and the Vishwanath temple, the clash of the Holi and Muharram festivals *and* the destruction of the Lat Bhairav.

these events fitted; and the description of violence as a means of describing native character.

IV

The colonial obsession with ethnic and doctrinal signs for the identification of rival crowds is perhaps best illustrated by the Banaras *Gazetteer*'s remarks on the military-police feud that followed the riots of 1809. We have already noted the *Gazetteer*'s contention that this feud 'originated, no doubt, in religious differences'. There is nothing, however, in the original correspondence of the Magistrate, the military commanders and other people in Banaras at the time, to suggest even remotely that the clashes between military and police personnel in 1810 had anything to do with religious matters.

If there was a connection with October 1809, it was that the behaviour of the police at that time had rendered the name of the police, in Bird's words, 'generally obnoxious, but particularly to the Sepoys, whose meritorious conduct entitled them in a manner to feel contempt for the cowardice of the police'.[30] When the military guard was finally withdrawn in 1809 and the police restored to their normal functions in Banaras, sepoys going into the city reportedly poked fun at the police. Some of them also persistently defied a magisterial order against the carrying of arms in the streets of Banaras. The incidence of disputes between military and police personnel on account of these pin-pricks increased in August and September 1810. As the season of *melas* associated with the Dasehra celebrations approached, the civil authorities were understandably perturbed about the possible consequences of such quarrels between the two arms of the law and the state, and they urged their military counterparts to ensure strict discipline.

That—the approach of an important religious festival and the apprehensions aroused by it—was the extent of the 'religious' dimension to this feud, which degenerated in the course of time, as the *District Gazetteer* has it, into 'a long succession of affrays... with Hindus and Muslims indiscriminately mingled on either

---

[30] (IOL) Bengal Criminal Judl. Prog., Range 130, vol. 22, Bird-Dowdeswell, 13 October 1810 (Consultation no. 46 of 24 October 1810). The rest of this paragraph is based on the same consultation.

side'. The failure of the indigenous population to conform to the colonial stereotype of Hindu and Muslim crowd (or for that matter, individual) behaviour could only be 'indiscriminate'.

It is perhaps one of the important features of colonialist writings on Banaras 1809 that such crude representations first became fixed here and accepted as self-explanatory categories. The process of thinking through stereotypes can be seen evolving even in some of the earliest reactions to the events of 1809–11. Consider the contemporary officials' reports on the great anti-house tax *hartal* of December 1810–January 1811. This extraordinary act of protest was described as follows in a letter from the Banaras Magistrate, dated 28 December 1810:

An oath was administered throughout the city both among the Hindus and the Mohommedans, enjoining all classes to neglect their respective occupations (until the tax was withdrawn).... The Lohars, the Mistrees, the Jolahirs, the Hujams, the Durzees, the Kohars, the Bearers, every class of workmen engaged unanimously in this conspiracy . . . during the 26th, the dead bodies were actually cast neglected into the Ganges because the proper people could not be prevailed upon to administer the customary Rites.[31]

To which Mill added, colourfully: 'the very thieves refrained from the exercise of their vocation although the shops and houses were left without protection—the people deserting the city in a body.'[32]

In trying to make sense of this staggering popular protest, the officials turned to their experience of 1809 and their 'common sense' about the dynamics of the local society. 'Men of all classes and description, from the highest to the lowest, whether Mohammedans or Hindoos, Jolahirs, Raujpoots and Goshains included, were all of one mind, and engaged by oath to promote the common cause', Bird wrote in January 1811.[33] The echoes of 1809 are clear.

[31] Board's Collections, vol. 323 (F/4/323), no. 7407, Bird–Dowdeswell, 28 December 1810. Many of the letters and documents from this volume that are referred to here are also reprinted in Dharampal, *Civil Disobedience & Indian Tradition. With Some Early Nineteenth Century Documents* (Varanasi, 1971).

[32] Mill, *History, vol. VII*, p. 334. For an important recent account, see Richard Heitler, 'The Varanasi House Tax Hartal of 1810–11', *IESHR*, ix, 3 (September 1972).

[33] F/4/323, no. 7407, note on verbal communication made by Bird to Macdonald at conference held at Mr Brooke's house on 13 January 1811.

Then Brahmans, Rajputs and Gosains were seen as being the most active elements on the Hindu side, and Julahas on the Muslim side. Now, those who have risen are described as 'Muhammedans (and) Hindoos, Jolahirs, Raujpoots and Goshains included'. Following the same logic, the commander of the troops stationed at Banaras expressed the fear that the Rajputs, Gosains, 'Muslims' and other 'fighting cast[e]s' [sic] might take up arms, especially if the blood of Brahmans or other 'religious orders' were spilt.[34] The Magistrate spoke of how the 'religious orders' had exerted their full influence in favour of the agitation and 'men of rank and respectability' encouraged the huge crowds;[35] and Heber later wrote of *dharmpatris* issued by 'the leading Brahmins' as being central to the process of mobilizing the people.[36]

In all this, the colonial observers neglected the evidence that they had before them of the very different sections of local society that formed the vanguard of the rising in 1810–11 as compared to 1809. The Rajputs, who are described as the 'moving spirits' behind the Hindu actions in 1809,[37] hung back in 1810–11: indeed, on the latter occasion, many Rajput landowners assisted the colonial authorities in their attempts to disperse the crowds.[38] And while many of the 'leading native inhabitants' and 'religious orders' of Banaras were certainly involved in the anti-house tax agitation, they appear to have conceded the leadership, at least in the initial stages of the protest, to artisans, skilled workers and other sections of the lower classes.

I have quoted earlier the first detailed report regarding the crowds that had assembled, which listed the Lohars, Mistris, Julahas, Hajjams, Darzis, Kohars and Kahars as the 'seven classes of people'· who, '*attended by multitudes of others* of all ranks and descriptions', gathered in the vicinity of the city.[39] The Lohars, in particular, were singled out as prime movers of the uprising. 'The Lohars, who

[34] Ibid., Macdonald–Bird, 12 January 1811, and note on conference held at Mr Brooke's house on 18 January 1811.
[35] Ibid., Bird–Dowdeswell, 4 January, 8 January and 28 January 1811.
[36] Heber, *Narrative, vol. I*, p. 327.
[37] *Benares Gazetteer*, p. 207.
[38] F/4/323, no. 7407, Bird–Dowdeswell, 8 January 1811, and Dowdeswell–Bird, 11 January 1811.
[39] See n. 31 above. Emphasis mine.

originally assembled for another purpose, soon took a principal part in the conspiracy, and have collected here in great number from all parts of the Banaras province', Bird reported on 2 January 1911.[40]

W. O. Salmon, the Collector, confirmed this in a communication to the government on the same day:

If one party be more obstinate and more determined upon extending the mischief than another, the Lohars, or blacksmiths, may be so charged, for they were not only the first to convoke the assembly of their near brethren, but they have far and wide called upon other Lohars to join them with the intent that no implement of cultivation or of harvest (which is fast approaching) be either made or mended, and thus that the zemindars and ryots may be induced to take part with the malcontents, in short that the whole of the country shall directly or indirectly be urged to insist on the repeal of the tax. *With these Lohars almost all other cast[e]s, sects and persuasions are in League,* and I am informed under a most binding oath amongst each other.[41]

Many of the most familiar features of Orientalist knowledge are already in evidence here: the typecasting ('fighting cast[e]s' like 'Rajputs', 'Gosains', 'Muslims'!), the centrality assigned to the 'religious orders', the charge of manipulation by élite groups or 'leading native inhabitants'. This reductionist tendency naturally influenced colonial descriptions of crowd action as well. Consider once more Cape's matter-of-fact statement on the 1809 riots: Holi and Muharram clash. There is 'some street fighting'. The defeated 'Muhammadans' revenge themselves by retreating into 'Aurangzeb's mosque' and breaking down the Lat Bhairava. 'The Hindus' pull down a mosque. And then, the military intervenes. The message is transparent: *this* is the natural order of things in this society. The sequential order is fixed, as an order of mimesis; and it is accepted by all colonial writers for the writing up of such events.

It is the same understanding that informs the Banaras *Gazetteer*'s, and thence the Government of India's 1928 remarks on what followed the breaking down of the Lat Bhairav in Banaras in October 1809:

[40] F/4/323, no. 7407, Bird-Dowdeswell, 2 January 1811.

[41] Ibid., Salmon-Secretary, Government of India, Revenue Department, 2 January 1811 (emphasis added).

Great crowds of Hindus attacked the mosque of Aurangzeb, set it on fire and put to death every Muhammadan of the neighbourhood who fell into their hands. The entire city was given up to pillage and slaughter, and order was not restored by the troops until some fifty mosques had been destroyed and several hundred persons had lost their lives.[42]

Another expression of the essentializing process noticed above is found in the colonial writers'historicization of the Banaras events of 1809. Given the nature of 'Hindus' and 'Muslims', 'Hinduism' and 'Islam', a violent conflict between the two was always on the cards. The riots of 1809 are represented as part of a continuum, a tradition: 'one of those convulsions which had frequently occurred in the past owing to the religious antagonism of the Hindu and Moslem sections of the population'. Or as Francis Younghusband put it in a book entitled *Dawn in India*, published in 1930, 'the animosities of centuries are always smouldering beneath the surface'.[43]

Judging by colonial accounts of the strife in Banaras, 1809 sees only a development in degree, an intensification. 'Towards the close of 1809 an open rupture could no longer be delayed' (Mill). 'The ill-will between the rival religions [*sic*] culminated in a sudden outbreak of great intensity in October 1809' (Nevill).[44] In certain instances, the tradition of conflict is seen as growing out of an actual historical experience—in the Banaras case, Aurangzeb's iconoclasm. Thus in a 'Handbook' on Banaras published in 1886, the Rev. J. Ewen notes that the Lat Bhairav stands on a site appropriated for Muslim worship in Aurangzeb's time but continues to be used by Hindu worshippers as well. He then simply adds: 'The dispute between the parties reached a climax at the end of the last century [*sic*].'[45]

An 'ill-will' that exists from the mid-seventeenth century, if not earlier, 'culminates' for no obvious reason, 'reaches a climax' in a 'sudden' outbreak of rioting in 1809. In this kind of history, 'violence' always belonged to a pre-colonial tradition: the imposition of British rule, the displacement of an earlier balance of power,

---

[42] *Benares Gazetteer*, pp. 207–8.

[43] F. Younghusband, *Dawn in India* (London, 1930), p. 144.

[44] Mill, *History, vol. VII*, p. 336; Nevill, *Benares Gazetteer*, p. 207.

[45] J. Ewen, *Benares: A Handbook for Visitors* (Calcutta, 1886), p. 40.

the raising of new hopes and fears, had nothing to do with it. This 'tradition' of strife becomes, indeed, the justification for colonial rule. By the later nineteenth century, it is no longer the power of the English sword, nor simply the superiority of English science and commerce, but also the argument that the 'natives' are hopelessly divided, given to primitive passions and incapable of managing their own affairs, that legitimizes British power.[46] Hence the Rev. James Kennedy, after his sojourn in northern India in the 1870s and '80s: 'The antagonism [between Hindu and Muslim 'systems'], though generally latent, every now and then breaks out into fierce strife, which but for the interposition of Government would lead to civil war.'[47]

V

I have left to the last what is possibly the most striking feature of the colonial writings under discussion and also perhaps the least investigated, in part because it has passed without much change into nationalist writings and a good deal of recent historiography. This is the reduction of Indian history to the history of the state. In colonialist writings a distinction was first made between the history of local society—wild, chaotic, liable to unexpected explosions—and the history of the state. The impressive efforts at state building in the past were noted, and the early British rulers of India self-consciously modelled themselves on their claimed 'predecessors', the Mughal emperors (and, to some extent, different Hindu ruling dynasties in southern India). But above all in these writings, it was the new, colonial state that stood out in contrast to the primitive, pre-political, one might even say proto-historic character of the local society.

We have earlier quoted the Rev. M. A. Sherring's comments on the history of Banaras/India: 'While its career has been of long duration, it has not been of a character to awaken much enthusiasm or admiration. It cannot be said that either the moral, or the social,

[46] This line of argument is, of course, already put forward for the annexation of Awadh and in other such cases even earlier.

[47] J. Kennedy, *Life and Work in Benares and Kumaon, 1839–1877* (London, 1884), p. 335.

or even the intellectual, condition of the people residing here is a whit better than it was upwards of two thousand years ago . . . '. In other words, they *had* no history. However, Sherring goes on, 'while I look with profound regret on much of the past history of India, I look forward to its coming history with strong hope and confidence'.[48]

The *Gazetteer* of 1907 also set off this 'past' history of Banaras against what Sherring called its 'coming' history. 'The history of Benares during the first part of the nineteenth century is mainly a record of administrative development under British rule. The only disturbance of the public peace occurred in 1809 . . . [etc.]'. James Mill had made the same point much earlier, when he wrote that the maintenance of peace and order in that city was 'for some time' a 'troublesome' and 'imperfectly' accomplished task. But the 'unrelaxing firmness' of British rule, a 'better knowledge of the British character' and the 'improving intelligence' of the Indians (no less!)[49] 'lightened the labour'—presumably the divinely ordained British task of bringing 'law and order' to these domains—so that ten years after 1809, 'Benares was regulated with as much facility as any other city in the territories of the Company.'[50] The altered speed of time here is striking. The 'pre-history' of Banaras, like the history of all India before the coming of the British power, is chaos. And then, within ten years, 'history' supervenes, order is established.

The representation of all popular politics as a problem of law and order, and their assimilation thereby to the history of the state, is a commonly observed feature of colonialist writings on India. In Banaras 1809, it is worth noting in this context, the origins of Hindu–Muslim strife were seen as lying not only in the peculiar religious sensibilities of the people but also in an 'unwarranted' act of assembly on the part of the Muslim weavers. The dispute over the consolidation of a Hanuman shrine at the Kapal Mochan was apparently followed by an agreement between local Hindu and Muslim leaders to wait until the Dasehra holidays ended on

[48] See n. 7 above.

[49] Compare Sherring's statement on the intellectual stagnation of the Indian people for two thousand years, in the preceding quotation.

[50] Mill, *History, vol. VII*, pp. 338–9.

19 October 1809 and then refer the matter to the court. However, on the evening of 20 October, the Magistrate's report tells us, 'the Joolahirs, *instead of referring, assembled suddenly at the Laut to decide their differences in person*'[51] and took those actions that led to riots on the following day.

Nine months later, while discussing measures that might be adopted to prevent a recurrence of such disturbances, the Magistrate wrote to the government: 'The disturbance [of October 1809] is found to have originated in the abuse of that privilege which the Natives have been permitted to enjoy, of *assembling among themselves to deliberate on questions of common interest.* I found it expedient to prohibit all assemblies of this nature without previous application to the police. . . . '[52] So that along with its disarming of the population of Banaras in 1809, the colonial regime also at this very early date imposed strict limitations on the right of assembly of the subject people.

The colonialist accounts of the anti–tax agitation of 1810–11 are no less instructive in this respect. We find a great deal of writing on the extraordinary caste solidarity, the diversity of castes involved and, as we have noticed, the 'leadership' of the religious orders and the use of religious injunctions, that went into the making of this remarkable dharna and hartal. Having established the ethnic identity and the religious motivation of the crowd to their own satisfaction, the officials then turned to their other major concern—the question of law and order. One official observed that 'instead of appearing like a tumultuous and disorderly mob, the vast multitudes came forth in a state of perfect organization: each caste, trade and profession occupied a distinct spot of ground, and was regulated in all its acts by the orders of its own punchayet'.[53] But the dispersal of the assembly, an active assertion of people's power, was nevertheless a matter of the greatest urgency. The Magistrate's report of 20 January 1811 is couched in familiar terms: 'It becomes every day an object of greater importance to disperse the people,

[51] F/4/365, Bird–Dowdeswell, 30 October 1809, para 3 (emphasis added).

[52] Ibid., para 7 (emphasis added).

[53] *Selections of Papers from the Records of the East India House relative to Revenue, Police, Civil and Criminal Justice under the Company's Government in India,* vol. II (London, 1820), p. 89.

and compel them to put an end to their *seditious and unwarrantable proceedings*'.[54]

There is a return here to precisely that sequential order that we mentioned earlier. Law and order is indeed the only kind of 'order' that is allowed to emerge out of the colonial writing up of the Bañāras events. The appropriation of all of this history to the history of the state proceeds by glossing over, underplaying, even omitting significant areas of the people's, not to mention the state's, experience and activities. Of the two parts that go to make up the story of a riot in the colonialist account—the circumstances and manner of its outbreak, and the process of its suppression—it is only the first that survives as a major presence, an example, in later colonial writings. The significance of the second part increasingly lies in its brevity—what appears as the clinical efficiency of colonial administrative practice. Notice, for instance, the Banaras *Gazetteer*'s silence over police inefficiency and the possibility of military disloyalty in 1809. The contrast in this respect with the earlier colonial writings is remarkable (see Table 2:2).[55] The immediate reports 'from the front' in 1809 and 1810 expressed serious concern over the collapse of the police force and the possible repercussions on the military. The police were pronounced guilty of a 'most culpable neglect of duty' and 'highly criminal conduct'; 'both Hindus and Mahomedans composing it' 'exerted themselves to inflame the passions' of their co-religionists.[56] The military sepoys luckily held firm: but there was considerable anxiety among civil and military officials in Banaras at the time as to which way the wind would blow.

For about twenty days in October and November 1809, the sepoÿs were not allowed time off to bathe, dress, or prepare their food. 'It was deemed advisable', wrote the Magistrate, 'considering the delicate nature of the service they were engaged in, to *prevent them* as much as possible *from communicating with the people*. For

[54] F/4/323, Bird-Dowdeswell, 20 January 1811.

[55] Cf. also Sir John Malcolm's discussion of the 'alarming' nature of the opposition to the Government in Banaras in '1812', as in Dacca, Bareilly and other places a few years later, in his *Political History of India from 1784–1823 in Two Volumes* (London, 1826), vol. I, pp. 577–80.

[56] F/4/365, Bird's letters of 6 and 11 November 1809.

this purpose they were provided with *mithaie* [local sweetmeats] that they might be at all times within the control and observation of their officers.' On 21 November 1809, when a reinforcement of troops arrived from Danapur, the authorities withdrew a good many sepoys from the city, but it was still thought advisable to retain the entire contingent of European officers 'to prevent all intercourse between the Seapoys and the people'.[57]

It was as if all this had been completely forgotten by the end of the century. Nevill's *Gazetteer* of 1907 referred to the sepoys in passing as having restored 'order' in Banaras after some fifty mosques had been destroyed and several hundred people killed. Nevill did not so much as mention the police in his description of the events of 1809. There was not the faintest suggestion here that these forces could have done anything but obey orders, that they were—even in the earliest years of British rule—anything more than cogs in a well-oiled colonial machine that arrived fully assembled and functioned with perfect efficiency from the moment of its installation. ('The history of Benares during the first part of the nineteenth century is mainly a record of administrative development.')

Mill had of course admitted otherwise; the maintenance of peace and order in Banaras was 'for some time' a 'troublesome' and 'imperfectly' accomplished task. But the 'unrelaxing firmness' of British rule, a 'better knowledge of the British character' and the consequent improvement in the intelligence of the 'natives' had cured all that. Here Mill and Nevill occupy the same ground. Firmness, Character, Intelligence. These are the hallmarks of British rule; this is the history of the 'perfect' state that is the colonial regime in India. What the nineteenth-century colonial writings on Banaras seek to do, almost without exception, is to promote a picture of the colonial state as a wise and neutral power, ruling almost without a physical presence, by the sheer force of its moral authority. By the end of the nineteenth century this is established with the aid of a few blind spots: the colonial regime pretends to have no allies, no local collaborators (Mill, by contrast, had

---

[57] Bengal Criminal Judl. Progs, Range 130, vol. 19, Bird-Dowdeswell, 11 July 1810 (emphasis added); F/4/356, Macdonald's letter of 31 October 1809; and F/4/365, Watson-Government, 21 November 1809, para 15

mentioned the opportune intervention of the Maharaja of Banaras in 1810–11) and a minimal armed force.

These blind spots are of course nothing compared to those that came to mark the history of the political activities of the colonized as told by the colonizers. One gets some idea of the extent of the distortion of that history from the omission of any meaningful reference to the dharna of 1810–11 from the *Gazetteer*'s summary of the history of Banaras in the early nineteenth century. I have earlier quoted Heber's account of the 1809 dharna involving 'all the brahmins in the city, amounting to many thousands'. Other accounts report the participation of the 'superior orders', the 'principal inhabitants', the Gosains, and so on. According to Heber, Bird who was 'one of the ambassadors [of peace]' on this occasion, recalled that 'the scene was very impressive and even aweful. The gaunt squalid figures of the devotees, their visible and apparently unaffected anguish and dismay, the screams and outcries of the women who surrounded them, and the great numbers thus assembled, altogether constituted a spectacle of woe such as few cities but Benares could supply'.[58]

In his account of the Banaras events of 1809, Heber devotes nearly as much space to this dharna as he does to the incidents of violence and rioting, and his account is followed closely by later colonial writers like Mill and Buyers, Sherring and Havell. Not so by the compiler of the *Gazetteer* of 1907, who does not mention the dharna at all. The *Gazetteer* is equally dismissive of the anti-house tax agitation of 1810–11, during which (by Heber's account) Banaras witnessed a dharna 'exceeding', as 'spectacle', even the dharna of 1809.[59]

Heber is sufficiently moved by what he learns of the popular protest in 1810–11 to devote several pages of his journal to a discussion of the agitation against the house tax. He writes without reservation of the strength and unity of the rising. After elaborating what he understands of the traditional Indian practice of dharna, the Bishop notes: 'Whether [or not] there is any example under their ancient princes of a considerable portion of the people taking this strange method of remonstrance against oppression [*sic*] . . . in

[58] Heber, *Narrative, vol. I*, p. 325.
[59] Ibid., pp. 325–6.

this case it was done with great resolution, and surprising concert and unanimity'.[60]

Heber's comments on the apprehensions of the Government also merit quotation:

The local government were exceedingly perplexed. There was the chance that very many of these strange beings would really perish, either from their obstinacy [in fasting], or the diseases which they would contract in their present situation. There was a probability that famine would ensue from the interruption of agricultural labours at the most critical time of the year. There was a certainty that the revenue would suffer very materially from this total cessation of all traffick. And it might even be apprehended that their despair, and the excitement occasioned by such a display of physical force would lead them to far stronger demonstrations of discontent than that of sitting dhurna.[61]

Even in this 'sympathetic' colonial account, however, it is the colonial regime that emerges as the hero of the tale. Of the two sides involved in this confrontation, one is made up of an emotional population—'strange (obstinate) beings' with 'strange methods', seething with 'anguish', 'dismay', 'despair'. Their 'remonstrance against oppression' too is in a sense passive. For in comprehending protest as despair, Heber relates the event to 'being' rather than to social and political circumstances, to unreflective response rather than deliberate action.

The active part in this confrontation is performed by those who make up the other half of Heber's history. The point is best made in the Bishop's own words. The 'wise and merciful' conduct of the officials stationed in Banaras who refused to do anything to provoke the crowds into violence, and the 'wisdom' of the 'Supreme Government' in repealing the 'obnoxious tax'—nothing said here about who imposed the tax and what made it 'obnoxious' in the first place—'ended [the] disturbance which, if it had been harshly or improperly managed, might have put all India in a flame'.[62]

In the less sympathetic colonial account contained in the Banaras *Gazetteer* of 1907 and carried into the reports of the Indian Statutory

[60] Ibid., p. 326.
[61] Ibid., pp. 326–7.
[62] Ibid., pp. 328–9.

Commission and other authorities, the colonial regime becomes the exclusive subject of modern Indian history. The *Gazetteer* devotes precisely five lines to the anti-house tax movement of 1810–11, less than one complete sentence: '. . . before peace had been restored fresh riots arose with the introduction of the house-tax under Regulation XV of 1810, and it was again found necessary to station troops throughout the city to repress the popular disorder till the withdrawal of the obnoxious measure in the ensuing year'.[63]

It will be noticed that the history of the state makes its entrance here almost bashfully. What we are presented with is a caricature of all that belongs to the history of the community, which succeeds in assimilating the life of the community to the development of the colonial administration—'peace', 'law' and 'order'. The reduction of the history of society to the history of the state is complete.

Let us quickly re-read the *Gazetteer*'s summary of the history of Banaras for the first half of the century.

— 'The only disturbance of the public peace occurred in 1809 and the following year'. Notice '*and* the following year'. Does this refer to a conflict that lasted from 1809 well into 1810? Or, what is more likely in the circumstances, to a more extended state of being?

— 'A curious sequel' to the 1809 strife was a military-police feud that 'originated, no doubt, in religious differences, but these appear to have been dropped in the course of time and a long succession of affrays ensued, with Hindus and Muslims indiscriminately mingled on either side'. 'Curious' perhaps because Hindus and Muslims had got so confused about their identities as to mix with one another; but of course this made no difference whatsoever to the essential 'irrationality' of their feuds, nor to their form which could only be 'affrays', 'riots', 'convulsions'.

— 'The trouble subsided with a partial reorganization of the city police in October 1810; but before peace had been restored fresh riots arose. . . .' Surely a novel understanding of the term 'riots' and how they occur or, rather, 'arise'! Nothing remains in the five-line entry on the 1810–11 events of the great crowds

---

[63] *Benares Gazetteer*, p. 209.

that gathered, the manner of their gathering, the remarkable mode of their protest, the consultation and decision-making, the perplexity and fears of the government and, one need scarcely add, the feelings of the people of Banaras when they were confronted with the new house-tax. The entry reverts, instead, to the theme of violence and disorder as the normal state of affairs and the consequent need for British intervention to establish peace and orderly behaviour.

Here, all political action undertaken outside the domain of British administrative initiative is represented as a 'convulsion'. Politics before the era of English-style constitutions in India is banished to the domain of the irrational, indeed the pre-political—'spontaneous', un-'conscious', 'fanatical'. It is a tradition that historians are still struggling to relinquish.

We may read on:

- 'Nothing' occurrred in Banaras after 1810–11 that was 'worthy of record' until the 'riots of 1852' (when some Nagar Brahmans organized protests against an alleged proposal to introduce common messing arrangements for prisoners in the jail, and clashes occurred with the police).[64]

Astonishingly, given the evidence of its ability to smell out a 'riot' in the most unlikely of places, the *Gazetteer* has nothing to say about the events of 1891 in Banaras; perhaps the entry on the history of the city had already become too long. But Crooke, writing a general account of the *North-Western Provinces of India* in 1894, made up for this lacuna: 'Only three years ago, the weavers of Benares, always a turbulent, fanatical class, took advantage of a quarrel over an almost deserted Hindu shrine, with which they had no possible concern, to spread rapine and outrage through the city'.[65] Once again, this remark is made in the course of a discussion of Hindu-Muslim conflict, and it is worthwhile to note what some of the other surviving evidence from this period tells us about 1891.

At the back of this particular incident lay the opposition of a large

[64] See (IOL) NWP, Criminal Judl. Progs, Range 233/vol. 36, no. 1466 of August 1852.

[65] W. Crooke, *The North-Western Provinces of India*, p. 187.

section of the Hindu population of the city, including many prominent citizens and even a few municipal councillors to the proposed demolition of all or part of a temple dedicated to Ram in order to clear the ground for a water-pumping station. A Temple Protection Committee was set up, the Sujan Samaj (or 'Respectable People's Society') took up the cause, 'thousands' of applications were sent to the Collector and numerous meetings held between November 1890 and April 1891 to protest against these plans. It was the refusal of the authorities to pay any heed to these popular representations, the acquiescence of the majority of the Indian municipal councillors in the authorities' plans, the closure of one of the two roads leading to the temple and, finally the demolition of the temple steps and the commencement of digging all around its walls even before a 'final decision' had been taken on the question of demolition, that led to the violence of 15 April 1891.[66]

There is evidence that this protest was connected, at the start, with the desire to ward off further taxation, and to the fairly widespread opposition to the administration's ham-handed implementation of its new water-supply scheme which affected not only Banaras but other cities like Agra and Kanpur as well.[67] The prevailing condition of food scarcity and high prices, adding as it did to the hardships of the lower classes,[68] appears to have fuelled the

[66] This discussion is based on the fairly detailed reports found in the RNP for the North-Western Provinces and Oudh, and for Bengal, in 1891; and L/P&J/6/301, no. 907 of 1891. See also K. N. Shukul, *Varanasi Down the Ages*, pp. 289–94, and Vijayshankar Mall, ed., *Pratapnarayan Granthavali*, part I (Kashi, 1958), pp 410–13. The role of the municipal councillors, and public reaction to it, is discussed further in Chapter 5 below.

[67] See, e.g., *Hindustani*, 22 April 1891 in RNP, NWP & O, w.e. 30 April 1891, pp. 301–2; *Hindustani*, 29 April 1891 in ibid. of 7 May 1891, pp. 315–16; *Azad*, 8 May 1891 in ibid. of 14 May 1891, pp. 333–4. Also the Chicago newspaper's comment, cited in the epigraph to this chapter, which goes on to say: 'Water-works are very useful to all cities, but here [in Banaras] at least they can scarcely be compensative for so venerable and so great a sacrifice, apart entirely from the prospective danger from disturbing the fierce prejudices of the large native population' (see n. 1 above).

[68] The large community of Muslim weavers in Banaras was said to have been especially hard hit at this time owing to the fall in demand for their rich fabrics and the prevalent high prices of all kinds of food grains; see L/P&J/6/301, no. 907 of 1891. RNP, NWP & O for April and May 1891 contains many comments on the extent of distress among the lower classes generally.

people's anger further. But added to all this was another, perhaps deeper concern. The proposal to demolish the Banaras temple came in the wake of the demolition of a Hindu temple in Darbhanga the year before, and hard on the heels of the Age of Consent Bill.[69] Coming together, these developments generated growing fears of a new government policy aimed at undermining Hinduism (and Islam), and heightened the agitation among Banaras Hindu and Muslims.[70] The attempted demolition of a mosque in Shyambazar (Calcutta), which led to violent protest in that city within a month of the Banaras riots, would only have confirmed these fears.

There is nothing in the official or unofficial records of the time to suggest that a Hindu-Muslim clash occurred in Banaras in April 1891, over the question of the Ramji temple or any other matter. On the contrary, one contemporary newspaper after another spoke of the local Muslims' sympathy with the Hindus and noted the participation of many Muslims in the anti-Government actions of 15 April.[71] What the *Hindustani* of 27 May wrote about the Shyambazar, Calcutta, riots could, with Hindu and Muslim numbers reversed, easily have been written about the Banaras riots: these were not Hindu-Muslim riots, as alleged by

[69] For the anti-Consent Bill agitation, see Amiya Sen, 'Hindu Revivalism in Action: The Age of Consent Bill Agitation in Bengal', *IHR*, vII, 1–2 (July 1980–January 1981).

[70] See RNPs for NWP & O, and for Bengal, from April 1891 onwards, e.g. article entitled 'The Destruction of Our Religion Under British Rule' in *Bharat Varsha* (Bithur) for May, in RNP, NWP & O, w.e. 23 July 1891, p. 512. The *Brahman* (Kanpur monthly) for March remarked that attempts would probably soon be made to destroy 'the most famous and sacred temples' of Vishwanath (Banaras), Jagannath (Puri) and Badrinath. Therefore, Hindus should protest strongly against the proposed demolition of the Banaras temple and appeal to Parliament if necessary, and 'the Musalmans and other Indian communities' should support them; ibid., w.e. 7 April 1891, p. 257. The *Azad* (Lucknow) of 8 May 1891 noted that the Muslims of Banaras joined the Hindus in their protest because they knew that they were sailing in the same boat: 'a Muhammadan mosque might anyday be treated in the same way as the Hindu temple'; ibid., w.e. 14 May 1891, p. 333.

[71] In addition to the references in n. 70, see *Bharat Jiwan*, 13 April 1891 in ibid., of 21 April 1891, p. 282; *Hindustani* of 22 April 1891, ibid., 30 April 1891, p. 302; *Hindustani* of 27 May 1891, ibid., 4 June 1891, pp. 386–7, which also notes that sixty-three Muslims were arrested for participation in the riots; and also numerous reports in RNP, Bengal for the same period.

officials (Crooke, in the case of Banaras), but 'between the Musalmans assisted by a number of Hindus on the one side and the police on the other. . . . Nothing could be more preposterous than to call the rioters bad characters. . . . .' Their entreaties to save their religious building having been ignored, 'they [had] resolved to sacrifice their lives on its behalf.'[72]

In the Banaras case, indeed, the Magistrate of the city spoke of the 1891 outbreak as the result of a 'league or covenant' between Muslims and Hindus for the future 'mutual protection' of their religious buildings which might be threatened by the extension of water-works and drainage schemes. As it happened, even this suggestion of the Magistrate was questioned by the acting Commissioner in his report on the riots. He acknowledged that the Muslim weavers were in difficult circumstances and had recently assembled in strength at the collectorate to demand some relief. 'But the remonstrance of the Julahas about the high prices, though made by a large crowd', he wrote, 'was not made in any spirit of lawlessness'. And

there is no evidence whatsoever to connect them *as a body* [emphasis original] with these outbreaks. Muhammadans were undoubtedly to be found in the crowd of rioters, as is only natural [*sic*]; but we may safely assert that had the Julahas as a body joined the Hindus, the results would have been far more serious. An excited Muhammadan mob is one of the most dangerous elements in society, and bad as things were in the late disturbances, experience tells us what fearful scenes might have been enacted had the industrious but poverty stricken Julahas joined the well-nourished lazy crowd of 'budmashes' who live on the pilgrims and toil not. . . .[73]

Here, the senior official reveals a marvellous ability to challenge the facile logic of his subordinate without throwing away any of the underlying assumptions—the elements—of colonialist knowledge about Indian society: those 'most dangerous' Muslim mobs that create 'fearful scenes', the badmash or criminal elements that abound in great cities like Banaras, 'rumours such as are always

[72] RNP, NWP & O, w.e. 4 June 1891, p. 391.
[73] L/P&J/6/301, no. 907 of 1891, J. H. Wright, Offg. Commissioner—Chief Secretary, Government of North-Western Provinces and Oudh, 28 April 1891, para 9.

afloat throughout the length and breadth of Indian cities'.[74] It was out of such ingredients, found in all official reports, and out of official 'common sense' about the people they governed, that Crooke concocted his statement regarding the 'turbulent and fanatical' weavers of Banaras who spread 'rapine and outrage through the city' in 1891.

One could go on. But this much of the writing on nineteenth-century Banaras should suffice to indicate that a methodical reordering of Indian history was in process as the colonial regime set out to systematize its knowledge and consolidate its power.

VI

It is perhaps unnecessary to multiply instances to show how widely this process of the rewriting of Indian history occurred. However, I shall briefly cite two other examples from the Bhojpuri region and one from outside to illustrate how the structure of the master narrative appears again and again in the writing up of the history of Hindu–Muslim relations, which is taken to be the history of the community *tout court*—the Indian 'past'—at least in northern India. The first of these examples comes from the Shahabad district of Bihar. It is one of the 'Notes' contained in a (Secret) 'Supplementary Report to the Government of India regarding the Origin of the Bakr-Id Disturbances of 1917' in that district.[75] The note is dated 31 May 1919 and is written by an official who was posted in Shahabad for a few months in 1893 on special duty in connection with the anti-cow-killing agitation.

The author invites attention to the 'curious parallel' between the events of 1893 and 1917. In both years,

the riots began in the Patna district, but though they were sufficiently formidable there, they never reached anything like the widespread violence and rapid extension of those in Shahabad . . . on both occasions, the Dumraon Raj, alone of all the great Baronial families of Bihar, was deeply implicated to the point of moral conviction, though short of actual proof. . . . Though the disturbed area during 1893 was comparatively small in Shahabad itself, the disturbances covered all the territories of the Dumraon Raj on the north bank of the Ganges in the districts of Ballia and Azamgarh of the United Provinces.

[74] Ibid., para 8.
[75] (Bihar State Archives, Patna) Political Special Dept, file no. 223/1919.

He notes further that the great zamindars of Tirhut, Darbhanga, Ramgarh, Bettiah, Hathwa, Tikari and so on, who were acquitted of complicity in the riots of 1893, 'are either Brahmins or Bhumihar Brahmins. Dumraon on the contrary is a Rajput.'

In 1893, the official goes on to say, the Maharaja of Dumraon's involvement was partly accounted for by personal interest. Brahmans and cow-protectionists were said to have persuaded him that 'his inability to beget a son was due to "the complaint of the cow".... The Maharajah of Rewa (since dead), who married the late Maharajah [Dumraon]'s daughter, was a fanatical supporter of anti-kine-killing propaganda, and had even made himself conspicuous within British territory in this connection.[76] It is believed that he has since blackmailed the present [Dumraon] Zemindar'.

There is a fascinating stitching together of motifs here. 'Personal interest' is a compound of a raja's deep desire for a son, the extraordinary influence of a son-in-law (from a related princely family), and the use of blackmail. In the events of 1917, however, it would appear that Dumraon was moved more by his ambition to be the undisputed leader of the zamindars of South Bihar. 'The late Maharajah of Dumraon was utterly uneducated and boorish, a man of very limited knowledge and intellect. The present man is of a far superior type [sic], socially and intellectually, and it may well be believed that his thoroughly experienced European Manager, Mr Wilson, was able to do a good deal to steady him and to open his mind to the reality of facts.' But in 1917, the war was not going too well for Great Britain, and Dumraon may well have feared that his traditional rivals, the Jagdishpur zamindars, might not only enrich themselves but add considerably to their status by taking a leading part in the anti-cow-killing agitation. 'On the whole, therefore, . . . there is every ground to believe that the [Dumraon] Raj played exactly the same part as in 1893, i.e., every facility was given to the movement, and the Raj sowars and officials not only did not obstruct but took an underhand part in it, while at the same time every precaution was taken to keep the Maharajah's personality out of the matter. . . .'

[76] Though no larger than Dumraon and other similar *zamindaris* in Bihar and Bengal, Rewa was a small princely state in central India (now Madhya Pradesh).

Finally, the note suggests, in both 1893 and 1917 'Extremist politicians' had a hand in the agitation. The Nagpur Congress of '1892 or 1893 [*sic*] . . . was followed immediately by a meeting in the same Pandal in support of the agitation against kine killing, and the riots of the following year were consequently attributed to the decision then taken.' In 1917, as in 1893, Extremist politicians used 'the unquestionably genuine feeling among Hindus on the subject of the cow, as well as . . . the lawless instincts of the disorderly portion of the population, notably in districts like Shahabad and Saran which had formerly been favourable recruiting grounds for the Army.' Ras Bihari Mandal, an important local Extremist, 'headed a large organisation of Goalas, of whom there are many in the affected areas, and who are notoriously as prone to dacoity and rioting as the Rajputs of that area.'

The history of the 1917 strife in Shahabad is here reduced to the machinations of big zamindars and a few 'extremist politicians'. The motives of these 'ringleaders' are to be found not only in their personal ambitions, but also in their *essential character* as a caste or community. Ras Bihari Mandal is a man of 'rascally private character and low birth'. The present Maharaja of Dumraon, in spite of his western education and the steadying influence of a thoroughly experienced European manager, is after all 'a Rajput'.

The circumstances, the consciousness, the aspirations of the people of western Bihar disappear without a trace, except in so far as the Hindus in general have an 'unquestionably genuine feeling' about the cow, which can be fanned into flames at will; and certain communities are cogenitally prone to lawlessness: 'the disorderly portion of the population, notably in districts like Shahabad and Saran which had formerly been favourable recruiting grounds for the Army',[77] and the Ahirs or Goalas 'who are notoriously as prone to dacoity and rioting as the Rajputs of that area'.

The specificity of the historical experience of 1917 is also wiped out. 1917 was no different from 1893. In both these instances, the riots began in Patna district (it is not at all clear why this is taken to be so significant) and spread in a far more virulent form to

[77] Cf. the Bihar Governor's observation in 1942 on the 'notoriously . . . criminal district of Saran, in N. Mansergh, ed., *The Transfer of Power, 1942–47: volume II 'Quit India'* (London, 1971), p. 789.

Shahabad. In both, the Dumraon Raj was deeply implicated (although the 'disturbed area' in 1893 was 'comparatively small in Shahabad itself'). In exactly the same way, the organization and activities of extremist nationalist politicians were behind the riots on both occasions.

A very similar line of argument is put forward in a comparison of the 1874 and 1893 riots in Bombay, in a despatch of 26 October 1893 from the Bombay Judicial Department to the Secretary of State for India in Council. On both occasions, the despatch notes, the first group to turn to violence were the Muslims and the scene of the outbreak was near the Jama Masjid. However, the outbreak of 1893 was on a much larger scale. On 13 February 1874 officials dispersed the gathering with comparative ease, and the crowd broke up with apparently no plans of further violence, for it was not till the 15th that further trouble occurred near the Muslim cemetery.

The outbreak in 1893 was more 'serious', 'widespread' and 'uncontrollable' than that of 1874. The dispersal of the crowd that initially attacked the Hanuman Temple would appear 'to have had the effect of arousing the Muhammedan population of the city generally; and, as will always happen on such occasions, the criminal classes . . . were not slow to avail themselves of the confusion. Much of the looting, and probably some of the deaths, are due rather to the depredations and violence of these classes than to religious excitement'. And so on. [78]

Before discussing these accounts further, it may be well to take up our final example of colonialist writings on communal riots in the nineteenth century. This piece of writing relates to a small habitation, not far from Banaras and like it a centre of handloom production conducted in the main by Muslim weavers, but in every other respect vastly different from that great Hindu pilgrimage centre. Established probably in the eighteenth century at the instance of some Sheikh Muslim zamindars of the neighbourhood, the weaving *qasba* of Mubarakpur in Azamgarh district was a place of no special sanctity or great renown. The parallels between the colonialist writing up of the history of the people of Mubarakpur and their reconstruction of the history of Hindu-

---

[78] (IOL) L/P&J/6/362, no. 10 Judl. Dept., Bombay—Secretary of State in Council, 26 October 1893.

Muslim relations in Banaras are, therefore, all the more striking. The two-page entry on Mubarakpur in the 1909 *Gazetteer* of Azamgarh district records that the qasba had a population of 15,433 people in 1901, of whom 11,442 were Muslims and 3,991 Hindus. It then proceeds to sum up the 'past' history of social relations in the locality as follows:

The Muhammadans [of Mubarakpur] consist for the most part of fanatical and clannish Julahas, and the fire of religious animosity between them and the Hindus of the town and neighbourhood is always smouldering. Serious conflicts have occurred between the two from time to time, notably in 1813, 1842 and 1904. The features of all these disturbances are similar, so that a description of what took place on the first occasion will suffice to indicate their character. In 1813 a petty dispute about the inclosing within the grounds of a Hindu temple of a little piece of land near a Muhammadan *takia* [*tazia*] platform was followed first by the slaughter on the spot of a cow by the Muhammadans and then by the defiling of the platform and of a neighbouring *imambara* with pig's blood by the Hindus. The Muhammadans retaliated by cruelly murdering a wealthy Hindu merchant of the place named Rikhai Sahu, by plundering and burning his house and by defacing a handsome temple which he had erected. Hereupon the whole Hindu population of the vicinity rose and a sanguinary battle ensued in which the Muhammadans were overpowered after many had been killed and wounded on both sides. The inhabitants of the town fled and the place was given up to plunder for some days till a magistrate arrived with troops from Gorakhpur and restored order. Similar disturbances occurred in 1893–94 and punitive police were quartered on the town for several months.[79]

Let us note first that this history of Mubarakpur appears as part of a notice on a small and fairly 'ordinary' place in a district gazetteer of handbook; whereas the history of Hindu–Muslim strife in Banaras that we have examined earlier in this chapter appears not only in the *District Gazetteer* and other histories of Banaras but in more general historical statements on British rule and on continuing Hindu–Muslim 'disturbances'.

As regards the entry on Mubarakpur, I have written elsewhere of the fact that the alleged 'disturbances' of 1893–4 in the qasba

[79] D. L. Drake-Brockman, *Azamgarh: A Gazetteer, being vol. XXXIII of the District Gazetteers of the United Provinces of Agra and Oudh* (Allahabad, 1911), pp. 260–1.

exist nowhere except in the imagination of the writer of this notice (they are, in this respect, not unlike the 'Hindu–Muslim' riots of 1891 and the 'undoubtedly religious' origins of the military-police feud in Banaras in 1810, which we have referred to earlier).[80] In the next chapter, I deal at some length with the figure of the 'fanatical (or bigoted) Julaha' that appears in this passage as in Crooke's comments on Banaras. Here I shall refer only to the common structure of the colonial argument on the history of Indian society, whether this is represented in the qasba of Mubarakpur or the populous city of Banaras or, for that matter, the rural areas of Shahabad.

The first, and perhaps most obvious, point to note is the characterization of the 'past', the pre-British period, as essentially chaotic and unruly. In Mubarakpur, as in Banaras/India, the 'fire of religious animosity' was 'always smouldering'. In Mubarakpur, as in Banaras/India, as in 'districts like Shahabad and Saran' (with their 'disorderly . . . population(s) . . . notoriously prone to dacoity and rioting'), that was what the British administration— 'enlightened', 'orderly', 'rational', 'experienced'—was up against from the beginning.

The communal riot narrative, as exemplified in these instances, ranges freely through time and space, unfettered by either. In it, all riots are the same—simply the reflexive actions of an irrational people ('fanatical and clannish' Julahas/Muslims, riot-prone Ahirs and Rajputs, 'the whole Hindu (or Muslim) population' that rises blindly when a religious building is attacked, or such an attack is beaten back, 'criminal classes' who take advantage of this; and so on). The geographical location of an outbreak does not appear to make very much difference, as I have already remarked in connection with Cape's identification of the site of the Banaras riot of 1809; the principal features of the narrative are the same for the qasba of Mubarakpur as they are for a *mohalla* in the city of Banaras or Bombay, as they will be for Shahabad or Kanpur or Calcutta. Nor does the date of a clash very significantly alter the plot: the changing conditions of state power are scarcely noticed after the early nineteenth century, the rise of new social identities and aspira-

[80] 'Encounters and Calamities: The History of a North Indian Qasba in the Nineteenth Century', in R. Guha, ed., *Subaltern Studies III* (Delhi, 1984).

tions is practically inconceivable, the emergence of new social and political movements appears only to feed into pre-existing loyalties and tendencies. It is well after the end of the nineteenth century that the stubbornness of colonialist historiography gives even a little in this respect.

Throughout the nineteenth century and for long afterwards, the colonial narrative on communal strife tends to proceed by identifying the 'first' major riot, that is, usually the first recorded after the establishment of British rule (1813 in the case of Mubarakpur, 1809 in that of Banaras), and then tracing a straight line through to the 'last'—which of course keeps changing with the date of the writing (1904 in the case of the entry on Mubarakpur in the Azamgarh Gazetteer of 1909; Kanpur 1931 in the Government of India file on 'Communal Disorders' prepared in the early 1930s).

In this mode of history writing one may take any two 'serious riots' and they will stand in for one another, irrespective of conjuncture or locale. All that can be usefully compared is magnitude. For a casualty list of the same order as that in the Kanpur riots of 1931, one has to go back to the 'grave Benares riots' of 1809, even though, the official 'Note' adds, 'conditions were *presumably* so different then as to make the two cases not really comparable'.[81] 'Presumably' is a significant word. In such a long time, a good deal ought to have changed. In this slow-moving country, however, it is remarkable how much goes on being just the same.[82] So a description of the 'first' outbreak—1813 in Mubarakpur—suffices to indicate the character of all subsequent strife, just as 1893 more or less adequately explains what happens in Shahabad in 1917, and 1874 what happens in Bombay in 1893 (or 1911, or 1929).

Repeated metaphoric interventions make up for the lack of

[81] L/P&J/7/132, 'Notes' of 19–20 May 1931 (emphasis added).

[82] Hence the same 'Note' compares the pattern of rioting in Bombay and Calcutta and Kanpur. The Bombay riots of 1929, it says, 'originated in fights between oil-strikers and Pathans employed in their places and gradually developed into general murderous assaults by Moslems on Hindus and Hindus on Moslems. *As in Calcutta in 1926* there was a second phase [of rioting in April-May 1929 after the initial outbreak in February] and a *further resemblance with those riots (and those at Cawnpore)* lies in the fact that the disturbances consisted of murders in side lanes rather than riots in the ordinary sense of the word'; ibid. (emphasis added).

consistent metonymic connections in the communal riot narrative.[83] In the absence of detailed description, it is the essentialist signs that represent Mubarakpur/Shahabad/ Banaras/India that enable the narrative to move along. Thus, 'fanatical and clannish' entities, 'disorderly sections of the population', communities 'prone to dacoity and rioting', 'fires of religious animosity', 'indiscriminate affrays'—these are the phrases that make for the history of Mubarakpur or Banaras or Shahabad in the nineteenth century as told by colonialist writers at the beginning of the twentieth.

This is of course *not* a history, to repeat a point already made, for evidently *nothing* ever changes in this community. The communal riot narrative cannot but be a history of the state, first because everything in it revolves around the question of 'law and order', and equally because if any change occurs in the local society it will occur, by this account, as a result of the efforts and the influence of the colonial state (for example, the education of the young Maharaja of Dumraon and the 'steadying influence' of his English manager).

An outstanding feature of this discourse is its distancing of 'us' and 'them'. In the communal riot narrative, as in colonialist discourse more generally, 'rioting', 'bigotry', 'criminality' are of a piece—the marks of an inferior people and a people without a history. Naturally, even the violence of the subject population is distinguished from the often unacknowledged but, in any case, 'controlled', 'rational' and 'legitimate' violence of the colonial state. 'Native' violence has parallels with the violence of the eighteenth- and even nineteenth-century European mob—hungry, displaced, turbulent—which also on occasion turns to rioting.

[83] Cf. R. Guha's comments on 'primary', 'secondary' and 'tertiary' discourse in 'The Prose of Counter-Insurgency' in *Subaltern Studies II* (Delhi, 1983). The metaphorical charge is high, as we have seen, even in 'primary' colonial discourse, the 'battlefront' reports of officials on the spot at the time of a 'riot'. But indexical interventions seem to increase significantly as the history is written up for a wider public, even if this is done within days of the outbreak in question. For an extraordinary example of such writing-up, see 'The Disturbances at Benares—August 1852', a contribution to the *Benares Recorder* made by the Commissioner of Banaras, E. A. Reade, in early August 1852, reprinted in E. A. Reade, *Benares City* (Government Press, Agra 1858), pp. 63–71.

(Happily, the promoters of this view at the turn of the century might have said, Europe was fast 'civilizing' its lower classes.) But the violence of the 'native' has other, specifically Oriental characteristics. It is a helpless, instinctive violence, it takes the form of 'convulsions' and, in India, these are more often than not related to the centuries' old smouldering fire of sectarian strife. That is all there is to the politics of the indigenous community. That is the Indian past.

Chapter Three

The Bigoted Julaha

The Julaha generally bears the character of being cowardly, pretentious, factious and bigoted. They [sic] took a leading part in the recent Benares riots and some of the worst outrages in the Mutiny were their work.

—William Crooke, 1896

As might be expected, the emergence of an identifiable colonial historiography of the Indian 'past' was accompanied by the development of a distinct sociology of India's 'present'. This colonial sociology has been subjected to close scrutiny by sociologists and anthropologists in recent times.[1] The historicity of this body of knowledge and the concerns that went into its construction may, however, require further emphasis. This chapter seeks to underline this historicity and these concerns through the examination of a colonial caste-stereotype which was frequently used in the analysis of sectarian strife in the Bhojpuri region.

It should go without saying that just as the colonial construction of the history of Banaras/India took time to mature, so the colonial

---

[1] See B. S. Cohn, *An Anthropologist among the Historians and Other Essays* (Delhi, 1987), esp. 'Notes on the History of the Study of Indian Society and Culture' and 'The Census, Social Structure and Objectification in South Asia'; R. S. Smith, 'Rule-by-Records and Rule-by-Reports: Complementary Aspects of the British Imperial Rule of Law', *Contributions to Indian Sociology*, n.s. 19, I (1985); Rashmi Pant, 'The Cognitive Status of Caste in Colonial Ethnography: A Review of Some Literature on the North-Western Provinces and Oudh', *IESHR*, 24, 2 (1987); Sekhar Bandhopadhyaya, 'Caste in the Perception of the Raj: A Note on the Evolution of the Colonial Sociology of Bengal', *Bengal Past and Present*, vol. CIV, nos. 198–9 (1985); R. Inden, 'Orientalist Constructions of India', *MAS*, 20, 3 (1986); and several contributions in N. G. Barrier, ed., *The Census in British India: New Perspectives* (Delhi, 1981). For earlier, influential statements, see the writings of M. N. Srinivas and Irawati Karve.

construction of Indian society changed over time, reaching its apparently fixed and 'developed' form only in the later nineteenth century. The considerable experimentation that went into the making of the early colonial records, the extensive consultation with local informants and the consequent 'openness' of some of the earlier colonial attempts at understanding and analysing Indian society have been noted by several scholars.[2] By the later nineteenth century, it has been pointed out, there was a pressure towards greater uniformity, and far greater reliance on records and reports already put together—as the upper (British) and lower (Indian) layers of the bureaucracy came to be more clearly separated.[3] All this was indicative of the changing character of the colonial state. Along with the altered needs of the colonial economy, as the colonial interest in revenue and 'tribute' pure and simple came to be matched by a desire for markets and raw materials, it brought about a significant change in the colonial understanding of Indian society.

In the early nineteenth century the 'village community' had been the prime candidate for the role of *basic unit* of Indian society— that which symbolized its essence.[4] By the latter half of the century 'caste' had taken over that position. It was largely after the 1840s that 'caste' emerged as the central organizing principle in the colonial records, from village level upwards. In 1849 a Governor-General had singled out the 'village community' as central to the local (though he might better have said 'administrative') scheme of things, and hence especially worthy of official support. Subsequently the village remained the unit of local administration. But the needs of uniform administration and statutes, the pressure to legislate for wider groups of people, the necessity of aggregating India and Indians into more manageable blocks than the tens of

---

[2] See the references from Cohn, Smith and Pant cited above. The following discussion of the place of caste in colonial sociology relies heavily on these three writers.

[3] Smith, 'Rule-by-Records', p. 163.

[4] On the village community, see E. T. Stokes, *The English Utilitarians and India* (London, 1959); Louis Dumont, 'The "Village Community" from Munro to Maine', in his *Religion/Politics and History in India*; C. J. Dewey, 'Anglo-Indian Images of the Village Community', *MAS*, 6, 3 (1972).

thousands of villages and small towns could provide, drew increasing attention to another feature that was seen as being not only unique but also central to Indian society—and that was 'caste'.[5]

However, as one anthropologist after another has pointed out, the question 'What constituted a caste?' was not easily answered; 'caste' was far from being anything obvious, fixed or readily grasped. It required fairly rigorous, and of course arbitrary, principles of selection before certain 'castes' (or 'caste-clusters' or even simply caste-names) could be picked out as generalizable, significant in local society, worthy of governmental notice. As already indicated, the primacy accorded to caste, as to the village community, was related directly to the problems of identifying the centres of productive (hence, revenue-generating) capacity and of maintaining law and order. But the balance between the two appears to have shifted as the nineteenth century progressed, with the weight being transferred more than just a little from the concern with revenue to the concern for law and order.

With 'castes', even more than with 'villages', colonial sociology set out to map those qualities of the subject population that were most germane to the business of administration—not only a group's productive capacity, its traditional occupation, its (established or reputed) efficiency, laziness, etc., but also its criminality, military prowess, truthfulness, litigious tendencies, rebelliousness, and so on. The criteria by which the colonial regime picked out the castes to be noticed, studied and officially watched were quite explicitly stated in connection with census operations during the last decades of the nineteenth century. These had to do with the numerical strength of the groups concerned, and with the question of support for or threat to law and order. 'The British were only willing to record minorities like the Agarwals, Marwaris, Ramoshis', to quote a scholar writing on U.P., 'who, though few, had a wide intra-[inter?] regional network. They also recorded minorities that were recalcitrant towards British law and order (such as Ramoshis, Thugs and other "criminal tribes") or those essential

---

[5] Cf. Smith, 'Rule-by-Records', who also notes that 'laws could be enacted in terms of caste or agricultural tribe only after a synthetic vision of the whole of Indian society had been officially constructed and disseminated within the ruling classes', p. 172; and Pant, 'Cognitive Status of Caste', p. 149.

to maintaining it, like the Gurkhas....'[6] The notional 'Indian individual', writes another scholar, was thus stripped of his place in the 'village community' and clothed instead in 'caste': an individual's rights (and, one might add, liabilities) now 'depended on his [her] status in society, as defined by the Government'.[7]

This is where the category of the 'criminal' and 'martial' tribe, the agricultural caste, and so on, protected or hounded by legislation or by unlegislated administrative interest, in a word the caste-stereotype, came into its own. In the following pages I seek to investigate the origins of one such colonial stereotype, that of the 'bigoted Julaha', and its importance in the explanation of sectarian strife in northern India. The larger question, which is here dealt with only tangentially, is that of the relationship in colonialist discourse between 'sociology' and 'history'—'caste' and the politicized 'religious community', or, in other words, 'caste' and 'communalism'.

II

The Julaha reputation for bigotry, which was well established in colonial sociology by the end of the nineteenth century, was clearly related to Julaha involvement in sectarian strife in the preceding period. Let us begin, therefore, by looking at the evidence regarding such strife in northern India during this period. The record of Hindu-Muslim riots under colonial rule stretches back, as we have seen, to the earliest decades of the nineteenth century. The occasions for strife were many and varied. In Banaras 1809, the quarrel broke out over the 'neutral' space between a Muslim mosque and an older Hindu structure. In Ayodhya (Faizabad), where another much-talked-about riot occurred in 1855, the issue was a similar contention over the domination of a site where a Muslim mosque stood

---

[6] Ibid., p. 150. The author goes on to note: 'In this context, too, must be located the large amount of information on caste divisions, caste rituals, etc., which was given in Army Recruitment Handbooks on each of the "martial races". The handbook, *Garhwalis*, for instance, was mostly concerned with identifying which subdivisions of Rajputs and Brahmins were amenable to military discipline and especially with regard to observance of caste rules on dining.'

[7] Smith, 'Rule-by-Records', p. 173.

adjacent to an old Hindu temple. In Bareilly the coincidence of the Muharram and Ramnaumi festivals in 1837 and 1871 is said to have been the occasion for Hindu-Muslim rioting. In smaller towns, too, like the two major cloth-producing centres of Azamgarh district (Mubarakpur and Mau), violence broke out time and again during the nineteenth century: in 1813, 1834 and 1842 in Mubarakpur on account of the defilement of a mosque, an *imambarah*, a temple; and on the issue of cow-slaughter in Mau, in 1806 and on several occasions from the early 1860s onwards.

In most of these instances, and in many others, large numbers of Julahas were actively involved in the quarrel on the Muslim side. As early as 1837, then, Thomason wrote in his report on the settlement of Azamgarh district that the Julahas of Mubarakpur, Mau, Kopaganj and other such places in that region were 'a weak and sickly-looking people, but mostly possessing firearms, and very liable to be excited to riot by anything which affects their religious prejudices. They have of late years been particularly turbulent, in consequence of the spread amongst them of the tenets of Syed Uhmud [Saiyid Ahmad]'.[8] Muslim weavers were prominent again in the Baqr'Id riots of 1893 in eastern U.P. and western Bihar, as the following comment in the Ghazipur *District Gazetteer* testifies: 'The Julahas are the most bigoted of all Musalmans and... a turbulent and lawless race, as was amply illustrated during the conflicts between Hindus and Muhammedans in 1893 and on other occasions.'[9]

One scarcely needs to point out the extreme onesidedness of this statement. The Muslim weavers' involvement in Hindu-Muslim strife is obviously only a part of the history even of their role in public agitations in the nineteenth century; and their participation in Hindu-Muslim quarrels, when such quarrels occurred, was hardly surprising, given the fact that they constituted the largest segment of the numerically small Muslim community of the region and that they were concentrated in towns where the possibilities of serious and violent conflict were always greater. One could add that when riots have occurred in any urban concentration

[8] J. Thomason, *Report on the Settlement of Chuklah Azimgarh* (Agra, 1837), p. 130.

[9] *Ghazipur District Gazetteer* (Allahabad, 1909), p. 90.

anywhere in the world, the densely-populated, ill-serviced and poorer localities of the lower classes have generally burned most fiercely. It is remarkable, in this context, that the extract from the Ghazipur *Gazetteer* quoted above takes the mere involvement of Julahas in the violent conflicts of 1893 as evidence of their 'turbulence' and 'lawlessness', although then, as on many other occasions, the weavers were not the attackers but the besieged.

It is also the case that, because of the nature of their occupation, weavers everywhere have been commonly dependent on money-lenders and other middlemen and vulnerable to the play of market forces, all the more so in the era of the advance of industrial capitalism. Because of their presence in manufacturing and marketing centres they have been more exposed than most other groups in pre-industrial societies to the political currents of the time. Some of Marx's comments on the rising of European weavers in the 1830s and 1840s are pertinent: 'Because it thinks in the framework of politics the proletariat [here the reference is specifically to weavers] sees the cause of all evils in the will, and all means of remedy in violence and in the overthrow of a particular form of state.'[10] It is not especially surprising, therefore, to find the north Indian Muslim weaver actively involved in a whole variety of nineteenth-century political movements, from the zealous reformism of Saiyid Ahmad's Wahabis to the revolutionary dreams of 1857.

One point that needs particular emphasis is that the struggle for power and status, which in colonial India often took the form of a contest over the boundaries of ritual space and 'traditional' authority, was reinforced by the rapid and unpredictable shifts that took place during the nineteenth century in the general social, economic and political condition of the people of northern India. A good deal is now known about the severe economic and social dislocation that occurred in Bihar and U.P., as elsewhere in the country, with the onset of colonialism.[11] It is unnecessary here to

[10] *Collected Works of Marx and Engels*, vol. 3 (Moscow, 1975), p. 204.

[11] For some of the most important statements on this region, see E. Whitcombe, *Agrarian Conditions in Northern India, vol. 1: U.P. under British Rule, 1860–1900* (California, 1971); Asiya Siddiqi, *Agrarian Change in a Northern Indian State, U.P. 1819–33* (Oxford, 1973); Shahid Amin, *Sugarcane and Sugar in Gorakhpur: An Inquiry into Peasant Production for Capitalist Enterprise*

reproduce in detail the evidence regarding that dislocation. Suffice it to say that the weaving communities of the north Indian hinterland were subjected to many new hardships.

In major centres of cloth production such as Lucknow and Banaras, or Mau and Mubarakpur (in Azamgarh district), the weavers and spinners faced violent fluctuations in the conditions of their trade in the immediate pre-colonial, as well as the early colonial, period. A sharp increase in the demand for their goods and skills in the later eighteenth and early nineteenth century was followed by a progressive erosion of their markets. One result in the long term was a forced shift from the manufacture of fine cloths to that of coarser and cheaper varieties; the silk industry of Banaras stands out as a notable exception in this respect, but even here new markets arose some time after the collapse of the old and the weavers were not able easily to protect themselves from fluctuations in demand.[12]

It was the quality cloth industry that was most directly affected by the competition from mill-made goods, but the manufacture and trade of the coarser varieties of cloth were also subjected to powerful new pressures as distant economic (and political) forces came to bear on the economy of the countryside.[13] Increased prices

---

in Colonial India (Delhi, 1984); T. R. Metcalf, *Land, Landlords, and the British Raj: Northern India in the Nineteenth Century* (California, 1979); C. A. Bayly, *Rulers, Townsmen and Bazaars: North Indian Society in the Age of British Expansion, 1770–1870* (Cambridge, 1983); and the relevant essays in Cohn, *An Anthropologist among Historians*, and E. T. Stokes, *The Peasant and the Raj* (Cambridge, 1978).

[12] See my 'Economic Dislocation in Nineteenth Century Eastern U.P.', in P. Robb, ed., *Rural South Asia: Linkages, Change and Development* (London, 1983); and my 'Structure and Conditions of Artisanal Production in Colonial North India', *Proceedings of Conference on Urbanism in Islam* (Tokyo, 1989).

[13] Bayly observes, for example, that until the early nineteenth century the inhabitants of Banaras acquired much of their ordinary cloth either from weavers within the city or from the two entrepot and weaving villages of Baragaon and Shivpur (1.5 and 2 miles from the city), from where individual weavers brought goods to city retailers. 'This sort of relationship between an external productive or entrepot unit and a nearby town was typical of the north Indian city in the period before village products began to feel the pressure of European imports'; Bayly, 'Indian Merchants in a "Traditional" Setting: Benares, 1780–1830', in C. J. Dewey and A. G. Hopkins, ed., *The Imperial Impact: Studies in the Economic History of Africa and India* (London, 1978).

from the middle of the nineteenth century and the growing (Indian and foreign) factory demand for raw cotton created new problems for the local artisans. Thus, during the cotton famine of the early 1860s, an enquiry into the 'slackness of demand for European cotton goods' produced distressing reports of weavers' conditions from all over U.P. In Jaunpur the number of looms at work was down from 3012 to 1986, and weavers had taken to 'the work of coolies, or servants, or to begging'. In Ghazipur brokers believed that whereas some 10,000 maunds of the cotton annually imported into the district was 'normally' retained for production within the district, the figure was down to 5000 or 6000 maunds in 1863. 'Many of the Julahas of this district have of late migrated to the Mauritius and elsewhere', the Collector reported, 'and many others, having abandoned their original occupation, have become bhistees, laborers, hawkers of cloth, and beggars'. In Allahabad the number of looms at work had declined from 10,000 in 1860 to 4000 in 1863. 'In a few of the pergunnahs, where cotton is grown, the diminution is comparatively small.' In towns where the diminution was great, 'the unemployed operatives may be seen seeking for service as Bhisties or Coolies. In the outlying villages they have taken to agricultural labour'. In the Lalitpur district of Jhansi division, 'The weavers, though battling the best they could to gain a livelihood at their trades, have broken down. The anticipation now prevalent amongst this class is, that even the few looms now at work must also be given up in a short time.' The local Collector referred to whole families of weavers flocking to get work as casual labourers: of the 150–200 coolies employed on the Doodhai dam in the Balabehut forest, more than two-thirds were weavers 'who have had to give up their looms and take to the pick-axe and shovel'.[14]

It was at this time that the weavers of Mau told the Commissioner of Banaras that they would make cloth of the finest quality for him and it would be 'cheaper than the coarser, as the latter required more cotton thread'.[15] Their labour and skills had become an entirely subsidiary consideration as compared to the cost of the

[14] *Selections from the Records of Government, North-Western Provinces, pt.* XL (Allahabad, 1864), art. IV, 'Information regarding the Slackness of Demand for European Cotton Goods', pp. 148, 151, 147, 146.

[15] Ibid., p. 148.

raw material. It was one striking indication of the weavers' decline into new, semi-proletarian conditions.

It should be made clear, too, that this was not a one-off, freak decline produced by the unusual crisis of the 1860s. The history of the north Indian weavers in the nineteenth century is, in E. P. Thompson's phrase from another context, 'haunted by the legend of better days'.[16] And in this matter, as in so much else in history, the legend was at least as important as whatever we may believe to have been the 'reality'. 'Fifty years ago', said an officer of Raza, a seventy-year-old weaver of the large weaving village of Usia in Ghazipur district, 'he was far better off than he is now'; for the demand for country cloth had greatly declined because of the competition from European goods. 'This is undoubtedly true', reported the officer who had interviewed Raza (for an inquiry ordered by Dufferin in 1888 into the proportion of the Indian population that starved), 'and is one cause why the weaver has to a great extent found his occupation gone'.[17]

'Fifty years ago . . .'; the remark on Raza echoes a note that is found in many other reports of the turn of the century. 'The weavers of Lucknow have been ruined by the import of English goods', William Hoey wrote in 1880. 'The Julahas of Lucknow are fast leaving the city . . . and seeking a livelihood in service.'[18] East of Lucknow, the *jamdani* or figured muslin weaving of Tanda and other places in Faizabad district was also under severe pressure. The town of Tanda, perhaps the most important of the traditional cloth-producing centres of the truncated kingdom of Awadh taken over by the British in 1856, had in that year exported cloth valued at over Rs 1.5 lakhs to Nepal alone. By 1880 it was sending less than half that amount. In 1862 there were approximately 1125 looms at work in the town. Less than two decades later, the number was

[16] E. P. Thompson, *The Making of the English Working Class* (Pelican, London, 1968), p. 297.

[17] Rev. & Agr. Dept., December 1888. Famine, Progs. nos. 1–24, *Reports on the Condition of the Lower Classes of the Population of India*, letter no. 2420/vii–49, from Collector, Ghazipur to Commissioner, Benares Division, 10 April 1888 (enclosed with Commissioner's Report of 14 April 1888), para 17.

[18] W. Hoey, *A Monograph on Trade and Manufactures in Northern India* (Lucknow, 1880), p. 28.

reckoned to be 875. An official survey of artistic handicrafts in U.P. in1883–4 could only say that the industry of producing muslin cloth in Tanda 'still lives'. Barely, one has to add, for there were only six families of weavers in the town still producing jamdani in the 1890s.[19]

Jais and other centres of cloth production in Rae Bareli district suffered a similar fate. In the 1840s Jais had 600 families of Julahas, all supporting themselves on the proceeds of weaving. By the 1880s the numbers involved in fine cloth and carpet manufacture had fallen to 50 workmen plying 40 looms. In the 1890s, there were 200 Julaha families left in the town, of whom only 20 worked the looms. In 1931 the Census Commissioner for U.P. reported that 'the fine muslim [muslin?] weaving of Jais, Nasirabad and other places (in Rae Bareli district) is now . . . extinct'.[20]

The cotton cloth production of the major weaving centres in Azamgarh, still in the later nineteenth century the most important cloth-producing district in U.P. excluding Banaras, appears to have held up a little better. In the 1890s the local industry was described as 'still moderately flourishing' though 'to some extent on the decline'.[21] The opening of a railway line through the district, and through its major weaving town, Mau, in 1898 occasioned some 'revival'.of trade: fewer weavers now left Mau, it was noted, 'to seek employment in the mills of Bombay, Cawnpore and Calcutta'.[22]

This widespread decline in the weaving trade, averted only in the case of Banaras and 'to some extent' Azamgarh, and there too through a recovery that took place mainly in the twentieth

---

[19] A. F. Millett, *Report on the Settlement of the Land Revenue of the Fyzabad District* (Allahabad, 1880), para 516; C. A. Silberred, *A Monograph on Cotton Fabrics produced in the North-Western Provinces and Oudh* (Allahabad, 1898), pp. 32, 46; *Report on the Railway-Borne Traffic of the North-Western Provinces and Outh, during the year ending 31 March 1884* (Allahabad, 1884), Appx. A, p. iii.

[20] Ibid., Appx. A, p. iv; Silberrad, *Monograph on Cotton Fabrics*, p. 47; *Census of India, 1931: United Provinces of Agra and Oudh, vol. XVIII, pt. 1. Report* (Allahabad, 1933), p. 426.

[21] Silberrad, *Monograph on Cotton Fabrics*, p. 46.

[22] Drake-Brockman, *Azamgarh District Gazetteer*, p. 255.

century,[23] occurred moreover over a period during which other sources of income for the people living in the plains of eastern U.P. and Bihar were reduced quite sharply. The closing down of native courts and *zamindari kachahris* meant an end to an important avenue of employment as soldiers, officials, agents, and suppliers; indeed, the decline in the fine cloth trade was also partly connected with this shift in the locus of political power and patronage. In the latter half of the nineteenth century many of the labouring, cultivating and zamindari communities of the region were also deprived of the opportunity to seek service in the colonial army and police,[24] as more and more caste qualifications were introduced. Nor was economic expansion, or for that matter educational and bureaucratic expansion under the Raj, such as to soak up the mass of the 'de-industrialized' and uprooted.[25] Indeed, the density of the population, and the recording and buying up of all rights in land, together with the imposition of a rigorous new law and law-enforcing authority, meant that it became increasingly difficult for many communities to eke out a living in and around the lands where they had lived for generations or, more often, centuries.

The full impact of the decline of handicrafts like spinning and weaving, rice-milling and oil-pressing, on the economy of this colonial hinterland may be judged from Grierson's 'Notes' on the district of Gaya. Grierson made a detailed study of the economic condition of the cultivators of Gaya in the 1880s, recording statistics of area, outturn, rent, cost of production of different crops, and so on, for over 3500 holdings. 'One of the most remarkable facts about cultivation in Gaya', he wrote after the conclusion of his survey,

is that it does not, as a rule, pay for its expenses . . . *If we exclude other*

[23] See G. Pandey, 'Structure and Conditions of Artisanal Production', cited in n. 12 above.

[24] The Bhojpuria *sipahi* had been a prominent symbol of the pre-1857 colonial armies in north India. There would, however, have been no ground for nicknaming the Indian soldiers 'Pandies' (from 'Pandey'—a common Brahman surname in eastern U.P. and Bihar) in the case of any later Mutiny.

[25] On 'de-industrialization' in this region, see esp. A. K. Bagchi, 'De-industrialization in Gangetic Bihar, 1809–1901' in Barun De, ed., *Essays in Honour of Professor S. C. Sarkar* (Delhi, 1978), and J. Krishnamurthy, 'De-industrialization in Gangetic Bihar during the Nineteenth Century: Another Look at the Evidence' *IESHR*, XXII, 4 (October–December 1985).

sources of income, 70 per cent of the holdings of the district do not support their cultivators. Those of them who have sufficient clothing and two meals a day must, in addition to cultivation, have other sources of livelihood.[26]

As regards sources of supplementary income, Grierson found from a smaller survey that the most important were, first, cattle-farming and, then, 'service', closely followed by artisanal work. It is striking that the income from 'service'—as *chaukidars*, peons, domestic servants, workers in factories, in the district of Gaya or further afield—was already greater than that from artisanal industry. 'The Howrah mills', commented Grierson, 'are full of Gaya Julahas'.[27]

Conditions in Gaya were not markedly different from those that obtained in the adjoining districts of the Bhojpuri region. In the later nineteenth century large numbers of the urban and rural poor in these districts—impoverished peasants and labourers, small zamindars and artisans—turned to the only major avenue of alternative employment now left to them, migrating with their Gaya counterparts to the industrial belt around Calcutta, the tea gardens of Assam, and plantations abroad. An official report on Azamgarh noted that during the decade of the 1890s emigrants from the district had remitted an average of Rs 13,00,000 per annum to their relatives at home: it was probable, the report went on, that 'but for this addition to their earnings, it would be impossible for the people to support themselves by agriculture alone'.[28]

In 1881 the number of non-Bengalis living in the four districts

[26] G. A. Grierson, *Notes on the District of Gaya* (Calcutta, 1893), pp. 91 and 95 (emphasis in original).

[27] Ibid., p. 107.

[28] Drake-Brockman, *Azamgarh District Gazetteer*, p. 118. S. H. Fremantle, *Report on the Supply of Labour in the United Provinces and in Bengal* (1906), para 30, noted that in the Kanpur Cotton Mills in 1905, 42 per cent of the labour force was Muslim, and a third of these were Julahas. 'After Musalmans come Koris, the Hindu handloom weaver caste. . . . This caste . . . predominates not only in the weaving sheds, but all over the mill, over any other Hindu caste and forms more than one-fifth of the whole number of workmen.' *The Census of India 1961*, vol. *XV, pt. VI, no. 23*, 'Survey of Village Lohta' (near Banaras), p. 4, reported that out of 52 Ansari (or Julaha) families resident in the place, 8 men were working as weavers in mills in Bombay or elsewhere.

of the Calcutta metropolitan area was found to be 279, 621, or 7 per cent of the total population of these districts. In the twenty years from 1891 to 1911 the number of immigrants from U.P., Bihar and Orissa swelled by over 100 per cent to 695,855. U.P. alone provided about a third of the immigrants throughout this period: 95,346 in 1891, 188,543 in 1901, and 235,487 in 1911. Of the U.P. migrants, by far the largest number came from the handful of Bhojpuri-speaking districts in the east of the province, notably Ghazipur (which accounted for nearly 29,000 migrants in 1901), Azamgarh and Ballia (nearly 25,000 each in the same year), Banaras (over 20,000) and Jaunpur (over 17,000).[29]

One might add that this history of migration cannot simply be read as a case of certain men and women changing one occupation for another by choice. It has been argued persuasively that the migrants from these areas had little choice in the matter.[30] The nature of this migration was without precedent in the history of the subcontinent. It was predominantly the forced migration of individual men. It long retained something of the quality of a 'temporary' move even when the migrant—and following him his brother/son/nephew and, in some cases, their wives and children as well—had been in the distant industrial location for decades. And the crises that it produced in the family and the local community—though we know precious little about all this yet—were entirely new.

The recent folklore of the Bhojpuri region certainly provides ample testimony to this. The poet Bihari Thakur's *Bidesiya*, a lament for the loved one who has gone 'abroad', acquired a remarkable popularity in villages and towns throughout this region.[31] 'Calcutta' quickly became a metaphor for the husband's paramour, the wife's greatest rival. The 'East'—rather different from that of the Orientalists—became the land where one could make one's fortune, but also the land which could break up one's family:

[29] R. Das Gupta, 'Factory Labour in Eastern India: Sources of Supply, 1855–1946', *IESHR*, xiii, 3 (1976).

[30] L. Chakravarty, 'Emergence of an Industrial Labour Force in a Dual Economy: British India, 1880–1920', *IESHR*, xv, 3 (1978).

[31] The *Bidesiya*, composed by Bihari in early twentieth century, quickly attained the status of a folk-form: many recensions may be obtained in the small towns and the cities of eastern U.P. and western Bihar.

Poorab ke deshwa men kailee nokaria,
Te Karee sonwan ke rojigar jania ho.

(One who obtains service in the East can fill his house with gold)

and

Railia na bairee
Jahajia na bairee,
Nokaria bairee na

(Railroads are not our enemy,
Nor are the steamships:
Our real enemy is *naukri*, i.e. service away from home.)[32]

The massive rearrangement of economic benefits under colonialism, and of the rules to be observed for survival and prosperity,
was surely of consequence in many instances of strife between
beneficiaries and losers in northern India. Thus, in Mubarakpur
in 1813 and 1842 the defilement of the Hindu temple was accompanied by an attack by the weavers and their associates upon
the houses and account-books of some of the bigger traders and
moneylenders. On the former occasion, the chief merchant-
moneylender of the qasba, Rikhai Sahu, was killed.[33] On the latter,
the homes of five moneylenders were attacked and those of the
two principal targets, Bicchuk Kalwar and Bhawani Prasad, were
not only plundered but burnt, a number of their relatives and
servants perishing in the flames.

In Mau clashes occurred between various parties of Hindus and
Muslims at the beginning of the century, when 'traditional' authority and the customary distribution of ritual space, and with this a
ban on cow-slaughter in the town, was brought into question
with the establishment of the new colonial power. The Banaras
Court of Circuit, trying the cases that arose out of these 'riots',
ordered a re-institution of the earlier ban on cow-slaughter in

[32] Cited in D. P. Saxena, *Rururban Migration in India. Causes and Consequences*
(Bombay, 1977), pp. 175, 178. For Calcutta as a symbol of separation, see
Rahi Masoom Raza, *Aadha Gaon* (Delhi, 1966), p. 10. The importance of the
local 'community' is discussed further in chpt. 4 below.

[33] Ali Hasan, *Waqeat-o-Hadesat: Qasba Mubarakpur* (Urdu ms., n.d.), p. 13,
notes that many of the weavers who attacked Rikhai Sahu in 1813 were his
'clients'.

Mau. There is no record of any violent clash between members of the two communities for the next five decades. The renewal of strife in the 1860s began with the erection of a new temple in October 1862, which was perhaps seen as another instance of the assertion of their money power by moneylenders and other rich Hindus and hotly contested by the weavers and other local Muslims as having no customary sanction.[34]

In Bareilly the major incident of the 'troubles' in 1837 was the murder of a wealthy Hindu dealer by a Muslim carpet weaver.[35] It is at least likely that the friction arising out of an exploitative relationship, which lay behind the Mubarakpur Julahas' attacks upon their Hindu moneylenders in 1813 and 1842, may also have been at work here.

In Shahabad (then part of Sandila, now of Hardoi district), to take an example of Hindu-Muslim strife in which Julahas were not involved, the violence of 1849 was related by observers to the refusal of further loans by a Hindu moneylender, Sabsukh Rai, 'the most respectable merchant in the district', to defaulting Pathan Muslim debtors. In retaliation apparently for what was seen as Sabsukh Rai's arrogance, the procession of *tazias* on the tenth Muharram halted outside his house, the processionists raised slogans against him, broke into his house and plundered property valued at over Rs 70,000.[36]

It is evident, for all that, that religion and religious feeling had a great deal to do with such outbreaks. I shall have more to say about the new political order that heightened the contention over ritual spaces, routes of processions and the like. Suffice it here to note that

[34] This account is based on B. N. Dar, *An Appeal to the English Public on behalf of the Hindus of the N.W.P. and Oudh* (Lucknow, 1893); and 'Petition of Hindu Inhabitants of Mhow to Secretary of State for India in Council' (n.d., 1893?) with its numerous appendices which provide detailed extracts from official reports and court judgements relating to conflicts in Mau. (I am grateful to Shri D. N. Pandey of Mau, Azamgarh, for permitting me to consult this document which is preserved in the library of his late father, a prominent public man of the town.)

[35] See H. R. Nevill, *Bareilly: A Gazetteer. Being vol. XIII of the District Gazetteers of the United Provinces of Agra and Oudh* (Allahabad, 1911), pp. 168–9.

[36] W. H. Sleeman, *Journey through the Kingdom of Oude, vol. II* (London, 1858), pp. 47–8.

quarrels over religious questions—the desecration of a temple or mosque, the refusal of passage to a Muharram procession, the demand to stop cow-sacrifice—provided the immediate issue in most of the instances of strife mentioned above. Religious symbols, religious practice and display of piety provided a major means for the expression of status, and of claims to higher status, throughout this period. So Bichchuk Kalwar sought to establish his position among the élite of Mubarakpur through careful trading and money-lending, certainly, but also through what could easily be described as excessive zeal in the matter of religious practice; or again, Angnu Kalwar and Manohar Das Agrawal, merchant-moneylenders of the generation immediately before and immediately after Bicchuk, made attempts to build temples inside the qasba where none had existed.[37] Or, to take an example of collective revenge rather than individual social climbing, the Pathans of Shahabad, having looted and destroyed Subsukh Rai's property, completed their task by building a small miniature mosque at the door of his house with some loose bricks. 'Poor Subsookh Rae has been utterly ruined', commented Sleeman in January 1850. 'The little mock mosque, of uncemented bricks, still stands as a monument of the insolence [*sic*] of the Mahommedan population, and the weakness and apathy of the Oude Government.'[38]

[37] See secn. VII of my 'Rallying Round the Cow: Sectarian Strife in the Bhojpuri Region, *c.* 1888–1917', in R. Guha, ed., *Subaltern Studies II* (Delhi, 1983); also chpt. 4 below.
[38] Sleeman, *Journey II*, p. 47. Notice the echo of Buyers' comment on the mosque built by Aurangzeb at the site of the Vishwanath temple in Banaras: 'a monument of Moslem pride and intolerance, and of Hindu humiliation in former times'. If these were purely official 'readings' at some stage, they certainly seem to have coloured local perceptions in the course of time: witness Bhartendu Harishchandra:

मस्जिद लखी बिसुनाथ धिग परे हिये जो घाव

and

जहाँ बिसेसर सोमनाथ माधव के मन्दिर,
तहाँ महजिद बनि गयीं होत अब अल्ला अकबर ;

Bhartendu Granthavali, II, pp. 684, 699, cited in Sudhir Chandra, 'Communal Consciousness in Late Nineteenth Century Hindi Literature', in Mushirul Hasan, ed., *Communal and Pan-Islamic Trends in Colonial India* (Delhi, 1981), p. 182, n. 9.

The evidence regarding north Indian weavers in the nineteenth century gives us a picture of a community that was cruelly tossed about as their dependence on a whole range of intermediaries— moneylenders, lawyers, recruiting sardars—significantly increased. The beneficiaries of the new conditions in the cloth trade included, prominently, a large group of Hindu merchants and moneylenders who came to attain a perhaps unprecedented hold not only on the trade but on the weavers themselves.[39] There can be no doubt that this heightened strength of the merchants/moneylenders, their powerful position in law under the new colonial dispensation, and their increasing arrogance as the lower classes often saw it, caused much annoyance to the 'losers'—not only to lower classes like the weavers, but also to the declining class of small zamindars and service gentry who claimed a 'traditional' authority and status.[40] It is but a small step from there to saying that weaver/moneylender (or weaver-merchant) conflict inevitably followed, and, since the weavers were mainly Muslims and the moneylenders mainly Hindus, this took the form of Hindu-Mislim strife. But it may be well to take this small step slowly.

III

The assumption that we should perhaps start with is that religion in pre-modern societies is not a surrogate for anything else (except insofar as it may be taken as an index of the inability of human

[39] The evidence on this question is of course contradictory, and the difficulties of comparison with earlier periods hazardous, but the rigour and rigidity of the new regime is perhaps generally recognized. For some of the major contributions on these questions, relating to northern India, see Hamida Hossein, *The Company Weavers of Bengal. The East India Company and the Organization of Textile Production in Bengal, 1750–1813* (Delhi, OUP); K. N. Chaudhuri, 'The Structure of Indian Textile Industry in the Seventeenth and Eighteenth Centuries', *IESHR*, XI, 2–3 (1974); S. Bhattacharya, 'Industrial Production, Technology and Market Structure in Eastern India, 1757–1857', in D. Kumar, ed., *Cambridge Economic History of India, vol. II* (Cambridge, 1983).

[40] Cf. C. A. Bayly, 'The Small Town and Islamic Gentry in North India: The Case of Kara' in K. Ballhatchet and J. Harrison, eds., *The City in South Asia* (London, 1980); also his *Rulers, Townsmen and Bazaars.*

beings to grasp the content of their own potential).[41] But 'religion' is also not fixed for all time, unchanging, unchangeable. Rather, new issues gain importance, new questions become central, the 'preservation of religion' acquires different meanings in different social and political contexts. In northern India in the nineteenth century, the presence of a new colonial regime and its drive towards obtaining the most comprehensive knowledge possible of the subject population were of much consequence in determining the character of public religion and religious issues. The regime's attempt to catalogue everything, 'public' and 'personal', 'sacred' and 'profane', and to record for succeeding generations 'established' custom and 'normal' practice that had always had a great deal of fluidity built into it, reinforced positions on such matters as procession routes, timing, musical accompaniment, and made issues out of questions that had not been the subject of such serious, or continuous, contention before.[42]

The outstanding example of this kind of stimulation and shaping of new disputes is provided not by 'religion' as such but by an institution closely tied to religion in India, 'caste'. The late nineteenth and early twentieth centuries saw a mushrooming of caste associations and caste movements, of claims to new (higher, purer) status and demands for new names to be registered in the administrative record. Without doubt, this process was considerably accentuated by the Census Commissioner's decision in 1901 to classify 'castes' and 'communities' all over the country in accordance with their ritual purity and standing in local society.

A statistically-minded Census Commissioner in Bihar in 1911 commented on the flood of petitions he had received asking for a change in nomenclature and a higher place in the order of precedence, and noted that the weight of the paper alone amounted to 1.5 maunds. Here, as elsewhere, it was not Hindus alone but Muslims as well who were agitated and assertive. As the same report noted, Muslim Rajputs in large numbers 'suddenly' (?),

---

[41] I am thinking here of Marx's notion of religion as alienation.

[42] See M. Roberts, 'Noise as Cultural Struggle: Tom-Tom Beating, the British and Communal Disturbances in Sri Lanka, 1880s–1930s', in Veena Das, ed., *Communities, Riots, Survivors: The South Asian Experience* (Delhi, OUP, forthcoming).

between 1901 and 1911, took to calling themselves Pathans, the title Singh yielding place to Khan. 'Practically all . . . [Muslims] of low degree'—weavers, oil-pressers, barbers and so on—aspired to the status of Sheikh, though 'the better class Musalmans would not recognize them, nor would they recognize each other as such'.[43]

There was much, apart from economic hardship, in the existing conditions of the Julahas to encourage them to wage a struggle to upgrade their status as a 'community'. Widely scattered and internally differentiated as they were, one obvious feature that the Muslim weavers had in common, apart from their occupation, was their lowly social standing in the eyes of both Muslims and Hindus of the upper castes and classes. This was the result, evidently, of their comparatively recent conversion to Islam and their position as manual labourers who were generally poor and illiterate.

One of the more obvious status-markers in nothern India in the nineteenth and twentieth centuries, as perceived by the locally dominant classes and by outside observers, was the distinction between the *sharif* (plural *ashraf*, the respectable classes) and the *razil* (or labouring people). The former category appears to have included all those who did not soil their hands with the messy business of labour: the Brahmans, Rajputs and Bhumihars (i.e. the 'zamindari castes' of the region), together with the 'true' Saiyids and Sheikhs (i.e. those who could demonstrate some sort of descent from 'noble' Arabic ancestors), Pathan converts from Rajput clans, and some smaller Hindu castes like the Kayasthas who were prominent in bureaucracy and the 'learned' professions. All the rest, from the 'clean' cultivating castes like the Kurmis, Koeris and Ahirs, and equivalent Muslim castes like the Zamindaras (or Rautaras) of Azamgarh, to the 'unclean' labouring and artisanal castes, Chamars, Dusadhs, Lohars, Julahas and so on, were classified as razil.

---

[43] *Census of India, 1911, vol. V. Bengal, Bihar and Orissa, and Sikkim. pt. I* (Calcutta, 1913), pp. 440, 446. For another illustration of government stimulation of caste and community identifications and aspirations—in this instance provided by the government's utilization of caste and community categories in the granting of public appointments and political representation, see Lucy Carroll, 'Colonial Perceptions of Indian Society and the Emergence of Caste(s) Associations', *Journal of Asian Studies*, xxxvii, 2 (1978).

Perhaps the most important indicator of a community's razil status thus was the performance of menial and other tasks for the upper castes and landowners. Orr exaggerated, but not wildly, when he wrote on *begari* in the mid-nineteenth century: 'The Chamar, Lodh, Kurmi, and all inferior castes are the prey of all, caught at every hour of the day or night, made use of as beasts of burthen, beaten and abused, treated as if incapable of feeling pain or humiliation, never remunerated.'[44] But there were other indicators too: the incidence of widow remarriage, for example, or the proportion of a group's womenfolk that went out to work, which was far greater among the lower castes than the higher. It was found in Bihar in 1911 that there were but 8 female workers to every 100 male workers among the Bhumihars, 10 to every 100 among Rajputs and 12 among Brahmans. By contrast, the statistics were 52 in every 100 for the Kurmis, 54 among the Ahirs and the Koeris, and as high as 69 and 71 among the Julahas and Dusadhs respectively.[45] On this calculation, then, the Julahas came out ranked with some of the lowest of the Hindu 'untouchable' castes. Several pronouncements of Muslim learned men in the nineteenth century also placed them on par with the Dabgars, a Muslim caste equivalent to the Chamars, and the Bhangis.[46]

The division that existed between Julahas and other 'low-born' Muslims on the one hand, and the sharif or 'respectable' Muslims

[44] Cited in H. C. Irwin, *The Garden of India* (London, 1880), p. 153.

[45] *1911 Census, vol. V, Bengal, Bihar & Orissa, pt. I*, pp. 576–80. The category of 'worker' here is problematic, since definitions changed and the censuses never took account of women's work in households, not only in the case of the upper castes but also in that of the lower, except it would seem where women were fully in-charge of a particular stage in the process of production or distribution—e.g. selling milk and vegetables in the case of Ahirs and Koeris, or spinning and reeling in the case of weavers' households. But the general point still holds: to let women go out to work, or to *admit* that they worked, was taken as a mark of low status.

[46] Maulvi Kamruzzaman (interview, Mubarakpur, 6 November 1980) referred to several examples of this, including Ahmad Raza Khan Barelvi's *Fatwa Rasviya*. Cf. R. V. Russell and Hiralal, *Tribes and Castes of the Central Provinces, vol. III* (London, 1916), p. 249; also 'Information Regarding the Slackness of Demand for European Cotton Goods', Appx., Mirzapur Collector's Report, p. 149.

on the other, was reflected also in some of their religious practices. That popular Islam in India paralleled popular Hinduism in remarkable ways from very early days is now widely recognized. Kunwar Muhammad Ashraf wrote of pilgrimages to the graves of reputed saints that characterized popular religious practice among the Muslims of northern India in the period of the Sultanate. In Sindh, pilgrimages of this kind brought together such great crowds that 'there was hardly any room to stand'. The sexes mingled freely and the atmosphere was decidedly festive, a situation disliked by the orthodox, and especially the theologians. But, as the author of the contemporary *Tarikh-i-Tahiri* observed, 'the custom has so long prevailed among these people and what time has sanctioned, they never relinquish'.[47]

Such practices continued in the centuries that followed. 'Three figures have loomed very large in the imagination and the life of the common [Muslim] people', writes Mujeeb; 'they and their graves are not only revered but worshipped. Sayyid Salar Mas'ud Ghazi, whose grave is at Bahraich, is the oldest'.[48] The *Hadi aqat-ul-aqalim* of Murtaza Husain of Bilgram, composed in 1780–81, noted that thousands of Muslims flocked every year to Salar Mas'ud's tomb in Bahraich 'to invoke the deceased soldier's aid in the fulfilment of their worldly objects'.[49] Until the end of the nineteenth century, and into the twentieth, Muslims and Hindus of many different castes continued the annual pilgrimage to the tomb of Saiyid Salar Mas'ud Ghazi or 'Ghazi Mian', and a *Ghazi Mian ka mela* was enthusiastically celebrated at many places in eastern U.P. and western Bihar. Prominent among the followers of Ghazi Mian were the Julahas: they 'reverence the flag of Ghazi Mian . . . to whom they ascribe the conversion of their ancestors', as one writer observed in the 1870s.[50]

The figure of Ghazi Mian had also long since been incorporated into the Panchpiriya sect which was followed, we are told, by 'the

[47] K. M. Ashraf, *Life and Conditions of the People of Hindustan* (2nd ed., Delhi, 1970), pp. 240–1, 243.

[48] M. Mujeeb, *The Indian Muslims* (London, 1967), p. 303.

[49] A. L. Srivastava, *The First Two Nawabs of Oudh* (Lucknow, 1967), p. 268.

[50] J. R. Reid, *Report on the Temporarily Settled Parganas of the Azamgarh District 1877* (Allahabad, 1881), p. 35.

mass of the peasantry' in eastern U.P. At the end of the nineteenth century Ghazi Mian was reckoned to be foremost among the Panch Pir (Five Saints) 'whose names differ from district to district, and [who] form a most remarkable collection including both Hindus and Musalmans'. The 1901 census recorded fifty-three castes in U.P. that were said to be worshippers of the Panch Pir. Of these forty-four were described as being 'wholly or partly Hindu'. The number of Hindu followers alone was put at over 1.75 million, and this took account only of those who declared the Panch Pir to be their 'principal' object of worship. Wilfrid Blunt, a close observer of the local scene, reckoned that the total number of people actually worshipping these saints around 1920 was more like 13.5 million. At the turn of the century the annual Ghazi Mian ka mela in Bahraich regularly drew an assembly of over 100,000 people.[51] It was attended by low-caste Hindus as much as by Muslims, Kalwars—some of whose caste fellows were prospering as they advanced from selling liquor to wider money-lending and trading activities—as well as Julahas—some of whose brethren were migrating in search of work to Bombay and Calcutta.

The powerful attacks launched against these syncretistic, un-Islamic practices by religious reformers and revivalists alike are certain to have reached most weaving towns and qasbas in the nineteenth century. Early in the century, officials reported the spread of Wahabi influence among the weavers of Mau, Mubarakpur and Kopaganj.[52] As the century advanced, and the debate between the new theologians and the orthodox deepened, the pressure to reform and become 'pure' Muslims is likely to have grown. Rafiuddin Ahmed has documented this process superbly for Bengal in the later nineteenth century. There, as he shows, the orthodox–reformist debate spread to the remote countryside, aided by the rise of new 'institutions' like the *bahas* and the prolifera-

[51] The above is based on H. R. Nevill, *Bahraich: A Gazetteer, being vol. XLV of the District Gazetteers of the United Provinces of Agra and Oudh* (Allahabad 1903), pp. 149–50; W. Crooke, *Religion and Folklore of Northern India* (Oxford, 1926), pp. 166, 169; E. A. H. Blunt, *The Caste System of Northern India* (reprinted Delhi, 1969), p. 292; Irwin, *Garden of India*, pp. 73–4.

[52] See n. 8 above; also 'Village Crime Register', Mubarakpur, pt. IV, entry for 1909–10.

tion of religious tracts (*puthis*). The consequence was a general rise in the level of an 'Islamic' consciousness and a marked drive towards self-improvement and Ashrafization, which included not only a stricter observance of practices enjoined by the *shariat* but also a growing use of Arabic and Persian names.[53]

To these kinds of pressure was added, as we have already noted, the pressure of a colonial government out to classify *everything* and to fix the status, character and administrative usefulness of one and all by means of a public record. Many groups of Muslims in nothern India, too, were therefore moving quickly by the turn of the century to shed 'Hindu' names and establish for themselves a 'purer' Islamic status. As an important part of this trend, Muslim weavers came together in an endeavour to change their caste appellation, overthrow the derisive views about them which the upper classes (Hindu and Muslim) helped to promote,[54] and gain an equal standing in the fraternity of Islam.

The word 'Julaha' was in all probability of Persian origin (*julah*— weaver, from *jula*—ball of thread). In India in the nineteenth century many observers sought to trace the name to the Arabic *juhala*, meaning the 'ignorant class', to bring it in line with their notions of the weavers' stupidity. Julaha spokesmen countered with the argument that the term in fact came from *jal* (net), *jils* (decorated) or *ujla* (lighted up, or white); hence also the name which local weaving communities sometimes used for themselves even in the early nineteenth century, *nurbaf* or 'weavers of light'.[55] They claimed Adam as the founder of their craft—when Satan (or, in some versions, Eve, or a fairy) made him realize his nakedness, he learnt the art of weaving and later taught it to his sons—and declared that their ancestors came from Arabia. From the later decades of the nineteenth century Muslim weavers in many places came to reject the name Julaha altogether, and insisted that they be called 'Momin' ('the faithful', 'men of honour'), 'Ansari' (after

---

[53] R. Ahmed, *The Bengal Muslims, 1871–1906: A Quest for Identity* (Delhi, 1981), *passim*.

[54] See n. 46 above; G. A. Grierson, *Bihar Peasant Life* (1885, reprinted Delhi, 1975), pp. 69–70. See also chpt. 4, section IV below.

[55] See (IOR) F/4/365, 'Memorial of the Mussulmans of the City of Benares, presented to the Magistrate on 27 November 1809'. The name *Safedbaf*, or 'weavers of whiteness', was also sometimes used.

a claimed Arabic ancestor who practised the art of weaving), 'Momin-Ansar' or 'Sheikh Momin'. By 1911 they had succeeded in having themselves recorded under these names in the census.[56] Today, it is rare for anyone in Banaras or Patna, Mubarakpur or Mau, to use the name 'Julaha' to refer to any member of this community.

The Muslim weavers' efforts to 'purify' themselves and upgrade their social position were, of course, in line with social reform and protest movements among many other lower and middle-ranking groups and castes at this time. In Chhatisgarh, a movement of 'purification' and upward mobility arose among the lowly Chamars in the 1820s. This had developed into a powerful struggle against the upper classses of the region by the later nineteenth century. Claiming to be followers of the one True God (*Satnam*), the Satnamis—as the reformist Chamars called themselves—decided to give up liquor, meat and certain red vegetables (because they had the colour of blood), refused to work cattle for irrigation or ploughing after midday (a kindness to the animals so employed that was already in force among the neighbouring Gonds of Bastar), and demanded the abolition of caste and an end to idol worship. They also asserted their right to a fair share of the produce and to hold more land, as owners or tenants.[57]

There is evidence of bitter and extended conflict between 'Hindu' landlords and 'Chamar' tenants in this region after the 1860s, leading to numerous court cases and many instances of 'rioting' and murder. Conversion to the Satnam or other independent religious persuasions—the Kabirpanth too acquired a large number of supporters from among the Chamars of Chhattisgarh[58]—was

---

[56] *U.P Census 1911, pt. I*, p. 360; *Bihar Census 1911, pt. I*, p. 446; C. A. Silberrad, *A Monograph on Cotton Fabrics produced in the North-Western Provinces and Oudh* (Allahabad, 1898), p. 1; Crooke, *Tribes and Castes, III*, pp. 69–70. In the early 1930s, the Jamiat-ul-Ansar-ul-Hind, also known as the All-India Momin Conference, was established as an apex organization to represent the social and political interests of the weavers.

[57] It should be noted that the Chamars of Chhattisgarh were able to launch such a movement because they were in a slightly better position than their caste-fellows elsewhere, on account of their numerical strength and the lands they had come to hold (as owners or tenants), probably in the recent past.

[58] It may be worthwhile to record that the Kabirpanth, which may be thought to have a substantial following among Muslim weavers, given Kabir's

part of a growing spirit of revolt within this low-class and low-status community. As a local 'Chamar' convert to Christianity is reported to have said when told to perform some menial task, 'I have become a christian and am one of the Sahibs; I shall do no more *bigar*.'[59] By the end of the nineteenth century there was a deep division in the Chhatisgarh countryside between the upper-caste Hindus and landowners on the one side, and the Satnamis on the other. 'Over most of India', wrote one official, 'the term Hindu is contrasted with Muhammadan, but in Chhattisgarh to call a man a Hindu conveys primarily that he is not a Chamar, or Chamara according to the contemptuous abbreviation [*sic*] in common use'. The same official noted the solidarity of the local Chamars: 'If a proprietor once arouses the hostility of his Chamar tenants he may as well abandon his village for all the profit he is likely to derive from it.'[60]

Significant social reform efforts were also initiated among the traditional 'cultivating' communities of northern India,[61] such as the Kurmis and Ahirs, which led on in the early twentieth century to the establishment of important inter-regional caste associations. The Bihar Census Commissioner wrote as follows about the Gwala Movement which developed among the Ahirs of Shahabad and

---

own origins and life among the Julahas of Banaras, was by the later nineteenth century being seen as an exclusively Hindu preserve. Older weavers in Banaras today state that no one in the community knows the name of Kabir, except for some young weavers who may have picked it up through a 'secular' education in school or college or through exposure to television—a comment, perhaps, on the successful process of Islamization that took place among the weavers in the nineteenth century, along with the appropriation of Kabir by Hindu literary and religious circles.

[59] Russell and Lal, *Tribes and Castes of C.P., I*, p. 316. (*Bigar* or *begar* is forced, unpaid labour).

[60] Ibid., p. 315.

[61] Cf. the successful case of upward mobility by the great cultivating caste of Gujarat, the Kanbis who, increasingly over the late nineteenth and early twentieth centuries, came to be called Patidars; D. F. Pocock, *Kanbi and Patidar: A Study of the Patidar Community of Gujarat* (Oxford, 1972), *passim*, and D. Hardiman, *Peasant Nationalists of Gujarat: Kheda, 1917–34* (Delhi, 1981); also the work of Sekhar Bandhopadhyaya on 'Caste and Politics in Bengal—A Study of the Namasudra Movement' (Ph.D. thesis, Centre for South-East Asian Studies, Department of History, Calcutta University, 1984).

other districts of Bihar, and which he described as the most important of the lower-caste movements for social uplift that had arisen
in the province:

Sessions are held once a year and are attended by several thousands of
persons. . . . A considerable body of literature has accumulated in support of
the claim of the Ahirs to Kshatriya origin and it is stated that 'nothing less
than Kshatriya position will satisfy it [the community]' . . . a number of
Ahirs have assumed the sacred thread. . . . The men of this caste refuse to
do *begari* [forced labour] for their landlords or to permit their women
folk to attend the markets to sell milk and ghee.

Other reports speak of instructions laid down by the Gwalas
for members of their community at numerous local meetings—
among them the injunction to wear the sacred thread, to protect
cows, to end the practice of early marriage, to contribute one
anna per *bigha* of land held to a common fund for the education of
Gwala children, to refuse to perform begar for zamindars, and to
maintain unity among themselves.[62]

If the donning of the sacred thread represented one aspect of
this rising, which derived from imitation of the upper castes and
classes, the withdrawal of women from work in the marketplace
represented not only such imitation but also a refusal to expose
lower-class women to sexual exploitation and harassment. The
refusal to perform begar was an equally emphatic blow against
exploitation by the landowners, while the appeal to members of
the community to end early marriage and pay attention to education
went against the trend of much orthodox upper-class opinion
(most clearly on the question of early marriage) and represented a
clear-cut recognition of the need for change and a new vision. This
was 'Sanskritization' as resistance, and—as in the case of the
Satnamis and Julahas—the whole movement was suffused with
religion.

Ahir claims to a higher status were bolstered by statements
pointing to the community's political importance and its protection of the *dharma* in bygone days. The members of the community

[62] Hetukar Jha, 'Lower-Caste Peasants and Upper-Caste Zamindars in
Bihar, 1921–25', *IESHR*, xiv, 4 (1977), pp. 550 and 555; and (Bihar State
Archives, Patna), Govt. of Bihar & Orissa, Political Dept. Special Secn.
(Confidential), File no. 238 of 1923.

generally spoke of their descent from the 'cowherd god', Krishna. Elliot recorded that the Ahirs of the North-Western Provinces (most of U.P. today) 'all trace their origin to Mathura, or places a little to the west of it'. Krishna himself, according to Ahir spokesmen, belonged to the tribe of Yadavas, or descendants of Yadu, a nomadic people who tended cattle and were believed to have made an early settlement in the Mathura region.[63]

The caste's claims of noble descent were often elaborately made. *Ahir Itihasa ki Jhalak*, a volume edited by D. S. Yadav and published in Lucknow in 1915, argued that in this *kaliyuga*[64] the country, and with it the Ahir community, had fallen on bad times and become the home of poverty (material and spiritual), ignorance, fear and undesirable customs. The volume quotes a report from *The Statesman* (Calcutta) of 27 January 1914, presumably written by another Ahir spokesman, in support of its assertion that the Ahirs are Kshatriyas.

Originally the warrior caste of *kshatriyas* were the protectors of Brahmans and cows alike. But a division of labour came about in the course of time. . . . Some *kshatriyas* were at last confined to the protector [*sic*] of the sacred men, while the term Gope or Gopal (Ahir is another synonym used chiefly in Bihar where the caste are especially numerous) was used to designate the protector of the almost equally sacred animals.[65]

The term 'Ahir', we are further informed by the same writer, is wrongly translated as 'milkman' and 'wanderer'. In fact it comes from the Sanskrit roots *ahi* and *ir* meaning therefore one who fends off or kills demons, snakes, men of bad character, enemies. And, along with Krishna, the great Mauryan emperors Chandragupta and Ashoka are claimed as Ahirs.[66]

There is other interesting evidence from Shahabad and neighbouring districts of the appropriation of major Great Tradition deities—not only Krishna, but Ram as well—by their assimilation into the person of the most popular caste deity among the Ahirs

[63] H. M. Elliot, *Memoirs on the History, Folklore and Distribution of the Races of the North-Western Provinces of India, vol.* I (London, 1869), Supplementary Glossary, p. 3; Crooke, *Tribes and Castes, vol.* I (Calcutta, 1896), p. 50.

[64] The fourth great age, or *yuga*, predicted in the Hindu cycle of world development: the age of vice.

[65] D. S. Yadav, ed., *Ahir Itihasa Ki Jhalak* (Lucknow, 1915), p. 21 & *passim*.

[66] Ibid., pp. 10, 13–14.

of the region, Bir Kuar. The myth of Bir Kuar, as it appears in Ahir songs, seems to have had two distinct strands. The first is a local story, embellished and presented in numerous recensions, of the mythical Ahir hero Bir Kuar, who was killed by a tigress while defending his beloved buffaloes. The second derives from Great Tradition legends and, at times, merges Bir Kuar not only in Krishna but also in Ram.

Bir Kuar's birthplace, as given in different songs and stories, varies between Ayodhya and Bhojpur (a town in Shahabad district). He is supposedly reared in Brindaban, Palamau or Bhojpur. Sometimes he hunts in Brindaban (Krishna's country) and drinks in Ayodhya (Ram's capital).[67] As the verse of one song recorded by W. G. Archer in the 1930s has it:

> Where was the birthplace of Baba Birnath?
> He was born in Ayodhya
> He was reared in Brindaban
> His posts are everywhere
> And from his castemen he levies worship
> When will my castemen come?
> The hour of worship is passing
> Oh a hero is Birnath
> And a grazer of buffaloes . . .[68]

Thus, the 'territory' of the Ahirs is also marked out along with their claims to a noble status in the Hindu hierarchy: born in Ayodhya, reared in Bhojpur, hunting in Brindaban, their 'posts are everywhere' over this great tract.[69]

In all of these movements, one could say, politics appears in the form of religion, religion is at the same time politics. 'Sanskritization' and 'Islamization' were means of asserting an identity, demanding rights and self-respect, and they challenged the existing social order even as they encouraged religious orthodoxy and 'improvement'. Towards the end of the nineteenth century, movements such as these among the lower and intermediate castes of eastern U.P. and western Bihar received a considerable fillip

---

[67] W. G. Archer, *The Vertical Man: A Study in Primitive Indian Sculpture* (London, 1947), pp. 99ff.

[68] Ibid., p. 65.

[69] For the importance of the notion of a community's territory, see chpt. 4 below.

owing to the spread of the Cow-Protection movement, which challenged the right of Muslims to sacrifice cows as a central part of their religious obligations. Not surprisingly, the Ahirs (present in some strength in this region), Koeris and Kurmis took a leading part, along with the upper castes, in the recurring battles that took place for the protection of the cow, and the Julahas were equally active among those who defended their right to sacrifice the animal at the Baqr'Id.[70]

IV

In the preceding pages there have been more than a few references to the Julahas and the community of Muslim weavers in northern and central India. It is necessary to stress, however, a point that we have already made in passing, that this 'community' was far from being homogeneous or united for most of the period under study. Julaha solidarity was forged gradually and imperfectly through struggles against concrete disabilities, for concrete ends. The fact is of some importance if we are to fully appreciate the role of the weavers in the caste and community struggles of the nineteenth century, not to mention the extent to which they were successful in achieving proclaimed goals.

It is only to be expected that there would have been major differences in the economic well being of different groups among the Muslim weavers: between 'master-weavers' and ordinary 'independent' weavers, and weavers who worked on others' looms in Banaras, Mubarakpur, Mau and elsewhere.[71] Much more striking are the 'caste' (one would also have to say 'historical') distinctions that existed among Muslim weavers even at the end of the nineteenth century—distinctions that the colonial administration did everything to obliterate as it isolated the category of the Muslim Julaha with its supposedly fixed and identifiable caste characteristics. Ibbetson's *Punjab Ethnography* listed groups that styled themselves Koli Julahas, Chamar Julahas, Mochi Julahas and Ram-

[70] See my 'Rallying Round the Cow', secn. IV; also chpt. 5 below.

[71] See, e.g., *Report on the Railway-borne Traffic of the North-Western Provinces and Oudh during the year ending 31 March 1883* (Allahabad, 1884), p. 37. By the later nineteenth century some of the bigger master-weavers had set themselves up not only as traders but also as landowners.

dasi Julahas. There was little doubt, Ibbetson remarked, that in time these groups would drop the prefixes that indicated their lowly Hindu origins and become 'Julahas pure and simple': that is to say, the pressure of the censuses, and other political and social demands of the time, would lead them to do so. In U.P., at the time of the 1891 census, the Parsotiya Julaha of Rohilkhand was found to be a Hindu, related to the major Hindu weaving caste of Koris. The remaining Julahas in the province registered themselves under 244 divisions. There were Bais, Bania, Bhangi, Bisen, Chamar, Chauhan, Koli, Rajput, Teli and Tomar Julahas, for example, some who derived their sectional identity from a geographical area (the Chaurasia, Faizabadi, Purabiya, Sarwariya, Shahabadi, etc.) and others who claimed a more or less 'pure' Muslim descent, calling themselves Madari, Muhammadi, Momin, Mughal, Pathan, Shaikh, Siddiqi or Sunni Julahas—evidence enough of their mixed origins and still ambiguous position in the fraternity of Indian Muslims.[72]

Just as there were major differences in caste identification among the Muslim weavers of northern India, so there were differences in historical associations and historical memories. The weavers of Banaras, Mubarakpur, Mau, Tanda, Jais and other such centres had developed and long maintained special links with the nawabs of Awadh, the kings of Nepal and even more distant rulers like the Nizam of Hyderabad.[73] Even a relatively undistinguished place like Mau, not noted in the colonial period for the production of any exceptional fabrics, could trace its distinct traditions and the special position of its manufacturing population back to the days of the great Mughals.

Mau was mentioned in the *Ain-i-Akbari*, along with Banaras and Jalalabad, as being famous for the production of certain 'beautiful' cloths.[74] In the reign of Shah Jahan, the pargana of Maunath Bhanjan was assigned to the emperor's daughter, Jahanara Begum, 'for [her] supply with cloth and sugar, the two great staples of the place', and its chief town (Mau) appears to have been renamed

[72] Ibbetson, *Punjab Castes* (1916, reprinted Delhi, 1974), p. 302; Crooke, *Tribes and Castes of the N.W.P.*, vol. III, p. 69.

[73] See my 'Economic Dislocation in Nineteenth Century Eastern U.P.'

[74] H. K. Naqvi, *Urban Centres and Industries in Upper India, 1556–1803* (Bombay, 1968), pp. 140–1.

Jahanabad. Under the patronage of the imperial house, then and in the reign of Aurangzeb, the town flourished. 'Substantial buildings were erected, a large market place [or *katra*] built, and every means employed to induce persons to resort to the town and take up their abode there.' Mau quickly grew to have as many as 84 *muhallas* and 360 mosques. Julahas, Katuas (a specialized caste of spinners who were Hindus) and traders constituted the major part of its population. A 'great manufacturing industry in cotton cloth' thus came into being, and the subsequent establishment of an imperial customs post in the town indicates the volume of traffic that passed through it.[75]

It is among the weavers of such towns in eastern U.P. that Burn, Census Superintendent of U.P. in 1901, is likely to have found that small number of 'uneducated Musalmans' who, in his reckoning, still spoke Awadhi—the dialect that was used by the officials and army of the former nawabs of Awadh. 'These people', wrote Burn, '(who) are almost entirely Muhammadans . . . believe that they speak Urdu, as their language differs considerably from that of the people round them'.[76] The language—which they believed to be Urdu—was just one mark of the pride and 'independence' of the weaving populations of Mau and Mubarakpur, Lucknow and Tanda, Banaras and Sassaram.

By the later nineteenth century there were other marks, too. The weavers of Mau, Kopaganj and Mubarakpur Khas (this excludes, presumably, the weavers of the areas surrounding Mubarakpur) 'are not, like most other weavers, worshippers of Ghazi Mian and his flag', Reid wrote in his report on the settlement of Azamgarh district in 1877.[77] In other words, groups of Muslim weavers were by now making a point of standing aloof from those practices of their fellow weavers which consisted in joining lower-caste Hindus

[75] (U.P. Regional Archives, Allahabad) COG (Gorakhpur), Revenue (Azamgarh), vol. 27, file 331, J. Thomason-F. Currie, 22 June 1836, para 22; Reid, *Report on Azamgarh District 1877*, pp. 146–7.

[76] R. Burn, *Census of India, 1901, vol. XVI, North-Western Provinces and Oudh, Part I, Report* (Allahabad, 1901), pp. 177–8. Burn mentioned also a handful of private servants and 'illiterate government officials' who also still spoke Awadhi.

[77] Reid, *Report on the Settlement of Azamgarh District 1877*, p. 147n.

in propitiating the whole range of supernatural powers that could conceivably aid them or do them harm.

That this new mood was beginning to penetrate even beyond the weaving qasbas and towns that had attained something of a privileged position owing to their links with the courts in the past is made clear by Deepak Mehta's study of Muslim weavers in two villages of Bara Banki district.[78] This scholar notes the intimate connection between work and worship in the lives of the weavers, and the centrality of the weavers' major religious text (or *kitab*), the *Mufid-ul-Mominin*, in the practice of both. While Mehta does not mention this, it is more than likely that the *Mufid-ul-Mominin* came to occupy this place as *the* 'book' of the weavers fairly recently—not before the late nineteenth or the early twentieth century in any case, for it is only from that time that the name 'Momin' (i.e. the 'faithful') was claimed as their own by the weavers.[79]

The *Mufid-ul-Mominin* relates how the practice of weaving came into the world, at its very beginning. The story, as recounted by Mehta, is as follows:

Adam [is] expelled from *Jannat* [heaven] as punishment for having eaten wheat. Adam feels hungry and prays to Allah for food. Allah orders Jabril [Gabriel] to give Adam a wood named Salim, and a goat, and to teach him the work of agriculture. Adam and Hawwa [Eve] slaughter the goat and eat its meat. Adam next complains about his nudity. (Some weavers said that Hawwa taunts Adam about his nudity, while others argued that a *houri* [fairy], and not Hawwa, offers to marry Adam if only he can clothe

[78] Deepak Mehta, 'Work, Worship and Word: A Study of the Weaver's Loom', a chapter of his Ph.D. thesis, 'A Sociological Study of Gandhian Institutions: Work, Weavers and the Khadi and Village Industries Commission' (Ph.D., Sociology Dept., Delhi University, 1989). I am extremely grateful to the author for allowing me to see his chapter in draft form, and for permission to quote from his findings.

[79] 'Irshad-ul-Mominin' (pseud.), *Mufid-ul-Mominin* (translated into Urdu from Persian by Maulvi Murtaza Khan, published by Maktaba Aijaza Mohammadi, Lucknow, n.d.). In conversation with me, Deepak Mehta expressed the opinion that the Mufid-ul-Mominin may well date from the post-Independence period; but he also recalled that one seventy-year-old weaver in Bara Banki had claimed that he was given a copy of the book by his grandfather, which suggests that it was available in the early part of this century.

himself fully.) Adam feels ashamed and complains to Allah about his nakedness. Allah orders Jabril to give Adam a box full of weaving instruments and to teach him the craft of weaving. . . .

Adam then asks Jabril to teach him how to weave. Jabril says that there are certain prayers to be recited in the process of weaving, equivalent to reciting the Holy Qoran one thousand times, or feeding two thousand needy people and setting free one thousand camels in God's name. In retaining these prayers in his memory the weaver is protected from calamity. If, however, he practices his craft without reciting such prayers and continues to call himself Momin (faithful Muslim) he is a liar, barred from entry into the Muslim community on the day of judgement.

The *Mufid-ul-Mominin* goes on to list the nineteen supplicatory prayers to be uttered in the different stages of weaving. These are given in the form of answers to questions that Adam asks of Jabril. The prayers are notable for their extreme simplicity and their straightforward message of the greatness and grace of the one God and his Prophet, Mohammed: 'Allaho Akbar', 'La Ilaha Illa Allah', 'Mohammad: o Rasul-Allah'. As Jabril says in the story, the recitation of these prayers in the process of weaving is 'equivalent to reciting the Holy Qoran one thousand times, or feeding two thousand needy people and setting free one thousand camels in God's name'.

Mehta finds, from his close study of the life-processes and work of the weavers, that four distinct practices are associated with the weaver's loom. The first, and most obvious, is commercial production. A second is cloth production for the dying, the weaving of the *kafan* or shroud. Unlike with the first, this practice is not thought of as a right but as 'an obligation that every Julaha is required to fulfil at some point in his or her life'.[80] The third and fourth practices have to do with the reproduction of the weaving community—the initiation of male children, and the transmission of the loom. During the initiation of the novice, all the prayers associated with the loom are recited in their sequential order and also repeated. 'The male headweaver, in whose household this initiation takes place, reads out all of Adam's questions and Jabril's answers from the *kitab* during the first six days of the month when

---

[80] Mehta notes that though women do not actually work on the loom, they are required to reel bobbins in the course of this practice.

both the loom and the *karkhana* [workshop or work-room] are ritually cleaned.' When the loom is passed on from father to son, again, 'the entire conversation between Adam and Jabril is read out once by a holy man'.

I have dwelt at some length on the heritage and self-image of certain groups of weavers, as well as the mystic quality of the weaving process and the close interconnection between work and worship in the weavers' lives, because all this puts a rather different light on their reactions to the turns and twists of economic fortune in the nineteenth century. There can be no doubt that the weavers were involved in many struggles in which the conditions imposed on their trade, and the matter of the profits and losses to be made out of it not only by weavers but also by merchants and moneylenders (British and Indian) were of central if not exclusive importance. But, equally, there is little room for doubt that in many places the memories and pride of the weavers contributed substantially to the contemporary struggle to preserve the community's occupation and rights.

One of the first references to the north Indian weavers as a 'troublesome' community appears in the context of a struggle between local weavers and the East India Company to preserve, or extend, their rights over certain portions of the trade. The weavers concerned belonged to the region around Banaras and the quarrel arose over a new British regulation by which goods imported into the city of Banaras for personal use were exempted from duty only if they did not exceed Rs 10 in value. The government agents were soon complaining about the 'clandestine importation' of thread, cotton and other goods for commercial purposes: this was apparently done by distributing the goods into several hands to take advantage of the 'ten-rupee system'. The amounts involved were sometimes pathetically small: thus, for example, Barlow, Deputy-Collector at the Banaras customs house, detained three weavers for the possession of thread which he described as their 'aggregate joint property', but felt compelled to release them since the value of the thread was so small—no more than Rs 11–4 annas in all.[81] Nevertheless the officials complained of a 'systematic fraud'

[81] (IOR) Bengal. Revenue Board of Commissioners (Customs) Ceded & Conquered Provinces, 1815 (vol. 56, range 97), Consultations for 7 July–30 December 1815; no. 5 of 11 July 1815.

being practised on the government and pointed at the same time to the aggressive tactics adopted by the weavers.[82] As Barlow wrote,

This class of people who subsist by daily labour, are becoming so formidable that not an individual case occurs in which a weaver is concerned—but hundreds immediately assemble. Every summary proceeding is laid before the Magistrate [i.e. the Collector's decisions were challenged in the Magistrate's court] and whatever costs they [the weavers] may incur by the suit they are ready to pay.

And again: 'The Weavers come to the Chokey's [*chaukis*—checkpoints] sometimes singly but as frequently in a body' and have become 'exceedingly troublesome. . . . Whether I immediately release the property [*sic*], or have occasion to detain it, the case is immediately submitted to the Magistrate, by all Weavers who can be mustered together'.[83]

Even here, there are indications of a larger concern than the simple profit and loss of the individual or a group of individuals. There is emphatic protest against arbitrary changes being introduced into the conditions of the trade; and there is, beyond that, the question of the rights of the community as a whole: 'whatever costs they may incur by the suit they are ready to pay'. In other cases, there is even less evidence of any overwhelming concern with economic profit and loss, and indeed at certain times striking indications of a willingness to suffer economic loss for the honour of the community and the preservation of its life-style.

One may cite here some observations made by the collector of Saharanpur on the 'rather remarkable change' that had occurred in the local weavers' position as a result of the rise in cotton prices at the beginning of the 1860s. 'Formerly', he wrote,

the weavers in this district generally purchased the thread on their own account, ultimately realising the profits from the sale of the manufactured article. Since the rise in the price of the raw material, it appears that the weavers have, as a general rule, been unable to do this, and that they have consequently now assumed the position of daily labourers. . . .

[82] Ibid, no. 7A of 18 July 1815, Barlow—Collector, Govt. Customs, Benares, 6 July 1815.

[83] Ibid., no. 5 of 11 July 1815, translation of Roobookarry of the Dy. Collector, 23 June 1815; and no. 11A of 18 July 1815, Barlow—Collector, Customs, 8 July 1815.

Their employers included not only the shopkeepers and merchants who supplied them with thread and took the profits on the
sale of the cloth, but also zamindars and 'even cultivators' who
now engaged them for the manufacture into cloth of at least a part
of their cotton crop. 'The weavers naturally feel this change has
rendered their position by no means so independent as was formerly
the case. I generally found that *they viewed this as more serious than
the loss of income* which has undoubtedly been considerable.'[84] At
the end of the nineteenth century, again, we have evidence of a little-
known movement of resistance by weavers to the introduction of
the factory system. When a Kayasth entrepreneur tried at this time
to set up a factory for the production of cloth in Mau, he came up
against a serious obstacle—the local weaver refused to take up
employment in his factory 'even for double the wage that he earns
outside'. Another Indian entrepreneur had encountered exactly
the same difficulty a little earlier in Banaras.[85]

What the weavers protested here was the attempt to reduce them
from the position of proud, and to some extent 'independent',
craftsmen into that of faceless wage earners; what they resented
was 'the indignity of being ordered about'.[86] But there was perhaps
more to it even than that. The weaver's loom was the symbol of
the community, a means of offering prayers to the Almighty, a
gift from God. Deepak Mehta observes that 'weavers often express
the view that the mosque and the *karkhana* [work-place] are inter-
changeable spaces in the work of weaving [and, one should add,
worship]'.[87] The loss of a loom was therefore much more than the

---

[84] 'Slackness of Demand for European Cotton Goods', p. 148 (emphasis
added).

[85] *Papers Connected with the Industrial Conference held at Naini Tal* (1907), p. 40.

[86] Cf. Thompson, *Making of the English Working Class*, p. 338; S. Bhattacharya, 'Cultural and Social Constraints in Technological Innovation',
IESHR, III, 3 (1966). Nita Kumar, 'Popular Culture in Urban India. The
Artisans of Banaras, *c.* 1884–1984' (Univ. of Chicago, Ph.D. thesis, 1984)
also notes the extraordinary importance attached by the artisans of Banaras
to the notion of being 'masters of their own time' and the 'ideology of freedom'
that they have built up around this: 'Ansaris [Muslim weavers] are not afraid
of work. They will work twelve hours a day', as one of them said to her, 'but
they cannot do *naukri* [service]': p. 74, cf. pp. 126, 133.

[87] Mehta, 'Work, Worship and World'.

loss of an individual's or a family's means of livelihood. It was the loss of one's place in the world. This was one reason why weavers sometimes continued to ply the loom even at times and in places where it was plainly uneconomical to do so. One such example comes from Ghazipur during the 'cotton famine' of the 1860s. Here, as the Collector's report tells us, while not 'one-half of the usual number of looms' were now being worked, even of the reduced number, many were 'kept up merely in order that the children may not forget how to weave'.[88] The centrality of the loom as the most important signifier of the community and as the means of its reproduction is here underlined.

It is hardly surprising to find that as part of the weavers' fight to preserve (and improve) their economic and social status, a vigil was maintained by prominent groups of weavers in what they considered to be *their* towns, *their* mohallas, *their* mosques, to guard against any innovations that might go to reduce the importance of their religious festivals and places of worship. As Reid put it in writing about the Julahas of Mau, 'they are very touchy about anything that seems intended to hurt their religious feelings, and act as one man in anything that concerns them as a body'.[89] It was on account of these diverse, sometimes desperate and often long-drawn-out struggles by weavers in many different places that the north Indian Muslim weaving community acquired the reputation of being uncompromising, easily aroused, violent Muslims: a community of 'fanatical', 'clannish' and 'bigoted' Julahas. What the stereotype did, of course, was to decimate the weavers' history. It erased at a stroke the very noticeable differences in the self-image and historical circumstances of different groups of Muslim weavers in northern India. And it flattened flesh-and-blood, emotional, labouring and thinking people into one-dimensional, unvarying and 'irrational' entities.

V

It can be shown, I think, that the image of Julaha bigotry was drawn up in colonialist writings on the strength of a few examples of

---

[88] 'Slackness of Demand for European Cotton Goods', p. 152.
[89] Reid, *Report on Azamgarh Settlement*, p. 147. See chpt. 4 below for an illustration of this point about maintaining a vigil.

Hindu-Muslim riots in one small part of the Gangetic plain in which sections of the north Indian weaving community were involved. If we set aside for the moment the special circumstances and traditions of the weavers involved in these conflicts, and overlook also the many contemporary examples of cross-communal struggle against acts and institutions that were perceived as a common threat by all the people of a locality in which these same weavers participated,[90] it is still remarkable how the idea of the 'bigoted Julaha' makes its appearance in just a few official accounts of the nineteenth century close on the heels of, and in direct response to, outbreaks of Hindu-Muslim strife.

The Julaha stereotype as we know it appears to have been forged in U.P. This fact is surely not unrelated to the recurrent conflicts over religious practice and ritual precedence in this region that we have noticed earlier, and the fact that exclusively Muslim political organizations of a modern kind found their earliest roots here.[91] Yet, when the gazetteers for the different districts of U.P. were drawn up at the turn of the century, and the Muslim weavers came to be presented as a major factor in the explanation of 'communal riots', a striking contrast appeared between western and eastern U.P. It was in a handful of eastern U.P. districts alone that the 'turbulent' and 'bigoted' character of the Julaha was highlighted. Everywhere else a rather different Julaha character appeared.

Let us take western U.P first. In Bijnor, where the proportion of Julahas among the local population was the highest in all U.P., the Julahas were said to be 'often working as cultivators and attaining a fair proficiency as husbandmen'. From Saharanpur it was reported that 'with their scanty beards and almost bare cheeks, the Julahas are readily distinguishable and are to be seen in almost every village. Most of them still follow their hereditary trade of weaving, but hard times have driven large numbers to agriculture in which they have achieved fair success'. The report from Bareilly was along much the same lines, the local Julahas being described as 'remarkably careful and industrious' cultivators. In the Aligarh *Gazetteer* nothing notable is said about the community, nor again

[90] Note the examples of Banaras in 1810–11 and 1891, cited in the previous chapter.

[91] Cf. Robinson, *Separatism among Indian Muslims*; P. Hardy, *The Muslims of British India* (Cambridge, 1972).

in that of Moradabad—where the Julahas were simply weavers 'or else . . . tillers of the soil'.[92]

In eastern U.P., too, the 'bigoted' or 'fanatical' character of the community was not everywhere observed. For Jaunpur and Gorakhpur it was merely said that a great many of the Julahas still followed their traditional calling, some had migrated to Calcutta and other centres of the modern cloth industry, and others had become quite successful cultivators. The absence of any further comment in the Gorakhpur case is particularly noteworthy, not only because Gorakhpur was a fairly important centre of the Cow-Protection Movement but also because there was evidently considerable political unity among the local Julahas. 'Almost all . . . [Julahas] in this district describe themselves as Momins',[93] the *Gazetteer* noted in an observation that testified to the solidarity of the Muslim weavers of Gorakhpur.

Nor was any statement regarding Julaha 'bigotry' forthcoming from the districts of Awadh. The Gazetteer for Lucknow recorded only that most Julahas of the district lived in Lucknow city; for Bara Banki that 'in spite of their proverbial stupidity, they are careful and laborious cultivators'; for Faizabad that while many had taken to agriculture, the Julahas of the district were 'still very largely engaged in their peculiar occupation of weaving'.[94] It was left to the Gazetteers of precisely four districts on the eastern border of the province—Banaras, Ghazipur, Ballia and Azamgarh—to draw up the portrait of the 'bigoted' Muslim Julaha.

Here, as I have already suggested, the existence of many old centres of cloth production, the numerical strength of the weavers in these 'urban' localities, the self-image and pride of the weavers, combined with the economic, social and political dislocation of the colonial period and the renewed struggles for power and prestige that came along with this, brought the Julahas out in numerous acts of resistance and repeated outbreaks of fighting over the prized

[92] *Bijnor Gazetteer* (1908), p. 103; *Saharanpur Gazetteer* (1909), p. 108; *Bareilly Gazetteer* (1911), p. 91; *Aligarh Gazetteer* (1909), p. 83; *Moradabad Gazetteer* (1911), p. 78.

[93] *Jaunpur Gazetteer* (1908), p. 85; *Gorakhpur Gazetteer* (1909), p. 102.

[94] *Lucknow Gazetteer* (1904), p. 68; *Bara Banki Gazetteer* (1904), p. 79; *Fyzabad Gazetteer* (1905), p. 68.

symbols of Hinduism and Islam. Much the same applied of course to the district of Faizabad, with its major weaving centres of Tanda, Akbarpur, Jalalpur, Nagpur and Iltifatganj, and also to Lucknow city. But there was one crucial difference: neither Lucknow nor Faizabad was affected, as the districts of Azamgarh, Ballia and Ghazipur were, by the cow-protection riots that took place in 1893, a short while before the *District Gazetteers* came to be compiled. The inference of 'Julaha bigotry' was drawn directly from the experience of these riots (in which as I have already remarked the Julahas and other Muslims were, in fact, the besieged) and from another instance of strife in Banaras in 1891 (an agitation against the demolition of a Hindu temple in which large numbers of once again, as representative of 'Hindu-Muslim' conflict).[95] As the Banaras *Gazetteer* put it, 'though they are almost certainly of Hindu extraction the Julahas are the most bigoted and aggressive of all the Musalmans, and have always taken a prominent part in the religious quarrels that have from time to time arisen in Banaras'.[96]

The causal equation that is at work here can be traced back a fairly long way in colonialist writings on some places in eastern U.P. I have already cited Thomason's judgement in 1837 on the Julahas of Mubarakpur, Kopaganj and Mau, that they were 'very liable to be excited to riot by anything which affects their religious prejudices'.[97] This was written three years after a violent outbreak in Mubarakpur and in the midst of a growing dispute over the size of tazias for the Muharram processions in the qasba. Forty years later, when the next settlement of Azamgarh district was made, the new Settlement Officer, J. R. Reid, reported, amidst gathering tension over the issue of cow-slaughter in Mau, 'In former times, both before and after cession, the weaver population [of Mau] was inclined to be turbulent.' For Mubarakpur he added that 'like their caste fellows of Mau, the weavers of Mubarakpur are fanatical and clannish in the extreme'.[98]

---

[95] See chpt. 2 above, secn. v.

[96] *Benares Gazetteer* (1909), pp. 103–4.

[97] See n. 8 above.

[98] Reid, *Report on Azamgarh District 1877*, pp. 147, 149.

The structure of this argument persists in later writings. A riot .indicates fanaticism, nothing more nor less. As a magistrate put it in regard to certain zamindars of village Husainabad who were implicated in a riot in Mubarakpur in 1904, 'the matter is still *sub judice*', but there was 'strong reason to believe' that the zamindars were 'more òr less fanatical Mohamedans [*sic*]'.[99] In its turn, of course, fanaticism can only lead to riots. The Azamgarh *Gazetteer* compiled in 1909 merely follows this circular logic. The Julahas of the district were concentrated chiefly in the towns of Azamgarh, Mau, Mubarakpur and Kopaganj, it observed, 'and like their kinsmen *in other districts* [N.B.] they are a turbulent race, and it is to them that the conflicts between Hindus and Musalmans that have from time to time disturbed the peace of the district are generally attributed'.[100]

The Ballia *Gazetteer*, compiled a few years earlier, was slightly more specific about the evidence on which this characterization of the Julahas was based: '*Like their kinsmen in Azamgarh and Ghazipur,* the Julahas [of Ballia] are a turbulent and lawless race, and it is to them that the conflicts between Musalmans and Hindus, which have from time to time disturbed the peace of *the eastern districts* may generally be attributed.' The Ghazipur volume admitted the source of its findings even more directly. 'The Julahas are the most bigoted of all Musalmans and . . . a turbulent and lawless race, *as was amply illustrated during the conflicts between Hindus and Muhammadans in 1893 and on other occasions.*'[101]

By the same process, the image of the 'bigoted Julaha' passed into some of the more general writings on U.P. As Crooke wrote of his 'cowardly, pretentious, factious and bigoted' Julahas in *The Tribes and Castes of the North-Western Provinces and Oudh* published in 1896, 'they took *a leading part in the recent Benares riots* and some of the worst outrages in the Mutiny were their work'.[102]

[99] (Gorakhpur Commissioner's Record Room), dept. XIII, file 63/1902–5, Magistrate, Azamgarh—Commissioner Gorakhpur, 6 July 1904, with attached copy of Joint Magistrate's report.

[100] *Azamgarh Gazetteer* (1911), p. 91 (emphasis added).

[101] *Ballia Gazetteer* (1907), p. 80; *Ghazipur Gazetteer* (1909), p. 90 (emphasis added).

[102] Crooke, *Tribes and Castes III*, p. 70 (emphasis added). The 'recent Benares riots' is again a reference to 1891.

In a monograph on cotton fabrics produced in U.P., published two years later, Silberrad considered it unnecessary to advance any reasons for his judgement that the Julahas were 'very zealous' and 'much inclined to fanaticism', but his language was reminiscent of that employed by Reid which I have quoted in an earlier paragraph: they 'display a strong clannish feeling, helping one another [!], and to a great extent settling disputes between members of their own caste among themselves'.[103]

Thus the stereotype passed into the sociological record, and thence to the hands of the modern historian—for whom the Julahas became 'a most bigoted and turbulent community', 'renowned for their bigotry'.[104]

VI

If 'bourgeois ideology continuously transforms the products of history into essential types',[105] bourgeois colonialism seems to perform this task of transformation with a vengeance. The point that needs to be emphasized in this connection is not simply that the myth or 'essential type' distorts 'reality', but that it does so in a particular way—by taking history out of it. 'Myth', writes Barthes, 'is depoliticized speech.... It deprives the object of which it speaks of all History. In it history evaporates ... all that is left for one to do is to enjoy this beautiful [or ugly] object without wondering where it comes from. Or even better: it can only come from eternity.'[106]

[103] Silberrad, *Monograph on Cotton Fabrics*, p. 1.

[104] Cf. Robinson, n. 29 of chpt. 1 above.

[105] R. Barthes, *Mythologies* (London, 1979), p. 155. It may be interesting to cite here just two more examples of the 'essential types' conjured up by colonialism. An official characterization of the community of Brahmans in western India: an 'intriguing, lying, corrupt, licentious and unprincipled race of people'; G. W. Forrest, ed., *Selections from the Minutes and Other Official Writings of the Honourable Mountstuart Elphinstone, Governor of Bombay* (London, 1884), p. 260. And this incredible portrait of the Pathan tribes of the north-west frontier: 'perhaps the most barbaric of all races with which we are brought in contact ... bloodthirsty, cruel and vindictive in the highest degree; he [the Pathan] does not know what truth or faith is ... though he is not without courage of a sort'; Ibbetson, *Punjab Castes*, p. 302.

[106] Barthes, *Mythologies*, pp. 143, 151.

This is surely the end-result of the mythicization of the bigoted Julaha, the fierce Pathan, the intriguing Brahman, the turbulent Ahir and the criminal Pasi. The 'Brahman' (or 'Julaha' or 'Ahir'), to paraphrase Said, becomes 'a trans-temporal, trans-individual category, purporting to predict every discreet act of "Brahman" behaviour on the basis of some pre-existing "Brahmanic" essence.·... Each particle of the Brahman tells of his Brahman-ness, so much so that the attribute of being Brahmanical overrides any countervailing instance.'[107]

In colonial sociology, then, 'caste' becomes more than just the original and unvarying unit of Indian society. It appears also as the site of particular instincts, tendencies, urges—aggression, mendacity, love of intrigue—themselves no doubt the precipitate of the 'past'. It is by means of this quality of having innate, unchanging and uncontrollable properties or passions that caste feeds into communalism, which has in this reading less to do with 'community' (after all, 'castes' are also communities) than with a culture—of unreasonableness, narrowness, dogmatism and violence, all arising at bottom out of an irrational, primitive religiosity. For the colonialist, one might say in other words, if caste was the defining unit of Indian society, communalism was its defining culture.

'Caste' thus passes into culture or, more accurately, nature. This is the real, the essential condition of India, a condition that 'proves' the necessity of the imperial presence. By negating the history of the people, this sociology creates the ground for that foreshortened history of the state that I discussed in chapter 2. In Mill's *History of India* the portions on the 'Hindu' and 'Muslim' periods are included only as the *pre-history* of the colonial experience: they are but a part of the history of the 'British' period. In like manner, the 'essential type' forms a part of the history of the colonial state: arising out of those same 'pre-historic' conditions, it gains its significance in the later nineteenth century by its spelling out of the magnitude of Britain's task in India.

---

[107] E. Said, *Orientalism* (London, paperback edn., 1980), p. 231.

Chapter Four

Community As History

इधर कुछ दिनों से गंगौली में गंगौलीवालों की संख्या कम होती जा रही है और सुन्नियों, शीओं और हिन्दुओं की संख्या बढ़ती जा रही है । शायद इसीलिए नूरुद्दीन शहीद की समाधि पर अब इतना बड़ा मजमा नहीं लगता और गंगौली का वातावरण 'बोल मुहमदी—या हुसैन' की आवाज़ से उस तरह नहीं गूँजता, जिस तरह कभी गूँज उठा करता था ।

—राही मासूम रज़ा, आधा गाँव

The efforts of colonial historiography and sociology could not efface the signs of the local community and its history. The community—Indian society beyond the confines of the state—survived and demanded recognition as a dynamic, deliberative and far from insignificant force in colonial India.

The onset of colonialism was not the first moment of crisis in Indian history, and it was not met passively by a 'passive' society. Major political struggles had taken place in the past, not only at the level of invading armies and regional kingdoms, but at the local level, for control of lands, markets and other resources. New landholding communities had replaced old ones. New occupational groups had arisen. Castes had evolved, multiplied, come together, split up. 'Ancient', 'Medieval' and 'Modern' India were all rich with religious developments—new cults, new movements, new energies.[1]

---

[1] The literature on these themes is of course enormous. For some indication of the richness of recent research, see T. Raychaudhuri and Irfan Habib, eds., *Cambridge Economic History of India. vol. I: c. 1200–c.1750* (Cambridge, 1982), including its bibliography; Satish Chandra, *Medieval India. Society, the Jagirdari Crisis and the Village* (Delhi, 1982); R. S. Sharma, *Social Changes in Early Medieval India* (Delhi, 1981); Muzaffar Alam, *The Crisis of Empire in Mughal North India: Awadh and the Punjab, 1707–48* (Delhi, 1986); C. A. Bayly, *Rulers, Townsmen and Bazaars. North Indian Society in the Age of British Expansion 1770–1870* (Cambridge, 1983); B. S. Cohn, Structural Change in Indian Rural Society, 1569–1885' and other papers in his *An Anthropologist among the Histo-*

The crisis constituted by colonialism was, however, different from any that had gone before. Capitalism reduces the world to a single market, or seeks so to do. Modern colonialism, as the aggressive overseas arm of capitalism, partook of that levelling and homogenizing tendency. However, political compulsions and the calculations of metropolitan capital in the periphery made its drive to transform the world in its own image a half-hearted attempt, at best, in the colonies. The homogenizing and hegemonizing urge of the advanced capitalist powers appears to have overcompensated itself for this failure by setting up in these far-flung areas a considerably magnified state power, a political structure that was not only remarkably unified but also excessively top-heavy. No previous ruling power had sought to appropriate all that was political in the life of the people in quite the same way as the colonial state.

The British colonial regime in India, if it had its way, would leave to the local community nothing but its existence as a geographical, anthropological, to some extent economic, entity, by assimilating to the colonial state structure every trace of political initiative. Local society responded, however, by resistance at every level, and the assertion of an identity as an autonomous, political, cultural, in a word *whole*, community. This unyielding 'community' took many forms—of region and nation, of countrywide religious fraternity, of caste and other local solidarities.

Contrary to what Dumont has to say, I think it can be argued that a community in a pre-capitalist culture defines itself precisely by its *territoriality* and at the same time by *temporality*. The onset of colonialism, bringing with it profound changes in the material and spiritual resources available to the people, brought a redoubled emphasis on these defining characteristics. From the level of the nation (where 'Bharatvarsha', the 'eternal India', the idea of a natural geographical unity, came to be regularly invoked) to that

---

rians; Dilbhag Singh, 'Caste and Structure of Village Society in Eastern Rajasthan during the Eighteenth Century', *IHR*, II, 2 (1976); B. D. Chattopadhyaya, 'Origin of the Rajputs: The Political, Economic and Social Processes in Early Medieval Rajasthan', *IHR* III, 1 (1976); Irfan Habib, 'The Political Role of Shaikh Ahmad Sirhindi and Shah Waliullah', *Enquiry*, no. 5 (December 1961).

of the region (Bengal, Bihar, Assam, Maharashtra, Tamilnad, Andhradesa, all of which developed a heightened and sometimes fierce regional consciousness) to the level of the tribal tract and the small town and village (*our* territory, *our* qasba, *our* village), the notion of rights over given territories was now obsessively brought forward.[2]

Myths, folk-tales, proverbs, genealogies, histories of caste, region, nation—a whole plethora of 'historical' statements was also thrown up to underline the temporal axis, the heritage, the popular consciousness of common traditions by which the local community defined its own identity and projected its image to others. Among the best known of these are accounts of the 'golden age' of ancient India or the glories of the Rajputs, Sikhs and Marathas at one end, and caste histories pointing to noble ancestry and often to misfortunes that had brought down a local group to its later 'humble' state, at the other.

Well-known writers and scholars contributed to this renewed interest in history through their writings, fictional and non-fictional, on the history and antiquity not only of particular regions and ruling dynasties but also of many lesser families and castes. For northern India, Bhartendu Harishchandra, 'father' of modern Hindi, provides a very good example of a 'classical' man of letters, poet, playwright and essayist who published a number of pamphlets and essays on historical themes. Among them there is the predictable history of Maharashtra, essays on 'Akbar and Aurangzeb', Kalhana's *Rajatarangini*, the ruling house of Bundi, the lives of Muhammad, Vallabhacharya, Socrates, Napoleon III, and so on. There are also a number of fascinating essays on the dating of 'historical' events, most notably 'Kaalchakra' (1884), which attempts 'the chronological placement of all the great events that have taken place in the world'. Finally, there are a number of

[2] Even though the notion of a community's 'territory' became, in many cases, more diffuse than before, owing to the very enlargement of scale; see, e.g. the case of the Ahirs discussed in chpt. 3, section III above. My emphasis on the importance of territoriality for the pre-capitalist community owes much to discussions with Ranajit Guha. For the importance of territoriality in the life of the peasant community in colonial India, see his *Elementary Aspects of Peasant Insurgency in Colonial India*, chpt. 7.

significant writings on the origin and development of particular castes/sub-castes in northern India.[3]

In 1871 Bhartendu produced a fairly detailed genealogy regarding the origins of his Agrawal sub-caste. The account is based, as the author tells us, both on oral tradition and on 'ancient writings', and especially on the story of the Mahalaxmi *vrata* contained in the latter part of the *Bhavishya Purana*.[4] Bhartendu writes of the glory and wealth of the Agrawals in the past, and of how Raja Agra or Agrasen (after whom the Agrawals are supposedly named) once even got the better of Indra, the king of the gods. In common with many lesser-known writers and spokesmen for the lower and inter-mediate castes, he also advances extravagant claims regarding the number of extraordinary people of the past who have belonged to the author's community. Thus the god, Krishna, on the one hand, and historical figures like Todar Mal and Maddhu Shah (two great luminaries of Akbar's court) on the other, are all claimed for the Agrawals—although, as the editor of a selection of Bhartendu's writings, Brajratna Das, points out, Raja Todar Mal is widely supposed to have been a Khatri.[5]

Later, in the 1870s, Bhartendu wrote a two-part essay on the origins of the Khatris. 'At this time', he wrote,

the people of numerous castes are actively engaged in portraying (re-presenting) the history of their development. For example, the Dhusara (whose 'Vaishya' status is itself doubtful since they permit widow remarriage) have declared that they are Brahmans, the Kayasthas (who are a hybrid Shudra community . . .) claim to be Kshatriyas, and among the Jats too, my friend the Raja of Beswan, Thakur Giri Prasad Singh, has decided that they are Kshatriyas. In this situation, it is necessary that this Arya community too should find its chronicler.[6]

He then proceeds to argue, on the basis of the 'English Histories of India' as well as the authority of the ancient Hindu texts, that

---

[3] A fairly comprehensive collection of Bhartendu Harishchandra's writings is now available in one volume, Hemant Sharma, ed., *Bhartendu Samagra* (Varanasi, 1987).

[4] Ibid., 'Agrawalon ki Utpatti', p. 583.

[5] Brajratna Das, ed., *Bhartendu Granthavali* III (Kashi, 2010 Vikram era), p. 12n.

[6] *Bhartendu Samagra*, p. 695.

the land from the Punjab to Allahabad was the homeland of the original Aryan settlers of India. 'If we call the ancient inhabitants of that region [he refers here to the Khatris] true Aryas, that is surely appropriate.'[7]

The question that remains is that of the *varna* that the Khatris belonged to. Here Bhartendu's answer is unambiguous: there is no doubt that they were Kshatriyas. How 'Kshatri' became 'Khatri' is 'a question on which there is much debate'. Among the many explanations that Bhartendu cites is the authority of the Sikhs' *Granth Sahib* which, he says, lists the four *varnas* as Brahman, Khatri, Vaishya and Shudra. Again, he notes that the 'Naga' language was widespread in Punjab, that many Naga words are still found in Punjabi, and that 'Khatri' is the Naga form of 'Kshatri'.[8] In conclusion he quotes at some length from the *Puranas* and *up-Puranas*, including the *Bhavishya Purana*, to prove the Kshatriya status of the Khatris:

We have demonstrated above that the Khatris are Kshatriyas, and also presented various alternative explanations [as to how the change from Kshatri to Khatri came about]. But we do not [here] simply present an alternative, for in the following verses . . . [from the *Puranas* and *up-Puranas*] the fact of their being Kshatriya is clearly stated.[9]

From the last decades of the nineteenth century, improved communications, the growth of the vernacular press and, not least, the colonial government's drive to record 'custom' quickened the pace of these attempts to recapture history, as more and more local groups sought to establish their identity and status by obtaining a public recognition of their genealogies, their 'traditions' and their rights in given territories. The Kurmis now proposed that their name derived from 'Kurma', the incarnation of Vishnu in the form of a tortoise, for as a cultivating caste *par excellence* they, like Kurma, supported the earth and all its people; or alternatively claimed that they were descended from and named after the great Kaurava kings of the Mahabharata.[10] The Chamars claimed that their progenitor was the youngest of four Brahman brothers

[7] Ibid., p. 696.
[8] Ibid., pp. 696–7.
[9] Ibid., p. 697.
[10] Crooke, *Tribes and Castes of the NWP&O*, vol. III, p. 346.

who, being youngest, was sent while the brothers were bathing in a river to rescue a cow that was caught in the quicksand. Since the cow unluckily drowned before the boy could reach her, he was compelled by his brothers to remove her carcass and was then turned out of caste and given the name Chamar.[11] The history of exploitation is written into the claim of noble ancestry.

The Noniyas or Luniyas (salt-makers) of northern and central India similarly traced their ancestry to a noble source, the line of Prithviraj Chauhan, king of Delhi. When Prithviraj was defeated and killed by Muhammad Ghori, his Chauhan kinsfolk, resisting and fighting the invader to the last, were, according to their story, punished with special severity. The survivors were allowed to live only by entering the lowly profession of salt-making, and through generation upon generation of poverty and humiliation the community lost sight of its rightful place and identity. 'What a change of circumstances!', declares the *Bans Prabodhni*, the principal book of the Noniya Chauhan movement, published in the 1920s:

The descendants of those who were once respected as kings and warriors are now struggling for their very existence, and are called people of low caste. Those. . . who are actually Rajputs, have forgotten their past, and poverty has led them to even worse situations. They have left their work according to the varnas.[12]

Here I propose to take up for detailed discussion the example of a slightly different kind of local history from the Bhojpuri region which represents just one attempt among many in the nineteenth and twentieth centuries to bring 'history' to the witness-stand and assert a community identity in terms both of temporality and territoriality. My example comes from the weaving qasba of Mubarakpur in Azamgarh district, which we have already

---

[11] Russell and Lal, *Tribes and Castes of the C.P.*, vol. II, p. 405. See also Crooke, *Tribes and Castes of NWP&O*, vol. II, p. 170, and M. A. Sherring, *Hindu Tribes and Castes as represented in Benares*, vol. I (1872; reprinted Delhi, 1974), p. 393, for slightly different traditions.

[12] Cited in W. L. Rowe, 'The New Cauhans: A Caste Mobility Movement in North India', in J. Silverberg, ed., *Social Mobility in the Caste System in India* (The Hague, 1968), p. 74. The above account of the Noniya Chauhan movement is based on Rowe's paper. For some other examples of such newly constructed caste histories, see chpt. 3, section III, above.

encountered at several points in the preceding pages, and takes the form of a history or chronicle of events in the qasba prepared in the 1880s by a scion of a local Muslim zamindari family, a text whose importance I shall try to illustrate by drawing on alternative reconstructions of the same history as found in other sources.

II

It is my submission that the real alternative to colonialist historiography in the nineteenth century is to be found in the historical memory and accounts of the 'little community', an example of which is the text we examine here—Sheikh Muhammad Ali Hasan's *Waqeat-o-Hadesat: Qasba Mubarakpur*.[13] What is the starting point of this historical reconstruction? Ali Hasan notes in a prefaratory statement that the idea of putting together a chronicle arose out of a conversation in the Middle School at Mubarakpur one day in the early 1880s, when the talk turned to the 'unprecedented' and 'unrepeated' bloodshed of 1813 and Sheikh Gada Husain, a respected zamindar of the place, asked Ali Hasan to undertake the task of compiling this 'history' as 'a labour of love'.[14] I shall have more to say about the moment of crisis that the bloodshed of 1813 constituted for the qasba. Let us note for the present only that 'a labour of love' is a significant phrase, pointing to the entirely different spirit that animated this history from any that might have moved the colonialist historian. The compilation of the *Waqeat-o-Hadesat* is not part of a long-standing cultural tradition of writing up local histories of the kind that existed in England, nor an academic exercise conducted from the outside. It is an insider's view of his *own* community, albeit (as we shall see) a community that is constructed from the standpoint of his class. The love that is invoked here is not for the 'pure' knowledge that

[13] *Waqeat-o-Hadesat*, which literally means 'Events and occurrences', is perhaps better rendered as 'Encounters and Calamities', which seems to me to convey somewhat more adequately the sense and the rhetoric of the title of Ali Hasan's MS. This Urdu MS is maintained in the personal collection of Qazi Atahar Mubarakpuri of Mohalla Haidarabad, Mubarakpur, Azamgarh, to whom I am deeply indebted for allowing me access to the document and for invaluable help in translation.

[14] *Waqeat-o-Hadesat*, 1.

the colonialist ethnographer, for example, claimed to be setting out to amass; nor is it very obviously related to that desire for maximum control that necessitated so much of the colonialist administrator's accumulation of knowledge. It is, rather, a love for the qasba and its traditions, as defined by Gada Husain and Ali Hasan.

What is highlighted in the *Waqeat*, as we shall see presently, is the pride, the glory, the 'traditions' of the qasba, and its identity as a community that has pulled together through good times and bad. What constitutes this history is the affirmation of community, the preservation of its name (we could again say 'traditions') and identity against grave challenges. It is a history of 'calamities'— indicated in the title of the chronicle—that are warded off by judicious leadership and the collective spirit of the inhabitants of Mubarakpur. It is they, the inhabitants, the 'community' of Mubarakpur, who are the subject of this history, its protagonist, its hero.

The *Waqeat-o-Hadesat* is, therefore, poles apart from colonialist historiography where, as I have suggested, it is the colonial state that becomes the subject of Indian history. In that colonialist perspective, the history of Mubarakpur in the nineteenth century is a history of 'calamities' all right, but 'calamities' that constitute a threat to colonial 'order', not to the life of the community. This will be evident from Table 4.1 which sets side by side the chronology of historical events in nineteenth-century Mubarakpur as these appear in the official colonial records and in Ali Hasan's chronicle.

What we have represented here is the difference between two kinds of catastrophic history. The same phenomenon looks quite different when seen from the indigenous community's point of view as against the ruling bureaucracy's. Since, in the colonial regime's perception, there is no political life other than the life of the state, a disruption of order within a local community can be understood only as a lapse in Law and Order. What appears as a catastrophic disruption in communal life to Ali Hasan is necessarily and inevitably perceived as a breakdown of Law and Order by the colonial official.

It will be seen from the chronicle of events in nineteenth-century Mubarakpur, as reproduced in Table 4.1, that the vast majority of entries in the colonial column relates to outbreaks or threatened outbreaks of violence owing to the desecration of religious symbols—proof in the colonial view, as already noted, of the essential religiosity, irrationality and fanaticism of the local people, ingredients that would ensure a return to anarchy if ever the controlling hand of the colonial power were to be withdrawn.

It is evident that what makes an Event in the colonial reckoning is a marked positive or negative correlation with the question of 'law and order'. Everything in the colonial account is dated from 1801, the date when the British took over the administration of this part of the country. It is a date which apparently divides darkness from light, days of 'order' and 'improvement' from the previous regime of 'anarchy' and 'misrule'. Often the later colonial records hark back to 1813, the year of 'the great disturbances' in Mubarakpur when 'disorder reigned for several days unchecked';[15] 1857 is a notable Near-Event, for in this dangerous moment, when 'order', 'progress' and 'civilization' were threatened all over northern India, Mubarakpur remained peaceful. Horne, the Magistrate of Azamgarh, reported in September 1857 that the Muhammadabad tahsil (in which both Mubarakpur and Mau lay) was the 'best' in the district, with 'crime' low and roads safe. It was a matter for self-congratulation, as 'there is great distress at present in Mubarakpur and Mhow, in each of which places there are about 5000 Julahas, who have lost all their capital by the robbery of their stocks of manufactured goods, which had been sent out for sale at the time of the outbreak'. Moreover, 'these people are generally very turbulent'. On this occasion, however, they had been 'excellently kept in order by the tehseeldar Mohamed Tukee, who deserves• great credit every way'.[16]

Ali Hasan's *Waqeat-O-Hadesat* covers the same chronological ground but offers us a very different history. It is not the British 'accession' to power in this region in 1801, but '1813' that marks the starting point of Ali Hasan's history, as we have already observed.

---

[15] (U.P. Regional Archives, Allahabad), COG, Judl. Azamgarh, vol. 68, file 47, Thomason—Currie, 23 May 1835 and letter no. 96, Sessions Judge, Azamgarh—Commissioner 5th Division, 29 May 1844; cf.*Azamgarh Gazetteer*, pp. 260–1.

[16] *Parliamentary Papers, House of Commons, Accounts and Papers, vol. 44, pt. 3, 1858–8*, memo. on Azamgarh, 11 September 1857, p. 571.

Table 4:1. Chronology of Events in Mubarakpur in the Nineteenth Century*

Event	Date	Nature of Occurrence	Remarks	Event	Date	Nature of Occurence	Remarks
I	Late 1790s	Shia–Sunni riot. One killed.	Pro-Shia stance of local Nawabi officials.	1	1801	'Accession'. Establishment of direct British administration in Azamgarh and eastern U.P.	Establishment of law and order.
II	1810 (1226 Hijri)	'Nakku Shahi'. Shia–Sunni quarrel; Nakku seriously wounded.					
III	1813	'Rikhai Shahi'. Great Hindu-Muslim clash. Arson and looting for nine days. Rikhai Sahu and numerous others killed.	Growing insolence of Hindu money-lenders. Bravery of the Mubarakpur Muslims.	2	1813	Great 'disturbance', sanguinary battle and plunder for days until British magistrate and troops arrived.	Religious fanaticism. Breakdown of law and order.

IV	n.d.	Suicide of a Brahman. Cow killed, head placed on platform. Riot averted by local officials.	Greatness of British rule.
N1	n.d.		
V	n.d.	'Katuaru Shahi' Katuaru, a tailor, apprehended and killed during a burglary.	
VI	n.d.	'Ali Shahi'. Quarrel between two teams of wrestlers. One killed.	
VII	1832 (1247 H.)	'Daka Zani'. Several dacoits apprehended and killed while attacking a moneylender's house.	Bravery of the townsfolk.

Table 4:1. (Contd.)

Event	Date	Nature of Occurrence	Remarks	Event	Date	Nature of Occurence	Remarks
VIII	1834	'Sukhlal Shahi'. Piglet killed and Sharif. Sukhlal Singh, Hindu *barkandaz* wounded, succumbed to injuries.		3	1834	Dead pig on Panj-i Sharif. Hindu *barkandaz* sent to investigate received several sword-cuts.	Near breakdown of law and order.
N2	1834–41	Successful tenure of Mirza Wali Beg as thanadar of Mubarakpur.		N1	1835	Dead pig on a *chauk*. *Thanadar* had it quickly removed.	Near breakdown of law and order.
IX.	1842	'Bicchuk Shahi'. Clash between Muslims and Hindu moneylenders. Several of the latter killed.		4	1842	Serious riot. Several killed.	Religious fanaticism. Breakdown of law and order.
X	1849 (1265 H.)	'Doma Shahi'. Quarrel between two teams of wrestlers. One killed.					

XI	n.d.	'Karima-Shahi'. Murder of a girl and theft of her jewellery.	
XII	1850 (1266 H.)	'Daka Zani'. Dacoits attacked a moneylender's house. Chased away by townsfolk.	Solidarity and bravery of the townsfolk.
XIII	n.d.	'Tilanga Shahi'. Suicide of a sepoy carried away by his grief while participating in the lamentations at Muharram.	
XIV	1851 (1267 H.)	'Baqridu Shahi'. Baqridu killed in a game of *kabaddi*.	
XV	n.d.	'Amanullah Shahi'. Amanullah, *hajjam*, apprehended and killed during burglary.	

Table 4:1. (Contd.)

Event	Date	Nature of Occurrence	Remarks	Event	Date	Nature of Occurrence	Remarks
XVI	n.d.	'Faqruddin Shahi'. Faqruddin killed a pig and placed its carcass on the Jama Masjid, nearly causing a riot.					
XVII	1857	Mubarakpur threatened repeatedly by the rebels, but preparations and warnings staved off any attack.	Renowned bravery of townsfolk. Courageous leadership of the zamindars and sardars of the qasba.	N2	1857	No disturbance, though great distress among the weavers.	Near breakdown of law and order. Yeoman service by local officials.
				5	1860	Introduction of local administration under Act XX of 1856. Local revenue to pay for police and 'improvement'.	Extension of local self-government and works of 'improvement'.

XVIII	1877	'Manohar Shahi'. Prolonged dispute over Manohar Das Agrawal's building of a temple inside the qasba.	Qasba tradition defended.
N3	1860–80s	Repair and extension of Jama Masjid, Imambarah, etc. through contributions of all castes and communities.	Qasba tradition honoured.
6	1893–4	'Religious disturbances'.	Religious fanaticism. Breakdown of law and order.
7	1904	Riot.	Religious fanaticism. Breakdown of law and order.

★ '*Remarks*' in the Table refer to observations that are explicitly made or inferences that are implied in the relevant records.

'N' = '*Near*-Event', i.e. an occurrence or incident that is mentioned in the records but not ranked as a major 'Event'.

Everything in this account flows from the tragedy of 1813—such a blood-bath, writes the chronicler, that 'God save every Musalman from such a fate'.[17]

The significance of 1813 for Ali Hasan's community lay, not as British officials cynically interpreted it, in the 'delightful licence' to plunder that the outbreak of that year had provided.[18] Otherwise, 1857 should have been welcomed as another excellent opportunity for indulgence in this pastime: instead, as we shall see, the people of Mubarakpur prepared themselves to defend the qasba's money-lenders when rebels in the vicinity threatened an attack upon the latter. What constituted the 'tragedy' of 1813 was the extraordinary threat to the life of the *qasba*: it was a moment of madness when the community almost destroyed itself, a moment in which a large part of the lives and property of the people of Mubarakpur literally perished. Verily, as the conversationalist in the Middle School in the early 1880s had it, 'unprecedented' and 'unrepeated'.

What brought about the conflict was a dispute over a stretch of land between a Muslim *chabutra* (or platform, on which *tazias* were placed during Muharram) and a Hindu *thakurdwara* (small temple), which led to the slaughter of a cow and the throwing of some pigs' carcasses on the platform and, thereafter, to open battle between Muslims and Hindus. Rikhai Sahu, 'a Mahajan of considerable wealth who was considered to be the chief person residing in that neighbourhood', and Devi Dube, 'second to him in point of wealth and influence and more intimately connected with the surrounding zamindars from his having the management of landed property to a considerable extent in the neighbourhood', were prominent in the proceedings leading to the outbreak.[19] They were instru-

[17] *Waqeat*, p. 18.

[18] COG, Judl. Azamgarh, vol. 68, file 47, Sessions Judge Azamgarh—Commissioner 5th Division, 29 May 1844.

[19] (U.P. Regional Archives, Allahabad), MG4, Judl. Series i, acc. 169, vol. 168, R. Martin, Magistrate Goruckpore—G. Dowdeswell, Camp Mobarruckpore, 25 April 1813 (hereafter, Magistrate's Report, 15 April 1813), para 6. Ali Hasan's *Waqeat* mentions the prominent part played by the Dubes of Amlo, a habitation adjacent to Mubarakpur; and an '*Arzi ba Adalat Gorakhpur, ba silsila-i-jang Mubarakpur* (Saturday 17 April 1813 A.D.)', signed by Sheikh Shahabuddin and four other weavers of Mubarakpur on 7 June 1813, specifically mentions Hardayal, son of Debi Dube, as one of the leaders of

mental in arranging the purchase of the land in question by Angnu Kalwar, owner of the thakurdwara, from two Muslim zamindars of Mubarakpur who were in debt to Rikhai Sahu. Other Muslims objected to this land being attached to the temple. But Angnu Kalwar was undeterred, and Devi Dube and Kanhaiya Lal, brother of Rikhai Sahu, personally supervised the commencement of the building of a wall to enclose the disputed ground.

This act led immediately to 'meetings and consultations' among the general body of Muslims and a few days later, on 17 April 1813, to the slaughter of a cow on the chabutra by a weaver who claimed to have offered a *minnat* at the place which necessitated such sacrifice.[20] Hindu retaliation, in the form of the killing of a number of pigs and the placing of their carcasses on the chabutra, was answered by a large-scale Muslim attack in which the temple belonging to Angnu Kalwar and the nearby house of Rikhai Sahu were burnt down and Rikhai himself killed.

From the following day, huge parties of Hindus from the surrounding areas began to converge on Mubarakpur, and the local Muslims assembled with arms to defend themselves as best as they could. On the same day, the Daroga of Sagri *thana* arrived to assist the Daroga of Muhammadabad, which was the nearest police-station, but 'so numerous was the assemblage of people that (the police) did not venture . . . within a considerable distance of the parties'.[21] The police estimated that there were 25,000 armed men involved in the combat. Ali Hasan put the number of Hindus alone at 40,000—a 'river of human beings', in his own words.[22] Early on the next morning, 19 April, 'Trumpets were sounded

---

the Hindu rioters. (Qazi Atahar made a copy of this petition from a copy he found in rather poor condition in the possession of the late Maulvi Hakim Abdul Majid of Bakhri, Mubarakpur, and very graciously translated for me from the Persian.)

[20] The practice of doing *minnat* (praying for a particular blessing, and promising a particular offering if the prayer is fulfilled) is a popular religious practice among the lower classes of this region and elsewhere in India. In this instance, a weaver called Boodhan was said to have offered a minnat at the disputed chabutra and promised the sacrifice of a cow if his wish was fulfilled.

[21] Magistrate's Report, 25 April 1813, paras 8–9.

[22] Ibid., para 1; *Waqeat*, p. 15. The details and quotations in the rest of this paragraph are taken from the Magistrate's Report.

and the attack was commenced by the Hindoos on the Musalmaans assembled in a place surrounded by a small ditch and a hedge'. From the time of this battle, 'the town was deserted by its inhabitants, set fire to in every direction and given up to plunder'. Arson and loot continued for a couple of days even after the arrival of a Magistrate and troops from Gorakhpur on 24 April 1813. By the time they were successful in putting an end to the looting and killing, scores, or possibly hundreds, of people had lost their lives and 108 of the 968 houses in the qasba had been gutted. It was chance and the fact noted by the Magistrate that almost all the houses had tiled roofs, that prevented the fires from spreading and razing the whole place to the ground.

The response of the people of Mubarakpur, both Hindus and Muslims, immediately after this disastrous outbreak was in line with Ali Hasan's prayer to God to ward off the repetition of such a blood-bath. As soon as peace—or sanity—had been restored, there was a closing of ranks, and the Muslims and Hindus of the area refused to co-operate in the official investigations that followed. Eight months after the 'riot', the Gorakhpur Magistrate reported his failure to obtain the kind of evidence that was required in the cases arising out of the outbreak, in spite of the transfer of two sets of officials suspected of being insufficiently energetic in the pursuit of their enquiries. He felt that further delay in the commitment of the trial was pointless. In part this may have been because, as the Magistrate put it, both sides, 'having been guilty of great outrage', were afraid to come forward. As significant, however, was his observation that 'the parties have now mutually agreed to adjust their grievances'. Further:

The accounts existing between the Muhammadans and Hindoos which were destroyed by the fire or otherwise have been re-adjusted and new bonds and agreements have been entered into by the parties concerned, and I am of the opinion that a considerable quantity of property plundered must have been restored or that an understanding exists between the parties that it shall be when an opportunity offers....[23]

Whether or not this conciliatory mood flowed from contrition at actions that had brought upon them such a calamity, the appalling

[23] MG4, Judl. series I, acc. 169, vol. 168, Magistrate's letter of 17 December 1813, paras 7–8.

days of 1813 appear to have become a point of reference for the people of Mubarakpur for a long time afterwards. Hence, in N1 of Ali Hasan's *Waqeat-o-Hadesat* (see Table 4:1), the *thanedar*, Mirza Karam Ali Beg, promises that what had happened in the 'Rikhai Shahi' of 1813 would not be allowed to happen again. Or, more strikingly, in Event VII, the armed dacoity of 1832, we learn from Ali Hasan's account that Muslim youths of the town, led by Fateh and his associates, moved to defend the house of Babu Ramdas, *mahajan*, but only after some hesitation because the dacoits were Hindus (mainly Rajputs) and the youths were wary of arousing Hindu fears of another 'Muslim' attack upon 'Hindus'.[24]

The fear of threats to the unity of the qasba, and its obverse, pride in the solidarity and strength of the qasba community, is the central motif of Ali Hasan's story. 'Events' in his narrative are those that either threatened or affirmed the community—and did so dramatically. Thus, regarding the Event just mentioned, the 'Daka Zani' of 1832, Ali Hasan writes that the townsfolk turned out in great numbers as soon as the members of the mahajan's household raised the cry for help. Such a crowd gathered that 'it was difficult to find standing space' not only inside the house but also anywhere around it. The gang of dacoits was hemmed in, attacked, and a number of its members killed.[25]

Pride in the qualities of the qasba's people is expressed in several ways. In 1832, the *Waqeat* tells us, an arrested dacoit told the Magistrate of the district that the gang included such renowned and dreaded dacoits as Bagi Singh and Chatar Singh, that they had attacked and looted all sorts of places in the past, including the government treasury, but no one had stood up to them until they encountered the 'warrior' (*jangi*) folk of Mubarakpur.[26]

In 1857, again, Rajab Ali, the rebel landowner of village Bamhur, a couple of miles south-west of Mubarakpur, announced his intention of plundering the mahajans of the qasba in a letter addressed to Sheikh Gada Husain, zamindar, and Baksh Mehtar, *sardar nurbaf*, the head of the weavers. 'Everyone' in Mubarakpur was enraged, writes Ali Hasan, and after consultations Gada Husain

[24] *Waqeat*, p. 30.
[25] Ibid., pp. 30–2.
[26] Ibid.

threw back the challenge to Rajab Ali with the warning that if the rebels tried to enter Mubarakpur to loot the mahajans they would have to bear the consequences. 'Do you think that the inhabitants of Mubarakpur are dead that you have made this decision (to loot the mahajans)? If ever again such a threat [*kalma*, literally "word"] escapes from your mouth, then you should prepare to defend your own village. Let us see who has the greater abilities in war.' And, regarding a further message (possibly a ruse) in which Rajab Ali expressed his desire to make an offering at the Panj-i-Sharif and Raja Sahib's *mazar* in Mubarakpur, the 'Mubarakpur people together' wrote in reply that four or five persons could come, unarmed, and fulfil this wish for prayer. But if a larger number came, or any were armed, then: '*tum apnon ko misl shirini-niaz ke tassawur karna* (you can think of yourselves as sweets which will be distributed and eaten). We have 1700 guns and 9 maunds of powder and shot ready for you'.[27]

It is in this light, too, that we may appreciate the significance of N3 in Table 4:1, which relates to the repair of the mazar of Raja Mubarak Shah, a Sufi saint of the eighteenth century after whom Mubarakpur was named, and the repair and extension of the Jama Masjid and Imambarah that had been built adjacent to it. The *Waqeat-o-Hadesat* recognizes both the division and the unity that existed between the Hindus and Muslims of the qasba in its statement that all castes and communities, Hindu as well as Muslim, contributed to this work of repair and extension. But it is the unity that is emphasized. Ali Hasan writes that the Hindu mahajans of Mubarakpur revered the memory of 'Raja Sahib' (Raja Mubarak Shah), and that along with others they lit lamps and made offerings of sweets at his mazar every Thursday. But the dilapidated condition of the walls of the Jama Masjid, which shared a common compound with the mazar, meant that dogs and cats got to these offerings and often also put out the lamps. Sometime in 1866–7 (Hijri 1281), therefore, Sheikh Gada Husain appealed to the mahajans to help in the repair of the buildings.

The chronicler records that the mahajans responded very generously indeed, then and for years after that. The work of repair and extension had gone on for twenty years and more from 1866–7

[27] Ibid., pp. 63–4.

until the last pages of the *Waqeat* came to be written. 'The entire wall along the length of the mazar was built through the donations of the Hindus.' And, owing to the co-operative efforts of the townsfolk, work estimated to take all of six months for repairing the walls and the floors, as well as for the construction of a washroom and the digging of a well adjacent to the mosque, was completed in four.[28]

A shorter entry of a similar kind in the chronicle is N2. This refers to Mirza Wali Beg's 'memorable' tenure as thanedar of Mubarakpur. One of the things that made it memorable, according to the *Waqeat*, was that Wali Beg, a Shia, called excellent *marsia* readers to participate in the Muharram celebrations in the qasba: people still recalled their outstanding compositions forty years later when the *Waqeat* was written.[29] We know from other sources of the central place occupied by Muharram celebrations in the life of habitations such as Mubarakpur. Mirza Wali Beg's term as thanedar was, therefore, a notable bright spot in the nineteenth century history of the qasba. Like the repair of Raja Mubarak Shah's mazar and the Jama Masjid, it had strengthened and promoted the traditions of the community and its corporate existence.

III

As in its purpose, so in its narrative technique the *Waqeat-o-Hadesat* is fundamentally different from the standard histories to which we have become accustomed since colonial times. The author makes no attempt to authenticate the chronicle that he presents: the narrative evidently needs no substantiation.[30] A collective catalogue, it is the inherited knowledge of the qasba—or at least those sections

---

[28] Ibid., pp. 86, 88. See C. A. Bayly, *Rulers, Townsmen and Bazaars* chpt. 9, esp. pp. 366–7, for another statement regarding the importance of such corporate identity and pride in other Muslim qasbas, and the role of Sufis in their establishment.

[29] *Waqeat*, p. 35. For the central place of the Muharram in the life of other Muslim communities in the region, see, for example, Rahi Masoom Raza, *Adha Gaon* (Delhi, 1966), *passim*.

[30] For the importance of 'shifters' and authorial intervention in modern historical discourse, see R. Barthes, 'Historical Discourse', in M. Lane, ed., *Structuralism: A Reader* (London, 1970).

of it that for Ali Hasan represented the qasba. It is perhaps necessary to say something more about how this collective (or community) is constituted in the *Waqeat*.

With all the references to 'the people of Mubarakpur together', it is clear that there are certain other principles of identification at work in Ali Hasan's compilation of the history and tradition of the community. The *Waqeat-o-Hadesat* is, first of all, a Muslim perception of a particular history, written at a time when the small-town Muslim gentry (the established leadership of the qasba) was in decline.[31] The fact that it is a 'Muslim' account is possibly the reason why N1 in Table 4.1 above, an incident in which a cow was killed and its head placed on a *chauk*, and an explosive situation developed, is mentioned but not given the status of an independent Event, whereas no. XVI which is very similar—a piglet being killed and placed on the Jama Masjid, and tension mounting—is discussed as a major Event, the 'Faqruddin Shahi'.

The nature of the discussion on this Event is even more revealing. Ali Hasan begins by saying that now he has to write about a great outrage, an insult to Muslims, perpetrated by a Muslim (Faqruddin): 'but since the *Waqeat* [occurrences, misfortunes] of the qasba are being related, it is necessary to include this incident too'.[32] 'Faqruddin' means 'the pride of religion', but this man should have been called 'Faqrushsheyatin'—'the pride of the *shaitans* (devils)' for he betrayed his religion by this base deed in the hope of profiting from the plunder that would very likely follow. Fortunately such a calamity was averted. Faqruddin was discovered to have been the rogue responsible for the act, arrested and sentenced to three years' rigorous imprisonment. On his return he was not accepted back into the community, for he was '*zalil-o-khar*' (base and disagreeable). He was still alive when Ali Hasan wrote, had become a *faqir*, wandered from village to village and was known as Pakhurdia *badmaash*.[33]

---

[31] The decline of the Muslim gentry is now fairly well documented. For some details from the U.P. region, see C. A. Bayly, 'The Small Town and Islamic Gentry in North India: The Case of Kara', in K. Ballhatchet and J. Harrison, eds., *The City in South Asia* (London, 1980), and Bayly, *Rulers, Townsmen and Bazaars*, pp. 354–8.

[32] *Waqeat*, p. 56.

[33] Ibid., p. 60.

Event xiii, the 'Tilanga Shahi', is interesting for similar reasons. This relates to the suicide of a sepoy who was on leave, visiting his sister in Mubarakpur, and who killed himself in mourning on the eighth day of Muharram—so completely absorbed was he in the spirit of lamentation generated by the crowds at the Qadam Rasool. If this was suicide, its historical significance lay in the circumstances of its occurrence. 'Could there be deeper commitment to the faith than such martyrdom?' the author asks implicitly. Of course, the incident may have generated fears of further disruption as well, for as the *Waqeat* has it, when the soldier drew his sword and killed himself, the crowds immediately scattered in confusion. But the thanedar, Khwaja Habibullah Khan Sahib, was able quickly to establish the circumstances of the occurrence, there were no untoward repercussions and no one was prosecuted. Following a post mortem in Azamgarh, Ali Hasan tells us, the body was buried at the spot where the soldier sacrificed his life for the Imam (Imam Husain).[34]

The remaining Near-Events that are chosen for inclusion in the record (N2 and N3 in the above Table) are equally significant, as is Event xviii, the 'Manohar Shahi' of 1877, another Event that is unaccompanied by unnatural death or grievous injury. I mention this because the majority of events recorded as historical in the *Waqeat-o-Hadesat* are marked by violence and unnatural death, features that perhaps served to indicate the dramatic character of an occurrence.[35] I have already said something about N2 and N3,

[34] The incident takes on even greater significance if we believe, with Qazi Atahar Mubarakpuri, that the soldier in question was a Hindu. If this was not the case, Qazi Atahar said to me while discussing the *Waqeat*, there would have been little point in including the incident as a major Event in the chronicle. It is worth noting that active Hindu participation in the major Muslim celebrations in the qasba continued at least till 1947, as several local people affirmed in interviews.

[35] Thirteen of the eighteen Events recorded in the *Waqeat* (see Table 4.1) i.e. all except Events ii, xii, xvi, xvii, and xviii, involved the violent death of one or more persons, killed in the course of quarrels, riots, dacoities and, in two cases (iv and xiii), suicide. Of the five 'excepted' Events, too, two involved casualties. In Event ii the 'Nakku Shahi', Nakku was badly beaten up and left for dead, though Ali Hasan tells us that he died a natural death shortly after the termination of the court case that arose out of the incident (*Waqeat*, pp. 6–7). In Event xvii, which relates to 1857, there was much fighting and killing in

which deal respectively with the thanedar who invited high-quality marsia readers to the qasba at every Muharram and the upkeep and extension of Raja Mubarak Shah's tomb and the Jama Masjid. Event XVIII, the 'Manohar Shahi', was a long-drawn-out dispute that arose when a mahajan named Manohar Das challenged qasba tradition by building a *shivalaya* (or small temple dedicated to Shiva) within the boundaries of Mubarakpur. The entry on this Event leads on to another perspective which the evidence presented above should already have suggested, and which points to what is perhaps the underlying principle of selection at work in the construction of this 'history'.

The *Waqeat* is the work of a member of the locally dominant class of Sheikh Muslim zamindars, who had established the qasba of Mubarakpur in the eighteenth century, gained for it the patronage of the Nawabs of Awadh and organized its major public celebrations and customs. If 'Mubarakpur', rather than 'British rule' or even the 'Muslim community', emerges as the real hero of his story, it is this 'Mubarakpur', fostered and built up by wisdom of its zamindars.

Ali Hasan's description of the defence of the traditions of Mubarakpur during the 'Manohar Shahi' of 1877 is instructive in this respect. The 'Manohar Shahi' was an instance of a conflict between the Hindu moneylenders and the Muslims of Mubarakpur which followed on a number of incidents of the same kind, some of them resulting in violence, earlier in the century. In the very first decade of colonial rule in the area, Angnu Kalwar had built a shivalaya[36] inside the qasba as an expression, perhaps, of the moneylenders' increasing prosperity and a new-found self-confidence in the altered political circumstances of the day. Perhaps it was another reflection of uncertainty in the new political situation that the local Muslims evidently did nothing about the shivalaya for several years. Then, in 1813, an attempt to extend the boundary of the

---

places far and near, and Ali Hasan takes care to note what he calls 'the only death of the Mutiny period' in Mubarakpur—that of a young lad called Magrooh, attacked by some constables from the local police outpost as he was returning one night from the Katra bazaar, possibly on account of some personal grudge (*Waqeat*, p. 73).

[36] This is referred to as a *thakurdwara* in the official reports on Mubarakpur in 1813.

shivalaya became the immediate cause of that 'unprecedented bloodbath' in which the shivalaya was destroyed and a great many lives lost. In the years before the outbreak of 1842, again, there had been extended friction between the mahajans and the Muslims after Bicchuk Kalwar and Babu Ramdas Agrawal had extended a wall thereby creating an obstruction in the path of the tazias taken out in procession during the Muharram.[37]

Following on all this, when it was discovered in 1877 that Manohar Das had built a shivalaya inside the compound of his house, anger flared up among the Muslims of Mubarakpur. Sheikh Gada Husain and other Muslim leaders questioned Manohar Das about the new building and, unsatisfied by his response, reported the matter to officials in charge of the police station at Muhammadabad and to the District Magistrate in Azamgarh. The Magistrate left immediately for Mubarakpur, an indication of the fear of another breakdown of 'law and order' generated by the earlier history of the place, and undertook an on-the-spot enquiry along with another English official who happened to be there. Some of the exchanges that Ali Hasan reports as having taken place on this occasion are of the utmost interest.

Manohar Das argued before the magistrate that he had built the temple within the compound of his own house and the zamindar had nothing to do with that land. He pointed out, too, that the Muslims of Mubarakpur built mosques and other places of worship wherever they liked, without objection from any source; that no more than five or seven months ago, Faqir Kunjra had erected a masjid close to a place that was sacred to the Hindus and 'we did not object'. Yet the Muslims wished to destroy the small shivalaya that he had built inside his own house: this was nothing but 'a show of power and tyranny'. To this, Muslim leaders replied that Faqir Kunjra had built his masjid with the permission of 'us zamindars': all the zamindars of Mubarakpur were Muslims, none Hindu—so 'what right had the Hindus to object or allow'?[38]

Gada Husain put the rest of the case against Manohar Das's new shivalaya as follows: Raja Mubarak was 'the guiding light of

[37] See my 'Rallying Round the Cow', section 7, for further details of this dispute.
[38] *Waqeat*, pp. 77–8, 81–2.

his age' and the founder of Mubarakpur. It was Raja Sahib's 'blessing' that had maintained the prosperity of Mubarakpur, and it was his *farman* (injunction) that 'when any person shall try to rise higher than me in this habitation [i.e. erect a building that rises higher than the height of Raja Sahib's mazar], he and his line will be no more'. The qasba had many great and very wealthy mahajans, and many rich Muslims as well, Gada Husain said. But because of Raja Sahib's farman, 'no one has a two-storied house'. Only once was this injunction defied, when Angnu Sahu had a shivalaya built inside the town. He spent a great sum of money and all the Hindus of the town worshipped there. But, Gada Husain went on, the shivalaya lasted less than ten years.

The religious injunction invoked here is significant as yet another indicator of the religious logic that dominated the thinking of the people. Indeed this logic went so far in the hands of the Muslim zamindar, Gada Husain—or in his hands as perceived by a younger member of another zamindari family, Ali Hasan—as to suggest that the worst fate that could befall a Hindu, too, was for him or her to give up Hindu ways and be deprived of religion. In the plunder, arson and bloodshed of 1813, which raged for nine days and nine nights, Gada Husain is reported to have said, Angnu Kalwar's shivalaya was destroyed and Angnu himself killed while his son 'so lost his mind that he began to eat the food of the Musalmans, and perished in his madness. Now no one survives from that family'.[39]

It is this same feature, of the overriding need to maintain qasba traditions, that appears to guide Ali Hasan's comments on the coming of British rule. The *Waqeat* contains no reference to the 'accession' of 1801, that favourite date of colonial administrators in the region. In this narrative, as we have observed, the Great Event or 'turning point' is the 'Rikhai Shahi' of 1813. There is a statement in the discussion on Event II, the Shia-Sunni quarrel recorded as the 'Nakku Shahi', that the British regime was already in saddle. But it is with Event III, the 'Rikhai Shahi', that meaningful British rule appeared in the area. It was in 1813, we are told, after the riots associated with the name of Rikhai Sahu, that a thana was

[39] Ibid.

established in Mubarakpur and courts in Azamgarh.[40]

What follows by way of comments on British rule is an appreciation of the benefits of administrative control. Here, the author of the *Waqeat* appears to share common ground with the colonial authorities. The importance of having good local officials is stressed (see N1 and N2). There is implicit recognition of the strength of the British power: thus, when writing of how groups of men from Sikhthi (a village adjoining Mubarakpur) joined in the plunder of 1857, the author remarks that they had not stopped to consider what would happen to them afterwards.[41] Again, Ali Hasan expresses much admiration for individual British officials—'Penny'[42] who emerges as the hero of 1857–8, fighting bravely and successfully against very great odds, or Tucker, officiating Magistrate at the time of the 1842 outbreak in Mubarakpur, who was 'a very worthy (capable) Englishman'.[43] We have indeed a direct acknowledgement of 'the greatness of British rule'. In the incident listed as N1 above, when a cow's head was placed on a chauk in the qasba, the thanedar, Mirza Karam Ali Beg, handled the situation with great efficiency and tact. As we have mentioned earlier, he assured the inhabitants that the disastrous proceedings

[40] Ibid., p. 20. However, the details here appear to be incorrect. It was only in 1820 that a deputy magistracy under the Jaunpur collectorate was established at Azamgarh, and Muhammadabad pargana (which included Mubarakpur) was then part of Ghazipur district. Event if a thana was established in Mubarakpur sometime in the early nineteenth-century, it must have been downgraded later, for the *District Gazetteer* of 1911 refers only to a police outpost.

[41] *Waqeat*, p. 61. What happened afterwards is recorded by Ali Hasan in the following words: 'The people of Mubarakpur, especially the Nurbaf [weaving] community, *on behalf of the Government* and *at the orders of both Penny Sahib and the Tahsildar of Muhammadabad*' took a prominent and profitable part in the loot of Sikhthi; ibid., p. 69 (emphasis added).

[42] This refers almost certainly to Mr Pennywell, Deputy Magistrate of Azamgarh in 1857, but Ali Hasan appears to have confused his story with that of the European indigo planter E. F. Venables. It is the latter who appears as hero and saviour in British accounts of the Mutiny in Azamgarh, and it was he—not 'Penny', as Ali Hasan believed—who was fatally wounded in an encounter with the forces of Kunwar Singh in April 1858; S. A. A. Rizvi, ed., *Freedom Struggle in Uttar Pradesh, Source Material, vol. IV* (Lucknow, 1959), pp. 5–6, 77, 85, 139–40, 466.

[43] *Waqeat*, p. 36.

of the 'Rikhai Shahi' would not be allowed to occur again, that no one from the countryside would be able to invade Mubarakpur as the Rajput zamindars of the surrounding tract and their followers had done on such a fearsome scale in 1813, and that the people of Mubarakpur should not panic and flee. To back up this promise, he sent an urgent message to the District Magistrate, who came with a troop of sepoys and camped in the qasba for several days. Thus 'a riot was averted'. 'All this was the greatness of British rule.'[44]

However, this expressed admiration for individual officials and aspects of British rule does not in any sense make Ali Hasan's chronicle a part of colonialist discourse, which is occupied centrally with the history and interests of the colonial state. The concerns of the *Waqeat* are, as we have seen, entirely different. There is evidence of this even in the course of Ali Hasan's comments on the British. While Ali Hasan recognizes the importance of having fair-minded and experienced officials appointed by the state, he emphasizes also the wisdom and influence of local leaders which is recognized only obliquely in the colonial account. Writing about Event I, a clash between Shias and Sunnis in the qasba, he accuses the Nawab's *amil* of favouring the Shias because he was, like the Nawab himself, a Shia. But Shahab Mehtar, the head of the Mubarakpur weavers, 'wise and respected', 'the like of whom is not to be found in our times', who had had to journey to Lucknow before the Nawabi officials agreed to act at all, now saved the situation and restored anity between the sects.[45] At the time of Event II, another Shia–Sunni conflict, Shahab Mehtar 'who was still alive' again intervened, unravelled a complicated court case and obtained the release of the innocent men who had been arrested by the police of the Muhammadabad thana.[46]

In 1857–8, to take just one more instance, it was in Ali Hasan's view the determination and foresight of the zamindars and *sardars* (leaders) of Mubarakpur that was responsible for the maintenance of peace in the qasba: in the colonial account we may recall, this

---

[44] Ibid., pp. 22–3.

[45] Ibid., p. 5.

[46] Ibid., p. 7. We may note in passing that the earliest detailed report on Mubarakpur to be found in the colonial records acknowledged the influence of Shahab Mehtar.

achievement was credited to the tahsildar of Muhammadabad, Mohammad Taqi. If 'Penny Sahib Bahadur' had lived, Ali Hasan comments, the local zamindars and sardars would certainly have been rewarded and decorated.[47]

The problem of authority pervades the pages of the *Waqeat-o-Hadesat*. What is presented to us here, I suggest, is the claim of a particular class of Muslim gentry to authority over the community. The *Waqeat* reflects the sharpened contradictions of the nineteenth century, the crisis of 'legitimate hierarchy' that came with the political and economic changes brought by colonialism. The authors of the *Waqeat*—and we may, I think, legitimately use the plural form—were people from an impoverished zamindari background, acquainted with Arabic and Persian and Islamic theology, beginning to pick up elements of a 'modern' English education, having to reckon with the increasing wealth of moneylender-traders and other 'upstarts', sometimes sharing a belief that was gaining ground among better placed sections of the Muslim élite in U.P. that British power alone could now defend their life-style and their culture—even if it was under British rule that their power and positions had been eroded. Their chronicle underlines the importance of 'traditional' leadership and 'Muslim' unity, and with these the 'benefits' of British rule. It harks back to Shia–Sunni conflicts that supposedly plagued the qasba both before and immediately after the establishment of the colonial regime (Events I and II). One wonders whether this has more to do with Shia–Sunni and other sectarian differences that came to the fore in the later decades of the nineteenth century than with the state of affairs as it existed in the last years of Nawabi administration.[48]

[47] Ibid., p. 73.

[48] For late-nineteenth century sectarian differences and developments in Muslim politics, see P. Hardy, *The Muslims of British India* (Cambridge, 1972); F. C. R. Robinson, *Separatism among Indian Muslims*; Barbara Metcalf, *Islamic Revival in British India: Deoband, 1860–1900*; Rafiuddin Ahmed, *The Bengal Muslims, 1871–1906*; and M. Mujeeb, *The Indian Muslims* (London, 1967), chpt. 18. The 'Village Crime Register' for Mubarakpur, pt. IV, entry for 1909 or 1910, notes that the Muslims of the qasba were divided into four sects—'Sunni, Hanfi, Wahabi (also known as Ahl-i-Hadis) and Shia'. It adds that 'All these sects have their own separate mosques. They do not pray in one another's mosques. All take part together in the *taziadari* [at Muharram]

Shahab Mehtar, 'the like of whom is not to be found in our times', and 'the greatness of British rule' is a curious juxtaposition. Yet it is not quite so curious if one bears in mind that 'collaboration', too, has complex and often contradictory motivations. What is honoured in the *Waqeat-o-Hedesat* is a body of traditions, customs and values that were, for Ali Hasan, the life of the qasba. There is a fundamental consistency here. British officials are saluted, as is the memory of Shahab Mehtar, for both served (or might serve) in their different ways, more or less efficaciously, to uphold these traditions and the position of the class that was above all responsible for creating them.

IV

The zamindars of course constituted a very small segment of the population of Mubarakpur. By far the most numerous class here was that of the handloom weavers and their dependants. In 1813 the population of the qasba was estimated to be between 10,000 and 12,000. Of these, 3000 were supposed to be 'weavers of the Mussulman cast'. According to the census of 1881, the population was 13,157—9066 Muslims and 4091 Hindus. By 1901, the number had risen to 15,433 inhabitants—11,442 Muslim and the remaining 3991 Hindu. In 1881 the weavers accounted for very nearly half of the 'male' working population recorded in the census, 1877 out of a total of 3774 'working males'. The other principal groups were a good deal smaller: among them, 560 'cultivators, tenants', 254 'general labourers', 143 'landholders', 49 *pansaris* (condiment sellers), 43 *halwais* (confectioners), 40 gold and silver smiths, 39 inn-keepers (*bhatiaras*), 37 butchers, 36 'cloth merchants' (plus another 22 'cotton merchants' and 10 'moneylenders and bankers' or mahajans), 36 barbers, 32 government and municipal employees, 32 corn and flour dealers, 32 fruit and vegetable sellers, 29 oil-makers and sellers, 29 washermen, 27 palanquin keepers and bearers, and 44 'beggars'.[49]

---

but the Ahl-i-Hadis do not participate in this at all'. Qazi Atahar's researches also indicate that Shia–Sunni and other sectarian differences among the local Muslims became more pronounced in the later nineteenth century: see his *Tazkara-i-ulema-i-Mubarakpur* (Bombay, 1974), pp. 30–3.

[49] *Supplement to the Report on the Census of the North-Western Provinces and*

If it was the bazaar and the palace, the 'Islamized trader' and the 'Hinduized aristocrat', who in Geertz's phrase 'stamped (their) character' on the Indonesian towns of Modjokuto and Tabanan,[50] it was the weaving of silken fabrics and the 'Islamizing' Julaha that gave to Mubarakpur its distinctive figure. Ali Hasan recognizes the centrality of this figure in the local community when he ends his *Waqeat* with the invocation, 'God grant the weavers of Mubarakpur such wisdom that through their courage and determination they may keep the funds of the *golak* [a public subscription system established for the upkeep and extension of the *mazar* and the Jama Masjid] ever flowing'.[51]

To what extent did the lower classes in Mubarakpur, and especially the Muslim weavers, share Ali Hasan's perspective on the history of the community. Given the marked distinctions of status and privilege among both Muslims and Hindus, in the qasba and outside, it would be surprising if there were no variations in outlook between the upper and the lower classes. I have referred to the distinction between the sharif ('respectable') and the razil ('lowly') that was observed all over this region. Ali Hasan indicates the importance of this kind of distinction, based on ancestry and caste, to people of his class when he writes of the Mubarakpur people's anger on the receipt of Rajab Ali's letter, threatening an attack on the mahajans in 1857: how could 'this Rautara' ('new Muslim' zamindar, i.e. someone recently converted to Islam) dare to contemplate such action against the 'noble' zamindars of Mubarakpur and their associates?[52] Here, Ali Hasan generalizes his own feelings of contempt for the 'new Muslim', expresses these as the feelings of all the Muslims in the qasba (the majority of whom were themselves converts of a not too distant past), and

---

Oudh taken on 17 February 1881, compiled by E. White (Allahabad 1882), Table XIII, p. 227.

[50] C. Geertz, *Peddlers and Princes: Social Change and Economic Modernization in Two Indonesian Towns* (Chicago, 1963), p. 18.

[51] *Waqeat*, p. 89. The centrality of the figure of the Muslim weaver remains to this day, at least in the eyes of 'outsiders'. As a Hindu contractor of Azamgarh put it after visiting Mubarakpur with me, '*Mujhe to in lungi walon se dar lagta hai*' ('As for me, I am scared of these lungi-clad people', i.e. the weavers!).

[52] *Waqeat*, p. 62.

makes them out to be the basis, at least in part, of the towns-
people's anger on this occasion.

There were several indications of the Julahas' separate, and lower,
status. In Mubarakpur, as in other habitations where they formed
a sizeable part of the population, the Julahas had their separate
mosques, though they were of course entitled to worship at the
bigger mosques established for the use of the Muslim community
at large. On the occasions when they did go to the bigger mosques,
however, they were not allowed to lead the public prayers or,
indeed, to sit in the fore of the congregation. This informal prohibition continued well into the present century.[53] Their religious
practice itself remained the butt of many jokes. The barbed
comment of Maulana Ashraf Ali Thanvi of Saharanpur is only
one example: 'If a Julaha reads the *namaz* for two days, he begins
to think of himself as the Chosen One'.[54]

The weavers, in their turn, recognized the considerable gap
that existed between those with wealth, education and social
standing, and those without. Thus Abdul Majid, a weaver of
Mubarakpur whose 'diary' (or occasional notes) from early in this
century has been preserved by his family, writes as follows about
the riot of 1904: 'It occurred at the instance of the notables [*bade log*,
literally "big people"]'. 'The lower classes [*chote log*, "small" or
"unprivileged" people]' were caught unawares. 'If the latter had
known that they would in their haste commit excesses and be
punished for them [in place of the notables who had instigated the
disturbance], they would certainly never have taken such action.'[55]

A more general comparison of Abdul Majid's 'diary', begun
within two decades of the compilation of the *Waqeat-o-Hadesat*,
with Ali Hasan's chronicle brings out something of the differences in outlook and interest between the weavers and the more

[53] Interview with Maulvi Kamruzzaman, Mubarakpur.

[54] Ashraf Ali Thanvi, *Arrafiq-fi-sawa-i-tariq* (Thana Bhawan, 1366 Hijri),
p. 25. (I am grateful to Maulvi Kamruzzaman for this reference, and for
translation from the Arabic.) For some other examples of the Julaha's proverbial stupidity, see G. Grierson, *Bihar Peasant Life* (1885, reprinted Delhi,
1975), pp. 69–70.

[55] The 'diary' of Sheikh Abdul Majid (*c.*1864–193?) is kept in the house of
his descendant, Sheikh Wazir Ahmad of Muhalla Pura Sofi, Mubarakpur.
The above quotations are from an entry headed 29 May 1904.

privileged Muslims of Mubarakpur. What the advent of colonialism meant for the people of Mubarakpur is perhaps not unfairly summed up in the following terms: more rigorous administrative demands and control, following the establishment of a centralized colonial power; improved communications, increased traffic, and a significant change in the direction of the cloth trade; and higher prices of food and of the raw materials needed for the local cloth industry, at least for important stretches of time. Of these new trends, however, it is only the first that finds place in Ali Hasan's 'history'. The fortunes of the cloth trade, and the question of food and living standards are nowhere discussed.

Large stocks of finished goods were lost by the weavers of Mubarakpur in 1857–8.[56] The generally pitiable condition of weavers, in Mubarakpur as elsewhere, is well known and now amply documented.[57] Yet neither their general condition, nor their decline in the nineteenth century, features anywhere in Ali Hasan's chronicle. It is true that 'processes' are not expressed as historical Events in the *Waqeat*. But what of the loss of substantial stocks by the weavers in 1857? There is no hint of the longer-term process, or of this sudden loss, even in the not inconsiderable space devoted by the author to 'Near Events', some of which appear as being no more dramatic or arresting than this particular development.

Ali Hasan was concerned, of course with compiling a 'history' of the 'community of Mubarakpur'. It is striking, however, that in his construction of that community and its history, the fortunes of the cloth trade and the living conditions of the weavers find no place. It is unlikely that a 'history' written by a local weaver could have neglected such a large area of the community's life and experiences. In any case, Abdul Majid's sketchy 'diary' or 'notes' offer a sharp contrast to the *Waqeat* in this regard.

Abdul Majid has much more to say than Ali Hasan about everyday occurrences in the qasba—births, deaths ('natural' as well as 'unnatural'), marriages and scandalous affairs. Without doubt, the genre itself has something to do with this; for a 'diary', as opposed to a 'history' (and even a 'local history'), is supposed

---

[56] See n. 6 above.
[57] See above, chpt. 3, section II, and the references cited there.

to have more room for the trivial and the titillating. What is more relevant for our purposes, however, is Abdul Majid's manifest concern with the cloth trade and price movements more generally—a concern that is entirely missing from the *Waqeat*. The haphazard entries in the diary contain numerous detailed statements regarding the price of different kinds of cloth and of silk thread, as of grain and other necessities, and comments on their implications. Thus, on 10 August 1919:

This year the trade has been such that Mubarakpur has become prosperous [*aabaad*, literally, 'populated' or 'full of life']. Until this year there has never been such a (prosperous) trade—nor will there be (again). . . . And this year as many as 142 members of our brotherhood have proceeded to Hajj-i-Kaaba from here.

Again, in July 1920: 'This year the outlook for the trade is not so happy. Silk thread has become very expensive'.[58] Or, on a different subject, referring to the soaring prices of goat-skins in November 1916, the price having touched Rs 3 to Rs 4 per skin by this time: 'Many of the big and wealthy Muslims have taken to trading in these skins'.[59]

It is notable, too, that the 'community' the weavers turned to in times of crisis or for the resolution of intractable problems was frequently the community of Muslim weavers alone. There is evidence of the leadership and influence of the Julaha *panchayat* from the early nineteenth century to today. Officials in Banaras had recognized the solidarity of the lower-caste panchayats, Hindu as well as Muslim, in 1809–10. Salmon observed in connection with the house-tax *hartal* that 'each caste has summoned its brethren [from the surrounding countryside] and adjured them to unite in the cause', in consequence of which the crowd was 'daily increasing'. Erskine noted that in the vast assembly that congregated to protest against the tax, 'each cast, trade and profession [*sic*] occupied a distinct spot of ground, and was regulated in all its acts by the orders of its own punchayet, who invariably punished all instances of misconduct or disobedience on the part of any of its

---

[58] Both these entries appear under the date, 10 August, 1919, but the second is an addition made in an appended paragraph.

[59] Entry for November 1916.

members'.[60] But it was some Lohars who, in conversation with the Collector, Salmon, provided the most striking testimony to the importance of caste organization. Here is Salmon's report of the conversation:

Having . . . explained to them that the tax in question would not be a hard one upon them, that I would exert myself to recommend that they should not be subjected to the two cesses of Phutuckbundee [*Phatakbandi*, a tax levied for the maintenance of a system of night watchmen in the city of Banaras] and house tax, and that if they would break up their 'Mujlis' and repair to their homes, I would listen to every single complaint of every individual as to the rate of the tax being excessive upon him, and as far as possible would consult their advantage; they replied that they were *one and indivisible* and *if their 'Punch' would consent, they would.* . . .[61]

Bird had also indicated the local officials' belief in the power of the caste panchayats by sending, early in the development of the demonstration against the house-tax, for the *chaudhris* or headmen of 'the respective classes engaged in the conspiracy'.[62] He had written specifically of the influence of Dost Mohammad and Fateh Mohammad, the principal chaudhris (or *mahtos*) of the Muslim weavers in those localities that were most affected by the riots of 1809.

It appears that these two persons exercise in their respective Mehals undisputed authority over every one of their own description, on all questions of common interest, particularly of religion. No general assembly can be convened but in their name singly or conjointly, and they preside in person at every general consultation.[63]

The authority of the weavers' panchayat was recognized in Mubarakpur too in 1813. Months of sustained investigation after

[60] *Selections of Papers from the Records of the East India House Relative to Revenue, Police, Civil, and Criminal Justice, under the Company's Government in India,* vol. II (London, 1820), p. 89; (IOR) F/4/323, Benares Collector—Secretary, Revenue Department, Government of Bengal, 2 January 1811.

[61] Ibid. (emphasis added).

[62] F/4/323, Bird—Dowdeswell, 28 December 1810.

[63] F/4/365, Bird—Brooke, 14 April 1810. The influence of the weaver's panchayat and their chaudhris appears to be just as strong in Banaras today. I was told repeatedly by weavers in Madanpura that no action of any importance to the community could be taken without the sanction of the *bawani*

the riots in April that year turned up little of use to the prosecution in building up its case against alleged rioters. But they did produce the significant observation that Shahab Mehtar, the head of the weavers (who appears in the Magistrate's report as 'Shah Mahter, the Surdar of the Musulmans residing in Mobarackpore') was at the time of the outbreak away in Gorakhpur, and the firm opinion that had he been present, he would probably have prevailed on the weavers not to take the action—the killing of the cow—that sparked off Hindu retaliation and general violence.[64]

At the end of the nineteenth century, observers again noted that the Muslim weavers of eastern U.P. and Bihar had an organized system of caste government on par with that operating among lower and intermediate Hindu castes. 'None of the Musalman groups approach[es] so closely to the Hindu caste system with its numerous restrictions as the Jolahas', the Bihar Census report for 1911 commented.[65] The Julaha panchayat in the countryside covered ten to fifty houses, its sphere being usually coterminous with a village but sometimes covering several villages.[66] In Mubarakpur there was a panchayat, headed by a mehtar, for each of the twenty-eight mohallas in the qasba. There were also institutions with a wider jurisdiction, for example, the 'panchayat of twenty-eight' encompassing the entire weaving community of Mubarkpur, the *baisi* (or panchayat of twenty-two) often covering an area of ten to fifteen square miles and the *chaurasi* (panchayat of

---

panchayat or panchayat of 52 (mohallas). Even participation in a recent inter-regional handloom weavers' strike had occurred after approval at a general meeting of that body. For further evidence of the authority of the weavers' panchayats today, see Nita Kumar, 'Popular Culture in Urban India: The Artisans of Banaras, *c.* 1884–1984'.

[64] MG4, Judl. Series I, Acc. 169, vol. 168, Magistrate's letter of 17 December 1813, para 6. Cf. Reid's 1877 evidence on the Julahas of Mau cited in the previous chapter: 'They are very touchy about anything that seems intended to hurt their religious feelings, and act as one man in anything that concerns them as a body'; n. 89 of chpt. 3 above. Note also that in 1857, Rajab Ali sent word of his intention to attack the mahajans of Mubarakpur to both Sheikh Gada Husain, zamindar of the qasba, and Baksh Mehtar, 'Sardar Nurbaf'; *Waqeat*, p. 61.

[65] L. S. S. O'Malley, *Census of India, 1911. vol. V. Bengal, Bihar and Orissa, and Sikkim. pt. I* (Calcutta, 1913), p. 461.

[66] Ibid., p. 489.

eighty-four) which could cover forty to fifty square miles. During the Khilafat–Non–Co-operation Movement, decisions regarding the weavers' participation in the programme of boycotting foreign cloth were taken at meetings of the 'panchayat of twenty-eight' and of the chaurasi—attended by the weavers of Mubarakpur as by others.[67]

However, it is not the case that this weaver identity and solidarity was exclusive of solidarity with other Muslims or with other inhabitants of the weavers' villages and qasbas more generally. Indeed, in terms of the principles of ethical conduct accepted by the local people—which were shaped by belief in the primacy of the collective honour over individual interest, attachment to a common faith and shared 'traditions', the notion of the duty of service to kith and kin, and so on—these 'communities' were similarly constructed. It is not surprising, therefore to find that the weavers and other lower-class Muslims of Mubarakpur shared many of their privileged Muslim neighbours' concerns for the faith and traditions of the qasba.

V

There is considerable evidence of this common concern in Abdul Majid's diary itself. The earliest incident recorded here, under the title '*Mubarakpur ka waqea*'—'An [or *the*] event in Mubarakpur', is the dispute relating to the temple built by Manohar Das in 1877, which is Event XVIII in Ali Hasan's *Waqeat.*[68] Of the *balwa* or riot of 1904, of which the final scenes at least he saw in person, Abdul Majid writes that it was all the outcome of a selfish intrigue in which Khuda Baksh, the Muslim zamindar of a neighbouring hamlet, planted a pig's head in a small, unfinished mosque in Mubarakpur, in the hope of using the commotion that would ensue to settle scores with a rival (Hindu) zamindar. The diarist notes the spon-

[67] Abdul Majid's 'Diary', entries for 12 December 1919, 8 February 1920 and July 1921. It might be noted however that the figure of 'twenty-eight' (as in Mubarakpur) or 'fifty-two' (as in Banaras) was frequently notional, referring perhaps to the number of mohallas, or other units, that originally came together to constitute the particular panchayat in question.

[68] The date of the event is given as 1875–6 in Abdul Majid's 'Diary'.

taneous anger of the Muslim weavers on the discovery of the pig's head—'The Musalmans' anger couldn't be contained'—and writes in moving terms of his and his companions' reactions when they saw a copy of the Qoran thrown out into a courtyard and trampled underfoot by a police search party: 'We were present there. We were profoundly wounded by this sight.' And, in words reminiscent of Ali Hasan's when he wrote of the vile character of Faqruddin in the 'Faqruddin Shahi' (Event XVI), he condemns Khuda Baksh, the originator of this outrage, as a '*kam-zāt*', 'base' person of 'low birth'.[69]

In other entry, Abdul Majid accuses the Muslim police official during whose tenure, in 1906, the Hindus of Mubarakpur were first permitted to blow *shankhs* (conch-shells) during prayers, of having taken a bribe from the Hindus.[70] Here greed is said to have been responsible for breaking down the tradition of the *qasba*. It is notable that on an earlier occasion, in 1842, when Bicchuk Kalwar, a prominent moneylender of the place, had quarrelled with the local Muslims precisely over this question of liberty to blow the shankh and the Muslim thanedar had taken the side of his co-religionists, the thanedar had been transferred at the instance, it was said, of Mir Muhammad Hasan (a police official?) of Muhammadabad-Gohna. In terms almost identical to those of Abdul Majid, Ali Hasan had in recording this incident accused Muhammad Hasan of accepting a bribe from the Kalwar moneylender: 'in truth', he wrote, 'the thirst for money is bad'.[71] And again, as Ali Hasan had written of the Muslims who gave evidence against other Muslims after the riot of 1842, so Abdul Majid comments on Muslim witnesses against Muslim 'accused' during the Khilafat–Non-Co-operation Movement; 'These Musalmans are responsible for having sent other Musalmans to jail'.[72]

---

[69] 'Diary' entry for 29 May 1904.

[70] Ibid., entry for 29 June 1906. It would appear that the blowing of shankhs by Hindus at prayer-time was given up again afterwards, for the 'Village Crime Register', Mubarakpur, pt. IV, entry for 8 June 1949, says that shankhs were not blown in the qasba till Indian independence.

[71] *Waqeat*, p. 37.

[72] Abdul Majid's 'Diary', entry for 19 June 1922.

We may expect a weaver who maintained a 'diary' to have been a person of some wealth and status, or at any rate culturally privilleged enough to be literate and 'historically' inclined. The evidence on this point is a little unclear, however. An entry in the local police register has it that 'Abdul Majid, resident of Pura Sofi, although he is an ordinary person [i.e. of no great wealth or distinction], always informs police officers of any secret [? meetings: the page is torn at this point] in the qasba that he comes to know about'.[73] It may even be that Abdul Majid's links with officialdom had something to do with his keeping a diary. In any case, the evidence cited above, of concern for the honour of the Muslim community, is perhaps all the more striking in that it comes from a person who might, as a police informer, be said to be isolated from his community, and who may on occasion have himself been instrumental in 'sending other Musalmans to jail'.

Other evidence indicates that Abdul Majid's views and outlook contained much that was shared by the general run of weavers in Mubarakpur throughout the nineteenth century. A petition presented to the Gorakhpur court by Shahab Mehtar and other weavers, 'representatives of those who have suffered', in the wake of the 1813 riots speaks for the Muslims not only of Mubarakpur but of all Hindustan. 'Upto now', it argues, 'all over Hindustan, Hindus and Muslims lived together—in amity—practising their respective religions and rituals freely. . . . But since the Hindus have gained *amaldari* [i.e., become *amils* or important government officials], since then the killing of Muslims has begun'.[74] Rhetorical though it is, the petition speaks plainly of the weavers as they sometimes saw themselves, especially in 'prominent' places like Mubarakpur, as the representatives of the Muslims at large. In the later part of the century, as we have noticed, the weaving community of Mubarakpur took a leading part in raising contributions for and supervising the work of repair and extension of Raja Mubarak Shah's mazar and the Jama Masjid and Imambara attached to it.

The weavers were prominent too, as the reader will be well aware by now, in the many violent clashes between Hindus and Muslims in the qasba that arose out of actions which were cons-

trued as being insults to Islam or challenges to the traditions of
Mubarakpur. The Magistrate's report tells us, as I have earlier
noted, that in 1813, when the Hindu moneylenders began construction to wall in a compound that contained a Muslim chabutra,
'meetings and consultations' immediately took place among the
general body of Muslims. The report notes also that, after the
Hindus' slaughtering of pigs and polluting of the chabutra in
retaliation for the slaughter of a cow at the same site, 'the whole of
the Musulman inhabitants of Mobarackpore assembled in arms'
and proceeded to sack Angnu Kalwar's temple and Rikhai Sahu's
house.[75] Ali Hasan, in his turn, reports that the pollution of the
tazia platform (or chabutra) generated fury among the Muslims,
'young and old', 'high and low': many of them asked, 'How does
anyone have the right to do this in our town?' and called on all
who 'cared for the faith' to come out in its defence.[76]

In the 'Bicchuk Shahi' of 1842 (Event IX in Ali Hasan's chronology), as in 1813, the weavers were quick to take up arms in defence
of what they conceived to be the honour of the community. The
'simultaneous attack' on the houses of five Hindu merchants and
moneylenders on this occasion, launched by 'several thousand'
Muslims 'headed' (as the colonial records have it) 'by old offenders',
occurred 'within fifteen minutes' of the carcass of a pig being found
on the Qadam Rasool (the Imambarah, according to the colonial
records) at daybreak. It was, indeed, so quick and so single-
minded that the Azamgarh Magistrate saw in it evidence of
'design, unanimity and previous arrangement... throughout'[77]
and even suspected that the dead pig was planted on the building
by the Muslims as the pretext for an assault—a suggestion that the
weavers and other Muslims of the town indignantly rejected.
Yet, the evidence (gathered mainly by colonial investigators) speaks
unmistakably of a large number of angry Muslims gathering at
the spot to discuss their course of action, and points, if anything, to commonness of emotion rather than the unanimity of a
'conspiracy'.

[75] MG4, Judl. Series I, acc. 169 vol. 168, Magistrate's letter of 17 December
1813, paras 3 and 4.

[76] *Waqeat*, pp. 11–12.

[77] COG, Judl. Azamgarh, vol. 68, file 47, Craigee—Morrieson, 25 March
1842.

Ali Hasan, who is a careful reporter of the inherited knowledge of the qasba with regard to its internal differences, records that the large body of agitated Muslims who assembled at the Qadam Rasool were convinced that this act of pollution was instigated by Bicchuk Kalwar, the moneylender who had been quarrelling with the local Muslims over ritual precedence for several years prior to this, and that they said, 'We cannot eat or drink until he is finished'. He goes on to tell us of the intervention of a low-caste Muslim woman as a crowd of Muslim men and youths from Shah Muhammadpur and other mohallas marched on Bicchuk's house and then debated what to do.

Mariam, the woman mentioned, was a Qasai (member of the butcher caste), living in the mohalla of Dewan Pura. Unlike the upper-caste women of the qasba, she was not restricted to the confines of her house, and perhaps like the majority of lower-class women she worked for a living along with the male members of her household. 'Although she was a woman', observes Ali Hasan in patriarchal condescension, Mariam could take on a hundred men in verbal jousting and repartee. Now, as the male members of her religious community hesitated at the door of Bicchuk Kalwar's house, she spat upon them: 'Shame on you. You call yourselves *men*. Our religion has been destroyed, and all you do is stand and watch'. Having said this, writes Ali Hasan, she called upon the people gathered there to burn down the house and, without waiting for a response, pulled out some straw and herself set it alight.[78]

In 1877 again it was a general body of Muslims at prayer (*namaaz parhne wale*) who, on noticing the *trishul* at the top of Manohar Das's recently completed shivalaya, went to ask of Gada Husain whether he had given permission for the building. The Hindus, they remonstrated, would sound the shankh and bells in the temple morning and evening; these and the bhajans would disturb the namaaz. And the threat of violence weighed heavily with the Collector when he decided to order the dismantling of the shivalaya.[79]

[78] *Waqeat*, p. 38.

[79] Ibid., p. 78, records the Magistrate's warning to Manohar Das that he was creating 'the conditions for a riot'. On the beginnings of the Muslim agitation in this instance, see also Abdul Majid's diary, entry on 'Mubarakpur ka waqea: Purani Basti'.

Similarly, in 1904, it was some weavers of Pura Sofi who discovered that a small unenclosed mosque which was being constructed by them in the open fields outside the qasba had been desecrated with the carcass of a piglet. They returned immediately to raise the matter in one or two mosques in their mohalla. A party went out to consult the zamindars of Sikhthi, in whose estate this section of Mubarakpur fell. An attempt was also made to get the local police to take action and a deputation of weavers went out to Muhammadabad to report the matter at the police station there. The brief consultation with the zamindars of Sikhthi was followed by further discussions in their own mohalla, and for the most part the weavers appear to have acted on their own—gathering a large crowd at the defiled mosque by the sound of a drum, marching north to Gujarpar where a temple was defiled by the killing of a cow seized on the way, and then marching back to the town and through it (inviting 'neighbours and friends' to join them) onto the Mubarakpur temple which lay just beyond its southern extremity, where a cow belonging to the priest and a calf confiscated on the way south from Gujarpar were slaughtered and the idols smashed.

Bechu, a weaver of Pura Sofi, testified in evidence that, on the discovery of the pig's carcass at the time of the early morning prayer, he and other Julahas talked over the matter at the mosque in their own mohalla. He added that after the visit to Sikhthi to consult the Sikhthi zamindars, there were other discussions in his mohalla before a drum was heard near the desecrated mosque and Bechu made his way there. That the Julahas, or weavers, were the main rioters was clearly stated in the 'first information reports' lodged by the chaukidars of Gujarpar. In the opinion of the judge before whom the case went for hearing, all the evidence pointed to the 'overweening arrogance of the [weaving] community over religious matters'.[80]

This judgement is, of course, in line with three quarters of a century of official statements on the weavers of Mubarakpur,

---

[80] (Gorakhpur Commissioner's Record Room), dept. XIII, file 63/1902–5, Judgement in Mubarakpur Riot Case, signed J. R. Pearson, 19.12.1904 (forwarded with Magistrate of Azamgarh's letter to Commissioner, Gorakhpur, 5.1.1905).

Mau and Kopaganj—'very liable to be excited to riot by anything which affects their religious prejudices', 'fanatical and clannish in the extreme'. But the evidence adduced above does show that the 'community' invoked by Ali Hasan in the later nineteenth century finds an answering call in the outlook of the weavers of Mubarakpur. The boundaries of the 'community' are flexible. What is not is the question of the honour of the collectivity—defined by a territory, a 'tradition' and a faith that is shared.

'Our religion has been destroyed', as Mariam put it. And: 'Who gave permission for the building of a temple in *our qasba*?' These statements reflect a solidarity developed in the pre-capitalist conditions of eighteenth and nineteenth-century India through common residence, shared cultural activities and a recognition of the mutuality of interests of different segments of the local population— Muslim zamindars and weavers, and even (though this appears to become less and less true through the colonial period) Hindu merchant-moneylenders. Nineteenth-century developments appear to have reinforced certain aspects of this solidarity at the expense of others.

VI

I have argued above that 'history' became a means for asserting the identity of a community and identifying its rights and status. It scarcely needs to be said that such 'histories' were never uncontested. It is evident that the greatly sharpened contradictions of the colonial period provided the context for the production of histories like the *Waqeat-o-Hadesat: Qasba Mubarakpur*. The widespread social and economic dislocation, powerful new movements of religious revival and reform in the nineteenth century, and the intrusive character of the colonial state combined to produce a crisis of 'legitimate hierarchy' within the local community. It was the contest over 'legitimate' authority that created the need to narrativize events, to make them 'speak for themselves' or be represented as if they could tell their own story—in other words, the need for 'history'.[81] As these contests developed through the changes and chances of the colonial world, 'history' itself became

[81] Cf. Hayden White, *The Content of the Form* (Baltimore, 1987), p. 19.

a site for struggle between the contesting parties. Not only the colonial regime, but other sections of the local society tended to challenge every reading of history that was put forward. A striking illustration of this is provided by developments in Mau (Azamgarh) in the wake of the serious riots that took place there at the Baqr'Id of 1893.

On 8 June 1893 the Officiating Magistrate of Azamgarh, Dupernex, had directed the Muslims of all villages in the district in which there was 'danger of disturbance' at the Baqr'Id to report to their local police stations within a week whether they intended to sacrifice kine on this occasion. This directive, which was apparently supposed to go out only to villages where the police apprehended trouble, was in fact transmitted to all parts of the district; and, in consequence, 426 Muslims 'gave notice' of their intention to sacrifice cattle (347 cows and 79 buffaloes). On the same date, Dupernex issued another order asking the 'leading Hindus and Muhammadans' of potentially troublesome villages to appear before a magistrate 'so that it might be settled in what villages sacrifice should take place'.

The 'leading Hindus' who responded to this order were made to sign a statement which read, 'We have no objection to the sacrifices taking place according to *established custom*. If the Muhammadans do *anything new* we shall inform the police'. 'Leading Muslims', in their turn, put their signatures to a statement saying, 'We shall sacrifice only in accordance with *established custom*, and shall do *nothing new* in contravention of usage'.

The emphasis throughout these proceedings was on recording and following 'established custom'. On 21 June, Dupernex reaffirmed the official position in this regard as the district busied itself with final preparations for the festival: 'Hindus and Muhammadans are to be made to understand that the festival should be performed as in previous years, and that nothing new or contrary to old-established custom will be allowed to occur.'

A government report prepared after the outbreak of riots declared that no compulsion of any kind was used to get Hindus to consent to '(any) sacrifice which was not customary', nor any sanction given anywhere for a departure from established practice. But, as the same report noted, there were no means of ascertaining whether the number of 426 cattle was 'more or less than the number which is customarily sacrificed by the Azamgarh Muhammadans at the 'Id. It is possible that in the existing state of feeling which prevailed in the district [on account of claims and counter-claims in the preceding years as regards 'Hindu' and 'Muslim' rights], some Muhammadans, who had not been in the habit of sacrificing kine, may have recorded their names at the police stations'.[82]

These official orders, and the riots that followed, immediately set off a whole new train of claims and counter-claims as to what the established custom was. Thus Bishan Narayan Dar, leading lawyer and Congressman of Lucknow, speaking as he said for all 'the Hindus of the North-Western Provinces and Oudh', joined leading Hindus of Mau in their bid to overturn the official position on the 'customary' status of cow-sacrifice in the town. Between them, they appealed to everyone from the Indian public to the English, as well as to the authorities of state from the local magistracy up to the Secretary of State for India in Council, and recounted the 'whole history' of cow-slaughter in Mau in the effort.[83]

This is a summary of that history, as they told it. As far back as 1806 (or 1808) a dispute over the question of cow-killing arose in Mau. The Magistrate decided at the time that the evidence showed that cow-sacrifice 'was not permitted (in Mau and certain other

[82] (IOL) W782, *East India (Religious Disturbances)*. *'Copies or Extracts of Reports relating to the recent conflicts between Hindus and Muhammedans in India, and particularly to the Causes which led to them'* (London, 1894), Letter from Chief Secretary, Government of N.W.P&O—Secretary, Government of India, Home, 28 August 1893. The preceding paragraphs are based on this report.

[83] B. N. Dar, *An Appeal to the English Public on behalf of the Hindus of the N.W.P. and Oudh, with an Appendix containing (a) Full and Detailed Account of the Cow-Killing Riots in the United Provinces and All Public Documents upon the same* (Lucknow, 1893)—this 'Appeal' was also published in Urdu, obviously for another 'public'; 'Petition of Hindu Inhabitants of Mhow, to Secretary of State for India in Council' with detailed appendices giving extracts from Govt. reports and Judgements relating to Hindu-Muslim conflicts in Mau on the question of cow-slaughter (n.d., 1893?). (I am grateful to Shri D. N. Pandey of Mau, Azamgarh, for permitting me to consult this document which is preserved among the books and papers of his late father, a leading Hindu personality of the town.) The following account of the history of Hindu-Muslim conflict in Mau is based on these two documents.

places in the region) under the government of the Nawab Vazir in consequence of the religious abhorrence of the Hindu inhabitants to such sacrifice';[84] and the higher courts confirmed his decision. In 1863, when some Muslims of Mau applied for permission to kill cows, permission was refused both by the Magistrate and the Appeal Court. But by 1865 a tussle had developed between the district authorities and the Sessions Judge as to whether local Muslims were at liberty to kill cows for food or not, the former holding that they could, and the latter that they could not.

'In 1866', writes Dar, 'the district authorities . . . had departed so far from the Governor-General's order of 1808 that they constructed a slaughterhouse for the purpose of killing cows, calves, bullocks, & c.'[85] In 1885 Mullock, who was then the Magistrate of Azamgarh, while convicting three Muslims of Mau for the public killing of a cow, expressed the opinion that the original government order of 1808 prohibited the slaughter of kine for sacrifice alone, and not for food. 'Ever since 1885 the relations between Hindus and Mahomedans in the Azamgarh district (have) been anything but friendly, and the climax of religious fanaticism excited and inflamed by the indiscretion of the officials was reached in the bloody riots of the 25th June [1893].'[86] 'The *custom* of killing cows in Mau', Dar concludes, 'is by no means of an older date than 1866 when the slaughter house was built; the custom of killing cows in [private] houses originated in 1885'.[87]

This was of course what would come to be called the 'Hindu' version of events relating to cow-slaughter in nineteenth-century Mau, and it was necessarily and immediately challenged by a 'Muslim' version. What was new in this situation was the very

---

[84] *The Dainik-o-Samachar Chandrika*, 21 August 1893, claimed that the prohibition existed from an even earlier time—the reign of Akbar. Bhartendu Harishchandra also held this opinion about the prohibition of cow-slaughter in northern India, writing in 1884 that Akbar's ban on cow-slaughter, which was celebrated in bardic tradition, had now been confirmed by documentary proof in the form of a letter from a contemporary Hindu Raja; see 'Akbar aur Aurangzeb' in Kesari Narayan Shukla, ed., *Bhartendu ke Nibandh* (Varanasi, 1952), p. 14ff.

[85] Dar, *Appeal to the English Public*, p. 17.

[86] Ibid.

[87] Ibid., p. 18 (emphasis Dar's).

writing up of these histories and their publication for widespread advertisement of one set of rights or another. It was this very matter of the recording and publicizing of 'history' or 'custom' that led to the terrible riot of 1918 in Katarpur village (in Saharanpur district). In this instance the trouble began when Harnam Singh, the representative of the Chauhan Rajput zamindars of the village, admitted in a discussion with local officials and Muslim leaders that cows had been sacrificed in Katarpur on the occasion of the Baqr'Id for some years past. On hearing of this, other Chauhan Rajput zamindars of the place upbraided their leader in the following terms—'You are the owner of three-quarters share [of the village] and you are causing such a thing to occur [i.e. acknowledging that cows have been sacrificed in a Chauhan Rajput village]. . . . Go and drown yourself'—and began the preparations that led to the killing of some 30 Muslims of the village at the Baqr'Id of 1918.[88]

Struggles of the same kind took place widely, and not only between 'Hindus' and 'Muslims'. When the Muslims of Mubarakpur asserted their right to decide whether a temple could be built inside the qasba, or the shankh sounded at the time of Hindu prayers, they questioned the assertion of a contrary right, based on a different reading of recent history, by the merchants and money-lenders of the place. Likewise, the assertion at different times of the Noniyas, the Ahirs and other such lower-caste groups of their right to don the sacred threat was quickly challenged by the upper castes. When the decision of the Noniyas of the village of Senapur in Jaunpur district to wear the sacred thread became known in the 1930s, the kshatriya landlords of the village reacted with anger—beating the Noniyas, tearing off their sacred threads and imposing a collective fine on the caste.[89] The Ahirs, whose Gwala movement in Bihar has been mentioned in the last chapter, had suffered similar attacks and humiliation in the 1920s, and it is interesting to learn that upper-caste Muslim zamindars were as affronted as the upper-caste Hindus at the Ahirs' new assertion of autonomy and self-respecting status.

In February 1921 certain Muslim zamindars of Bihar subdivision

[88] (IOL) L/P&J/6/1557 of 1918, Judgement in Katarpore Riot Case.
[89] Rowe, 'The New Cauhans', p. 76.

in Patna district instituted a number of cases against the Gwalas who were now refusing to supply them with ghee, curds, etc. at rates lower than those in the market. Later an anti-Gwala movement was organized by 'upper caste' zamindars, its first meeting being held in October 1922 in the house of a Muslim zamindar, Maulvi Muhammad Wali. 'The organizer of this movement', Hetukar Jha tells us, 'was also a Muhammadan (Maulvi Muhammad Masood of Marija) . . . a *zamindar* of some influence and a non-cooperation leader'.[90] In Muzaffarpur in 1923, 'the annoyance caused to the higher castes by the determination of Goalas, Koeris, Kurmis, etc., to wear the sacred thread and to attach "Singh", "Rai" to their names' culminated in two riots in the Shoohar and Belsand thanas. In Darbhanga the move by local Gwalas to wear the sacred thread, following the example of their fraternity in Muzaffarpur and Patna districts, brought them into collision with the Brahmans and Babhans, resulting in a riot in Chak Salem village in 1922. 'The Babhans [Bhumihar Brahmans] who disliked the idea of the Goalas claiming to be their equal assaulted a Goala girl and left her naked. She lodged a complaint before the S.D.O. [Sub-Divisional Officer] at Samastipur who dismissed it without enquiry.'[91]

What was involved in all such cases was the denial by a traditionally privileged or 'superordinate' classes of a 'history' that was claimed as their own by the 'subordinate' classes. I qualify the terms 'superordinate' and 'subordinate' because in cases like the conflict between Hindu merchant-moneylenders and Muslim zamindars in nineteenth-century Mubarakpur, it was no longer very clear which was which. Where the class position of the contending parties was less in doubt—as between landlords and peasants in Katarpur or Senapur or Samastipur—the denial of 'history' frequently amounted to a denial of human dignity. How could these 'inferior' people even entertain notions of autonomy and self-respect? How could they have a history? The thinking of the Indian élite was in line with that of the colonial rulers in this respect. Just as the colonial regime would, if it could, appropriate to itself the entire political

[90] H. Jha, 'Lower-Caste Peasants and Upper-Caste Zamindars in Bihar 1921–25', *Indian Economic and Social History Review*, XIV, 4 (1977), p. 550.
[91] Ibid., pp. 551–3.

life of the subject people, so the local élite would, if it had its way, appropriate the whole life and history of the local community. Neither was quite prepared perhaps for the resistance it encountered.

Chapter Five

Mobilizing the Hindu Community

पतिया चला गौ लोक से । हिन्दू भाई के पास मिनती [विनती] है.... मुसलमान के छन [संग] गौ
देखे तो ले लेने का धरम है । पाँच पतिया लिख भेजने का धरम है । न भेजे तो गौ मारे का हत्या हो....
हिन्दू को लाज़िम है.... मुसलमान का घर लूट लेवें और मुसलमान को मार दें और पतिया पाँच गो
देहात में फैल[1] देवें । न पतिया फैलावें और न लूट मार के [करें], तो बेटी पर चढ़ें, जोरू के मूत
पियें, व भगनी पर चढ़ें । इस से बेहतर है के मातारी के मुसलमान से ब्याह कर दें...

Oh Hindu brothers, help us. . . . Those who are Hindus should assemble for cow
protection and should write and make over 5 'chitthis' to others, Failing which he will
be sinful of killing 5 cows.

—(Patias—'circular letters'—distributed during the
Hindu–Muslim riots in Shahabad, September-October 1917)[1]

Historical reconstructions of the kind discussed above were clearly
part of a more general assertion of community and status by many
different groups and classes. What such assertions and counter-
assertions did, paradoxically, was to transform the very sense of
'community' and redefine it at every level. In an earlier period the
discourse of community had perhaps been stronger, in the sense
of being more universal and unchallenged by any other discourse.
At the same time, however, the sense of the individual community
had also been 'fuzzier'[2]—capable of apprehension at several different
levels (sub-caste, sect, dialect and other regional or religious
groupings) and not greatly concerned with numbers or the exact
boundaries between one community and the next. Much of this

---

[1] For the full text of these patias, see Appendix I below.
[2] See Sudipto Kaviraj, 'Imaginary History', Nehru Memorial Museum &
Library, New Delhi, Occasional Paper', 2nd series, no. VII (September 1988)
and more generally his forthcoming work on Bankimchandra Chattopadhyaya. This paragraph and the next owe much to discussions with
Dr Kaviraj.

survived, as we know, into the late-nineteenth and even the twentieth century. But the balance of forces was against its long survival in the old form.

The new 'communities' were now often territorially more diffuse than before, less tied to a small locality, less parochial, on account of the changes in communications, politics and society more generally. They were at the same time historically more self-conscious, and very much more aware of the differences between themselves and others, the distinctions between 'Us' and 'Them'. The new 'community', or 'enumerated community' as Sudipto Kaviraj calls it in contradistinction to his 'fuzzy' community, also became increasingly a part of a rationalist discourse—centrally concerned with numerical strength, well-defined boundaries, exclusive 'rights' and, not least, the community's ability to mount purposive actions in defence of those rights.

Once again, this is not to suggest that collective actions in defence of a community's claimed or assumed rights had never occurred before. But the explicit statement of objects and rights now became a feature of such actions, their scale expanded, and they brought diverse 'communities' into more and more frequent confrontation with the state. In Mubarakpur, as the preceding chapter will have indicated, opposition to the encroachments of the state constituted an important aspect of the local community's acts of resistance in the nineteenth century. It is noteworthy that in the long-drawn-out dispute between the Hindus and Muslims that followed the building of a *shivalaya* in the qasba in 1877,[3] the state had ultimately to back down under the pressure, as it were, of the 'traditions' of Mubarakpur. This in spite of the expressed opinions of the officials on the spot (most of whom, in 1877, happened to be Hindus) and the British District Officer's initial decision to let the shivalaya stand—on the ground that it was inside the compound of a Hindu moneylender's house and that the buildings round about were mainly the dwellings of other Hindus.

We have observed already that the threat of violence weighed heavily with the administration in their reversal of this initial position. The Muslims pointed out repeatedly that since the qasba

---

[3] Discussed above in section III of the previous chapter.

was established, there had never been a temple or shivalaya inside the habitation. The one instance when this tradition was ignored led to the nine days and nights of bloodshed that occurred in 1813. Apart from this, their leaders stated, 'article number 20' of the 'Zamindari Law' lays down clearly that the *riyaya* have no right to construct any building without the permission of the zamindar(s). 'You have created the conditions for a riot', the Magistrate now told the builder of the shivalaya. Eventually, after a court case that dragged on for months, and the continuous efforts of district officials to arrange some sort of compromise, the Mubarakpur Muslims had their way and the shivalaya was dismantled.[4]

A similar retreat by the state occurred after the Banaras outbreak of 1891, which I have referred to in section v of chapter 2. What was in question here, as in so many other areas, was the right of the state to intervene where it had not intervened before. Such intervention created new grounds of contention, and focused the question of who was to have control over a whole range of activities in a whole range of areas—'government' or 'public', and, implicitly, which 'public'? The Age of Consent Bill, the demolition of a temple in Darbhanga, the proposal to demolish the Banaras temple, the decision to close the access road to the public—these events, coming in quick succession, brought matters to a boiling-point in Banaras.

Following the resulting confrontation, the administration was forced to back down in this instance too. Large numbers of Hindus and Muslims in Banaras were united in their anger and resistance to this colonial encroachment. The Municipal Councillors who had acquiesced in the administration's plans were widely condemned and written off as toadies and traitors: some of them also had their property attacked in the riots. This movement, and others like it around this time, signalled the end of the era of Sir Syed Ahmad Khan and Raja Shiva Prasad. What else could one expect from loyalist 'leaders' such as these, it was now openly asked.[5] A different kind of leadership was called for.

[4] Ali Hasan, *Waqeat-o-Hadesat*, pp. 74–84; also Abdul Majid's diary, entry on '*Mubarakpur ka waqea: Purani Basti*'.

[5] See RNP, NWP&O for May and June 1891. The north Indian press almost universally blamed the Municipal Councillors for allowing the officials to bring matters to such a pass, calling Raja Shiva Prasad, Raja Shambhu Narayan Singh, Babu Bireshwar Mitra and others 'anglicised Rajas and Babus',

Three days after the violent protests of 15 April 1891, an important meeting was held at the Divisional Commissioner's house. The provincial government sent a special representative. The object of the meeting was to take steps to invite some pandits to attend a Municipal Council meeting two days later. The pandits were to be asked to declare under oath whether, according to the Hindu scriptures, an idol in a temple could be removed to another place or not. In the event other counsels prevailed. The meeting resolved that it was unnecessary to consult the pandits and decided that the temple should remain where it was. 'The decision gave general satisfaction and reassured the minds of the people', the local *Bharat Jiwan* reported.[6]

We have seen a striking example of such resistance by the community at a much earlier date, in the Banaras anti-house-tax hartal and dharna of 1810–11.[7] The boundaries between the rights of the state and the rights of the community were not easily settled, then or later. Nor were those between the rights of different communities, or indeed of different sections *within* the same community: and frequently the struggle to establish the boundary between one set of contestants spilled over into struggles regarding boundaries between other sets of contestants as well. In the following pages, I examine one of the more conspicuous examples of such a struggle in the period under study—the attempt to define

'sycophants' and 'chamchas'. The *Rafi-ul-Akhbar* (Banaras) of 20 July 1891 reported on the death of Babu Bireshwar Mitra, that he was 'an able lawyer, but very unpopular with the citizens. His death is viewed with satisfaction by all classes of people, especially Musalmans, with whom he had little sympathy'; ibid., w.e. 30 July 1891, p. 534. The *Naiyar-i-Azam* (Moradabad) wrote on 15 June 1891 in connection with the Shyambazar, Calcutta riots, that it was not known what Nawab Abdul Latif and Mr Amir Ali of Calcutta, 'who pride themselves as being the leaders of the Muhammadan community', had done for the 'martyrs'. Or Syed Ahmad Khan, who 'pretends to be a great reformer and even a prophet of the present century. He filled his paper (the *Aligarh Institute Gazette*) with accounts of the murder of Mr Quinton at Manipur, and expressed deep regret at the death of Mr [Theodore?] Beck's father in England, but he has not a word to say about the Calcutta martyrs'; ibid., w.e. 25 June 1891, p. 443.

[6] *Bharat Jiwan*, 20 April 1891, in ibid., w.e. 21 April 1891, p. 283.

[7] For a useful analysis of the context of this resistance, see Richard Heitler, 'The Varanasi House Tax Hartal of 1810–11'.

the identity and assert the rights of the 'Hindu community' at large in the later-nineteenth and early-twentieth centuries, through concerted action to protect the cow as a symbol of the Hindu religion and, hence, of the 'community'. In this, as in other instances of this kind, however, the attempted demonstration of unity also showed up the fissures in the community, and pointed to the persistence of other unities and solidarities that often acted in defiance of the unities sought to be established here.

The contradictory processes and tendencies that went to make up the struggle to establish an all India 'Muslim community' have attracted considerable scholarly notice.[8] The parallel struggle to forge a united 'Hindu community', with its own organizations and representatives, has received rather less attention—presumably because this 'community' was far more numerous, more widely dispersed, and, plainly, less in need of presenting the kind of 'unity' that sections of the Indian Muslim community were constrained to seek. In recent years, however, scholars have written at some length on the Urdu–Hindi controversy and the Cow-Protection movement as part of the attempt to construct the larger 'Hindu community' in northern India.[9] They have stressed, rightly, not

[8] See, e.g., M. Mujeeb, *The Indian Muslims* (London, 1967); Hardy, *Muslims of British India*; Robinson, *Separation among Indian Muslims*; Rafiuddin Ahmed, *The Bengal Muslims*; Aziz Ahmed, *Islamic Modernism in India and Pakistan, 1857–1964* (London, 1967); and David Gilmartin, *Empire and Islam. Punjab and the Making of Pakistan* (Delhi, 1989).

[9] Among earlier studies, see Robinson, *Separatism among Indian Muslims*; Bayly, *Local Roots of Indian Politics*; Paul Brass, *Language, Religion and Politics in North India* (Cambridge, 1974) and Jurgen Lütt, *Hindu Nationalismus in Uttar-Pradesh 1867–1900* (Stuttgart, 1970); also, Harold A. Gould, 'The Emergence of Modern Indian Politics: Political Development in Faizabad. Part I: 1884–1935', *Journal of Commonwealth and Comparative Politics*, XII, 1 (March 1974). More recent work includes McLane, *Indian Nationalism and the Early Congress*; Anand A. Yang, 'Sacred Symbol and Sacred Space in Rural India: Community Mobilization in the "Anti-Cow Killing" Riot of 1893', *CSSH*, 22, 4 (October 1980); Sandria B. Frietag, 'Sacred Symbol as Mobilizing Ideology: The North Indian Search for a "Hindu" Community', ibid., and her 'Religious Rites and Riots: From Community Identity to Communalism in North India, 1870–1940' (Ph.D. thesis, University of California, Berkeley, 1980); P. G. Robb, 'Officials and Non-officials as Leaders in Popular Agitations: Shahabad 1917 and other Conspiracies' in

only that these agitations encouraged a sense of 'oneness' among Hindus but also that, as a necessary corollary, they tended to divide 'Hindus' from all 'non-Hindus'.

Regarding Cow-Protection, Rafiuddin Ahmed notes that the question of the ritual slaughter of cows came to occupy centre-stage in the politics of the late nineteenth century 'not so much because the Muslims loved to sacrifice cows as because the militant Hindus [and, one might add, the colonial regime] made it an issue'. 'What used to be a quiet and private ritual', he notes further, 'now came to be celebrated with public éclat as an ostentatious response to the Hindu challenge'. McLane describes the movement for cow-protection as a 'species of sub-nationalism' that sought to shape and define the community in terms of the 'supremacy of Hindu custom' and, thereby, excluded Muslims from the 'primary community or nation' [*sic*]. Sumit Sarkar observes that the rioting that followed in the 1890s was on a 'quite unprecedented, almost country-wide, scale' and describes this as a poor augury for the national movement that was just getting into its stride.[10] Cow-protection was of special importance, too, as the scholars have noted, in bridging the gap between urban and rural Hindus and élite and popular levels of 'communalism'.[11] The question I wish to ask here is *how* all this happened: what did the call for cow-protection amount to, and how was it received by different sections of the putative Hindu community? I investigate these questions through a close examination of Cow-Protection activities and propaganda in the Bhojpuri region.

B. N. Pandey, ed., *Leadership in South Asia* (Delhi, 1977), and his 'The Challenge of Gau Mata: British Policy and Religious Change in India, 1880–1916', *MAS*, 20, 2 (1986); and G. Pandey, 'Rallying Round the Cow: Sectarian Strife in the Bhojpuri Region, *c.* 1880–1917', in R. Guha, *Subaltern Studies II* (Delhi, 1983).

[10] Ahmed, *Bengal Muslims*, p. 170; McLane, *Indian Nationalism*, p. 275; Sarkar, *Modern India*, p. 80.

[11] Ibid., p. 79; Frietag, 'Sacred Symbol as Mobilizing Ideology'. On p. 614 of the latter, Frietag writes: 'Only the sacred cow could have easily bridged the gap between Great and Little Traditions, between urban searches for community identity and rural values'. The basis of this far-reaching statement is, however, not clear.

II

The Cow-Protection movement arose in northern India in the wake of Kuka and Arya Samaj efforts to highlight the need for action on this issue. Stimulated by the writing and activities of Swami Dayanand Saraswati, the movement found organizational form in the Gaurakshini Sabhas (Cow-Protection Societies) of the early 1880s, first established in Punjab and then spreading to other parts of northern and central India. Nagpur in the Central Provinces was described as being the headquarters of the Gaurakshini movement at the end of that decade.[12]

Conflict over a municipal by-law forbidding the killing of cows and buffaloes within the municipality of Allahabad, and Allahabad High Court rulings denying legal protection to the cow as an object of religious worship, appear to have sparked off a new level of public debate and pushed the issue of cow-protection into the lime-light in eastern U.P. after 1887–8. With much increased activity on the part of urban-based Hindu publicists (and their merchant and *rais* patrons), urban officials and zamindars, and roving sadhus and sanyasis, the network of Gaurakshini Sabhas expanded and the movement spread rapidly in the countryside of eastern U.P. and western Bihar, as elsewhere, to become 'the question of all [questions] [and] the gravest danger that threatens us in India', as one official put it.[13]

In the Bhojpuri region, more especially in the districts of Azamgarh, Ballia and Ghazipur in U.P., Saran and Shahabad in Bihar (and the neighbouring districts of Gaya and Patna which lay just beyond the Bhojpuri-speaking localities), feeding as it did on pre-existing conflicts and aided by propaganda at the large religious and cattle fairs of the region, the agitation acquired unexpected social depth and remarkable militancy. It was here that some of the worst outrages associated with the Cow-Protection movement occurred, and these left a permanent mark on the relations between 'Hindus' and 'Muslims' both in this region and beyond.

[12] The outline of the rise and spread of the Gaurakshini Sabhas presented in these paragraphs largely follows the account found in the works cited in n. 9 above.

[13] Cited in McLane, *Indian Nationalism*, p. 290.

At the Baqr-Id of 1893, as already noted, the weaving centre of Mau in Azamgarh became the focal point of a large-scale attack upon Muslims mounted by great bodies of Hindus pouring in from the surrounding villages and districts. The evidence points to a concerted attack by Hindus from Ballia and Ghazipur upon the Muslims of Mau, Kopaganj, Ghosi, Chiriakot and other villages and qasbas in Azamgarh which were even further removed from Ballia and Ghazipur districts. In Mau, there was an armed confrontation between the Hindu attackers and local Muslims, mainly Julaha-Ansaris. The two sides, both armed with *lathis* and choppers, and also swords, bows-and-arrows and guns, were held apart for several hours by officials and mounted police and also a chance rainfall. But the Hindu attackers moved in on the Julaha quarter of Chandpura more than once, police firing was necessary, and two or three people were killed on each side before the attackers withdrew.

The object of the Hindu crowds was, first, to confiscate all the cows in the possession of the Muslims that were suspected of being intended for sacrifice, and second, to secure from the Muslims an undertaking not to sacrifice cows in future. The Hindu leaders rejected all official attempts to arrange a compromise agreement. Eventually, under enormous pressure, the local Muslim leaders gave in. The Hindus took possession of six or more cows and obtained a stamped agreement, signed by several prominent Muslims and initialled 'under compulsion', we are told, by a Deputy Magistrate and the local Tahsildar who were present.

Part of the crowd refused to rest content even with this total acceptance of their demands. As the crowds began to disperse, one section attacked and smashed the tiled roofs of houses in a particular Muslim quarter of Mau, and another—described as consisting of 'united Hindu forces' from the south and west of the town—attacked the small body of 150 or so Muslims who had remained outside the *mohalla* of Chandpura when the remainder of their fellows withdrew after the earlier battles there: of this group, six Muslims were cut off and beaten to death, while one other, seriously wounded in the attack, died subsequently.

Mau was the scene of some of the most brutal outrages in the course of the Hindu demonstrations at the Baqr-Id of 1893, but attacks and demonstrations of a similar kind, if on a smaller scale, occurred not only at other places in Azamgarh district but also in Ghazipur and Ballia, Shahabad and Gaya.[14] The Gaurakshini Sabhas established in the 1880s and '90s appeared to have collapsed after this, or at least gone underground, and it looked as though the movement had been effectively quashed by the fears of the local people and the precautions of the police. But cow-protection was far from dead as a political, agitational issue. It surfaced again in western Bihar in the years after 1910.

The recrudescence of cow-protection activities after 1910 coincided with the rise of the Ahirs' Gwala Movement, which we have discussed earlier.[15] The prevention of cow-slaughter appears to have become a point of some special importance with the Gwalas (or Ahirs) in the context of their struggle to upgrade their social status. This particular aspect of Gwala activities, however, readily found support among more privileged Hindu castes—Marwaris, Rajputs, Brahmans, Bhumihars and Kayasths (the last two, of course, themselves engaged at this time in trying to establish their 'pure' and 'noble' ancestry).[16] At the Baqr-Id of 1911, crowds of people, said to be mainly Ahirs and Bhumihars, collected to prevent the sacrifice of cows at several places in Patna district. In 1915 and 1916 large numbers of Hindus, armed with lathis, sickles and other agricultural implements, gathered towards the same end. In some places, where they could not stop the *qurbani*, these crowds took revenge by attacking Muslims and the police after the sacrifice had been performed: at Kanchanpur in the Fatuha *thana* of Patna

[14] In May 1893 it was reported from Gaya district that 'hardly a day passes without some cases of rioting or threatened breach of the peace on account of the anti-kine killing agitation'. The government also had to impose a punitive police force on Koath and 46 other villages of Shahabad district; (IOR)L/P&J/3/96. See Pandey, 'Rallying Round the Cow', section III, for further details regarding the riots at Mau and in other places; Yang, 'Sacred Symbol and Sacred Space' and *Trial of the Basantpur Riot Case in the Court of the Sessions Judge of Saran, 1893* (Calcutta, 1894) for details of the Basantpur case.

[15] See Chapter 3, section III, above.

[16] See N. Sengupta, 'Caste as an Agrarian Phenomenon in Twentieth Century Bihar', in A. Das and V. Nilakant, eds., *Agrarian Relations in India* (Delhi, 1979); Lucy Carroll's papers on the Kayasthas in *JAS*, xxxv (1975) and xxxvii (1978); and Swami Sahajanand Saraswati's important role in organizing the Bhumihar Brahman Sabha in Bihar.

district, in 1916, an estimated crowd of some 5000 'armed' villagers, 'arranged in some kind of military formation', launched an attack upon the Military Police and were repulsed only by heavy police firing in which a large number of the attackers were killed and wounded.[17]

Following on all this, there was a outbreak of violence in Shahabad in the following year on an altogether different scale, described by observers as 'unprecedented since 1857–58'. What began as a show of strength by Hindu demonstrators gathered in large numbers at the villages of Piru and Ibrahimpur on the occasion of the Baqr-Id, on 28 September 1917, developed in the days immediately after into a huge conflagration that engulfed a vast area. Officials spoke of 'civil war' and acknowledged that over 150 square miles of territory had passed out of their control.[18] Administrative fiat of a kind was restored by the calling in of heavy military reinforcements, but only after a week of frustrating warfare waged by armed police and troops, seeking to protect Muslim villagers and enforce 'law and order', on the one side, and thousands of Hindu peasants and zamindars on the other, wielding lathis and spears, congregating in a matter of moments and as quickly melting away.

As little has been written about this particular outbreak—less even than on the Cow-Protection agitations and riots of the 1880s and '90s[19]—it may be well to spell out some details of at least a few of the clashes and demonstrations that took place in Shahabad in 1917. Many thousands of Hindus streamed into the village of Piru from places all over the district, and even beyond, on 28 Septem-

---

[17] (IOR) Home Progs., Confidential 1919, vol. 52, Prog. no. 155, July 1919, 'Note on Previous Cow-killing Riots and Disturbances in Patna Division', 14 January 1918.

[18] Ibid., Pro. no. 154, Letter no. I-C, Oldham, Commissioner Patna—Chief Secy., Govt. of Bihar and Orissa, 31 December 1917/4 January 1918 (hereafter, 'Oldham's Report'), p. 20; (IOR) L/P&J/6/1507, Letter 168/I-C, H. McPherson, Chief Secy., Govt. of Bihar and Orissa—Secy., Home Dept., Govt. of India, Patna 11 March 1918 (hereafter, McPherson's Report), pp. 4, 10.

[19] Robb's 'Officials and Non-Officials . . . in Shahabad', one of the only detailed studies, is concerned chiefly with 'leadership' changes and price movements that, in his view, led to heightened rich peasant/landlord conflict around this time and that help to explain the outbreak of 1917.

ber 1917. This was the consequence of some weeks of preparation and propaganda for a demonstration, and the circulation of *patias* (or 'snowball' letters) on a large scale. The organizers of the demonstration claimed that it was intended to be peaceful and limited to the villages of Piru and Ibrahimpur. There is some evidence to support the claim that a limited demonstration was planned, for hundreds of Hindus marched through villages where qurbani was to be performed, and was performed without interference, to congregate at Piru and Ibrahimpur. The claim of 'peaceful' intentions is trickier, for demonstrations of this kind, even on a smaller scale, had often led to violence, and a new level of enthusiasm and determination is bound to have been generated by the mere assembly of such a large crowd—fed, as it was, on a whole variety of rumours regarding not only the practice of sacrifice at the Baqr-Id and 'justice' to the cow (and, thereby, to Hindus), but also the end of British rule, the impending arrival of German troops, and the coming of swaraj.[20]

In Ibrahimpur, meanwhile, the local Hindus and Muslims had succeeded in effecting a compromise on the question of qurbani. By an agreement signed on 27 September, the Ibrahimpur Muslims surrendered their right to sacrifice cows in deference to the religious feelings of the Hindus, and the latter agreed to provide thirty goats, to be sacrificed instead of cows, every year from then on. This was a considerable and meaningful achievement, and it is notable that

---

[20] See my 'Sectarian and Other Solidarities: Some Observations on "Communal" Mobilization in Modern India', *Proceedings of the Indian History Congress, Fortieth Session, Waltair* (1979). Official reports written soon after the riots emphasized the importance of 'Home Rule' propaganda and, more specifically, of 'Home Rule' meetings held in Patna and Shahabad in bringing about the Hindu rising. At one of these, held in Patna in December 1916 and attended by Bipin Chandra Pal, Babu Kalika Prasad Singh of Dalippur 'and other politicians', the idea is said to have been accepted that religion might be used to arouse the Biharis to political consciousness; (IOR) Home Progs. Confidential 1919, vol. 52, Pro. no. 165, Letter no. 2388-C, Chief Secy. Govt. of Bihar & Orissa—Secy. Home Dept, GOI, Ranchi, 18 June 1919; & Letter no. 1583-S.B., D.I.G. Crime & Railways—Chief Secy., 10 April 1919. There is also some evidence that meetings in Shahabad before the riots of 1917 provided a platform for both Cow-Protection and Home-Rule propaganda; Oldham's Report, p. 24.

through the worst phase of the outbreak the Hindus of Ibrahimpur not only took no part in the rioting but sheltered the Muslim men, women and children in their own houses.[21]

On 28 September local Hindu leaders, or at least some of them, sought to inform the assembled crowds of this compromise agreement and asked them to return home. 'But', to quote the inimitable language of the British policeman in India, 'the mobs having assembled were not to be denied their fun'.[22] The crowd of about 5000 Hindus at Ibrahimpur was 'very aggressive' and could not be pacified by the Deputy Superintendent of Police or by Hindu leaders. Ultimately over half this crowd rushed at the police party, assaulted the Deputy Superintendent and escaped with all the goats and cattle of the village plus a certain amount of movable property. On the same day, before any cow-sacrifice had occurred, the crowds also attacked and caused much damage to Bhagalpur and Milki, two villages near Ibrahimpur and Piru. They then threatened the larger Piru bazaar, and were stopped only by the challenge of the Sub-Inspector of Police, Lakshmi Narain Misr (until then among the chief organizers of the Hindu demonstration) to kill him, a Brahmin, first.

At this juncture the administration took the strange view, which they declared representative Hindu leaders accepted, that the attack by the Hindu crowds had violated the Ibrahimpur agreement and hence the Muslims were entitled to perform qurbani. After the arrival of armed police, a cow-sacrifice took place at Piru on the evening of 28 September, and a Sub-Divisional officer supervised the qurbani in Milki, Bhagalpur and Ibrahimpur on the following day, despite some evidence of reluctance on the part of the Ibrahimpur Muslims to perform the sacrifice.

This act of provocation appears to have marked the critical point in the unfolding of events. All through the night of 29 September a small but angry crowd stood at Bacchri Bridge, not far from where J. D. Boylan, the Superintendent of Police for the district of Shahabad, was camping in the Piru police station. Periodically

---

[21] Ibid., Appendix II & III (Letter no. 527C, Inglis—Commissioner Patna Divn., 29 September 1917, and 'Report' by S. Ahmad Ali, S.D.O. Sadr. 28 September 1917).

[22] Ibid., Letter no. 1583-S.B. from DIG Crime and Railways, 10 April 1919.

it raised threatening shouts and slogans. From dawn on the 30th rapidly swelling crowds congregated on Piru, calling for vengeance wherever cows had been slaughtered. Before long there was an enormous crowd on both sides of the police station, stretching 'in a dense mass from the cross roads in Piru Bazar for at least a mile along the Piru-Jagdishpur road'. Boylan reported that the crowd at this stage was so concentrated that the lathis above their heads were like a hairbrush; and from the area they occupied he estimated the assembly at about 50,000.[23]

Later in the morning, nearly all the Muslim houses in Piru, Ibrahimpur, Bhagalpur and Milki were looted and a major confrontation took place between the police and the Hindu crowds. The Superintendent of Police and his party of forty armed policemen were attacked and forced to withdraw into the police station, but in the end, following a number of arrests, the killing and wounding of several rioters in police firing, and threats of further and prolonged firing, the crowds dispersed. The District Magistrate felt that the worst was over: 'I do not anticipate any further rioting.'[24] The mass of the assembled Hindus had other ideas as they scattered in different directions, having failed to prevent the qurbani at Ibrahimpur and Piru, and having faced the police in an extended and, as it transpired, as yet undecided contest. A day later a huge Hindu backlash arose very soon to engulf the major part of the district.

An account of the assault on two villages in the Nasriganj thana—Mauna and Turukbigha—will perhaps serve to indicate the nature of the fighting and destruction that occurred in the district in the following days. Something of an island among a sea of large Hindu villages, Mauna was inhabited almost entirely by Muslims, among whom were its owners: the handful of Hindu residents belonged to the lower castes and were servants and tenants of the Muslim maliks. On 2 October Sita Dusadh and Pyari Ahir, two Hindu

---

[23] L/P&J/6/1507, report from *The Times*, 16 January 1918; Oldham's Report, Appendix v, Copy of First Information Report, Piru and Milki (sd. J. D. Boylan, S. P., Bacchri Bridge, 30 September 1917, 1–40 p.m.). The account of happenings in this area is taken from Oldham's Report, Appendix iii–v, viii and ix.

[24] Ibid., Appendix iv, Letter no. 531-C, Inglis—Commissioner (Arrah, Piro, 30 September—1 October 1917).

inhabitants, brought news of a patia threatening an attack on the village. A telegram was immediately sent to the District Magistrate, and the matter was reported at the Police Station of Nasriganj on the 3rd and again on the 4th. On the 4th Baldwin, the Special Magistrate at Nasriganj, rode out to Mauna with a private of the Somersets. After enquiries there, he warned the inhabitants of the adjacent Hindu village of Taraon to keep the peace. It may be noted here that a number of Taraon Hindus held land in Mauna on mortgage. At the same time, the Mauna Muslims held half of Parasia, another nearby Hindu village: and in the course of the Settlement of 1912–16, a dispute had arisen between a Muslim malik of Mauna on the one side, and, on the other, Girja Lal (*thekedar* of Parasia) and Saudagar Sunri, both of whom were subsequently charged with participation in the attack on Mauna. One other 'enmity' that was mentioned in this context by many local people may be noted; the Ahirs of Babhandi (the village adjoining Mauna on the east), many of whom again were accused and convicted of joining in the attack, were involved in various disputes with the Muslims of Mauna regarding the supply of milk and other matters; and some of these Ahirs held land in Mauna. There is no direct evidence that these pre-existing quarrels had anything to do with the attack on this village. Yet it is worth taking note of them for they may well have contributed to its scale and ferocity.

On his return to Nasriganj from Mauna on 4 October, Baldwin learnt of a serious attack that had been mounted on Turukbigha. The next day brought an assault on Nasriganj itself, which was fought off by the 25 Somersets stationed there. With Muslim villages thus being attacked all around, the administration was stretched beyond capacity and Baldwin 'was not in a position', as official reports later noted, 'to give effective help for the protection of Mauna'. But the Muslims of the village organized their own defence. Behind the seven barricades that they erected and with the few arms that they could quickly find, a party of some 50 Muslims and 15 Hindus fought off a huge body of attackers for many hours on 5 October before they finally surrendered.

About noon on that day, Hindu crowds attacked Mauna from the south (the direction of Taraon), and then from the east (where Babhandi lay). Both attacks were repulsed. The defenders evidently rushed from one barricade to another, depending on the direction of the main thrust of the attack at a particular stage. Both sides were armed with swords, spears, choppers and lathis; the Mauna Muslims also had one or two guns. With these they evidently accounted for a number of the assailants: even after several bodies had been carried away by the attackers, three were left on the ground. Around five in the evening, the attacking crowds began throwing bricks. The Mauna people found no way of countering this assault. Weak with exhaustion, they now gave way. Three Muslims were killed as they retreated through the village; another, a youth lying ill in a house, died of shock. A number of Muslims were injured, and the Judge suspected that there had been cases of rape though (as frequently happens in such circumstances) no one came forward to report any. Several houses were set on fire, being saved only by the damp left by recent rains, and prayer-carpets and copies of the Quran were defiled and burnt. However, most Muslims hid successfully in the houses of local Hindus, or outside the village. They reappeared only after the withdrawal of the rioters at night, but then hid again all that night and the next day owing to rumours of new attacks. Only, then, on the 7th were they able to reach the police station at Nasriganj to make a report. Baldwin, who now visited Mauna again, observed that the village had been 'absolutely sacked'.

My second example is the attack on Turukbigha, a hamlet of *mauza* Khiriaon which lay in the zamindari of Lalchattarpati Singh, one of the principal accused in the case that was instituted in connection with the Turukbigha events. On 28 September 1917, qurbani had been performed as usual in Turukbigha, quietly and without interference from any quarter. On 2 October, however, the hamlet was attacked by a crowd of some 2000 Hindus. This attack was beaten back. Two days later another crowd, again estimated at about 2000, renewed the attack. They were twice repulsed, but then, swelled by large reinforcements that came in from many sides, they succeeded in forcing their way into Turukbigha. Two Muslims were killed before they could reach the relative safety of the sugarcane fields around the village or places still further away, fields and homes where their women, younger children and older family members had already hidden. Baldwin, just back from his first visit to Mauna, met a 'panic-stricken mob' of Muslim men, women and children of Turukbigha two miles away from the village.

Judicial records suggest that there were some remarkable points of similarity in the attacks on Mauna and Turukbigha, although these may simply reflect to an extent the mechanical working of the 'due process of law' as practised by the colonial courts in India. In each case, there appears to have been a spirited defence by a small body of Muslims: in Turukbigha, the defenders were said to number 110 to 115, including boys. In both, the crowd that launched the final attack was said to be about 15000 strong: 'at any rate', the Judge wrote in the Turukbigha case as he had done in that of Mauna, 'there must have been many thousands'. In Turukbigha, as in Mauna, the flight of the Muslims was followed by large-scale plunder and the burning of Muslim houses, the fire being put out by rain, which fell in Turukbigha immediately after the riot. 'Every Muhammadan house [in Turukbigha] had been looted', Baldwin reported, 'and what was not worth taking away was broken'. But for the rain, he added, the entire *basti* (habitation) would probably have been gutted.[25]

The situation between 3 October and 5 October 1917 was such that ten or fifteen Muslim villages were being attacked daily in the Nasriganj jurisdiction alone; and like Mauna, many other villages must have gone without police protection. Where the police did appear in the course of an attack, they were sometimes met by stout resistance. At Hariharganj, a Muslim hamlet of Nasriganj, for example, on 5 October 1917 an armed force of two Gurkhas and twenty others opened fire on a crowd of about 1000: yet the crowd fought on, refusing to fall back until one person had been killed and six others lay seriously wounded (all of the latter died subsequently). Elsewhere, sections of the Hindu population not participating in the actual attacks showed open sympathy for the rioters. Thus on 3 October, near the village of Bagahi, local women directed Lieutenant F. C. Temple and his troop away from village Chakaria (Chakrahi) where the loot from Bagahi was at that very

[25] L/P&J/6/1507, Court of Commissioners of Special Tribunal of Arrah, Trial no. 5 of 1917, Emperor *vs.* Akhaj Ahir and others (village Mauna, P. S. Nasrigunj); Trial no. 6 of 1917, Emperor *vs.* Abilakh Ahir and others (village Turukbigha, P. S. Nasriganj); cutting from *The Times*, 4 March 1918.

time being stored. As it happened, the troops spotted bodies of looters and a large herd of cattle taken from Bagahi. The rioters then fled, dropping their spoil and leaving the cattle. 'The whole of the surrounding country was strewn with loot of various kinds', Temple reported, 'such as beds, doors, school books, clothes boxes, grain, etc. The most valuable stuff had been removed earlier and we only arrived when the low caste riff-raff were gleaning what was left by the principal looters'.[26]

The consequences of rioting and agitation on this scale were fearful. The immediate casualties and losses were high enough. Official statements had it that a dozen or so people were killed at Mau on 26 June 1893. Neither Hindus nor Muslims in the district of Azamgarh, or outside, accepted the figure. 'There is not the slightest doubt that about 250 men, Hindus and Mohamedans, were killed', wrote Dar.[27] A large punitive police force was stationed in Azamgarh district at an estimated cost of nearly Rs 84,000 for two years. In Ghazipur and Ballia, too, there were numerous arrests and punitive taxation for additional police. Warrants were issued for the arrest of 193 people in Ghazipur in connection with the 1893 riots, and a tax of Rs 21,275 levied (for collection in two years) for the maintenance of punitive police in the district.[28]

In Shahabad in 1917 officials estimated that 41 people had been killed and 176 injured, but admitted that these estimates were almost certainly too low; 124 villages were said to have been looted in Shahabad district, another 28 in Gaya and one in Patna. Property damaged, destroyed or stolen was valued at Rs 7 lakhs in Shahabad, Rs 1 lakh in Gaya; 1800 people were charged in connection with the riots in Shahabad, 400 in Gaya, 38 in Patna.[29]

But the fall-out from this agitation and strife was, in fact, much more widespread and enduring. By this date in the history of

---

[26] Oldham's Report, Appendix VI and VII.

[27] Dar, *Appeal to the English Public*, Appendix 'The Truth about the Azamgudh Riots', p. 5.

[28] (Gorakhpur Commissioner's Record Room), Dept. XVI, File 37/1898–1900, Letter 607/XVI-34, Magistrate, Azamgarh-Inspector General of Police, 23 August 1893; (IOL) W782, *East India Religious Disturbances*, pp. 56–7.

[29] *Progs. of Bihar and Orissa Legislative Council* (29 November 1917), reply to question by S. K. Sahay—extracted in Home Progs., Confidential, 1919, vol. 52.

colonial India, such instances of strife, even when they occurred in remote rural areas, were reported and commented on far and wide.[30] News of the attacks and killings in 1893 and 1917 spread very quickly indeed and had instant repercussions in distant parts of the country. The violence of June 1893 in eastern U.P. and Bihar was followed closely by riots in Junagadh and Bombay, where Muslims, some of them Julaha migrants from that very region, came out on the streets at least in part to take revenge for the attacks upon their co-religionists in Azamgarh and elsewhere. In 1918 again, in the first of what would become a long series of major Hindu-Muslim riots in Calcutta, migrant workers from northern India spoke of avenging the deaths of their Muslim brothers and sisters in Shahabad the year before.[31] All this served further to harden feelings and sharpen a widespread and growing sense of Hindu–Muslim antagonism. As McLane puts it, a trifle over-dramatically, for 1893, 'it seemed momentarily as if two nations were emerging in many parts of India'.[32]

III

What does this history of agitation for the protection of the cow, and the attendant conflicts and violence, tell us about emerging solidarities in the Bhojpuri region, about the place of religion in the politics of local Hindus and Muslims, about the growing

[30] See the extensive reporting of the Banaras 1891 incident in the Bengal press, RNP, Bengal 1891, and the equally active interest generated in the U.P. press by the Shyambazar, Calcutta violence, RNP, NWP&O. There were appeals for funds in far-flung places, and calls for support from 'all Hindus' and 'all Muslims'. See also n. 5 above.

[31] McLane, *Indian Nationalism*, pp. 320–1; K. Macpherson, *The Muslim Microcosm: Calcutta 1918–35* (Wiesbaden, 1974), pp. 37, 40. See also reports on Shahabad 1917 in *Pratap*, 8 October 1917, 15 October 1917, etc., and in *Abhyudaya* for the same period. The Shahabad riots became a point of reference in Indian politics for some time after this: thus, in the context of the questions raised by the Mappila uprising of 1921, Gandhi repeatedly referred to the pillage and murder in Shahabad as evidence that 'wrongs' had been committed on both the Hindu and the Muslim sides; cf. *Young India*, 29 September 1921, 26 January 1922, 29 May 1924.

[32] McLane, *Indian Nationalism*, p. 322.

importance of identifying oneself as 'Hindu' or 'Muslim' in the late-nineteenth and early-twentieth centuries? Since the movement was long-lasting and widespread, changed over time and had many centres and many different kinds of organizers and participants, it may be useful to begin by noting some of the points that existing analyses of the movement have already made. Some recent writers have sought to distinguish two phases in the Cow-Protection movement—an urban and a rural, corresponding perhaps to a less militant phase, under a moderate, 'upper class' leadership, and a more militant one that was guided by 'extremist' leaders from less privileged backgrounds.[33] One writer has also suggested that the movement in its earlier, urban phase was more unambiguously 'ideological', i.e. concerned with religion, distinction between people on grounds of religion and attacks upon people of other religious persuasions. It is said that this 'ideological' component of Cow-Protection activities was not quite so marked in the country-side, concerns were more parochial in this later phase and the villains of the piece in Cow-Protection propaganda included a whole variety of local castes, Hindu as well as Muslim.[34]

There is some evidence that the Cow-Protection movement became more aggressive as it advanced from the 1880s to the 1890s and from Punjab and the Central Provinces to eastern U.P. and Bihar, although this shift did not correspond very closely to a move from 'urban' to 'rural'. The great majority of the Gaurakshini Sabhas not only in Punjab and the Central Provinces, where no major violent clashes occurred, but also in the areas where serious riots broke out in the 1890s, were established in order to set up *gaushalas.*(homes for sick and aged or deserted cattle) and propagate the usefulness of cattle and the religious and other reasons for protecting the cow. They gained support not only from prominent Hindu rajas and landlords, traders and bankers, but also from Hindu officials, honorary magistrates and members of local boards and, in the form of attendance and participation at Cow-Protection meetings, even from Muslim and English local officials.[35] Many

[33] Pandey, 'Rallying Round the Cow'; Frietag, 'Sacred Symbol as Mobilizing Ideology'.

[34] Ibid., p. 607; also her 'Religious Rites and Riots', pp. 127ff.

[35] McLane; *Indian Nationalism*, p. 309; L/P&J/3/96 (Bodleian Library,

of these wealthy and highly-placed patrons appear to have taken a back-seat as the Gaurakshini Sabhas became more militant, turned to coercive practices and threatened 'law and order'.

The Magistrate of Darbhanga district observed in October 1893, for instance, that many of the Gaurakshini Sabhas in his district had come up because of financial support from the Maharaja of Darbhanga, one of the 'great' landlords of Bengal and Bihar, and from other rich notables. The Maharaja was still President of the Darbhanga Sabha and continued to exercise a controlling hand: 'beyond protecting and taking care of cows not much activity is observable'. But there were other Sabhas in the district where 'a very different state of affairs is visible'. Such was the Madhubani Gaurakshini Sabha, which now denied all connection with the 'parent' Sabha in Darbhanga. The Madhubani Babus, substantial landlords, were still joint Presidents. But they were mere figure-heads. The Sabha was actually run by its secretaries, Munshi Lal, a *mukhtar*, and Mahabir Prasad, a teacher in the Middle Vernacular School—both people with 'abilities far above the average, a fine capacity for organisation'—and was a 'most aggressive' body. This was something, the Magistrate added, that not one of 'the leading members of the Hindu faith [*sic*]' who originally supported the movement—such as the maharajas of Banaras, Dumraon, Darbhanga, Raja Rampal Singh and other big landlords of U.P. and Bihar—could have imagined or desired.[36]

Whatever the actual motives and sympathies of the great rajas and landlords, the experience of their withdrawal from the lime-light, along with that of sundry titled folk, English and Muslim officials, honorary magistrates and other aspirants to colonial patronage, was widespread; and the initiative in organizing Cow-Protection activities in the late 1880s and 1890s passed to people who were described officially as 'half-educated English-speaking agitators', small zamindars, professionals and traders with little direct bureaucratic connection, and a motley crew of swamis,

---

Oxford), Ms. Eng. Hist. d. 235, 'Confidential Correspondence' of Sir A. P. Macdonnell, Macdonnell—Forbes, 9 November 1893.

[36] Ibid., H. C. Williams, Magistrate and Collector, Darbhanga—Commissioner, Patna Division, 18 October 1893, and appended 'Note on Madhubani Gaurakshini Sabha'.

sanyasis and fakirs whose propaganda proved to be remarkably effective. 'One "Pahuari Baba" did more in a month to stir up disaffection [in the Patna Division]', wrote Anthony Macdonell, Lieutenant-Governor of Bengal, Bihar and Orissa in 1893, 'than the whole Native Press has probably done in a year'.[37]

The suggestion made by Sandria Frietag that with this move from lesser to greater militancy ('urban' to 'rural'?), the Cow-Protection movement also moved from a stronger 'ideology', greater clarity about the requirements of 'religion', to a more diffuse, parochial and, as it were, pragmatic appeal, seems to be more questionable. There are often specific, local conflicts that feed into wider movements which may explain the choice of particular targets for attack or the active participation of particular groups of people, as we have indicated in our discussion of the attacks on Mauna and Turukbigha in Shahabad in 1917. The choice of Ibrahimpur (along with Piru) as the site for the initial demonstration on the occasion of the Baqr-Id in that year may also have followed from a pre-existing quarrel between the original Muslim owners and the new Hindu zamindars of the village. In the years before 1917, the raiyats who had apparently remained loyal to the original malik and his descendants were reportedly under severe pressure from the new owners, and Nazir Beg (of the old zamindar's family) was 'subjected to much harassment, one act being to interfere with the long established custom of qurḅani in his house and mosque'.[38] In 1916 tension had been acute in the village and tempers had flared both at the Baqr-Id and at the local Hindu festival of Gai Darh when pigs were baited by cattle.

It is perhaps not surprising, then, that the Hindu co-owners of Ibrahimpur and the brother of their *patwari* (village records-keeper), who were present at district meetings to chalk out a programme of protest against cow-sacrifice at the Baqr-Id of 1917, should have suggested Ibrahimpur as the site for a Hindu demonstration. But the general proposition that pre-existing contradictions—

---

[37] Ibid., Macdonnell—Forbes, 9 November 1893. For further statements regarding this *baba*'s influence, see Yang, 'Sacred Symbol and Sacred Space', pp. 582, 589.

[38] Home Progs., Confidential, 1919, vol. 52, Prog. no. 165, letter no. 538, S.B., D.I.G. Crime and Railways—Chief Secy., 10 April 1919.

quarrels between landowners, tension between weavers and moneylenders, anger against shopkeepers or officials or police—feed into wider political movements applies as much to urban areas as to rural.

Frietag's other evidence for the 'parochial' concerns of 'rural' Cow-Protection—that in Gorakhpur, the Cow-Protectionists attacked the travelling and trading groups of Nats and Banjaras and the untouchable Chamars, along with the Muslims[39]—cuts both ways. Rather than representing a concession to some local resentments, in fact, these attacks appear to me to represent the demand of an increasingly aggressive and determined movement that all erring Hindus ('betrayers') must fall into line—those (like the Nats and Banjaras) who might conduct cattle from one place to another for sale to the commissariat or to individual non-Hindus, and those (like the Chamars) who sometimes responded to the degraded position assigned to them in Hindu society as cow-herds, lifters of carcasses and curers of animal-skins by turning to cattle poisoning and the sale of cattle skins.[40]

In any case, none of the evidence from the militant, 'rural' phase of the Cow-Protection movement suggests any lessening of the religious element in the appeal to the Hindus. Pratap Narayan Mishra's Kanpur monthly, *Brahman*, stressed in the 1880s that cow-protection was the supreme dharma of the Hindu, that the wealth of Hindustan too was largely dependent upon the welfare of the cow, and that without cow-protection the 'Hindu nation' and the country of 'Hindus' could never prosper. Mishra wrote also that the supreme importance of *gaumata*, the 'Mother Cow', was attested to by the invocation, 'Gaubrahman', in which Hindus made their obeisance to the cow even before they bowed their

[39] Frietag, 'Sacred Symbol as Mobilizing Ideology', p. 607, citing Hoey's 'Note on the Cow-Protection Agitation in the Gorakhpur District', in L/P&J/6/365, File 84 of 1894. See also 'Riots at Azamgarh District, 1893', U.P. Government General Department, Resolution of 29 August 1893, 'Abstract Translation of Papers found in the house of Parmeshri Dayal Singh'.

[40] Evidence of this is scattered through the colonial records for the later nineteenth century. See, e.g. (Allahabad Regional Archives), Commissioner of Varanasi, Bundle 39, File no. 148/1879; *Selections from the Records of the Government of India, Home, Revenue and Agricultural Department, . no. CLXXX*, Papers Relating to the Crime of Cattle-Poisoning (Calcutta, 1881).

heads to the repositories of the faith, 'those who are venerated universally', the Brahmans.[41] The 'rural' literature of the later phase of Cow-Protection—poorly printed leaflets, pictures and 'snowball' (or relay) letters—did nothing to dilute this religious appeal focused on the cow as mother: on the contrary it made the appeal even more direct and urgent.

Several motifs appear again and again in the broadcast appeals of the late 1880s and early 1890s. One is that of the cow as the 'universal mother', based on the proposition that all human beings drink the cow's milk: in consequence of this, the killing of a cow is represented as matricide. Another is that of the cow as the dwelling-place of all the major Hindu gods and goddesses, as a result of which cow-slaughter becomes doubly heinous in Hindu eyes. A third, which gains prominence by the end of the 1880s, is the representation of the Muslim—and to a lesser extent the Englishman, the Indian Christian and others—as the killer of cows and, hence, the enemy of Hinduism.

A picture displayed at a Cow-Protection lecture in Bahraich in 1893 combined two, or, if one accepts the interpretation of the local officials, all three of these themes. It showed a cow, inside which several Hindu deities were depicted, waiting to give milk to the assembled Hindus, Muslims, Parsis and Christians. Near the cow was a demon, half-human and half-animal, with a raised sword. A man representing Dharma Raj appeals to the demon: 'Oh! Demon of the iron age! Why art thou going to kill this useful animal. Have mercy on her.'

The *Hindustani*, reporting the case that arose out of the display of this picture, declared that the demon here was in the common form of such creatures in 'Hindu books'. But the Deputy Commissioner of Bahraich was convinced that the demon's animal head was that of a pig, and intended as a deliberate insult to Muslims.[42] Other pictures more simply portrayed a (Muslim) butcher ready to slaughter a cow, and Hindus of several different castes crying out to him to desist. 'The effect of this symbolical teaching on the rustic mind may be readily conceived', as a colonial official superciliously

---

[41] Vijayshankar Mall, ed., *Pratapnarayan Granthavali, pt. I*, pp. 178, 563, 601.

[42] RNP, NWP&O, w.e. 5 September 1893, pp. 350–1; Mclane, *Indian Nationalism*, p. 302.

commented, '[for] to the Hindu the symbol has in everything displaced the symbolised entity'.[43]

It was, however, not only the 'rustic mind' that was disturbed by all this propaganda. In an article on the anti-cow-killing agitation, Mohammad Ali wrote in 1911 of a picture that was printed in Bombay and then widely circulated in many different parts of the country. The picture represented a cow standing meekly with its head turned to one side, while 'a huge inhuman monster, a Malechh [*mleccha*, non-Hindu untouchable]' rushed forward, sword in hand, to kill the animal. A Brahman, 'with a look of mingled wrath and horror', stood with arms upraised in front of the cow to ward off the attack. Several gods and goddesses, as well as ordinary Hindu folk, were drawn 'in symbolical configuration across the body of the cow, with appropriate writings and texts to explain their significance'. Among them, Mohammad Ali noted, was an extract from the Koran in Devanagri characters, placed insultingly below the hind feet of the cow, 'A mere glance at this picture unmasks the real spirit in which the anti-cow-killing agitation has been conceived', he concluded.[44]

The 'religious' appeal remained just as central, but was in some ways even more strident in the course of the mobilization for Hindu demonstrations that turned into such a colossal outbreak of violence in Shahabad in 1917. This is amply illustrated by the contemporary patias that survive in the colonial records. These documents, small in number as they are, bear close scrutiny, and I reproduce them in Appendix I for the convenience of the reader.

The basic form of these patias appears to be the same. It consists of:

1. Invocation
2. Information
3. Appeal for (a) propaganda, and (b) action
4. Promise of support
5. Sanctions

This structure, and the remarkable brevity of the patias, is deter-

---

[43] L/P&J/3/96, 'Note on Agitation against Cow-killing', pp. 10–11.
[44] R. A. Jafri, ed., *Selections from Moulana Mohammed Ali's Comrade* (Lahore, 1965), p. 258.

mined to a large extent by the constraints of the form itself—the need to keep the relay-letter short and sharp for quick reproduction and further distribution. Recall the use of 'dharmpatris' for the mobilization of forces in Banaras in 1809 and again 1810–11. The process was described as follows by the local Magistrate:

Swift and trusty messengers run full speed all over the city, *proclaiming in a single word* the place of rendezvous, and *invoking infamy and eternal vengeance* on any who do not at the hour appointed repair to it. From the city the alarm is spread over the country. The first messenger conveys the symbol which is a Dhurmputree or paper containing a mystic inscription to the next village. From that to the next, till all know where, when, and wherefore they must meet. This practice is common not only among the Hindoos but the Mahomedans also and in the disturbances of 1809 and 1810 was the means of collecting together an innumerable multitude at one spot in the space of no more than a few hours.

And thus by Heber, with reference to the rising against the house-tax:

The leading Brahmins sent written handbills to the wards in Benares... and to some of the adjoining villages, declaring *very shortly* the causes and necessity of the measures which they were about to adopt, calling on all lovers of their country and national creed to join in it, and commanding, *under many bitter curses*, every person who received it to forward it to his next neighbour. Accordingly, it flew over the country, like the fiery cross in the 'Lady of the Lake', and three days after it was issued, and before Government were in the least apprised of the plan, above 300,000 persons [had assembled].[45]

The circular letters of the 1880s and early 1890s follow the same pattern:

In accordance with our orders and by the grace of the cow, an invitation is given to all Hindus to attend the meeting to be held on 22nd December 1889 for the purpose of establishing a Sabha. Whoever refuses to attend the meeting will be guilty of the sin of cow-killing. He who will help in the movement for establishing the Sabha, by erecting cattle sheds and by giving subscriptions, God will bless him with wealth and prosperity. All are to sign this invitation.

[45] (IOR) Home Misc., vol. 775, Report on Benares City by W. W. Bird, 20 August 1814 (pp. 451–506), para 12; Heber, *Narrative*, vol. I, p. 32/ (emphasis, in both quotations, mine).

Or again, in a longer circular from the Sadar Sabha of Ballia:

1. This Gaurakshani Sabha has been established by the order of Bhirguji, Baleshar, Ganga Maharani and Gao Maharani. . . .

2. By order of Ghulam Haidar Shah and Lakar Shah (the Muhammadan saints), all the Muhammadan residents of the district have been directed to join the Gaurakshani Sabha and help their Hindu brethren, and they have done so.

3. There are now 182 Sabhas in Hindustan and Bengal. The Rajas and noblemen and zamindars have prohibited cow-killing on their estates. By the direction of these Sabhas we have started a Sadar Sabha in Ballia, thinking it our bounden religious duty to do so. . . .

5. In your estates or villages you should persuade your people on the sanction of an oath to put a stop to cow-killing, and not to sell their cattle to an unknown person. . . .

6. Some people abandon their cattle without any cause; the animal wanders into another village and is impounded . . . [After a month or two in the pound] the cattle are sold to butchers and killed. . . . Any Hindu acting thus should be looked upon as a butcher born and . . . excommunicated.

7. In this manner lakhs of cows are being killed. If a cow is killed in a village inhabited by Hindus, that village should be overturned and destroyed by fire. Ill-fortune will pursue the inhabitants of such a village. The emasculation of calves should not be allowed. Whoever does so should be looked upon as a butcher born, and be placed out of caste. . . .[46]

The patias of 1917, prepared in haste in the midst of a rapidly growing confrontation, betray a greater sense of urgency. They begin usually with an invocation to Ram, probably the most popular deity among the Hindus of the Bhojpuri region, or to 'Mother Cow', which follows naturally from the matter at stake. The information that they go on to provide tends to be a bare minimum: that the cow, which has committed no sin, is dying at the hands of 'others' ('*dusre ke haath se marta hai*', patia no. 1), that fighting has broken out between Hindus and Muslims on the question of qurbani, that the cow has been publicly paraded and sacrificed in certain places to heap additional humiliation on the Hindus, that some Hindus (acting against the dictates of their

[46] For both these circulars, see 'Abstract Translation of Papers found in the house of Parmeshri Dayal Singh', cited in n. 39 above.

dharma) are sheltering and helping Muslims, that the village of Mauna is to be attacked, and so on.

There is an interesting progression in the temper and content of the patias that come from different stages of the Hindu mobilization, as one can see from a comparison of patias 1, 7 and 4, in that order. The first of these clearly comes from the early phase of the rising when the immediate object was only to exercise care and, if possible, thereby prevent the taking away and sacrifice of cows. 'Watch over the cow in every village and every home. Otherwise the cow will cry in pain and depart [be taken away/ killed].' The confiscation of cows found in the possession of Muslims was also ordered: '*le lene ka dharam hai,*' 'it is your religious duty [to take away any cow that you see in a Muslim's hands]'.

Patia no. 7 follows soon after no. 1, chronologically, but its tone is already more urgent as it identifies a particular village, Bikramganj, where a cow (or more than one cow) is being prepared for sacrifice, and urges Hindus to assemble in strength to save the life of the cow. Patia no. 4 comes from a later stage in the fight, when cow-sacrifices had occurred in many places, the call had gone out for revenge against the Muslims, and Hindu attackers had already encountered resistance from the Muslims in some villages. Such things have occurred, says the patia, that for the Hindu now, 'being alive is a curse'. 'Therefore, you must loot the houses of the Musalmans and kill the Musalmans and circulate five patias each in the countryside.'[47]

That appeal for action, of course, constitutes the next component of the patia, as we have analysed it. A part of the appeal is the simple one of passing on the information and message contained in the patia to other Hindus, the injunction to anyone reading a patia to relay it to 5, 10, 12, 25 or other given number of 'Hindu brothers'. The other part relates to the physical action to be undertaken: that Hindus must not allow cows to pass into the hands of Muslims, must prevent the sacrifice of cows already in Muslim hands, must not shelter Muslims in villages where qurbani has been performed or even that they must kill all Musalmans.

The promise of support from additional Hindu (and certain

[47] See Appendix 1 below.

interesting non-Hindu) forces is an unusual feature of the patias circulated in Shahabad in 1917, pointing to the quite remarkable expectations and anti-British rumours aroused by the exceptional circumstances of the First World War,[48] as well as to the fairly long-drawn-out nature of the fighting in Shahabad, the Muslim resistance encountered and the strength of military and police contingents that the rioters had to combat. Different patias thus contain the promise of calling in reinforcements from Hindu zamindars and rajas who were well known in the region, from distant kings (including the German), from the Bengalis (the particular force the authors have in mind here is unclear: the 'Bengalis' as a race were already being described as 'non-martial'), and of course from the great mass of the 'Hindu community'.

The patias almost invariably ended with a listing of the extreme consequences that would overcome those who responded or failed to respond to the appeals for action and propaganda contained in them: recipients could acquire the merit accruing from the gift of five cows or the de-merit flowing from the slaughter of five, or the consequences of a sin equivalent to sleeping with one's daughter, sister, mother or marrying any of these to a Musalman.

The sin of incest looms large in these patias. The violation of the chastity of women of one's family is repeatedly invoked as a spiritual punishment in these appeals for action to protect 'Mother Cow'. The fear of incest and the question of cow-slaughter are presented as being equally critical to the life of the community. The notion of the sacred duty of cow-protection, the sanctity of the *family* and the inviolability of the *community* are thus collapsed together. As in the case of the proposition that the killing of a cow (whose milk all human beings drink) is 'matricide', it is the image of the community—here, the 'Hindu community'—as a family that binds the elements of the patia together.

Prior to the sin of incest, and central to the demand to preserve the sanctity of the family and the community, is the insistence on action to prove one's faith. Action on behalf of the community appears in the patias as the one means of proving oneself a Hindu. 'We appeal to Hindu brothers . . .' (patia no. 1); 'Hindus have no

---

[48] See n. 20 above; also my 'Peasant Revolt and Indian Nationalism, 1919–22' in R. Guha, ed. *Subaltern Studies I* (Delhi, 1982), pp. 164–5.

choice . . .' (patia no. 4); 'If you are a Hindu, you must save the cow . . . (patia no. 6); 'Those who are Hindus should assemble for cow protection . . .' (patia no. 8); 'Whatever Hindu, on seeing this patia, will not come, shall incur the guilt of killing 7 cows' (patia no. 9); 'It is your duty (dharma) . . .' (patia no. 1).

If you do not do your duty, you forsake your dharma, you are no Hindu. For which Hindu would willingly take a step that is equivalent to the crime of killing a cow (or, worse, five cows, or seven), or sleeping with one's daughter, or marrying one's mother to a Muslim. Those who respond to the call at this time, they alone are Hindus: all others are traitors, enemies, Others.

It is difficult, then, to sustain the view that Gaurakshini propaganda was less religious (or 'ideological') in the 'rural' phase of this movement than in its urban. The appeal to Hindus to devote themselves to the service of the cow, to work for the care of sick and aged cattle, to do their utmost to prevent cow-sacrifice, was always religious, even if it was backed up by statements regarding the economic benefits to be obtained from 'Mother Cow'. In the later, more aggressive stages of the Cow-Protection movement, this appeal was reinforced, as we have seen, by the appeal to bonds of family and threats of excommunication. In spite of the forthrightness and urgency of Cow-Protection propaganda in the 1890s and the 1910s, and the terrible sanctions that were invoked alongside the appeal to 'all Hindu brothers', however, only certain sections of that 'community' called 'Hindu' responded readily to the appeal for action.

IV

It was a rather differentiated 'Hindu community' that the cow-protection movement addressed, and the pattern of its response appears to have been determined to a large extent by ties of caste and kinship. The detailed reports from local officials regarding the nature of the Hindu mobilization in Azamgarh in 1893 provide ample illustration of this.

Officials singled out four men as the 'principal instigators' of the disturbances in Azamgarh at the Baqr-Id of that year: Pandit Ghanshyam Narain Misr of Nimdand, Thakur Jagdeo Narain Singh of Nagra (in Ballia district), Thakur Sudhisht Narain Singh of Mau, and the fakir Khaki Baba or Khaki Das. Khaki Baba was an important orator for the Gaurakshini Sabhas in this region, apparently one of those itinerant sadhus or 'men of religion' who lent 'legitimacy' and at times fanaticism to the movement. Ghanshyam Narain Misr, as a Pandit (or Brahman), could also possibly have performed the role of such a 'man of religion'. But as a zamindar and owner of property in both Azamgarh and Ballia districts, he was important in other ways as well. That he played a leading part in organizing the Cow-Protection movement in Azamgarh district appears fairly clear. He was President of the Gaurakshini Sabha in the Sagri pargana, and all the subscriptions of the Nathupur division, notorious for its militancy on the question of cow-protection, were deposited with him. He was also observed mobilizing the crowds on the day of the riots in Mau, as we shall see. The two remaining zamindars in the above list of 'instigators' are of still greater interest in the context of the present discussion, for the evidence relating to them brings out well the role of this class in gathering the forces for demonstrations of the kind that occurred in Azamgarh in June 1893.

Jagdeo Narain Singh was a Bais Rajput of Nagra, once owner of 'a fair estate' which had however fallen into the hands of mahajans. President of the Ballia Gaurakshini Sabha, he was described as 'the soul of the movement' in eastern Azamgarh. He was particularly active in this area in the weeks immediately preceding the 1893 riots. A petition from 'poor Muslim residents of several villages in Azamgarh', sent to the Government of India a week before the Baqr-Id, named Jagdeo Bahadur, zamindar of Nagra, as chief of the assailants who were making preparations to 'take the head' of Muslims who sacrificed cattle at the Id.[49] According to a police guard, both Jagdeo and Ghanshyam Narain Misr were present at Adri, the village where men from Ballia district and elsewhere assembled before proceeding to Mau on 25 June. They were seen with other leaders 'on elephants, & c., marshalling the people'. Other evidence appears to confirm these reports about their involvement. One of the first prisoners arrested in Ghazipur

[49] Gorakhpur Commissioner's Record Room, Dept. xvi, File 37/1898–1900, 'Petition to Secy., Govt. of India, from poor Muslim residents of several villages in Azamgarh, 18 June 1893'.

in connection with the Azamgarh events said he had gone to Azamgarh on 25 June under the orders of his zamindar to attend a Sabha (meeting) of Jagdeo's. It was noted too that the Kshatriyas of Chiriakot and its neighbourhood, many of whom were convicted for their part in the demonstration against qurbani at Chiriakot, were closely connected with Jagdeo Narain Singh.

Sudishht Narain Singh of Mau—'the most influential Hindu in those parts . . . not a Hindu in the neighbourhood would dare to lift a finger if he ordered otherwise'—was said to have joined the other organizers of the 25 June demonstrations in their appeal for support from outside the district. Circulars were sent out to the neighbouring thana of Ghazipur district, calling on the Thakurs there to send in fifty men from each village to help the Hindus at Mau. As a man of property, and a real or affected well-wisher of the government, Sudhisht Narain staunchly denied this accusation. For this ambivalence, as it appeared, he was abused to his face by some of the Ghazipur men who congregated at Mau on the day of the Baqr-Id. In any case, the use of his name, whether on his own initiative or without his prior knowledge, remains a significant indicator of the kinds of people who took a leading part in this agitation and the manner in which they used caste and zamindari links to mobilize support.

There are other pieces of evidence pointing to the support lent to the movement by petty zamindars and co-sharers in many different parts of Azamgarh district. The Muslim petitioners mentioned above listed Sheo Das Singh of Mau, Imrit Singh of village Pradhan, Harjan Singh of Jafarpur Korthi (all three presumably Rajputs) and Beasji Maharaj of Kua Kopaganj as the four 'chiefs' for Azamgarh appointed by Jagdeo Narain Singh, and stated that the subscriptions raised as well as account books and detailed correspondence were maintained at the house of Imrit Singh.[50] In Nizamabad *pargana*, the entire *chutki* collections were said to be deposited in the hands of some of the local zamindars. In Sagri, the 'treasurers' were Ghanshyam Narain Misr for Nathupur and an Agarwal trader, Bhairon Prasad, for the western division. In the other seriously affected pargana, Muhammadabad, the proceeds were sent up to a fakir, two Gosains (probably, practis-

[50] Ibid.

ing 'men of religion') and a number of small Rajput and Bhumihar zamindars and co-sharers, including Jaggi Singh of Bhujohi and Sitlu Sing of Aldemau who, along with Girja Pande of Chiriakot, were described as the 'chief men' of the Sabhas in this area.[51]

Still within the pargana of Muhammadabad, the Thakur and Bhumihar co-sharers of Kasara and its neighbouring villages near Mau were reported to have 'taken up the anti-cow killing movement with vigour' at an early stage.[52] The same could be said of the Rajput zamindars of Gujarpar and other villages around Mubarakpur, their religious enthusiasm multiplied perhaps by their long-standing rivalry with the Muslim zamindars of that weaving centre. In Sagri, again, the Surajpur Babus, owners of the Surajpur taluqa and of other estates in Saran and Ghazipur, Bhumihars by caste and related to the Maharaja of Banaras, were said to have 'sympathized actively' with the Cow-Protection movement. The thousands of demonstrators who assembled at Ghosi on 25 June 1893, it was reported, came chiefly from the Nathupur division and from Ballia district beyond it; many of them (some 5000 according to one report) had come into Ghosi from the direction of Surajpur. 'What I wish to emphasize as regards the disturbances at Ghosi', wrote the Azamgarh Magistrate, 'is that it would have been next to impossible for such an assembly of Hindus to have gathered there without the connivance of the Babus of Surajpur'.[53]

In the numerous demonstrations and attacks on Muslim habitations that took place at the Baqr-Id of 1893 in Azamgarh district and elsewhere in the Bhojpuri region, the chief zamindari castes— Rajputs, Bhumihars and Brahmans—provided a large part of the fighting force, although they brought along with them tenants, servants and other 'dependants' belonging to a whole range of other castes.[54] In Shahabad in 1917, too, many of the most active

---

[51] L/P&J/6/357, Dupernex, Offg. Magistrate, Azamgarh-Commissioner, Gorakhpur, 7 July 1893 (hereafter Dupernex's Report); appendix on 'Ramifications of the Gaurakshini Sabha in Azamgarh District'.

[52] Azamgarh Collectorate, Dept. XIII, File 146/1894, Magistrate Azamgarh-Commissioner Gorakhpur, 19 January 1893.

[53] Dupernex's Report, p. 14.

[54] Apart from some information from the trials instituted after the riots, we have interesting evidence in the list of assailants presented in the Muslims'

elements appear to have come from the same groups. Colonial administrators, ready to smell a conspiracy anywhere, sought to dig up evidence of the unseen hand, of the bigger 'zamindars, pleaders and mukhtears attending meetings and encouraging the movement [in Shahabad] . . . [though] none of them appeared to have been in evidence during the disturbances'. What was beyond question according to their investigations, however, was 'the general support of zamindars and their agents . . . given to the movement throughout the affected area'.[55]

The investigating officials singled out petty zamindars belonging to Rajput and other clans for their leading part in the riots. 'Nearly all men of this class over half the district joined the movement. It was precisely these landholders of moderate position, men of good caste and good family, able to turn out two or three hundred *lathials* [dependants or servants skilled in the use of lathis or cudgels] each, who led the mobs in the important attacks', the Chief Secretary to the Government of Bihar and Orissa subsequently reported.[56]

The patias that we have discussed above appear to have been issued, at least in the initial stages, by upper-caste zamindari elements, and sent out to caste-fellows and village notables who could be expected to whip up a substantial following in a hurry. With two of the patias retained in the records from 1917–18, we have the names of the sender and the recipients. One, patia no. 5 (see Appendix 2), declares that it is sent, with salutations, by Jagdeo Singh, 'resident of Arrah', to Kali Singh Ji of village Gondpura. Another, patia no. 9, is written 'on behalf of' Brahmdeo Rai and Dharmadeo Rai, Bhumihars of Taraon to the Rajput Babus ('rulers', owners) of village Pauni; and the judicial record notes that

---

petition from Azamgarh, 18 June 1893 (n. 49 above). The caste breakdown of the men accused of preparing to use armed force against the Muslims is as follows: Bhumihars 94, Rajputs 31, Brahmans 16 (these three accounting for 141 of the total of 198), Banias 9, Sonars 5, Koeris 5, Kandus 5, Katuas 4, Gosains 3, Others 20, unidentified 6. See also the Basantpur references cited in n. 1 above, for a caste break down of rioters in a neighbouring district of Bihar.

[55] Home Progs., Confidential, 1919, vol. 52, no. 1583 S.B., D.I.G.'s letter of 10 April 1919.

[56] McPherson's Report, p. 7.

a copy of this patia was given on 2 October, three days before the attack on Mauna, by Ramjanam Rai of Taraon to Ramyad Singh, '*jeth raiyat*' (literally 'senior cultivator', i.e. the head of the cultivators) of the village of Pauni.[57] Evidence regarding some of the actual attacks on Muslim villages confirms the leading part played by the zamindari castes.[58] In connection with the attack on Turukbigha on 4 October 1917, it was noted that it differed from the attack on village Mauna a day later in that the men leading the former were 'not local cultivators or petty zamindars, but the zamindar [Lalchattarpati Singh] himself, and another well-to-do zamindar of the neighbourhood, Lobhi Upadhya [ya] of Mangraon'. After an initial assault on Turukbigha on 2 October was repulsed, Lalchattarpati Singh appears to have sent out messengers to Mangraon, Sabari and other nearby places, asking for reinforcements to enable a successful second attack. On this second occasion, Lobhi Upadhyaya appeared on an elephant. His brother Ramasrey 'and two other Brahmins' were said to have been on horseback. His son was also reported to have been seated behind him on the elephant, though he was ultimately to be acquitted of the charge of participation in the riot. A large number of the other men accused, and convicted, of joining in the attacks on Turukbigha were kinsfolk, servants and tenants of Lalchattarpati Singh and Lobhi Upadhyaya.

Again, Thakur Gopi Singh of Narainpur, whose name is still recalled in Arrah in connection with the riots of 1917, 'a well-to-do zamindar and perhaps the most important person convicted in connection with the disturbances',[59] was instrumental in making arrangements and providing food for the vast crowds that gathered on 28 September to demonstrate against the proposed sacrifice of cows in the villages of Piru and Ibrahimpur. In the case in which Gopi Singh was convicted, relating to an attack on the village of Katar on 2 October, 105 people were sent up for trial. Of these 15 (including Gopi Singh) described themselves as zamindars; two

---

[57] L/P&J/6/1507, note on patia translated in Judgement, Trial no. 5 of 1917.

[58] The next two paras are based primarily on L/P&J/6/1507, Court of Commissioners of Special Tribunal of Arrah, Trials no. 6 and 4 of 1917.

[59] Home, Confidential, 1919, vol. 52, no. 4222, S.B., D.I.G.'s letter of 5 September 1918.

were mahajans; and one, Rambaran Lal, the hereditary patwari of Katar. The attack upon Katar, a village owned by Muslim zamindars, appears to have been organized from Narainpur, which lay a few hundred yards to the south. Both Rambaran Lal, who was to the fore in the actual organization of the assault, and Gopi Singh were resident here; and among the Narainpur men found guilty of taking part in the attack on Katar were seven Rajputs (Gopi Singh, three relatives of his, and three others); five Kayasths (Rambaran, his brother, son and two other relatives); Madho Kumhar, a servant of Gopi Singh; and a Chamar, a Sunri and a Dhobi.

Many of the Hindu zamindars who took part in the attacks upon Muslim hamlets and villages in Shahabad in 1917 were 'smaller' men than Gopi Singh, Lalchattarpati Singh and Lobhi Upadhyaya. Thus, sixteen of the people accused in the case arising out of an attack on Mauna described themselves as zamindars, one was a patwari, two banias, one 'a banker' and one a Brahman chaukidar. In spite of this description, however, the Commissioners of the Special Tribunal trying the case decided to impose no fines 'as we are not aware that any of the accused are very well-to-do men'.[60]

Such men will nevertheless have had more than a little influence and standing in their own villages. But the point to emphasize perhaps is that they shared kinship and zamindari links with those who took a leading part in the agitation over qurbani at the Baqr-Id of 1917—most notably the Rajputs, the Brahmans and the Bhumihars, the three 'true-blue' zamindari castes of the Bhojpuri region. Here, the sense of the Hindu community was overdetermined by notions of caste and zamindari honour: the 'Hindu' attempt to recover prestige was also a zamindari attempt to assert status. Perhaps the most striking evidence in support of the point being made here is the fact noted by investigating officials that the area of Shahabad that burst into flame in 1917 'almost exactly coincides with the area affected in 1857–58', when the same Rajput, Brahman and Bhumihar landowning (and 'martial') communities had risen in revolt under the banner of Kunwar Singh. Observers also noted in 1917 that the Jagdishpur zamindari and its branch at Dalippur, the estates of the descendants and

[60] L/P&J/6/1507, Trial no. 5 of 1917.

kinsfolk of Kunwar Singh, were associated in the popular mind with the Hindu uprising: the slogan *Dalippur ke babu ki jai* was widely heard, and there were reports implicating other members of the Ujjainia clan of Rajputs.[61]

While it is necessary to emphasize the leading part played by upper-caste zamindari elements in organizing the Hindu demonstrations and attacks in September and October 1917, it would be a very one-sided statement that did not recognize a similar initiative (and leadership) on the part of rather less privileged communities who were organizing their own autonomous movements at this time and who were able to use the issue of cow-protection, perhaps, as another lever in the bid to improve their social status. I have mentioned the Gwala Movement among the Ahirs of western Bihar, which took the lead after 1910 in highlighting the question of cow-protection. I have also quoted the colonial official who, in summing up his experience of the strife in Shahabad in 1917, singled out Ras Bihari Mandal along with the Maharaja of Dumraon as being among the prime fomentors of the agitation: Ras Bihari Mandal, an 'important Extremist politician', a man of 'rascally private character and *low birth*', 'headed a large organization of Goalas (Gwalas) of whom there are many in the affected areas, and who are notoriously as prone to dacoity and rioting as the Rajputs of that area'. The other great cultivating castes of the Bhojpuri region, the Kurmis and Koeris, also appear to have played some part in Cow-Protection activities.

Most colonial officials, of course, were firmly convinced of the upper classes' monopoly of enterprise and brains, and paid little attention to the role of such subordinate groups in the rise and spread of large-scale political movements. Historians, with less excuse, have often reproduced this official view. Yet, in the local colonial records relating to Shahabad in 1917, there is clear evidence that the Ahirs of Bacchri (a village adjacent to Ibrahimpur and Piru) and the patwari of their village, Mathura Lal, took a major part in organizing the initial demonstration at Ibrahimpur and Piru on the day of the Baqr-Id. It was the Ahirs of Bacchri who allegedly initiated the protest against qurbani in Ibrahimpur in 1916; and Bhutan Ahir, a resident and chaukidar of Ibrahimpur, was described

---

[61] Oldham's Report, pp. 17 and 23.

as one of the prime movers of the agitation in 1916 and again in 1917.

In 1917 it was Mathura Lal and some Ahirs of Bacchri who got in touch with Laxmi Narain Misr, the Sub-Inspector of Police at Piru, and gained the support of the local Hindu policemen. They also joined Laxmi Narain Misr and other subordinate police officials of Piru, along with a number of local zamindars and zamindari agents in the meetings from which the first patias originated—to be sent out to other zamindars and 'men of influence' in the vicinity. Again, the crowd of 5000 or so men armed with lathis who congregated at Ibrahimpur village on 28 September was described as being composed 'mostly [of] Rajputs, Ahirs and Chatris [sic]' from the villages of Dalippur, Jetaura, Tewani, Balligaon, Kastar and Katar.[62]

The caste breakdown of those arrested for participation in the widespread rioting that followed confirms these indications of the special role of the Ahirs, a role that cannot be explained away by the suggestion that they were drawn in by the zamindari groups. Of the 140 trials instituted in consequence of the Shahabad riots, I have seen the detailed evidence and judgements in only seven cases. Out of 560 men sent up for trial in these, as many as 85 were Rajputs, 90 Brahmans and 55 Bhumihars.[63] Other upper castes, fairly thin on the ground in any case, were represented by a handful of Kayasthas and Banias from one or two villages. Ahirs, however, were 'very prominent' in the riots, 127 of them being convicted in these seven cases alone. Doubts about the representative character of any sample are heightened in this instance, of course, by the feeling that privileged men of the upper castes would be far more readily

[62] Ibid., Appendix III, 'Report' by S. Ahmad Ali, 28 September 1917, 7 p.m.

[63] L/P&J/6/1507, Court of Commissioners of Special Tribunal of Arrah, Trials no. 1, 3, 4, 5, 6 of 1917; and also case no. 486-G relating to an attack on Bithwa Rasulpur on 5 October; and Emperor *vs.* Algu Kandu, etc. relating to an attack on Bisaini Kalan on 5 October. In the last-named case, there was a large gap between the number of accused (253) and those convicted (83): in this case, therefore, I have taken account only of those convicted. Robb's 'Officials and Non-officials, Shahabad 1917' uses evidence only from the first five of the above-mentioned trials. The figures in his table on p. 191 also differ from those presented here, I suspect, because of the general difficulty of identifying men's castes through their names; Bhumihars, for instance, commonly took the title of either Rai or Singh.

noticed in the course of a riot. Yet, if this is granted, the identification of the lowly Ahirs in such large numbers becomes all the more significant.

I would suggest that we have evidence here of a relatively independent force that added a good deal of power to cow-protection activities in the Bhojpuri region—marginally 'clean' castes who aspired to full 'cleanness' by propagating their strictness on the issue of cow-slaughter. The strength of their autonomous mobilization was seen very clearly in Shahabad in 1917, but their militancy and independence were already in evidence in Azamgarh in 1893, in the demonstrations and clashes around Ghosi for instance. Here on three successive days, 25–27 June 1983, large crowds of Hindus assembled to demonstrate against qurbani. On 25 June Ahirs and Kurmis took the lead in confiscating a cow from Abdul Latif of Milkipur, and the crowd of 5000 or more that gathered was not pacified until the next day when Abdul Latif surrendered the other cow that he possessed and the qurbani was definitely abandoned.

On the same day, a crowd of an estimated 4,000 Hindus assembled at Karimuddinpur, and a small section of this crowd armed with lathis attacked the Tahsildar and Sub-Inspector of Police, who were both on horses, and the accompanying party of officials, peons and policemen, inflicting substantial injuries upon them and forcing them to retreat. On the following day, at 9.00 a.m., trouble was again reported to be brewing in Karimuddinpur. Rather than risk another confrontation, officials sent Sher Ali Khan, an influential local Muslim who was on good terms with the Hindus, and three or four Hindus to try and retrieve the situation. This enterprise took the entire day to accomplish and it was only at 5.00 p.m. that the crowd was persuaded to leave the field they had decided to plunder. But while other sections agreed, groups of Koeris and Ahirs refused to leave without completing the task of plundering. In the end, as the Tahsildar put it, 'the remaining low caste people made an assault at Mauza Karimuddinpur at the house of Haji Roshan, a wealthy merchant in the village'.[64] Later the Hindus 'of the riot' sought to attack the Hindus

[64] The details of these events are taken from L/P&J/6/357, Chand Narain, Offg. Tahsildar, Ghosi to Magistrate, Azamgarh, 28 June 1893.

who had intervened on behalf of the administration; rain seems to have foiled their attempt. Early on the following morning a huge crowd, now estimated at 7000, again assembled, but a major affray was avoided—partly, no doubt, because with the Baqr-Id over and qurbani staved off, the principal point of the rioters had been made.

Major cases of rioting are always likely to provide opportunities for plunder, or for the settling of old scores by poor and exploited groups. It is possible that such factors were partly responsible for the actions of lower-caste folk at Karimuddinpur; and something of the same nature was certainly operative in Shahabad in 1917 too, where the outbreak was of course on an altogether different scale. As we know, the initiatives of various zamindars, Ahirs and other groups, and the spate of patias and rumours that followed, produced a massive rising against the Muslims of Shahabad and the military and police force that sought to intervene. A very large proportion of the Hindu populace of the district appears to have become involved in this outbreak, spurred on no doubt by the fear of social boycott and ostracism, indeed of religious damnation, as much as by any anger over cow-slaughter or resentment against the foreign rulers. In the later stages of the outbreak, when the law-enforcing authorities had plainly lost control, whole gangs of men (many of them from the lowest castes and classes) also appear to have been drawn into the riots by the prospect of loot. Such would seem to have been the case with some Nonias of Katar who were found guilty, along with Gopi Singh and others, of participation in the riot there on 2 October: five of them were established as having been among the men and women who robbed the Katar Muslims who had hidden in the fields behind their habitation. Such, too, were the groups of 'rioters' encountered by Lieutenant Temple and his force when they reached the village of Bagahi on 3 October. On 10 October, again, by which time the worst of the Shahabad outrages were finished, portions of the district were still described as being in 'a disturbed state', and the men responsible for this were said to be 'low class [caste?] Hindus'.[65]

Whatever one might make of those later, confused stages of general rioting and looting, it emerges clearly from the evidence

---

[65] L/P&J/1507, Telegram, Viceroy to Secy. of State for India, 10 October 1917, and Trial no. 4; Oldham's Report, Appx. VII.

that the handful of upper zamindari castes and a few of the lower castes, like the Ahirs and Kurmis, took the dominant part in the actions to save the cow in the Bhojpuri region in 1893 and 1917. We have observed the same kind of circumscribed 'Hindu community' moving to the defence of a 'general' Hindu interest in Banaras in 1809.

In spite of the widely rumoured threat to major institutions of the Hindu faith in the city, the Lat Bhairava and the Vishwanath temple, and the appeal for action in their defence to all believers in Shiva and Kashi, it was the Rajputs, the Gosains and the Brahmans who were the chief combatants on behalf of the Hindus on that occasion. As the Banaras *District Gazetteer* put it, in its summing up of the forces involved on the two sides in the clash of 1809, 'on the one side were the Musalman Julahas and others of the lower classes . . .; while among the Hindus were many of rank and influence, the moving spirits being the Rajput inhabitants of the city.'[66] The evidence on this point is especially instructive because, as we have seen, lower castes among the Hindus—Kohars and Kahars, Koeris and Kurmis, Mallahs and Doms, and above all the Lohars—took a most impressive and prominent part in the defence of the interests of the local community (i.e. the community of Banaras, Muslim as well as Hindu) on the imposition of the new house-tax in the following year.

A similar picture emerges from another example a century later—the 'Hindu' attack upon Muslims in the village of Katarpur on the occasion of the Baqr-Id in 1918, which I have, again, referred to earlier.[67] Stung by a public admission that qurbani had been performed in the village in past years, as I have noted, the Chauhan Rajput zamindars of Katarpur began preparations to prove at the forthcoming Baqr-Id that *they* were the masters, and that cows could never be sacrificed in *their* village. In these preparations, the Chauhans were evidently advised and assisted by professional men, merchants and priests from the important Hindu pilgrimage

[66] Banaras *District Gazetteer*, p. 207. F/4/356, Board's Collections, vol. 356, no. 8500, Bird-Brooke (Senior Judge, Benares Court of Circuit), 14 April 1810, para 5, notes the involvement of the lower castes and classes in violence and looting, as in Shahabad. But the upper-caste initiative in organizing and generally leading the attacks seems fairly clear.

[67] See Ch. 4, section VI above.

centres of **Hardwar and Kankhal**, which lay at a short distance from Katarpur. Following on all this, thirty Muslims of Katarpur were butchered to death at the Baqr-Id in September 1918 by a large crowd of Hindus from the village, the towns of Hardwar and Kankhal, and other villages nearby—a calamity that the small police force present could apparently do nothing to prevent.

The caste background of the 165 men subsequently brought to trial, and in all but 20 cases found guilty of participation in the riot, is significant. Of them as many as 50 were Chauhan Rajputs. The rest were made up of 24 Brahmans, 17 Banias, 14 Sainis, 7 Mahants or priests (including three who were sentenced to death), 6 Jats, 6 Khatris, 4 Kayasths, 4 Kalals, 4 Gosains, 4 Banjaras— far the majority of these being men of the trading and priestly communities—and smaller numbers from other castes. That is to say that the great bulk of the accused came from the community of the Chauhan zamindars or of the merchants and priests in the nearby pilgrim towns. Not surprisingly, the largest number was from Katarpur itself: 33 men of the village were prosecuted, 27 of them were Chauhans, and the remainder are very likely to have been personal servants or other direct dependants.[68] Limited though the evidence is, it provides striking testimony to the general aloofness of the lower castes even in Katarpur (a village inhabited by 538 Hindus and 238 Muslims in 1911) from this defence of 'Hindu' interests.

V

All this is not to suggest that 'Hindu' (and 'Muslim') interests or the notion of a 'Hindu (or Muslim) community' had no meaning for the vast majority of local castes, in the Bhojpuri region or elsewhere. We have seen that quite the opposite was the case with the Muslim weavers of Mubarakpur, in spite of the strength of 'caste' feelings and of their own caste organization in the qasba and beyond. But the relevant point, perhaps, is that apperception at the local level during the early nineteenth century, and well into the twentieth, was very much in terms of *jati* and *biradari*, caste and kinship, that the strength of local caste and community orga-

---

[68] L/P&J/6/1557, correspondence and 'Judgement'.

nization mattered (in that decisions were most often taken and/or channelled through them), and that the feeling of belonging to a wider 'Hindu' or 'Muslim' community did not mean—in spite of all that colonialist historiography and sociology had to say on the subject—that 'Hindus' and 'Muslims' responded automatically and in unvarying ways to every appeal for action on behalf of 'Hindu' or 'Muslim' interests.[69]

The point possibly applies with greater force to the Hindu community than to the 'Muslim', because, unlike the latter, the 'Hindu community' was far from being small, concentrated in any particular localities, or bound by anything in the way of a 'revealed' book or a 'united' church. The all-India 'Hindu community' (and, to a large extent, the all-India 'Muslim community' too) was a colonial creation for, as I have argued, the social and economic changes brought by colonialism, Indian efforts to defend the indigenous religions and culture against western missionary attacks, the 'unifying' drive of the colonial state—which was marked at the level of administrative structure and attempted political control ('Muslims' must not be antagonized, 'Hindu' sensibilities must not be touched), and the very history of movements like that of Cow-Protection, widely publicized as they were by the end of the nineteenth century, tended to promote the idea of an all-India 'Hindu community' and an all-India 'Muslim community' which were supposedly ranged against one another for much of the time. In spite of a widely felt sense of 'Hinduness' and 'Muslimness', I would suggest that until the nineteenth century at any rate, people always had to work through caste, sect and so on to arrive at the unities implied in the conception of the 'Hindu community' and the 'Muslim community'.

Given the strength of local community solidarity until well into the late colonial period, and of collective decision-making at many levels, it is not surprising that in different conjunctures, and on different issues, different constellations of local groups, castes and communities are to be found coming together—'Hindu' or 'Muslim' or both. Of course the very act of coming together,

[69] For an argument similar to mine, but applied to the urban context and a slightly later period, see Chitra Joshi, 'Bonds of Community, Ties of Religion: Kanpur Textile Workers in the Early Twentieth Century', *IESHR*, 22, 3 (1985).

especially when this occurred repeatedly in particular combinations, gave rise to new feelings of solidarity and new strains in the indigenous society. And yet, in spite of the many instances of Hindu-Muslim strife in the nineteenth century, and the powerful movements that arose to promote 'Hindu' and 'Muslim' unity in northern India, the new solidarities that emerged did not everywhere and indubitably add up to 'Hindu' versus 'Muslim' We know this from the experience of the very region and the very castes that we have been discussing in this chapter.

In Bihar, in the rural heartland of the Hindi belt, Cow-Protection propaganda had been exceedingly effective in mobilizing large sections of the 'Hindu community' against a small and isolated 'Muslim community'. Here and in eastern U.P., the large Hindu cultivating castes of Koeris, Kurmis and Ahirs had teamed up with the upper castes of Brahmans, Bhumihars and Rajputs in the agitation to end cow-sacrifices in the 1890s and the 1910s. For all that, the latter were far from willing to accept the former as anything but a barely touchable, and pretty lowly group in the local society and in the community of Hindus more generally. And in the 1910s and '20s, as we have seen, when the Koeris, Kurmis and Ahirs became better organized and increasingly militant in pressing their demands for a more respectable status the upper-caste Hindu zamindars joined hands with the upper-caste Muslim zamindars of the region to keep these 'upstart' peasant castes in their place—through physical violence, rape or any other method that served their purpose.[70] That divide between upper and lower castes and classes, and the strife attendant upon it, remained the predominant feature of the rural political scene in eastern U.P. and Bihar, more marked than any perceptible rift between local Hindus and Muslims, at least until the 1940s.

[70] See p. 156 above.

Chapter Six

'Hindi, Hindu, Hindustan'

It is said that the Hindu Congress and the Muslim League, having embraced each other, all causes of serious friction will cease and there will be an unusual flow of love between the two communities; but strangely this year the Bakr-Id quarrels have been unprecedented both in intensity and extent. . . . It is hinted that the Mahomedan sub-divisional officer in Arrah is to blame for this outrage. The Mahomedans there have been the victims of acts of violence and therefore it is in keeping with the anti-Mahomedan spirit that their co-religionist the sub-divisional officer should not go scot-free. This is a foretaste of the overdue Home Rule.

—Letter from 'A Mahomedan' to the editor,
Pioneer, 27 October 1917

The responses of Muslims in Shahabad and its vicinity to the riots of 1917 tell us a good deal about the complexities of nationalist and communalist politics in northern India at the turn of the century. I have mentioned above that official accounts had drawn a direct link between Home Rule meetings and the Shahabad outbreak.[1] Whether as a result of this kind of official propaganda or because such a view was in fact more widely shared, numerous statements from local Muslims in the wake of the riots pronounced judgement simultaneously on the Home Rule movement and on the rioting.

Little more than a fortnight after the riots, on 21 October, a mass meeting of Muslims at Sassaram, the 'most important Mahomedan centre in the district of Shahabad', passed a series of resolutions declaring their 'unflinching devotion' to the British government even (especially?) at this moment of distress, dissociating themselves from the Home Rule League agitation, and disowning 'such Mahomedans, who, even after the fanatical outrage perpetrated

[1] Chapter 5, note 20.

on the innocent victims of the Shahabad riots, and the demolition of the mosque, and the desecration of the Holy Book, continue asking for Home Rule for India'.[2]

A week later the Anjuman Islamia of Gaya, at its inaugural meeting, substantially reproduced these resolutions, adding to them its disapproval of the All India Muslim League and the District Muslim League for joining forces with the Congress—a move that was said to be 'most injurious' to Muslim interests. It also appealed for the setting up of a fund for the relief of sufferers in the riots, but declared that no aid should be accepted from Hindus.[3]

A couple of days later, on 30 October, a public meeting at Koath (Shahabad), a storm centre of the riots in 1893 and again in 1917, brought together Muslims from eighteen villages around Koath. Hazrat Syed Jaan-i-Alam, *sajjada nashin* of Dargah Marehra in UP, who presided, exhorted Muslims to 'regard none but Christians as their true friends' [*sic*]. Among the resolutions passed unanimously by the meeting were the following: 'That the preorganised and widespread riots in Shahabad, with "Jai Mahabir!" and "Jai German!" as war-cries, have been at once a direct encroachment on the civil and religious liberties of the Moslem Community; and an indirect challenge to the authority of the Local Government, which is thus given a foretaste of the Home Rulers' plot or system of agitation'; that the Home Rule agitation was 'untimely as well as detrimental to the religious, social, and political interests of the Indian Musalmans'; strongly denouncing the Bihar Muslim League and its 'wirepullers' for signing the Congress creed 'without consulting the mass', which means 'forging the Home Rule demand in our name'; appealing to the ulema of different sects to issue fatwas

---

[2] (IOR) Mss. Eur. D. 1167/1, C.E.A.W. Oldham Collection, Cutting from the *Englishman* (the report from Sassaram is dated 22 October 1917). An earlier meeting, held at Arrah on 17 October, and attended by 6000–7000 Muslims, had also protested against the Home Rule agitation while condemning the acts of violence perpetrated against the local Muslims. It had further resolved to establish an Anti-Home-Rule League with branches all over the district. The meeting was attended, according to a newspaper report, by Muslims 'of all classes', most prominently zamindars, traders, vakils mukhtars, ulema and doctors; *The Pioneer*, 19 October 1917.

[3] *The Pioneer*, 1 November 1917.

against Home Rule; and appointing a committee to raise funds for the relief of Muslims who suffered in the riots.[4]

A day before the Koath meeting, a joint meeting of the Bihar and Orissa Provincial Congress Committee and the Bihar Provincial Association, held in camera at Bankipur under the chairmanship of Syed Hasan Imam, failed to mention the Shahabad riots in its public report of the proceedings. The report confined itself, instead, to announcing the formation of a sub-committee of twenty-four Hindus and five Muslims to prepare a 'joint representation' to be submitted to Lord Montagu in support of the Congress-League scheme and its application to Bihar and Orissa, and naming the members of a deputation that would meet the Viceroy and the Secretary of State for India in this connection.[5]

The purpose of citing this evidence is not to suggest that élite nationalist politics and popular political concerns could never find a meeting point. The exact opposite was to be demonstrated within three years of the Shahabad riots, through massive popular participation in the Rowlatt Satyagraha and the Non-Co-operation/Khilafat Movement—in Bihar and UP, as elsewhere. In the Bhojpuri region Muslims and Hindus from a wide variety of backgrounds, and many different castes and classes, came out in support of Gandhi and the Ali brothers, for Swaraj and a place in the sun. Large numbers of Muslim weavers participated in the Non-Co-operation Movement, and the political organization of the north Indian Muslim weaving community, the All-India Momin Conference, supported the Congress all the way through to the 1940s and beyond.[6]

[4] Mss. Eur. D. 1167/1, cutting from *The Statesman*, 7 November 1917. See ibid., for reports of other meetings of Muslims held in different towns and villages of Bihar around this time.

[5] *The Pioneer*, 1 November 1917. A joint conference of the All-India Congress Committee and the Council of the All-India Muslim League, held at Allahabad on 6 October 1917, had similarly failed to discuss or even take note of the Shahabad riots, which were just then being prominently reported in the press; *Pioneer*, 8 October 1917.

[6] See my 'Encounters and Calamities', in R. Guha, ed., *Subaltern Studies III*, pp. 266–8; also Venkatesh Narain Tewari, *Musalmanon ki Dalit Jatiyan* (Lucknow, 2002 Vikram), p. 3 and *passim*.

On the 'Hindu' side, the important role of cultivating communities like the Ahirs, the Kurmis and the Koeris in the Kisan Sabhas and in Congress-led or supported agitations in the 1920s and 1930s is now well attested.[7] Yet it is notable that in Shahabad, in 1934, precisely these three substantial agricultural communities came together in an unusual (and perhaps unprecedented) 'lower-middle caste' peasant association called the Triveni Sangh to oppose the oppression and the machinations of the upper castes and classes in the area. And in spite of considerable Ahir, Koeri and Kurmi sympathy for and participation in a variety of nationalist agitations during this period, the Shahabad Triveni Sangh, significantly, came out in support of the Government of India's War effort during the Second World War and opposed Gandhi's Quit India movement in 1942.[8] In a word, neither 'nationalism' nor 'communalism' was quite so easily 'made' or so triumphant as historians and others have sometimes assumed.

By the early years of this century, the sense of religious (as of caste) community was far more widespread and more keenly marked than ever before. Pushed by the reform movements, religious debates, administrative demands and, not least, the pressure of census operations and 'representative' politics, élite groups among the Hindus, Muslims, Sikhs and other communities moved quickly to appropriate the marginal groups ('untouchables' came to be classified as unambiguously 'Hindu' for the first time now by Hindu leaders), to purify their domains ('Muslims' must not be contaminated by 'Hindus', and *vice versa*), and to establish their separate identities (among religious communities, most notably in the case of the Sikhs).[9] The temper and pace of 'Hindu', 'Muslim', 'Sikh' and other communities' politics, therefore, greatly increased.

[7] See e.g. M. H. Siddiqi, *Agrarian Unrest in North India* (Delhi, 1978); Kapil Kumar, *Peasants in Revolt* (Delhi, 1984); S. Henningham, *Peasant Movements in Colonial India: North Bihar 1917–42* (Canberra, 1982); Arvind Das, *Agrarian Unrest and Socio-Economic Change in Bihar, 1900–80* (Delhi, 1983); and G. Pandey, ed., *The Indian Nation in 1942* (Calcutta, 1988), chpt. 4 and 5.

[8] Ibid., p. 152.

[9] For the Sikhs, see Khushwant Singh, *A History of the Sikhs*, vol. 2, 1839–1964 (Princeton, 1966); Paul Brass, *Language/Religion and Politics in Northern India*, part IV, and Richard Fox, *Lions of the Punjab*; for the 'untouch-

Nevertheless, as the preceding chapters should have established, 'Hindu' politics, 'Muslim' politics and so on still encompassed the exertions of many disparate castes, classes and local communities, struggling for status, searching for roots, for leadership and for adequate forms of self-expression. Both 'Hindu' and 'Muslim' politics appeared to be made up of makeshift responses to shifting crises, uncertain of long-term political goals, inconsistent and conflict ridden. Élite demands for more seats in education and the services, for simultaneous civil service examinations in India and England, for the preservation of the different literary languages of the 'Hindus' and the 'Muslims' (as it was claimed), seemed far removed from the concerns of the Hindu and Muslim masses; and it was on the basis of many unstable and contradictory demands and agitations that 'Hindu' and 'Muslim' leaders tried to construct united 'Hindu' and 'Muslim' communities in the late nineteenth century and after. Much the same kind of thing might be said for the Indian 'national' community and nationalist politics, to which we will now turn.

II

Along with the attempt to mobilize a wider Hindu community (and a wider Muslim community) in the later nineteenth and early twentieth century went an attempt—in places involving many of the very same men and women—to build up nationalist feeling and nationalist associations that went beyond the confines and concerns of the religious community. Bayly's close study of politics in the Allahabad region between 1880 and 1920 illustrates the point very well indeed.[10] This study draws our attention to the early development of a secular tradition in Allahabad's nationalist

---

ables', Cohn, *An Anthropologist among the Historians*; N. G. Barrier, ed., *Census in British India: New Perspectives* (New Delhi, 1981); Swami Sundarananda, *Hinduism and Untouchability* (1922; 2nd ed., Delhi, 1945); B. R. Ambedkar, *What Congress and Gandhi have done to the Untouchables* (Bombay, 1946).

[10] C. A. Bayly, *The Local Roots of Indian Politics: Allahabad, 1880–1920* (Oxford, 1975). See also Bayly's 1970 Oxford D.Phil. thesis, 'The Development of Political Organisation in the Allahabad Locality, 1880–1925', which contains much useful information on the Allahabad countryside and town-country links.

politics, built up around the towering personality of Ajudhia Nath Kunzru, the 'only leader of national standing' in the local Congress until his death in 1892, and inherited at a later stage by Motilal Nehru and his allies—widely described as 'friends of the Muslims'. But Bayly's work underlines at the same time another, at least equally important dimension of this early nationalist activity.

The author points to the close connections of the radical Congress leadership of the 1910s with 'Hindu sectional interest groups' that had been active for some time before then.[11] He writes of the 'strong conservative and "revivalist" strain in local nationalism during its early years',[12] and illustrates this by referring to the work of the Prayag Hindu Samaj (founded 1880) and the regional Madhya Hindu Samaj (founded 1884), both of which later constituted electorates for the annual sessions of the Congress. The annual sessions of the Madhya Hindu Samaj were held concurrently with the Indian National Congress until 1891 or 1892, he notes: and the Samaj's concerns reflected 'the whole drift of official policy during the 1880s, which had encouraged people to think beyond their localities . . . in the agglomerate categories of Hindu and Muslim. The overriding issues were the propagation of the Hindi [i.e. Devanagri] script and protection of cattle.'[13]

One may generalize the argument from another perspective too. From the earlier decades of the nineteenth century there arose in India Hindu and Muslim movements that were in large part an answer to a colonialism that challenged the validity of the indigenous forms of social existence in virtually every respect.[14] They represented an effort by people at many different levels of the society to overcome the marks of subordination and humiliation that had come with colonial rule. Even those who argued, as many Hindus did, that their decline and hence subordination and humiliation had occurred before the coming of the British, were made

---

[11] Bayly, *Local Roots*, p. 2n.

[12] Ibid., p. 106. Cf. Gould, 'The Emergence of Modern Indian Politics: Political Development in Faizabad, 1884–1935'.

[13] Bayly, *Local Roots*, p. 109.

[14] The Wahabi and the Faraizi movements, and even the later history of the Brahmo Samaj, serve to illustrate this. Cf. also C. F. Andrews remarks in *Swami Dayanand* (Arya Samaj publication, Calicut, 1924).

more acutely aware of their 'fallen' condition by the colonialist 'exposure' and denigration of their history and culture. Among Hindus, as among Muslims, then, the activities not only of religious organizations, traditionalist or reformist, but also of many western-educated 'secular' publicists, amounted to a kind of cultural counter-offensive against the colonialist, and especially missionary, attack on the 'backwardness' and 'barbarism' of Indian life and religion. The Arya Samaj, for instance, appealed most of all to precisely this group of western-educated Hindu Indians, with its statements regarding the advanced level of ancient Hindu civiliza-tion when all of Europe was still running around in bearskins, and its assertions regarding the unmatched 'scientific' temper and incredible scientific achievements of the early inhabitants of Hindustan.[15]

Much of the political activity that developed in the later nine-teenth and early twentieth centuries followed in these tracks, with cultural revival being of central importance in it. In eastern UP, which includes Allahabad and much of the Bhojpuri region, a Hindu revival and politics was rather more in evidence than a Muslim one on account of the relative numerical strength, access to resources and general prominence of the local Hindus. The Cow Protection movement was only one part of the effort made here to mobilize the 'Hindu community' in the last decades of the nineteenth century. Equally significant was the movement to promote a Sanskritized Hindi written in the Devanagri script (as opposed to an increasingly Persianized Urdu written in the Persian script) and the slightly later movement to establish a Hindu Uni-versity in northern India, movements centred on Banaras and Allahabad and linked most prominently perhaps with the names of Bharatendu Harishchandra, 'father of modern Hindi', and Madan Mohan Malaviya, symbol of the national movement in this area until the arrival of Gandhi (and, with him, the Nehrus).[16]

[15]See Swami Dayanand Saraswati's *Satyarth Prakash*; Har Bilas Sarda, *Life of Dayanand Saraswati* (Ajmer, 1946); J.T.F. Jordens, *Dayanand Saraswati: His Life and Ideas* (Delhi, 1978); K. Jones, *Arya Dharma: Hindu Consciousness in Nineteenth Century Punjab* (California, 1976).

[16](NAI) GOI, Home, Pol., Deposit, February 1921, no. 13, Extract from CID Memo no. 1052, dated 7 January 1921, 'Kisan Sabha in Allahabad', comments on how Gandhi had displaced 'the local hero', Malaviyaji. See

What Bayly's study of Allahabad shows is the coexistence in early Indian nationalism of an influential secular strain along with strong community concerns. At one level, the entire study is an attempted reconstruction of the origins of the two major nationalist groups that came to dominate Allahabad politics (and with it, the politics of a much wider tract) in the 1910s and 1920s—the one associated with the 'secular' Motilal Nehru and the other with the 'Hindu' Madan Mohan Malaviya. The author writes of the division that existed, from the very beginning, 'between the secular, and non-communal catch-cries used in the Congress publicity or official pronouncements, and the idiom adopted by their orators'[17]— 'religious migrants' and 'freelance publicists' whose use of emotive symbols and emotive issues like cow-protection was always liable to deepen sectarian attitudes. The point that is underlined is the internally varied character and the diverse roots of early nationalism.[18]

One implication of Bayly's work is that nationalism in India found it tactically necessary to wear two faces. This ambiguity in Indian nationalism has been viewed somewhat differently by others, as the result of an interaction between two idioms which go together to make up the score of the nationalist discourse. One of these is a 'modernist' idiom deriving from the metropolitan culture of the colonizers, the other a 'dharmic' idiom which derived from the pre-colonial traditions of the colonized. 'It is the coalescence of these two idioms and their divergence', writes Ranajit Guha, which determined the tensions and defined the character of the elements that went to make up the relationship of Dominance and Subordination in colonial India.[19] Many of the

---

also J. Nehru, *A Bunch of Old Letters* (Bombay, 1958), B. G. Horniman's letter to Jawaharlal, 1 July 1917 (p. 1), and Motilal to Jawaharlal, 27 February 1920 (p. 6).

[17]Bayly, *Local Roots*, p. 142

[18]This point is well illustrated also by the diversity of speakers found at nationalist meetings in Banaras and Allahabad, Lucknow and Aligarh in the 1880s and 1890s. For a few examples from 1892, see *Report from the Vernacular Newspapers: North-Western Provinces and Oudh, Central Provinces and Rajputana* for the weeks ending 2 November and 9 November 1982.

[19]R. Guha, 'Dominance without Hegemony and its Historiography', in *Subaltern Studies VI* (Delhi, 1989), p. 233. Dipesh Chakrabarty uses the terms

inconsistencies of nationalist discourse in India may be explained, perhaps, in terms of the coming together and contrary pulls of these different idioms.

It seems to me, however, that the internal contradictions of nationalist thought derive from another quarter as well. The discourse of nationalism is part of the post-Enlightenment discourse of modernity, of progress, of human capability: but as a discourse of modernity it bears the distinct marks of an earlier age. Consequently, nationalism has everywhere had a deeply divided relation to 'community'—whether it be the 'pure' Aryan race and language that supposedly constituted the 'natural' community of Germans, or the community/nation of Jews widely scattered throughout the world, or the religious communities of India. On the one hand, nationalism must speak in the language of rationality, of the equality of all individuals, and of 'construction', the possibility of making the world as *we* want it; on the other, it needs the language of blood and sacrifice, of historical necessity, of ancient (God-given) status and attributes—which is part of the discourse of community, as it were, and not of individual rationality.

In Indian political discourse at the end of the nineteenth century, there was yet another interesting peculiarity. Given the history of the subcontinent, its great size and evident diversity, as also the exigencies of colonial rule, the idea of the 'Indian nation'—its contours, its content and meaning—was still, at this time, in its early stages of construction: it was not, by any means, ready-made or fully formed already. At the same time, and somewhat paradoxically, the language of nationhood was the common language of the times at least in élite political circles. This language was used very widely indeed by Indian political leaders—people in very different political positions, with very different perspectives (loyalists as well as nationalists and, for that matter, even British colonialists). As so often in human history, political rhetoric— which plays an important part in moulding consciousness— outstripped political programme and action. This is itself one major

'discourse of civilization' and 'discourse of *dharma*', in his 'Colonial Rule and Domestic Order: "Home" and "Woman" in Bengali Nationalist Thought' (paper presented at workshop on 'Culture, Consciousness and the Colonial State', Isle of Thorns, UK, 23–27 July 1989).

reason why the political discourse of the period appears so confusing and inconsistent.

The relevant question for the historian of nationalism is perhaps this: How was the imagined political community of the future (commonly described by the late nineteenth century in the vocabulary of nationhood) being constructed by Indian nationalists at different times? The answer, I would like to suggest, is that it was *not*, in the earlier stages of the national movement, constructed in the way in which we in India have begun to 'think' the nation since the 1920s and 1930s. Before that time, the nation of Indians was visualized as a composite body, consisting of several communities, each with its own history and culture and its own special contribution to make to the common nationality. India, and the emerging Indian nation, was conceived of as a collection of communities: Hindu + Muslim + Christian + Parsi + Sikh, and so on.

Sometime around the 1920s this vision was substantially altered, and India came to be seen very much more as a collection of individuals, of Indian 'citizens'. The difference between these two positions was quite fundamental: and it is my contention that it was in the context of the change from one to the other that the concept of communalism was fully articulated. In other words, communalism and nationalism as we know them today came to acquire their present signification in the 1920s or thereabouts, to a large extent in opposition to one another, and in response to far-reaching changes that were occurring in the national movement as well as in the way in which Indian nationalism was being constructed.

None of this is to suggest that there were no intimations of a secularist, citizen-based nationalism before the 1920s or survival of a community-based conception of nationalism after that decade. Quite the contrary, as the whole history of our national movement and the disturbing developments of the last ten years serve to demonstrate. But it *is* to underscore the importance of the change that occurred around that time, and of the new contention within the discourse of nationalism that was then established.

III

For the later nineteenth century, at least, it is possible to describe 'community' and 'country' as the watchwords of nationalist politics, if not of all 'modern' politics in India.[20] If subjection to a single colonial regime constituted the *raison d'etre*, the for-long-unspoken ground of Indian nationalism, 'living in the same country' constituted the openly voiced, the fundamental basis of nationhood—and this was a perception that was shared by loyalists and nationalists alike. As Syed Ahmad Khan put it on several occasions in the first phase of his political career (up to the early 1880s), 'the word *qaum* ("people" or "nation") . . . is used for the inhabitants (*bashandun*) of a country.' 'Hindu and Muslim, are merely religious terms—the Hindus, the Muslims, and even the Christians constitute one nation by virtue of living in the same country.' Or as Gandhi put it in *Hind Swaraj*, 'The Hindus, the Mohamedans, the Parsis and the Christians who have made India their country are fellow countrymen'.[21]

Sometimes the communities that went to make up the nation were stretched or redefined in regional or even caste terms. But the basic proposition remained unaltered. The 'communities' (religious or other) together constituted the nation; and service to Community went together with, and indeed to a large extent implied, service to Country. Let me return for a moment to Madan Mohan Malaviya's career which so clearly demonstrates this proposition. Malaviya's range of activities is indicated by his establishment of major newspapers like the *Leader* and *Abhyudaya*;

[20]As already indicated, terms like 'nation' and 'community' were used ambiguously, and interchangeably, in Hindi, Bengali, etc., as well as in English, in the later nineteenth century. Noting this for Bengal, Sudipto Kaviraj writes: 'There is, remarkably, a great tentativeness, provisionality about this people [or nation] (*jati*)', 'Imaginary History', pp. 14, 16. While this is surely correct, it is equally remarkable how widespread the notion was, among Indian writers and politicians by the turn of the century, that India was one country and its people (by some definition) a nation.

[21]Hafeez Malik, 'Sir Sayyid Ahmad Khan's Contribution to the Development of Moslem Nationalism in India', *MAS*, 4, 2 (1970), pp. 137–8; M. K. Gandhi, *Hind Swaraj*, in S. Narayan, ed., *Selected Works of Mahatma Gandhi*, vol. 4 (Ahmedabad, 1968), p. 136.

his educational concerns reflected in the Hindu Boarding House at Allahabad (which 'created a nucleus of students drawn from all over northern India, Bengal, and Maharashtra' and soon became a centre of Extremist politics) and his life's work, the Banaras Hindu University (BHU); his attempts to promote 'Hindi, Hindu, Hindustan' through the Prayag Hindu Samaj, the Sanatan Dharma sabhas, the all-India Hindu Mahasabha and the Indian National Congress.[22]

Malaviya said of the Hindu Samaj established in Allahabad in the 1880s that its purpose was 'to encourage the unlift of the Hindus, to nurture their self-dependence, and to present a strong face to their enemies'.[23] But his political vision was obviously very much wider. Thus he wrote in 1905:

हिन्दुस्तान में अब केवल हिन्दू ही नहीं बसते हैं—हिन्दुस्तान अब केवल उन्हीं का देश नहीं है । हिन्दुस्तान जैसे हिन्दुओं का प्यारा जन्म-स्थान है, वैसे ही मुसलमानों का भी है । ये दोनों जातियाँ [24] अब यहाँ बसती हैं और सदा बसी रहेंगी । . . . इन दोनों जातियों में और भारत की सब जातियों—हिन्दू, मुसलमान, ईसाई, पारसी—में सच्ची प्रीति और भाइयों जैसा स्नेह स्थापित करना हम सब का बड़ा कर्तव्य है ।

(It is not the Hindus alone who now live in Hindustan. Hindustan is no longer exclusively their country. Just as Hindustan is the beloved birth place of the Hindus, so it is of the Muslims too. Both these communities now live here and will always live here. . . . To establish real affection and brotherly love among these two communities and all the communities of India—Hindu, Muslim, Christian, Parsi—is the greatest duty before us all.)[25]

Or again, speaking in the Imperial Legislative Council on the introduction of the BHU Bill in March 1915, Malaviya declared that BHU would be a denominational but not a sectarian institution.

Instruction in the truths of religion, whether it would be Hindus or Musalmans [*sic*], whether it be imparted to the students of the Banaras Hindu University or the Aligarh Muslim University, will tend to produce men who, if they are true to their religion, will be true to their God, their

---

[22]Bayly, *Local Roots*, pp. 180–1.

[23]Sitaram Chaturvedi, *Mahamana Pandit Madan Mohan Malaviya* (Varanasi 1936), p. 29, cited in ibid., p. 108.

[24]The use of the word *jati* for 'community' as well as 'nation', 'caste', etc., is characteristic of the period; see n. 20 above.

[25]Padmakant Malaviya, *Malaviyaji ke Lekh* (Delhi 1962), pp. 24–5.

King and their country.... I look forward to the time when the students who will pass out of such Universities will meet each other in a closer embrace as *sons of the same Motherland* than they do at present.[26]

Lala Lajpat Rai summed up this approach to nationalism in the following words as late as 1920: 'The Indian nation, such as it is or such as we intend to build [it], neither is nor will be exclusively Hindu, Muslim, Sikh or Christian. *It will be each and all.* That is my goal of nationhood.'[27] The broad parameters of this vision of Indian history and society appear to have been shared by a wide variety of politicians and publicists, Muslim and Hindu, Moderate as well as Extremist. Hence Syed Ahmad Khan's image of the Hindus and Muslims as the 'two eyes' of the 'beautiful bride' that was India appears alongside Pratap Narain Misra's metaphor of 'the two arms of Mother India' and the Moderate Congress leader, Bishan Narayan Dar's 'two indestructible factors of Indian nationality'.[28] This vision seems to have been shared by many whose political stance would be formally described as being 'loyalist'. Some of the ambiguity in Sir Syed Ahmad Khan's position itself indicates this. But let me illustrate the point more fully with another example from the Bhojpuri region, that of Bharatendu Harishchandra, the outstanding Hindi litterateur of the later nineteenth century.[29]

[26] *Speeches and Writings of Pandit Madan Mohan Malaviya* (G.A. Natesan & Co., Madras, n.d.), pp. 270–1. The conception of service to Country through Community is also illustrated well by Gandhi's 1911 support for a mosque in London and a Muslim University in Aligarh. Such a university, 'if properly conducted can only advance the cause of unity between the two great sections of the population of India'; *Indian Opinion*, 20–5–1911 (*CWMG XI*, p. 83). Five months later, reporting that Muslims and Parsis had come forward to support the Durban Hindus in their protest against a ban on fire-crackers at Diwali, Gandhi saw this as the way to build national unity. Muslims must come forward to 'sympathize with Hindus in what concerns the latter alone', Hindus likewise with other communities, and so on; *Indian Opinion*, 28–10–1911 (ibid., p. 175).

[27]P. Nagar, *Lala Lajpat Rai: The Man and His Ideas* (Delhi, 1977), p. 175.

[28]A. M. Zaidi, ed., *Congress Presidential Addresses. vol. 2, 1901–11* (Delhi, 1986), p. 479; Vijayshankar Mall, ed., *Pratapnarain Granthavali Pt. I*, p. 181.

[29]The following paragraphs owe a great deal to Sudhir Chandra's pioneering work on the social and political consciousness of Bharatendu Harish-

Bharatendu was a man of independent means who was born in a loyalist family which had protected British property in Banaras during the Mutiny of 1857. He was appointed an Honorary Magistrate at an early age, and became a prominent participant in a whole range of official functions and celebrations in Banaras in the 1870s and 1880s until his death in 1884. Nevertheless Bharatendu became an early critic of the drain of wealth to England, a strong advocate of swadeshi, a rediscoverer and historian of the Indian past, and a deeply concerned, even anguished, commentator on the country's existing subject condition. At the same time, he was a leader of the agitation to promote what he saw as the real indigenous language and script of northern India (Hindi in the Nagri script), as against Urdu and the Persian script (both of which he considered foreign); he was a believer in the need for a 'pure Hindu' university and a fervent advocate of cow protection.[30]

An examination of the argument put forward in Bharatendu's renowned Ballia lecture in 1884, 'भारतवर्ष की उन्नति कैसे हो सकती है' (How Can India Progress?) will perhaps suffice to indicate the character of his political thought. The full text of this address is reproduced in Appendix II. Here I shall refer only to the main points of the argument found in it. Bharatendu makes much of the opportunity offered by British rule to enable his countrymen and women to awaken, take their future in their own hands, and march forward to recapture a lost glory. 'Run!' he says, for whoever falls behind

---

chandra and his contemporaries, shortly to be published by OUP, New Delhi.

[30]The following comments on the cow question, contained in a letter to Babu Ramdin Singh, are typical:

अब की बकरीद में भारतवर्ष के प्रायः अनेक नगरों में मुसलमानों ने प्रकाश रूप से जो गोबध किया है इससे हिन्दुओं की सब प्रकार से जो मान हानि हुई है वह अकथनीय है । पालिसी परतन्त्र गवर्नमेंट पर हिन्दुओं की अकिंचितकरता और मुसलमानों की उग्रता भलीभांति विदित है यही कारण है कि जानबूझ कर भी वह कुछ नहीं बोलती, किन्तु हम लोगों की जो भारत वर्ष में हिन्दुओं के ही वीर्य से उत्पन्न हैं ऐसे अवसर पर गवर्नमेंट के कान खोलने का उपाय अवश्य करणीय है । इस हेतु आपसे इस पत्र द्वारा निवेदन है कि जहां तक हो सके इस विषय में प्रयल कीजिए । भागलपुर, मिरजापुर , काशी इत्यादि कई स्थानो में प्रकाशयरूप से केवल हमारा जी दुखाने को हांकाठोकी यह अत्याचार हुआ है जो किसी समाचारपत्र में प्रकाश भी हुआ है । आप भी अपने पत्र में इस विषय का भलीभांति आन्दोलन कीजिए । सब पत्र एक साथ कोलाहल करेंगे तब काम चलेगा । हिन्दी, उर्दू, बंगाली, मराठी, अंग्रेजी सब भाषा के पत्रों में जिनके संपादक हिन्द् हों एक बैर बड़े धूम से इसका आंदोलन होना अवश्य है, आशा है कि अपने शंका भर आप इस विषय में कोई बात उठा न रखेंगे ।

—(*Bharatendu Samagra,* p. 1077)

in this race is lost forever. 'फिर कब राम जनकपुर ऐहैं।'. (When will there be such an opportunity again?)

The argument is in fact advanced with remarkable vehemence. The writer speaks of his as an exceptional age in which western education and the inventions of science have opened up untold opportunities, and the old and the young are all racing forward, struggling to be the first to reach the heights of modernity. At this time, he notes with bitterness, the 'Hindu Kathiawadis' (here, probably meaning people made of wood) are standing by idly, 'digging the ground with their toes'. They are not ashamed to see that even the midget Japanese '*tattoos*' [i.e., ponies] have joined the race, and are panting as they run. The times are such that whoever is left behind now will never be able to catch up again.[31] And further, he says, if even under the rule of the British we remain trapped like frogs in a well, then we deserve all that we suffer.

Bharatendu urges his audience to give up superstition, belief in so-called learned men, pandits and mahatmas, to exert themselves, reform society and work for the welfare of every section of the nation (women, the old, the poor, and people of every caste). Dharma (religion, a religious life) is 'the source of all progress. Hence it is dharma that must first be advanced/elevated'. But there is a difference between 'true religion' and 'social religion'. The sincere worship of God, he says, is all that constitutes true religion. Fairs, festivals, fasts and other such rituals—all these are part of

---

[31]In one of his poems, Bharatendu had written (ibid., pp. 253–4):

रोम-ग्रीस पुनि निज बल पायो ।
   सब बिधि भारत दुखित बनायो ।
अति निरबली स्याम जापाना ।
   हाय न भारत तिनहुँ समाना ।

(Rome and Greece have found their strength again, [only] India remains prostrate in every respect.

Alas! [today] she cannot even match

   Exceptionally weak Siam Thailand and Japan).

Partha Chatterjee informs me that the same kind of reference to 'backward' Japan occurs in Bengali patriotic poems written in the Swadeshi period, the occasion for this being provided by Japan's military victory over Russia in 1904.

'social religion' which may be changed according to the changing needs and circumstances of the country.

Bharatendu next appeals for unity among people of all sects, religions and castes. The Vaishnavas, the Shaktas and others, people of diverse sects and persuasions must bury the hatchet. This is not the time for discord. Hindus, Jains, Musalmans must all unite.

Addressing his 'Muslim brothers', he says that it is necessary (literally, 'proper') that, living in Hindustan, they should stop thinking of the Hindus as inferior and should instead relate to them exactly as brothers do. They should give up practices that hurt the feelings of the Hindus. Many Muslim brothers, in his view, believe that the thrones of Delhi and Lucknow still survive. 'Friends! Those days are gone. It is time to bid farewell to laziness and intransigence. Come, join the Hindus [in the race for progress] for two are stronger than one.'

To his 'Hindu brothers' he says: 'Brother Hindus! You too must give up your insistence on minute details of belief and practice. Promote fellowship among all [who live here], and recite the following mantra. Whosoever lives in Hindustan, of whatever colour or caste he may be, is a Hindu.[32] Help the Hindus. Bengalis, Marathas, Panjabis, Madrasis, Vaidiks, Jains, Brahmos, Musalmans should all join hands.'

Finally, Bharatendu appeals to his countrymen and countrywomen to undertake such work as will generate wealth within the country and increase its industry. Your wealth flows to England,

---

[32]The point has been made that such an expansive use of the term Hindu was essentially communal; Sudhir Chandra, 'Communal Elements in Late Nineteenth-Century Hindi Literature', *Journal of Arts and Ideas*, no. 6 (1984), p. 12. While this argument has force in the context in which it is made, one may note that in the nineteenth century, the meanings and usages of such terms were still very fluid, so that Syed Ahmad Khan used the term 'Hindu' for 'the inhabitants of Hindustan' in a lecture in Lahore in the same year as Bharatendu's Ballia lecture, 1884; see *A History of the Hindu-Muslim Problem in India. From the Earliest Contacts Upto its Present Phase With Suggestions for its Solution. Being the Report of the Committee appointed by the Indian National Congress (Karachi Session 1931) to enquire into the Cawnpore Riots of March 1931* (Allahabad, 1933)—hereafter *Congress Kanpur Riots Enquiry*—p. 163; and Hafeez Malik, *Sir Sayyid Ahmad Khan and Muslim Modernization in India and Pakistan* (New York, 1980), p. 245.

France, Germany, America by a thousand routes, he says. Even an object as trifling as a matchstick is imported from there. There is no time to be lost. 'Brothers! Now at least, you must arise, and do all you can for the progress of the country. Read only those books, play only those games, have only those conversations that advance your interests [i.e. the interests of your country]. Give up the use of foreign goods and a foreign language. Fight for the progress of your country through your own language.'[33]

What was Bharatendu Harishchandra's answer, then, to the question of how India can progress? Social reform, swadeshi, hard and purposeful effort, and unity among all sects, castes and religions. It was a programme to which all nationalists in India, even in the twentieth century, could have subscribed. One difference from the militant nationalism of later days, however, was the extraordinary encomiums that Bharatendu showered on the British, the paeans of praise for the new opportunities brought by British rule, or as one might say, the evident loyalism of the text.[34] There was another feature that marked off his political vision from that of at least a substantial section of later nationalists. This was the underlying assumption that India was constituted, both historically and socially, by given communities called the Hindus and the Muslims—a view that colonialist researches and writings from the eighteenth century, and more especially in the nineteenth century, had done much to promote, and one that nationalists in the twentieth century would increasingly challenge.

An even more crucial difference with this section of later nationalists emerges from the totality of Bharatendu's work. For Bharatendu, the interests of Indian nationalism necessitated also

---

[33]The importance attached to language by Bharatendu was in line with many other incipient nationalist statements in India around this time. For Bankimchandra Chattopadhyaya's emphasis on a people's own language, see R. Guha, *An Indian Historiography of India: A Nineteenth-Century Agenda and its Implications* (Calcutta, 1988).

[34]The phrase is Ranajit Guha's, ibid., p. 54. Bharatendu himself wrote:

हम . . . स्वभावसिध्द राजभक्त हैं . . . राजभक्ति भरतखंड की मिट्टी का सहज गुण और कर्तव्य धर्म है. . .;

Bharatendu Samagra, p. 224. For a few other examples of Bharatendu's loyalist statements, see ibid., pp. 216, 470, 732.

the advance of 'Hindi, Hindu, Hindustan', to use the words of a slogan (or mantra) coined by his younger contemporary and literary disciple, Pratap Narain Misra.[35] This points to another paradox in early nationalist thought that requires some further consideration, before we return to the theme of the common ground of modern Indian political thought in the late nineteenth century and the prescriptions that flowed from it.

IV

If Bharatendu Harishchandra was an uncertain nationalist at best, there were other, more clearly established nationalist figures in the later nineteenth century—including more than a few Moderate leaders—who argued, like him, for the need to build up Hindu unity and strength even as they argued for Hindu-Muslim unity, and for the need to cement Hindu unity precisely in order to develop an Indian national unity. Many of them suggested also that the period of Muslim rule that had existed before the coming of the British had more than a little to do with bringing about this Hindu decline and disunity. As a consequence, there was a distinctly anti-Muslim tone in the writings of some even of the most supposedly advanced and secular sections of the Hindu nationalist intelligentsia in the last quarter of the nineteenth century. Let me try to demonstrate these propositions by reference to the work of two prominent Moderate leaders of this period, both of whom served as Presidents of the Indian National Congress—one from UP, Bishan Narayan Dar, a Lucknow lawyer, social reformer, Urdu poet and known 'friend of the Muslims' who was President of the Congress in 1911; and the other from Bengal, the renowned economic historian, 'Victorian Liberal' and progressive nationalist Romesh Chunder Dutt.

Dar was among the leading élite nationalist politicians of UP who were drawn into the debate on cow protection and the Cow Protection movement in the 1890s, as we have already noticed. I have referred in earlier chapters to his *Appeal to the English Public on behalf of the Hindus of the N.W.P. and Oudh*, produced in the

[35]See Sudhir Chandra, 'Communal Elements in Late nineteenth-century Hindi Literature'.

aftermath of the Hindu-Muslim riots in Azamgarh at the Baqr-Id of 1893. McLane uses this document to make the point that even liberal and 'non-communal' Congress leaders identified themselves with the 'Hindu' cause in this moment of crisis. 'Apparently the pressures within Hindu society [at this juncture] overcame even the least communal of Congress leaders who generally failed to speak out against the [cow-] protection movement.'[36] A closer look at Dar's *Appeal*, however, suggests that this kind of statement involved more than a mere concession to Hindu communalist pressure.

There are several standard arguments advanced by Dar which are common to the developing nationalist discourse of the later nineteenth century and are also found in the writings of Bharatendu Harishchandra. Dar notes the merits of the pre-colonial ('Mohamedan') regime, in spite of his assumption regarding the overall advantages of British rule. 'The rule which the present Government has supplanted was personal and despotic... but it had some merits which the British rule lacks. It was *the Government of Indians by Indians*; in other words, the Government was composed of those who knew the wants and requirements of the subject people' (*Appeal*, pp. 24–5).[37] 'The Mohamedan Government respected Hindu prejudices' (p. 18). Dar suggests that officials under India's pre-colonial governments came 'daily and hourly' into contact with the people. This made for a means of communication between rulers and ruled that went far to redeem 'the follies, the corruptions of the Mohamedan *regime*'. The British government in India, he goes on to say, 'is the opposite pole of this. It is *a Caste Government*, living *in perfect isolation* from, and in blessed ignorance of the subject race' (pp. 24–5).

But, again in common with Bharatendu and the whole range of

---

[36]McLane, *Indian Nationalism and the Early Congress*, p. 308. The statement refers to Ganga Prasad Verma, another leading Lucknow Congressman and close associate of Dar's. Verma accompanied Dar on his 'fact-finding' mission to Azamgarh, and they wrote a joint report after their visit clearing the Cow Protection societies of blame for the riots.

[37]The page numbers in parentheses in this and the following paragraphs refer to the English text of Dar's *Appeal to the English Public on Behalf of the Hindus of the N.W.P. and Oudh*. Emphases are mine, except where otherwise stated.

moderate nationalists of the late nineteenth century, Dar remains at bottom a believer in the providential good sense of British rule. And to sustain this belief he makes a sharp distinction between the government of the Queen-Empress and the government of British officials in India, between the British Parliament on the one hand and the 'Civil Service clique' on the other. 'At present in the Azamgarh District, the Government of the Queen-Empress does not exist, but the Government of Sir Charles Crosthwaite [Lieutenant-Governor of the North-Western Provinces and Awadh]; and therefore the authorities there can justly [*sic.*] and lawfully pit class against class and persecute the Hindus'. And again: 'Beneath all the showy liberalism and impartiality of the Indian Government there lies hidden the selfish spirit of the Civilian sect... even so, a general inquiry into the hidden principles of Anglo-Indian polity, held under the searching glance of the British Parliament, will detect, I am sure, those vices of the Civil Service rule, which have brought on us "all our woe"' (p. 32) Much as Bharatendu had said in an address to the 'beloved' Prince of Wales in 1877; 'We are by nature loyalists. How would the miserable Englishmen who make up the subordinate bureaucracy know anything about our character; they spend their time in trying to feather their nests'.[38]

It is the central proposition of Dar's *Appeal to the English Public* that the policy of 'Divide and Rule', initiated and promoted by the local colonial officials, is producing disastrous consequences for Indian society, and that the British people will live to rue the day when their official representatives adopted this policy in India. He holds the local representatives of the colonial regime 'wholly and solely' responsible for the 1893 riots (p. 3). Not these riots alone, 'all the religious disturbances of the last 10 or 12 years... are the first fruit of the policy of "Divide and Rule" which the Anglo-Indian bureaucracy has adopted in this country' (p. 1). 'Our present rulers have forgotten the lesson of Akbar and have adopted the policy of Aurangzib. But the policy of Aurangzib can end only in one way. Akbar founded and consolidated the Empire; Aurangzib shattered it to pieces. The conciliating policy of the one made the Hindus devoted supporters of the Mogul throne; the religious

[38]*Bharatendu Samagra*, p. 224.

fanaticism of the other produced the Mahratta power and sealed the doom of the Empire' (p. 23).

But Dar's concern is not limited to the fate of the British empire in India. He is even more deeply concerned to preserve the 'great fabric of Hindu and Mohamedan union' (p. 31) which colonial policies are tending to tear apart. Should the 'fabric of our civilization' be destroyed and social disorganization supervene, and the government of the country become an unprofitable business, he notes, the British will simply pack up their bags and leave. 'But we shall be ruined, the forces which will destroy our unity will destroy our society and seal the fate of our progress' (p. 30). The Muslims 'are bone of our bone and flesh of our flesh', declares Dar. 'They have lived with the Hindus for centuries, they have made India their home: ... The natural feelings of both communities are beyond doubt those of friendliness and mutual accord; but the British Government is by its short-sighted and selfish policy working a mischievous change in them' (p. 23).

Dar goes to some lengths to describe the political and cultural achievements, the qualities of head and heart, of those Muslims 'who have left their mark on Europe'. These were the ancestors of the Muslims who conquered India; and like the Muslim conquerors of south-western Europe and West Asia, the Muslim ruling class in pre-colonial India 'cultivated learning and art and made toleration one of the principal features of their policy'. Even under a despotic and military regime, and at a time when the 'religious spirit was much stronger than it is now', they practised religious tolerance. In colonial India, Dar observes, the Muslims have become 'poor' and 'backward in education': 'but their nature is not changed; they have not forgotten their ancient history, they have not altogether lost those qualities which made them rulers of men' (pp. 21–3).

It is in this context that we must consider Dar's comment on the Indian National Congress as 'the political movement of modern India' (p. 13) and note that the language of 'us' and 'them' which appears all the time in his discussion of the relations between Hindus and Muslims carries over into his remarks on the Congress and its politics. Since Dar speaks on behalf of 'the Hindus', the use of this language has a certain validity in his discussion of Hindu-Muslim relations: the Muslims 'are bone of *our* bone'; '*they* have lived with the Hindus for centuries, *they* have made India their home'. But from the standpoint of 'the political movement of modern India', the division between 'us' and 'them' is surely unacceptable when Dar comes to write about relations between Congress and 'the Muslims'. However, the division is made. It is the object of the Congress, writes Dar, 'to unite, not to divide the two races'. This is in answer to the colonialist charge that the Congress was behind the Cow-Protection movement and the strife that flowed from it. Pursuing this line of thought, he goes on to say that none of the propaganda of the government or its unofficial agents would 'shake *our* confidence in the good sense and patriotism of the Mohamedan community', or diminish 'the regard and affection' in which '*we* hold *it*' (p. 113). Here the Congress unwittingly becomes 'non-Muslim' (Hindu?) and the 'Mohamedan community' somehow external to it.

Another point that will have emerged even from the few extracts quoted above is that Dar invariably uses the form 'Hindus' and 'Mohamedans', suggesting a unity among Hindus and Muslims, the existence of interests common to all members of each community, and a common 'Hindu' and 'Muslim' perception of this identity of interests, as though these were, somehow, given from the very beginning. He speaks of a time when 'the Hindus' had greater 'national spirit' in them than they have now; of 'the Mohamedans who [uniformly] still feel the touch of the vanished hand of the Mogul Emperor'; and of the change that has come over 'the fortunes of the Mohamedans of India' (pp. 20, 22). He writes of the persecution of 'the Hindus' in the aftermath of the 1893 riots. 'The zeal of persecuting the Hindus has... overpowered the sense of justice' of the government of the North-Western provinces and Awadh (p. 10). 'In the Azamgarh district *a large number of respectable Hindus have left their villages out of fear and gone to some other districts.* Hundreds of families have been ruined; all business is stopped, and the Hindus are left, mere helpless, hopeless victims to the malice of the ignorant and injured Mohamedans and the greed and oppression of the Police' (p. 11, emphasis Dar's). 'I have seen the Hindus of the Azamgarh district lately. . . . *Terror and despair* are depicted in their faces and for the present they do not feel that they are in a land which they may call their own'

(p. 12, emphasis Dar's). And further: '[The Hindus] are doubtless a very quiet, orderly, and law-abiding people; their religious teachings are against all sorts of aggression. . .; but meekness and forbearance have their limits; . . . a spirit of sullen discontent and disquietude is beginning to rise among them, and may one day burst. . . forth with the force of pent up waters . . .' (pp. 28–9).

Dar condemns what he calls the colonial policy of favouring the 'Muslims' against the 'Hindus', and vice versa, in precisely the same terms. 'There was a time when Hindus were the favoured class, and Mohamedans were treated with contempt. . . . When the Star of the Mohamedans rose, that of the Hindus began to set' (p. 20). He goes on to warn his 'Mohamedan fellow subjects' (p. 12) against reposing too much faith in the sympathy and goodwill of the colonial regime. 'The Anglo-Indian Government is no particular friend of the Mohamedans . . . [and] no particular enemy of the Hindus.' Self-interest had induced the government to turn first to one 'community', and then to the other. 'The moment its [current] self-interest is served it would throw away the Mohamedans like squeezed oranges [sic] and turn to the Hindus' (pp. 20–1).

Let me recapitulate the argument as it has appeared thus far. The use of the language of 'us' and 'them' is a feature of Dar's discourse on the existing state of Hindu-Muslim relations. In spite of this and in spite of his emphasis on the difference between 'Hindu' and 'Muslim' character, this discourse is marked also by an urge to bring 'Hindus' and 'Muslims' together. Nothing that the British government or its agents do will 'shake our confidence in the . . . patriotism of the Mohamedan community' or affect the 'regard and affection' between 'Hindu community' and 'Muslim community'. The Muslims should realize, too, that the favour of the British is self-interested and usually short-lived, based entirely on the regime's calculation of its own best interests. Therefore, Hindus and Muslims must come together to demand the kinds of policies that are needed for the welfare of the country. 'Whenever India becomes one nation and it becomes difficult to get Indians to rise against their own countrymen, the present despotic form of rule will cease to exist . . .' (p. 19).

There is more to this question of bringing the 'Hindus' and

'Muslims' together to build one nation, however. In the case of the Hindus at least, Dar's *Appeal* represents an acknowledgement that this widely dispersed and diversified community still needs to be united—through political struggle, education and so on. Recall his observation that 'the Hindus' had once displayed more 'national spirit' than they displayed now (p. 22). Dar condemns, too, the persecution by the colonial government of 'those who are known to be concerned with movements calculated to unite the Hindu race more firmly than ever' (p. 10). It is in this context that he discovers a silver lining even in the riots of 1893 and the 'persecution' of the Hindus that ensued.

The riots and the persecutions which have followed upon them will go far to bind the Hindu community together more firmly then ever.... By passing through the burning ordeals of political persecution, the diverse sections of Hindus, the heterogeneous elements of east and west and north and south will be fused into one homogeneous whole, strong enough to *take care of itself and* to meet the effects of any disintegrating policy which Anglo-Indian officialdom may adopt towards *this country* (pp. 29–30, emphasis added).

'Hindu unity', like 'Muslim unity', appears to be a pre-requisite, in Dar's mind, for a larger national unity and for protecting the country as a whole from the worst consequences of colonial rule. A very similar position is found in the writings of R. C. Dutt, the second example that we take up in this section. We remember Dutt today chiefly as the economic historian of Indian nationalism, as we should. But, as Sudhir Chandra has recently reminded us,[39] there were other important dimensions to his political and intellectual career. Dutt was a novelist who wrote in the 1870s what might be called a 'Hindu Raj Quartet'—*Banga Vijeta, Madhavi Kankan, Maharashtra Jivan Prabhat* and *Rajput Jivan Sandhya*— stories of the rise of Maratha glory, the decline of the Rajputs and resistance to 'foreign' (i.e. Muslim) rule. In a later novel *Sansar* (published in Bengali in 1886, and then translated by Dutt into English and published under the title, *The Lake of Palms*, in 1902), he appears consciously to have erased the anti-Muslim tenor of

[39]Sudhir Chandra, 'The Cultural Complement of Economic Nationalism: R. C. Dutt's *The Lake of Palms', Indian Historical Review*, XII, 1–2, pp. 106–120.

his earlier, historical novels. But glimpses of the author's pride in the Hindu past—with all that this might imply in the contemporary political situation—remained even in this novel.[40]

Dutt was also, of course, and in his own mind most importantly, a historian of early India. And pride in the Hindu past is the guiding principle of the *History of Civilization in Ancient India*, written at the end of the 1880s, when the Indian National Congress had already been established and the question of Hindu and Muslim participation in nationalist politics had already emerged as an important public issue. 'For the Hindu student the history of the Hindu period should not be a blank, nor a confused jumble of historic and legendary names, religious parables, and Epic and Puranic myths. No study has so potent an influence in forming a nation's mind and a nation's character as a critical and careful study of its past history . . .', he wrote in the Preface to volume I of his *History*, dated 13 August 1888.[41] There was, then, a clear nationalist, political purpose to this 'critical history'. This purpose was reiterated two years later when the Preface to volume II came to be written.

Dutt took the opportunity offered by the writing of this Preface to answer the criticism, advanced by colonialist reviewers, that volume I of his *History* had described all that was 'robust and manly' in the Vedic Hindus but left out their 'coarseness and imperfections'. He had not done any such thing by design, Dutt wrote, but 'I confess that, like most modern Hindus, subject to all the drawbacks of a later and more artificial civilization, I feel a warm appreciation for the *manly freedom* of ancient Hindu civilization and life'. Both for the Vedic and later periods, he added, 'I have not hesitated to point out emphatically and repeatedly how much we lack in all that was healthy and free, unrestricted and life-giving in the ancient

---

[40]Ibid. One of the passages that Sudhir Chandra points out as indicative of Dutt's continuing Hindu pride does not, in fact, appear in the Bengali version of this novel. It appears to have been borrowed from a well-known novel of Bankim's—such borrowing being not at all unusual in the world of later nineteenth-century Bengali literature—and inserted by Dutt into the English version of his novel. I am indebted to Tanika Sarkar for this finding and for her general observations on the literature of the period.

[41]R. C. Dutt, *A History of Civilization in Ancient India. Based on Sanskrit Literature* (People's edn., Calcutta, 1899), vol. I, p. xv.

Hindu institutions and social rules. It is a truth which we Hindus need bear in mind.'[42]

If the argument presented so far is scarcely surprising as a part of the historiographical awakening of a subject people, Dutt's *History* had in it a rather more curious element. His declaration of Hindu pride represented not only an assertion of Indian greatness in the past, as against the denigration of Indian society by the colonialists. It had in it also a strong expression of regret at the decline of Hindu civilization (= India?), which he dated from the establishment of Muslim rule in northern India. In volume I Dutt accepted the characterization of the period 800–1000 A.D. as the 'Dark Ages' in northern India.[43] Alberuni's description of India at the end of that period, he wrote in volume II, leaves a sad impression on the 'Hindu' mind.

Great is the penalty which the Hindus have paid for their caste disunion and their political weakness. For six centuries after 1200 A.D., the history of the Hindus is a blank. They were the only Aryan nation in the earth who were civilized four thousand years ago; they are the only Aryan nation in the earth who are socially lifeless and politically prostrate in the present day.[44]

The statement here is not explicitly anti-Muslim, but might not the association of 'Hindu' decline with 'Muslim' rule amount to the same thing?

Dutt goes on, immediately after this statement, to talk about the signs of reviving life after 'six centuries of national lifelessness', and it is again worth quoting him at some length. 'There is a struggle

[42]Ibid., vol. II, p. VIII (emphasis added). Cf. Surendranath Banerjea, 'The study of the history of our own country furnishes the strongest incentive to the loftiest patriotism. I ask, what Hindu is there who does not feel himself a nobler being altogether, as he recalls to mind the proud list of his illustrious countrymen, graced by the thrice immortal names of a Valmiki and a Vyasa, a Panini and a Patanjali, a Gautam and a Sankaracharya? I ask, what Hindu is there whose patriotism is not stimulated, whose self-respect is not increased, as he contemplates the past history of his country? For ours was a most glorious past'; *Speeches and Writings of Hon. Surendra Nath Banerjea. Selected by Himself* (Madras, G. A. Natesan & Co., n.d.), p. 3.

[43]Dutt, *Ancient India*, I, p. 25.

[44]Ibid., II, pp. XI and 333–4.

in the land', he writes, 'to go beyond the dead forms of religion, and to recover what is pure, nourishing, life-giving. There is an effort to create a social union which is the basis of national union. There are beginnings of a national consciousness among the people.' This surely is a statement about the new social basis created (by common subjection to colonial rule?) for a new kind of composite nationalism. But Dutt stays with the metaphor of an ancient body being rejuvenated.

It may be England's high privilege to *restore* to an ancient nation a new and healthy life. . . . And if the science and learning, the sympathy and example of modern Europe help us to *regain* in some measure a national consciousness and life, Europe will have rendered back to modern India that kindly help and sisterly service which India rendered to Europe in ancient days—in religion, science and civilization.[45]

An 'ancient nation' rejuvenated, a new 'social union' as the basis of 'national union', and out of all this the 'beginnings of national consciousness'. In Romesh Chunder Dutt, as in Bishan Narayan Dar, the unity of all Hindus forms a necessary part of the process of building the unity of all Indians—conceived by both of them as being represented in the union of Hindus and Muslims.

V

I have said practically nothing so far about the perceptions of the Muslim political leadership in northern India during this period. It can be nobody's argument that the kind of vision and programme outlined in the preceding section squared comfortably with the political visions and hopes of non-Hindu publicists and politicians who were active at the time. Yet, as I have already suggested, there remained an important area of common concern and effort among all those who had begun to speak the language of nationalism or aspired to do so. It will help to say a little more at least about some of those prominent Muslim figures who were in this position.

It is evident that a slogan like 'Urdu, Muslim, Hindustan' would come less easily to a Muslim publicist in India than its equivalent of 'Hindi, Hindu, Hindustan' came to many Hindu leaders and writers at the turn of the century. This was not only because Islam,

[45]Ibid., II, p. 334.

unlike Hinduism, was not coterminous with India. In Muhammad Ali's well-known words, the problem facing the Muslim leader in India at the turn of the century was that he could not but be aware of belonging to two circles which were not concentric—that of Islam and that of Hindustan.

There were other reasons, too, for the difference in Hindu and Muslim positions. From the time that W.W. Hunter's *Indian Musalmans* was published in the 1870s, the belief had gained ground that the Indian Muslim community as a whole had fallen behind the Hindus in education, recruitment to government service, advancement in 'modern' industries and other economic activities, and, consequently, in social and political position as well as in a more general self-confidence. In an age when farsighted political leaders were expected to serve Community as well as Country, any public worker who professed interest in the 'Muslim community' would have to do everything possible to lift the community up by its bootstraps. That is precisely the task Syed Ahmad Khan would seem to have set himself in the period after the 1860s; and the same concern appears to have moulded the vision of other majoı Muslim leaders of northern India who followed in his wake.

Thus, Muhammad Ali noted in an article entitled 'The Communal Patriot', written in February 1912, that the Hindu 'communal patriot' 'sprang into existence with "swaraj" as his war-cry' and a full awareness of the importance of terms like 'India' and 'territorial nationality', which suited both his community's interests and his own privileged political and economic position. The Muslim 'communal patriot' owed his origins to 'a very different set of circumstances'. The 'Muslim community' had lagged behind the 'Hindu' in every respect, Muhammad Ali observed. 'When it made up its mind to accept the inevitable and move with the times, it suddenly [*sic.*] found itself face to face with a community vastly superior to it, in number, in wealth, in education, in political organisation and power. . . .' The 'Muslim conservative' was therefore pushed, in self-defence, according to the writer, into a position of 'communal patriotism'.[46]

As the statement suggests, the Muslim politician seeking to

---

[46]Afzal Iqbal, ed., *Select Writings and Speeches of Maualana Mohammad Ali*, vol. I (Lahore, 1944, 2nd edn. 1969), pp. 76–8.

represent the 'community' of Indian Muslims in the era of early nationalism was in a rather different situation from that of the Hindu politician seeking to represent the 'Hindu community'. The underlying logic of the different political positions adopted by Hindu and Muslim politicians in northern India, however, appears to have been the same. In this logic, the building blocks of the political community of the future were given. They were the long-existing religious 'communities', which needed education, organization, encouragement, protection in order to survive and prosper in this 'modern' age. Where conservative Muslims differed from progressive Muslims, and where large numbers of progressive (nationalist) politicians, Hindu and Muslim, appear to have differed among themselves, was chiefly over the *method* and *pace* of advance towards common 'nationhood' and, hence, self-government.

The 'loyalist' Syed Ahmad Khan argued consistently that Indian nationhood could be achieved only very gradually, that the 'Western' system of political representation on the basis of 'one man, vote' was not suited to pluralist countries like India, and that British rule should remain as an arbiter or controlling hand— holding the balance even between different communities and interests—for a long time to come. Yet, the object of his great dream and achievement, the Mohammadan Anglo-Oriental College which later became the Muslim University at Aligarh, was to provide that liberal education and leadership that would enable his religious fraternity to take their place by the side of other Indians in the advance to 'modernity'. 'The chief reason that induced me to found this college was, as I believe you know, that the Mohammedans were becoming more and more degraded and poor day by day. . . . I am glad to say that in this Institution *both the brothers* [Hindus and Muslims] get the same education. . . . There is no distinction between Hindus and Muslims.'[47]

On the other side, we may quote the nationalist Muhammad Ali, writing twenty-eight years later: 'Any true patriot of India working for the evolution of Indian nationality will have to accept the communal individuality of the Muslims as the basis of his

[47]Shan Mohammad, ed., *Writings and Speeches of Sir Syed Ahmad Khan* (Bombay, 1972), p. 162.

constructive effort. This is the irreducible factor of the situation. . . .'
And again, a year later:

Cooperation, free partnership, sense of mutual dependence and helpful-
ness will grow as soon as both the great communities begin to perceive
that neither of them is a negligible factor in any scheme about the future
of India. The recognition of communal individuality especially of the
less-favoured community, in the early stages of India's political development is an essential condition to that perception. . . .[48]

Indeed, nothing could more dramatically express the late-nine-
teenth and early-twentieth-century vision of Indian nationhood,
as built on the backs of a united 'Hindu community', a united
'Muslim community' and so on, than Mohammad Ali's call for a
Federation of Faiths and his fanciful dream of a 'United Faiths of
India' as the form of the future nation-state.[49]

To say this is not to minimize the major differences in political
perception and political prescription that existed between and
among Hindu and Muslim political leaders during this period.
Nor is it my intention to suggest that there were no fears among
the early nationalists about the implications of a political mobilization proceeding from 'Hindu', 'Muslim' and other such blocs. It
was precisely the fear of Hindu-Muslim discord that appears to
have led R. C. Dutt, in his later fiction, to tone down the anti-
Muslim tenor of his earlier historical novels. Fears of internal
dissension led, too, to the well-known resolution of the Congress,
at its fourth annual session in Allahabad in 1888, barring the discussion of any subject to which Hindu or Muslim delegates 'as a
body . . . unanimously or nearly unanimously' objected. Ajudhia
Nath Kunzru of Allahabad is also reported to have initiated a move,
as member of the Legislative Council in the late 1880s, to secure
'adequate representation' for the 'Muslim community' in local
self-government.[50] Yet these moves serve, perhaps better than
any number of quotations from the political writings of the time,

---

[48]Iqbal, ed., *Select Writings and Speeches, vol. I*, p. 80; R. A. Jafri, ed., *Selections from Moulana Mohammad Ali's Comrade* (Lahore, 1965), p. 419.

[49]Ibid., p. 268; Iqbal, ed., *Select Writings and Speeches*, p. 256; see also
D. Lelyveld, *Aligarh's First Generation: Muslim Solidarity in British India*
(Princeton, 1978), p. 341.

[50]Bayly, *Local Roots*, p. 133.

to underline the point that, to the nationalists of the later nineteenth century, 'Hindu' and 'Muslim' communities were given; and it was these 'great Indian communities', plus the Parsis, the Christians, and so on, that constituted the emerging Indian nation.

Those who feared the divisive potential that existed in such an approach to nationalist politics responded by constricting 'politics' in a very narrow channel. They did this through the sort of resolution mentioned above and by relegating a whole variety of public issues to the domain of the 'social'. As W. C. Bonnerjee put it in explaining the holding of the Indian National Social Conference in conjunction with the Indian National Congress from 1887 onwards, it was thought best to leave it to Hindus, Muslims, Parsis, etc., the delegates belonging to different religious denominations, to

discuss their respective social matters in a friendly spirit among themselves. . . . Social questions were left out of the Congress programme . . . the Congress commenced and has since remained, and will, I sincerely trust, always remain as a purely political organization devoting its energies to political matters and political matters only.[51]

I might add that it was the logic of this early nationalist position that led to the Lucknow Pact, the open espousal of separate electorates then and for a decade afterwards by both the Congress and the Muslim League—the representatives of the 'Hindus' and the 'Muslims' as it were; and indeed to the terms of the 'joint' Khilafat Non-Co-operation movement of 1920–2.

In sum, the evidence from the turn of the century points, on the one hand, to a political vision of emerging or potential unity based on the common interests of all Indians. On the other hand, it indicates the existence of a vision of society as already formed into discrete communities, each with its own priorities and interests and each with the right to determine its own ('social') future: 'India' was 'Hindu' + 'Muslim' + 'Sikh' + 'Christian', etc., and likely to remain so for a long time to come. The character of this latter equation speaks of the limits of Indian liberalism in the nineteenth and early twentieth centuries, a liberalism that was manifestly

[51]P. Sitaramayya, *The History of the Indian National Congress, 1885–1935* (Madras, 1935), pp. 117–18.

inadequate for its own project of building a liberal nation of free and equal citizens. It was not until the 1920s, however, that the making of such an equation was seriously, and consistently, called into question.[52]

[52]One should note, however, that the thrust towards a modernist, secular nationalism, separated from its communitarian moorings, probably gathered pace in some areas, such as Bengal, rather earlier than it did in northern India. In Bengal, the Swadeshi period would seem to have inaugurated this search for unity 'on a higher plane'; see Sumit Sarkar, *Swadeshi Movement in Bengal*, p. 495 and *passim*.

Chapter Seven

Nationalism versus Communalism

The brave [Ali] Brothers are staunch lovers of their country, but they are Mussulmans first and everything else afterwards. It must be so with every religiously-minded man.

—Gandhi, 24 September 1921

Nationalism is greater than sectarianism. And in that sense we are Indians first and Hindus, Mussulmans, Parsis, Christians after.

—Gandhi, 26 January 1922

As is well known, the 1920s made for a new conjuncture in the world of Indian politics. The 'masses' entered the organized national movement on an unprecedented scale. Congress leaders and workers got drawn into the villages as never before. The participation of peasants and workers in nationalist activities, and their appropriation and reinterpretation of nationalist symbols and slogans, greatly increased. Consequent upon all this, the demands of the disprivileged came to be voiced on nationalist platforms far more insistently and concretely than in the past.[1]

At the same time, however, the Khilafat/Non-Co-operation movement acted as a catalyst in certain other ways too to precipitate those compounds in Indian politics that have been handed down to us as 'nationalism' and 'communalism'. A national leadership that might already have been perturbed by the devastating Hindu attacks on the Muslims of Shahabad and Katarpur at the Baqr-Id of 1917 and 1918, respectively, but had brushed them aside as being of little consequence in the context of the immediate political agenda and the emerging unity among Hindu and Muslim nationalist politicians, was thrown into consternation by some of the

[1] See Sumit Sarkar, *Modern India*, for a comprehensive account of these developments.

events of the next few years. The massive agitation among Muslims of many different classes across the subcontinent on the specifically 'Muslim' political issue of the fate of the Khilafat, the Mapilla rising in Malabar, the Hindu and Muslim movements that followed in northern India to reclaim 'victims' and protect the 'faithful'— *shuddhi* and *sangathan, tabligh* and *tanzim*—and the spate of Hindu-Muslim riots from 1923 onwards, pointed sharply to the heightened dangers arising from community-based mobilization.

A nationalist survey of the Hindu-Muslim problem undertaken in the wake of the Kanpur riots of 1931 noted:

The following casual list of riots, which have been marked by increasing violence and cruelty, gives some idea of the proportions the problem has assumed during the last decade.

1921 — Malabar
1922 — Multan
1923 — Ajmere, Saharanpur, Multan, Amritsar, Sindh, Jubbulpur, Agra, and Rae-Bareli.
1924 — Delhi, Kohat, Nagpur, Indore, and Lucknow.
1925 — Calcutta, Allahabad, Sholapur.
1926 — Delhi.
1927 — Lahore, Multan, Betiah, Bareilly, Nagpur, and Cawnpore.
1928 — Surat, Hyderabad (Deccan), and Kalipaty.
1929 — Bombay.
1930 — Azamgarh, Dacca, Muttra [Mathura], Mymensingh, and Daravi.
1931 — Basti, Benares, Mirzapur, Agra, and last but not least, the great disaster at Cawnpore [Kanpur].[2]

The Hindu Mahasabha and other such sectarian organizations now attained a new importance and came to adopt far more extreme positions. Savarkar had expounded the notion of the Hindu Rashtra in his book *Hindutva*, written in an Andaman jail in 1917. The foundation of the Rashtriya Svayam Sevak Sangh (RSS) in 1925 indicated both the growing acceptance of such a view and the quite new aggressiveness of those who advocated it. As the founder of the RSS Dr K. B. Hedgewar is reported to have said, if there was no dispute about the English, the Germans and the French being

[2] Congress; *Cawnpore Riots Enquiry Committee Report* (1931), reprinted in N. G. Barrier, ed., *Roots of Communal Politics* (Delhi, 1976), p. 228.

the nation in England, Germany and France, why should there be any confusion about the identity of the nation in Hindustan? 'Hindu society living in this country since times immemorial is the national society here and the main responsibility of this country rests with this society. The same Hindu people have built the life-values, ideals and culture of this country and, therefore, their nationhood is self-evident.'[3] Thus there arose the idea of a Hindu Raj which would reflect the glories of the ancient Hindu civilization and keep Muslims in their place, to be matched in due course by the notion of a Muslim Raj which would protect the place of the Muslims. The Hindu-Muslim problem now became 'the question of all questions' (Gandhi); it 'dominated almost everything else' (Nehru).

II

The succession of events outlined above did much to bring about a new reversal in nationalist discourse, a reversal that in its turn helped to mould the contemporary debate and understanding of Indian society and politics. As we have observed, 'Hindu' and 'Muslim' political mobilization had been seen in the past as necessary, even inevitable, at least in the early stages of the building of an Indian nationalism. Such communitarian mobilization now came to be regarded by more and more nationalist observers as a distorted and distorting tendency. 'Hindu' and 'Muslim' politics, with all their divergent aspects, became from the 1920s the chief flogging horse of Indian nationalism—divisive, primitive and, in a far more general nationalist judgement, the product of a colonial policy of Divide and Rule. This was the birthplace of the nationalist version of the concept of 'communalism'.

Indian nationalism as we know it—a nationalism that stood *above* (or *outside*) the different religious communities and took as its unit the individual Indian citizen, a 'pure' nationalism unsullied, in theory, by the 'primordial' pulls of caste, religious community, etc.—was, I suggest, rigorously conceptualized only in opposition to this notion of communalism. In a way this is to challenge the received view that communalism develops after and in some senses

[3] D. R. Goyal, *Rashtriya Swayamsewak Sangh* (Delhi, 1979), p. 40, quoting C. P. Bhishikar, *Keshav: Sangh Nirmata* (Delhi, n.d.), p. 31.

in opposition to Indian nationalism, and that it is, as the report of the Congress committee appointed to enquire into the Kanpur riots of March 1931 has it, nothing but nationalism driven into religious channels.[4] Since communalism had come to be seen by the 1920s as the politics of the religious community, one might well argue the opposite, that nationalism was nothing but communalism driven into secular channels—and not sufficiently driven. More adequately, one would have to say that communalism and nationalism, as we understand them today, arose together; the age of communalism was concurrent with the age of nationalism; they were part of the same discourse.

'Hindu' and 'Muslim' politics had occasionally been analysed by the nationalists in the earlier period. From the mid-1920s such analysis became an urgent task as the search for a 'pure' nationalism was taken up with a quite new vigour. There were many leading nationalist thinkers, Gandhi among them,[5] who retained their belief in the centrality of religion and the religious community in Indian life. Even so, their analyses of Indian society, and of the basis of Indian nationalism, changed significantly.

For one thing, many of these thinkers now began to emphasize the distinction, as they saw it, between the 'essentials' of religion, which had to be upheld in any circumstances, and the 'non-essentials', which ought to be discarded in the interests of a larger unity.[6] Thus, Lajpat Rai said in September 1924:

If we really and honestly want a United India, we, i.e., the different religious communities in this country, shall have to make a clear distinction between the essentials and non-essentials in religion. . . . I do not

---

[4] *Congress Kanpur Riots Enquiry*, 'Foreword', p. iv.

[5] Ravinder Kumar has persuasively argued that Gandhi's understanding of India and also much of his political efficacy flowed from a recognition of the strength of 'community' loyalty (regional, religious and other); 'Class, Community or Nation? Gandhi's Quest for a Popular Consensus in India', reprinted in his *Essays in the Social History of Modern India* (Calcutta, 1983). See also n. 26 in chpt. 6 above.

[6] Late-nineteenth-century writers and publicists had made the same kind of distinction, but without laying quite the same kind of emphasis on the urgent need to discard 'non-essentials'. For example, see Bharatendu's distinction between 'true religion' and 'social religion' (p. 215 above; also J. Lutt, *Hindu Nationalismus in Uttar Pradesh*, pp. 93–4).

maintain that either Hindus or Muhammadans should sacrifice the essentials of their religion for the sake of unity. . . . I must, however, say frankly that unity is a dream never to be realised unless Hindus and Muhammadans, Sikhs and Christians, make up their minds to be more liberal and rational in their religion and social life than they at present are. . .[7]

Gandhi had made the same kind of distinction earlier, suggesting, for example, a trifle eccentrically, that visits to the temple were an *essential* part of his dharma, but not so the playing of music outside mosques.

Hindus may take it from me that it is no part, no essential part of Hinduism, that we should play music at any time. . . I yield to my Mussalman brethren in every non-essential because it is natural for me to do so, because my religion demands that I should live in peace with the whole world. . . [and because] the cornerstone of swaraj . . . is Hindu and Muslim unity.[8]

It was from around this time too, in the early 1920s, that Gandhi took up the cudgels against that great—and 'inessential'—blot on Hindu society, the 'sin' of untouchability; and it is perhaps not without significance that the call to fight against this evil was now repeatedly linked up in his writings and speeches with the call to establish Hindu-Muslim harmony. 'Truthful relations between Hindus and Musalmans, bread for the masses and removal of untouchability. That is how I would define swaraj at the present moment.'[9]

The nationalism of people like Gandhi also changed in another respect. They now began to stress more than just the possibility of a coexistence of loyalty to the Country and loyalty to the (religious)

---

[7] V. C. Joshi, ed., *Lala Lajpat Rai. Writings and Speeches, Vol. Two, 1920–8* (Delhi, 1966), pp. 180, 183. *The Congress Kanpur Riots Enquiry* made the same point (p. 46): 'The real ultimate cause of all communal tension is the exaggeration of non-essentials in the religions. If there is any way whereby in the present conditions of life, the religious, moral, and political practice of the people can be reformed, it is the inculcation far and wide of the fundamental truth that true self-government is Government by the higher self in all departments of life.' See also Radhakrishna Awasthi, ed., *Kranti ka Udghosh. Ganesh Shankar Vidyarthi ki Kalam se, Volume II* (Kanpur, 1978), p. 911.

[8] *CWMG, XIX*, pp. 539, 541.

[9] *CWMG, XXIX*, p. 396; cf. pp. 562, 564, 153: in the same volume.

Community: they stressed the primacy of the one over the other. The extracts from Gandhi used as an epigraph for this chapter show how, as late as September 1921, the Mahatma had spoken of his allies, the Ali brothers, as 'staunch lovers of their country, but Mussulmans first and everything else afterwards'. Four months later, when the full impact of the Mappilla outbreak was beginning to be seen, his position had undergone what looks like a complete reversal: 'Nationalism is greater than sectarianism', he now wrote. 'In that sense we are Indians first and Hindus, Mussulmans, Parsis, Christians after.'[10]

For others, a younger generation of nationalists who came of age precisely in this decade of 'communalism', as one might somewhat extravagantly call it, religion could not be allowed even this refuge in public life. Ganesh Shankar Vidyarthi speaks for this new generation:

मुस्लिम लीग और खिलाफत कमेटियाँ, हिन्दू सभा और आर्य समाज और सनातन धर्म सभायें . . . हैं, और अभी कुछ दिन तक रहेंगी । . . . परन्तु . . . कांग्रेस के प्रत्येक अनुयायी के लिए, देश की स्वाधीनता के प्रत्येक इच्छुक के लिये, इस समय और उस समय तक जब तक कि ये साम्प्रदायिक संस्थायें संकीर्ण दृष्टि से देखने, और संकीर्ण ढंग से काम करने के लिए विवश हैं, यह स्पष्ट कर्तव्य है कि वह इन साम्प्रदायिक संस्थाओं को तनिक भी महत्व न दें । [11]

(The Muslim League and the Khilafat Committees, the Hindu Sabha, the Arya Samaj and the Sanatan Dharma Sabhas . . . exist, and will continue to exist for a while. . . . But . . . for now, and until such time as these communal organizations are able to overcome their narrowness of vision and their narrow ways of working, it is the clear duty of every single follower of the Congress and every single person desirous of Indian independence to attach no importance to these organizations.)

We pray to God, he says further, that our leaders may learn to rely not on the weak crutches of religious organizations and diffident, Moderate political tactics but on the true (literally, infinite) strength of the country, which is to be found in her 'millions of children' (ordinary people).

परमात्मा करे, हमारे नेता टूटी-सी लकड़ियों पर सहारा करना छोड़ें और देश की अनन्त शक्ति पर, जो उसके करोड़ों बच्चों के रूप में है, अधिक विश्वास और भरोसा करना सीखें . . . [12]

---

[10] *CWMG, XXI,* p. 192 and *XXII,* p. 268.
[11] Vidyarthi, *Kranti ka Udghosh II,* p. 752 (article of 17 November 1924).
[12] Ibid., p. 753.

The days of religion and religious organizations are numbered, Vidyarthi argues, the 'trend of world history' and the 'future of India' are against them. 'Whosoever wishes to be a "Hindu" or a "Musalman" is welcome to be a "Hindu" or a "Musalman" inside the home. The newly rising nationalist forces will put up with these pastimes [*sic*] only so long as they present no obstacle to the . . . advancement of the *country and the nation.*'

(अपमे घर मे बैठे हुए, जो चाहे मुसलमान हो जाये और जो चाहे हिन्दू । इन खिलवाड़ी को उसी समय तक आगे चलकर उमड़ने वाली राष्ट्रीय शाक्तियाँ बर्दाश्त करेंगी जब तक कि वे देश और राष्ट्र के हित और उनकी उन्नति में, किसी प्रकार की बाधा उपस्थित नहीं करतीं ।) [13]

And again 'All Congress work should be for the welfare of the country, not for the benefit of any individual, religion or caste (within it). The Congress programme should be for *the common people*, not for religious communities, castes or prominent individuals. . . . The Congress's field of work should be *purely national*. The question of religious and caste rights should have no place in it.'

(केवल देश कल्याण की दृष्टि से कांग्रेस के समस्त काम हों, व्यक्ति , मज़हब या जाति के हित या उन्हें खुश करने के लिए नहीं । कांग्रेस कार्यक्रम सर्वसाधारण के लिए हो, सम्प्रदायों, जातियों और विशेष व्यक्तियों के लिए नहीं । . . . कांग्रेस का क्षेत्र शुद्ध राष्ट्रीय रहे । मज़हबी और जातीय अधिकारों को उसमें कोई स्थान न मिले । [14])

Thus the language of the 'purely national' raised the concept of the Indian nation to another level and pushed its foundations beyond the great individuals in history, beyond the religious communities, beyond caste. Ideas that had certainly existed in the decades before the First World War now became a principal theme in Indian political discourse, taking on a consistency and gaining an effectiveness that they never had before.

The repeated and widespread emphasis on the purely national was, of course, new. What was more striking still was the call to privatize religion (the separation of religion from politics, as we would put it today), the dissociation of the 'nation' from any pre-existing communities and the construction of the purely national unambiguously, in terms of a new kind of community—the 'India of our dreams'. Even Lajpat Rai, firm believer as he was in the

---

[13] Ibid., p. 741. Emphases in the translation are mine.
[14] Ibid., p. 908 (article of 23 May 1926). Emphases mine.

glories of the ancient Aryas and Aryavarta, adopted the new language for a while in 1924: 'India is neither Hindu nor Muslim. It is not even both. It is one. It is India.'[15]

What was new, too, was the emphatic association of that 'national' with the 'common people', the 'true strength of the country', the ordinary men and women working in villages and towns all over the subcontinent—in a word, the Indian citizen. As Jawaharlal Nehru put, it, 'The mountains and the rivers of India, and the forests and the broad fields, which gave us food, were all dear to us, but *what counted ultimately were the people of India . . .* spread out all over the vast land. *Bharat Mata*, Mother India, was essentially these millions of people.'[16]

Nehru was of course the chief unofficial, and in due course official, spokesman of this refurbished nationalism. His writings on nationalism and communalism have much to tell us about their altered signification. 'Hindu nationalism', wrote Nehru, 'was a natural growth from the soil of India, but inevitably it comes in the way of the larger nationalism which rises above differences of religion or creed'. '*Real* or *Indian* nationalism was something quite apart from these two religious and communal varieties of nationalism [Hindu and Muslim] and strictly speaking, is the only form which can be called *nationalism in the modern sense of the word.*' The basis of this 'real' Indian nationalism was the common economic interests of the mass of the people. 'The whole basis and urge of the national movement came from the desire for economic betterment, to throw off the burdens that crushed the masses and to end the exploitation of the Indian people.'[17]

So, too, the basis of communalism was the economic (and political) interests of the reactionary upper classes. Nehru wrote of Hindu and Muslim communalism: 'In neither case was it even

[15] Joshi, ed., *Lajpat Rai, vol. 2*, p. 221.

[16] J. Nehru, *Discovery of India* (London 1951), p. 44.

[17] Nehru, *Discovery of India* (Bombay, 1961), p. 286; *Glimpses of World History*, II, pp. 1129–30; *SWJN, 6*, pp. 4, 14. (Emphases added.) For further indications of the new 'economic' emphasis in nationalist discourse, see the 'Fundamental Rights' resolution passed at the Karachi Congress in 1931 and the debates around it, and Nehru's Presidential address to the 1936 Lucknow Congress.

bona fide communalism [i.e. the stirrings and demands of a community], but . . . political and social reaction hiding behind the communal mask'.

The political and economic aspect of the Hindu-Muslim question. . . was this: the rising and economically better-equipped middle class (Hindu) was resisted and checked to some extent by part of the feudal landlord class (Muslim). The Hindu landlords were often closely connected with their *bourgeoisie*, and thus remained neutral or even sympathetic to the middle-class demands. . . . The British, as always, sided with the feudal elements. The masses and the lower middle classes on either side were not in the picture at all. . . . The outstanding fact seems to be how, on both sides, the communal leaders represent a small upper class reactionary group, and how these people exploit and take advantage of the religious passions of the masses for their own ends.[18]

Just as the new *nationalism*—secular, democratic and, in time, 'socialistic'—was defined largely in opposition to a growing politics of communalism, so *communalism*—or the politics of the 'religious community' or 'communities', which gave rise to such tension, suspicion and strife—was defined in opposition to what was now conceived of as nationalism. Communalism became in this view part of a 'pre-modern' (if not 'pre-political') world that was shored up by the colonial regime in its own interests. Nationalism was all that was forward-looking, progressive, 'modern' in Indian politics. Communalism was all that was backward-looking, reactionary. Nationalism reflected the spontaneous urge of the Indian people for economic advancement and freedom from exploitation. Communalism reflected the machinations of the colonial regime and reactionary upper-class elements that played on the religious sentiments of the people to further their own, narrow interests.

The next step in this nationalist argument was that communalism, and with it ideas like Pakistan, were doomed from the start. Religion and religious organizations should read the writing on the wall, as Ganesh Shankar Vidyarthi had suggested; they were against the trend of world history, the wave of the future. Nehru hammered the point home:

The day of even national cultures is rapidly passing and the world is becoming one cultural unit. . . . The real struggle today in India is not

[18] Nehru, *Autobiography* (London, 1936), pp. 459, 463, 467-8.

between Hindu culture and Muslim culture, but between these two and the conquering scientific culture of modern civilization. . . . Everywhere religion recedes into the background and nationalism appears in aggressive garbs, and behind nationalism other isms which talk in social and economic terms.[19]

And elsewhere,

To think in terms of Pakistan when the modern trend is towards the establishment of a world federation is like thinking in terms of bows and arrows as weapons of war in the age of the atom bomb. The whole mentality behind this conception of bows and arrows and Pakistan is most dangerous and if we cling to such anachronisms, we shall never solve our problems.[20]

From the time of the Round Table Conference in London in 1931, Congress leaders repeatedly and vociferously stated that once the British left India the communal problem would disappear, that the 'political' question of swaraj had to be settled first before communalism or any other 'social' issue could be tackled. The 'politics of religion' came to be seen, from this viewpoint, as a politics that was irrelevant to the real needs of the country at this time, that was, in other words, not real politics at all.

The question of Pakistan, and any other such question, does not arise at present. The first question which should be in every Indian's heart at present is the question of the independence of the country. Pakistan and such other questions can only be decided after independence is achieved and the government restored to the people of the country. . . . I wonder how people in India can worry about sectarian problems of civilization and culture [sic.] when hunger and poverty are staring the nation in the face. It is an imperative necessity to relieve all this which vitally affects the country before people can apply themselves to any minor issues.[21]

The realm of the political was sometimes so defined as to exclude the forces of communalism altogether from its ambit. 'Whatever. . . [our] differences on the *communal* question might have been', Nehru wrote about Mohammad Ali, 'There were very few differences on the political issue. He [Mohammad Ali] was devoted to the

[19] Ibid., pp. 469, 470, 472.
[20] *SWJN* 14, p. 187; cf. *Discovery* (London, 1951), pp. 505–6.
[21] *SWJN* 7, p. 401 and *SWJN* 14, pp. 219, 221, 222.

idea of Indian independence.' In his presidential address to the Lucknow session of the Indian National Congress in 1936, Nehru observed: 'the principal communal leaders, Hindu or Muslim or others, are *political reactionaries, quite apart from the communal question*'. And again, in a report from Bihar in 1946, that the propaganda of the Muslim League and the Hindu Mahasabha 'did not affect the widespread popularity of the Congress among the Hindu masses *so far as the political issues* were concerned. *But it did produce communal feeling* and a tendency among the middle class to criticize the Congress for not supporting the Hindu cause as against the Muslim League'.[22]

III

Yet, political or not, the politics of the religious communities—now called communalism—encircled the nationalist dream like the coils of a snake.[23] Outside the North West Frontier Province, Muslim participation in the Civil Disobedience movement launched in 1930 was disappointingly small, especially by comparison with the Non-Co-operation experience. In March 1931, as the Karachi Congress met to celebrate the Gandhi-Irwin pact and to take in the significance of the suspension of civil disobedience, news came of the disastrous Hindu-Muslim riots at Kanpur—sparked off by the effort of local nationalists to enforce a hartal in protest against the execution of Bhagat Singh and the resistance that some Muslim shopkeepers offered to this.[24] Even before Kanpur, the stage was set for Jinnah's famous (or apocryphal)

[22] *Autobiography* (London, 1947), pp. 119–20; *SWJN*, 7, p. 190; Đurga Das, ed., *Sardar Patel's Correspondence, vol. 3* (Ahmedabad, 1972), p. 168 (Emphases added).

[23] The phrase, used in a somewhat different context, is Gandhi's; *CWMG, XVII*, p. 406, cited in Partha Chatterjee, *Nationalist Thought and the Colonial World*, p. 110.

[24] Officials described this as the worst riot since Banaras 1809 in terms of the casualties that occurred; see p. 24 above. David Page writes of 'the traumatic effect of this riot on the North Indian Muslim psyche. Never before in living memory had a riot of such proportions taken place'; *Prelude to Partition: The Indian Muslims and the Imperial System of Control 1921–32* (Delhi, 1981), p. 232.

statement regarding a parting of the ways. The disillusionment and isolation of Congress Muslims had increased to such an extent that Mukhtar Ahmad Ansari, T. A. K. Sherwani and Khaliquz-zaman had, early in 1930, resigned their various offices in the Congress, remaining only four-anna members, and Sherwani had even made attempts to come to terms with the Muslim League.[25]

It seemed as if 'Hindu' and 'Muslim' politics were gaining a stranglehold on the matter of Indian political advance; the experience of the Round Table conferences clearly deepened this impression. Secular nationalists could not but make determined efforts to break out of this stranglehold.

Open Congress opposition to separate electorates from the late 1920s[26] signalled the arrival of a new stage in the nationalist battle against a politics based on the religious community.[26] Twice, once in the mid-1930s and again a decade later, the Congress leadership even decided to take the issue of communalism to the masses. In 1934 Nehru took the lead in initiating a frontal attack on the communalist position. He accused sectarian parties of being 'blissfully ignorant' of the hunger and unemployment among the masses including the lower middle classes. 'The Muslim masses are probably even poorer than the Hindu masses', he wrote, 'but the "Fourteen Points" [put forward by Jinnah in 1929 as the minimum "Muslim" demand] say nothing about these poverty-stricken Muslims'.[27] A couple of years later, the Congress launched its Muslim Mass Contacts campaign. It was indicative of the hesitancy of the Congress in the face of sectarian politics, however, or should

---

[25] Ibid., p. 237. On the opposition to the Nehru Report after 1928, Page writes that both Shaukat Ali and Mohammad Ali now established themselves in 'the separatist camp', and it was not long before Mohammad Ali found himself 'on the same platform as Fazli Husain and Sir Mahommed Shafi'; ibid., pp. 183 and 184.

[26] The classic statement is of course the Nehru Report; *All Parties Conference 1928. Report of the Committee appointed by the Conference to determine the principles of the Constitution for India* (Allahabad, 1928).

[27] *Leader*, 7 January 1934. On Muslim mass contacts see Mushirul Hasan, 'The Muslim Mass Contacts Program', in R. Sisson & S. Wolpert, eds., *Congress and Indian Nationalism* (California, 1988).

one say the very strength of the sectarian arrangement of the Indian political world, that there had to be a separate 'mass contacts' programme for the Muslims and that only a Muslim, Kunwar Muhammad Ashraf, was judged fit to pilot it.

Ten years later, in the run-up to the 1946 elections, the Congress renewed the attempt to turn the tables on the communalist parties. In western UP, Nehru reported to Azad, then Congress President: 'I have found an extraordinarily favourable response from the Muslim masses. . . . I was surprised to find how popular the Congress was among the Muslim peasantry. In fact the Jamiat did not go far with them, it was the Congress that counted.' To Stafford Cripps he said in January 1946:

During the last three months we have again started approaching the Muslim masses and the results have been remarkably encouraging. Probably they will not affect the elections much as we have not had enough time. But they are laying the foundations of solid work among the Muslim masses which will make a difference before very long.

And to Krishna Menon:

As a rule city Muslims are for the League, especially the rougher elements. But it is also clear, especially in the UP and Bihar, that the Momins (chiefly the weaver class) and the Muslim peasantry are far more for the Congress because they consider the League an upper class organisation of feudal landlords, etc.

But there was a catch: as Nehru put it, 'An unknown factor, however, creeps in when God and the Koran are used for election purposes'.[28]

We shall return to this 'unknown factor' later in this chapter. The point to note here is that, from the early 1930s, secular nationalists took up in some earnest the political task of combating communalism, exposing the narrow interests and concerns of a very large number of Hindu and Muslim leaders and organizations, and mobilizing the masses, Hindu and Muslim, into their new role as citizens of an emerging Indian nation. From the 1930s, too, a growing section of the provincial-level and national Congress leadership joined socialists and communists in many parts of the

[28] *SWJN 14*, pp. 124, 141, 97.

country in calling for *economic swaraj* without which, they argued, *political swaraj* would have little meaning. They called for an assault on the central problems of Indian society—poverty, illiteracy, gross inequality. The attack against the reactionaries who fuelled the politics of communalism was a part of this general nationalist assault.[29] Their work in the Muslim mass contacts campaign and the run-up to the 1946 elections apart, Left nationalists of many hues were also involved in numerous peasants' and workers' struggles in the course of which they highlighted the common interests of Hindus, Muslims and other communities, and the importance of unity in the fight against oppressive regimes.[30]

Until the actual onset of Partition and Independence, however, when radically altered political conditions made the long-drawn-out struggles of Tebhaga and Telangana possible, these agitations could rarely be carried far enough or sustained for very long. The reasons for this are many and diverse, as so much recent research has shown: the repressive policies of the state, the class interests of the Congress leadership, the sectarian concerns and language of many of the grass-roots level nationalist cadres (and, sometimes, of the more senior leaders), the hope of carrying all sections of society with the Congress in the national movement, the fear that anti-communal campaigns (and, in places, even peasant agitation) might further alienate Muslim opinion and Muslim leaders and lead to greater strife.[31] But a detailed consideration of these obstacles

[29] See, e.g., Acharya Narendra Deva, 'The Communal Problem—A Socialist Viewpoint' in his *Socialism and the National Revolution* (Bombay, 1946), pp. 157–9; also Premchand's well-known views, as reported in Geetanjali Pandey, *Between Two Worlds. An Intellectual Biography of Premchand* (Delhi, 1989), p. 195.

[30] There were notable efforts by the Communists in the early 1940s, for example, especially in Bengal, to build up Hindu-Muslim unity in the course of their mobilization of the peasantry.

[31] For a guide to the literature on this question, see Sumit Sarkar, *Modern India*. More recent books that deal with some of these problems include Tanika Sarkar, *Bengal, 1928–34; The Politics of Protest* (Delhi, 1987) and Kapil Kumar, ed., *Congress and Classes* (Delhi, 1988). The point about hesitant support for peasant agitations in areas where Hindu-Muslim differences might arise is illustrated in Pandey, *Ascendancy of the Congress in U.P.*, pp. 189–91. For the important case of Congress's withdrawal of support from the popular movement in Hyderabad in 1938, see Sarkar, *Modern India*, p. 369.

would take us away from the central concern of our enquiry at this point. To round off our discussion of the nationalist response to sectarian politics and sectarian strife in this period, we need to give some account of the new nationalism's appeal to history.

The binary opposition between nationalism and communalism that was set up in the 1920s entailed, for the nationalists, a careful re-examination and presentation of the Indian past. Shorn of its 'Hindu' and 'Muslim' 'excesses', this reconstructed history was to emphasize not only the 'tolerance' and synthesizing capacities that had gone into the making of Indian civilization, which the early nationalists had also written about. The new nationalist historiography would also show the almost automatic commitment of India's inhabitants—older and newer, 'Aryan' and Scythian and Afghan—to the soil of this land, to the Indian state and indeed to the Indian 'nation' in the centuries past—the priority of a 'secular', 'national' loyalty, as it were, over any loyalty to religion, caste or race. The nationalist unity that was not adequately realized through political struggle in the present—partly because the nationalist assault on communalist and other reactionary forces always remained cautious, even in the 1930s and 1940s—was to be realized in the past, through a judicious reconstruction of Indian history.

The inaugural moment in this nationalist reconstruction of Indian history was the idea of the 'fundamental' unity of India. Something that had long been assumed, this notion was now advanced, in opposition to colonialist assertions about the impossibility of uniting Indians, as a 'scientific' and demonstrable truth. This fundamental, essential unity of India was based, it was said, on the natural geographical barriers that surrounded the subcontinent and marked it off from the rest of the world; an ancient (Hindu) culture and practice that linked together the most distant points in the land; and, in some later recensions, the economic self-sufficiency of India and the interdependence of its various parts.[32] Thus: 'There is no country marked out by the sea and the mountains so clearly to be a single whole as India. This geographical

[32] Radhakumud Mookerji, *The Fundamental Unity of India* (London, 1914), *passim*. Mookerji cites numerous colonial authorities from V. A. Smith to the 1911 Census Commissioner, E. A. Gait, on the 'natural' geographical unity of India. He adds the argument about economic self-sufficiency and interdependence in an 'Introduction' written for the second edition in 1954.

wholeness explains one of the central features of Indian history, the urge to political unification in defiance of vast distances and immense difficulties of transport and communication' (Beni Prasad). 'At almost any time in recorded history', wrote Nehru, 'an Indian from any part of the country would have felt more or less at home in any other part, but a stranger and an alien in any other country'.[33]

Part of the 'demonstration' of the feeling of oneness and the common cultural heritage of all Indians was provided by the old argument about the openness and tolerance of Indian civilization, which was now strongly underlined. 'Religious toleration has been one of the master characteristics of Indian history.' India's 'unity of spirit' arose without the aid of physical force, out of a culture of tolerance, assimilation and synthesis, the argument went. Each fresh incursion in early times made India more willing to receive. 'The same process of conflict and synthesis, but intensi- fied a thousand times, occurred with the advent of Islam in India'. 'As soon as the first waves of conquest, plunder and desecration had spent themselves, there began the operation of the forces, inherent in human [Indian?] nature, which interknit contacts into conational wholes and transform plurality into community.'[34]

These movements for unity, syncretism, synthesis, 'inherent' in the Indian condition, were said to have reached their climax, in the centuries of 'Muslim' rule, in the careers and thought of people like Kabir and Akbar.

Kabir's was the first attempt to reconcile Hinduism and Islam; the teachers of the south had absorbed Muslim elements, but Kabir was the first to come forward boldly to proclaim a religion of the centre, a middle path, and his cry was taken up all over India and was re-echoed from a hundred places. He had numerous Hindu and Muslim disciples, and today his sect numbers a million. . . . But it is not the number of his following which is so important, it is the influence which extends to the Punjab, Gujarat and Bengal, and which continued to spread under the Moghul rule, till a wise sovereign correctly estimating its value attempted to

[33] Beni Prasad, *The Hindu-Muslim Question* (Allahabad, 1941), p. 83; J. Nehru, *Discovery of India* (Bombay, 1961), p. 62.

[34] Beni Prasad, *Hindu-Muslim Question*, pp. 5 and 8. Humayun Kabir, *The Indian Heritage* (1946; 3rd edition, 1955), p. 61.

make it a religion approved by the State. Akbar's *Din-i-Ilahi* was not an isolated freak [idea] of an autocrat who had more power than he knew how to employ, but an inevitable result of the forces which were deeply surging in India's breast and finding expression in the teachings of men like Kabir.[35]

Akbar's was 'perhaps the first conscious attempt to formulate the conception of a Secular State', as another nationalist commentator put it. 'He also initiated a liberal social and religious policy which aimed at bringing about a fusion of the diverse elements which constitute the Indian people.'[36]

However, the notion of India's natural and long-standing unity was not dependent on positivist demonstration alone. The adjective 'fundamental' pointed to the axiomatic character of this nationalist proposition. In the nationalist discourse of the twentieth century, then, the unity of India appeared as a demonstrable but at the same time a metaphysical truth. 'India' became the nation personified. The 'essential unity' of the vast Indian subcontinent had '*seized the national consciousness*' and become a 'settled habit of thought' in ancient times, Radha Kumud Mookerji had written.[37] Jawaharlal Nehru reiterated the point on many occasions; 'Some kind of a dream of unity has occupied *the mind of India* since the dawn of civilization'; 'some powerful impulse, some tremendous urge, or ideas of the significance of life . . . was impressed upon *the subconscious mind of India* when *she was fresh and young* at the very dawn of her history'; 'Akbar became the great representative of the old Indian ideal of a synthesis of differing elements and their fusion into a common nationality. He identified himself with India and *India took to him* although he was a newcomer.'[38]

But how was this 'dream', this 'powerful impulse', realized in practice? It was in answer to this question that the new nationalists

---

[35] Tara Chand, *Influence of Islam on Indian Culture* (Allahabad, 1963), p. 165. About so-called 'syncretic' religions like Kabir's, the point should be made that they started as confrontational against the existing hierarchical order, and continued to have that critical edge for a long time. Nationalism appropriated them for its harmonizing purposes, seeking to make them part of the ideology of a non-problematic 'national unity'.

[36] Kabir, *Indian Heritage*, p. 18.

[37] Mookerji, *Fundamental Unity of India*, pp. 67, 79. (Emphasis added)

[38] Nehru, *Discovery* (1961 edn.), pp. 63, 147. (Emphases added)

made a significant departure from the nationalist accounts of the past that had been produced before. The new history emphasized not only the element of tolerance and adaptability in Hinduism, and Indian culture more generally; it emphasized along with this the importance of the great rulers of the state, in the realization of the Indian dream. On the one hand, the ideal of Indian unity, the idea of an Indian nationhood, was said to have been established in the distant past—'at the very dawn of [India's] history'. On the other, the idea was actualized, in this particular reading, by the exertions of India's—one should say, north India's—great rulers (Chandragupta and Ashoka, Samudragupta and Harsha, Sher Shah and Akbar), and apparently by their exertions alone. Chandragupta Maurya 'raised the old and ever-new cry of nationalism and roused the people against the foreign invader'; 'the old dream of uniting the whole of India under one supreme government fired Ashoka'; 'Akbar became the great representative of the old Indian ideal of. . . a common nationality', 'he might be considered the father of Indian nationalism', 'he may in many respects be regarded as the creator of modern India'.[39]

In 1931 the Indian National Congress appointed a committee to enquire into the Hindu-Muslim rioting that occurred in Kanpur in March that year. The committee's report contains perhaps the most elaborate contemporary nationalist statement on the history of Hindu-Muslim relations in the subcontinent. A consideration of its purposes and findings will help to further illustrate some of the points made above about the nationalist reconstruction of Indian history in the context of the battle between 'nationalism' and 'communalism'.

'The prevailing impression is that the Hindu-Muslim problem in its present form is an age-long problem', the committee observed in the foreword to its report. 'This is an extremely wrong impression, created by interested parties through deliberate misrepresentations, about the propagation of Islam in India, about the nature and incidents of Muslim rule, and generally about relations which subsisted during this period between the Hindus and the Musalmans.' It

---

[39] Ibid., pp. 126 and 136; Nehru, *Glimpses of World History*, I, p. 482; Kabir, *Indian Heritage*, p. 18.

was the purpose of the long historical retrospect included in the report to 'correct this view which is generally met with in school histories and other interested works'.[40]

The retrospect was divided into two major sections, covering the 'Muslim period' and the 'British period'. In the first the authors sought to indicate the affinities which existed between Hindus and Muslims up to the Mughal period and 'the broad synthesis towards which their life was moving'. In the second they set out to analyse how this synthesis was disturbed and to show the contribution of British policy towards the making of the present crisis.

On the latter question, the committee's conclusions were unambiguous:

All the main controversies which at present embitter and have latterly divided the two communities, for example, the cow question, Ramlila and Moharram, and other religious occasions or processions, music before mosque; as also the question of representation in services, in Municipalities and Councils, joint and separate electorates; safeguards; redistribution of Provinces and federal, as opposed to a unitary, basis of the constitution—all these did not and could not have existed during the Muslim period.

Much of this was true enough, indeed true almost by definition ('could not have existed during the Muslim period'). But the concluding sentence of the historical section of the report, which followed on immediately from the above—'They are all products of the British Period and of British Policy'[41]—was rather more open to question as it swept under the carpet of British policy the dust of many stirrings in India during the colonial period, and hinted at the termination of the British period as a ready solution to the problem of Hindu-Muslim antagonism.

The business of a Hindu-Muslim synthesis and colonial responsibility for recent disputes apart, the Congress Enquiry Comittee had a good deal to say about certain other forces that had contributed to Indian unity in the past and would presumably do so in the future. During the centuries that followed the establishment of 'Muslim' power over parts of northern India, the committee's

[40] *Congress Kanpur Riots Enquiry*, pp. xxvi–vii.
[41] Ibid., p. 110.

report noted, the efforts of Muslim rulers linked up with those of the Rajputs, as with those of 'Buddhists' and others earlier, 'to give India her political unity'. Gradually, 'centrifugal' forces were subdued and a central paramount power became feasible.

The Moghals inherit this colossal effort of over five centuries [*sic.*] and during the Moghal period *India realizes as she had never realized before* within historical times [*sic.*], except once, in the days of the illustrious Ashoka, the objective towards which *she had been consciously moving*. From the beginning, *her one mission had been* to weld her myriad children into a harmonious people by giving them a political, economic and cultural unity. During the Moghal period the foundations of this national synthesis were again strongly and deeply laid.[42]

It was the result of *eight hundred years of constant building* that within a century of [the establishment of] British rule India began to make herself felt as a political unity and . . . inspite of the utmost efforts of the British to the contrary, imbibed national idealism and began to move irresistibly towards securing Western representative institutions and freedom from foreign rule. There runs throughout this period *a continuity of constructive political development* of which any people may well be proud.[43]

The different subject positions constructed in the above narrative need to be properly noted. At the most obvious level are the rulers of different parts of India—the Mughals, the Rajputs, the 'Buddhists' and others earlier, who by their actions and initiatives had attempted to give India her political unity and been responsible for 'eight hundred years of constant building'. Behind them, however, at a deeper level, is the Spirit of India, the Essence, an already existing Oneness, seeking to realize its eternal mission. The nationalist historical narrative closes with an invocation of this spirit and a condemnation of those who have sought to divert her from her mission, that is, the realization of Indian unity.

This kind of rarefication resulted, of course, in a grave over-simplification of Indian history. It may be said that such over-simplification was an intrinsic part of the nationalist enterprise. Nationalism necessarily reconstructs its past to establish in it the unity, uniqueness and pride of the 'nation'. However, one needs also to ask the question whether all nationalisms reconstruct their

[43] Ibid., p. 76, emphasis added.
[42] Ibid., p. 75, emphasis added.

past in exactly the same way. In common with nationalisms elsewhere, nationalist discourse in India summoned to its side the Spirit of the Nation, its ancient character ('from the dawn of history'), the metaphysical truth of its unity. But the historical realization of this Truth was attributed, as we have noticed, to the great rulers of India—the Mughals, the Rajputs, the 'Buddhists' before them. What was missing from this reconstruction of the past was any sense of the common people as historical agents, of the peoples and classes of the subcontinent struggling to realize their many versions of truth, honour and the just life. There was no room here for an accommodation of local loyalties, for continued attachment to religion, or even appreciation of the vigorous struggles that had been waged against these; nor much allowance for the class-divided and regionally diverse perceptions of the 'imagined community', out of the struggle for which Indian nationalism and the Indian national movement arose.

By its denial of subjecthood to the people of India—the local communities, castes and classes—nationalism was forced into the kind of statist perspective that colonialism had favoured and promoted for its own reasons. In nationalist historiography, as in the colonial construction of the Indian past, the history of India was reduced in substance to the history of the state. In the colonial account, the state alone (and for all practical purposes this meant the colonial state) could establish order out of chaos, reduce the religious and other passions of Indians to 'civilized' proportions, and carry India into 'modernity'. So, too, in the nationalist account, the Indian state had performed the role of maintaining Indian unity in the past and would do so in the future. By the 1930s and 1940s, the importance of an 'enlightened' leadership was thus being stressed on all sides as the critical ingredient that was required in the bid to advance the 'backward' peoples of India. It had taken great leaders, a Chandragupta Maurya, an Ashoka, an Akbar, to actualize the dream of Indian unity in the past, and they had done so in the great states and empires that they established. It would take great leaders like Nehru and Patel to realize the newly desired unity of India, and the state would again be their major instrument.[44] The twentieth-century liberal, seeking to overcome the

---

[44] Cf. the dedication in Kabir's *Indian Heritage*: 'To Jawaharlal Nehru who like Asoka and Akbar has helped to discover and enrich the Indian heritage.'

limits of nineteenth-century Indian liberalism, could do no better than turn to statism.[45]

IV

It is obviously not the case that the nineteenth-century liberal, concerned with the interests of Community and Country, quickly went under. Nationalist thought—necessarily—remained full of contradictions, inconsistencies, ambiguities, even in its 'mature' phase. These contradictions operated not only at the level of the commonly perceived gap between precept and practice, brought about among other things by fear, interest or uncertainty. They operated also at the level of conceptualizing nationalism, and identifying both the preconditions for national unity and the obstacles in its path—of which, from the 1920s, the most threatening seemed to be communalism. In these concluding pages I wish to draw attention to some of these continuing conceptual uncertainties, an appreciation of which may contribute a little towards understanding why nationalism was never quite able to come to terms with 'communalism'.

We have referred above to the nationalists' redefinition of 'politics' in the 1930s and 1940s, and their exclusion of problems like communalism from the realm of the 'political'. This narrowing of the 'political' domain had a different context and meaning from the narrowing that had been undertaken by the early nationalists. The nationalists of the Gandhian era, unlike those of the earlier generation, were not, and could not be, satisfied with a mere separation of the 'social' from the 'political'. Their ideal political world—the mass of the people mobilized into a new national community—necessitated the subordination of the social—the religious and other pre-existing communities; and they had to work resolutely for the subjugation of the latter by the former. This subjugation of the social by the political could not, however, be achieved by the mere exclusion of communalism from the agenda of current political questions.

Indeed, as the previous sections of this chapter will have indi-

---

[45] Cf. Partha Chatterjee, *Nationalist Thought,* chpt. 5.

cated, the nationalists of this era were never quite able to decide whether communalism was to be treated as a political or a social problem. Communalism was sometimes seen as being organic, i.e. as the natural language of the people, and at other times as artificial. Even some of the most advanced and progressive nationalists of the period would appear to have had difficulty in deciding whether communalism was in fact artificial or organic, which is why they often spoke of it as backward, primitive, or, in other words, primordial.

Behind this lay a further difficulty. Secular nationalists, and with them the more recent historians of India, have appeared to misjudge the stratified character of religious discourse, forgetting that a 'religious' standpoint (like Gandhi's) sometimes satisfies an outlook that is not so much anti-nationalist as anti-rationalist or anti-Enlightenment.[46] In part at least this helps to explain the conundrums of Indian nationalism in the last phase of British rule: 'I wonder how people in India can worry about sectarian problems of civilization and culture when hunger and poverty are staring the nation in the face'; 'An unknown factor, however, creeps in when God and the Koran are used for election purposes.'

That unknown factor continued to affect all Indian politics both before and after independence. Indeed, there is evidence of compromise and vacillation among all variety of nationalists even in the course of the 1920s, i.e. at the very time when the new religion of secular nationalism was being expounded.

In 1924, as already noted, Lajpat Rai had begun to speak the language of the new nationalism, as he wrote of the need to dispense with the 'irrational', 'inessential' aspects of religion. But Lajpat Rai was also led, simultaneously, by the experience of the Kohat riots, by what he saw as the 'intransigence' of Muslim leaders at the subsequent Unity Conference in Delhi, and the attitude of the so-called secular Congress leadership, to give renewed thought to the question of 'Hindu unity' and to lend his active support to the Hindu Mahasabha. The Belgaum session of the Mahasabha, held in December 1924, resolved to establish a wider political role

---

[46] Partha Chatterjee makes the point about the anti-rationalist basis of Gandhi's philosophy and action very forcefully; ibid., chpt. 4.

for the Mahasabha and appointed a committee under Lajpat Rai's chairmanship to 'ascertain and formulate Hindu opinion on the subject of Hindu-Muslim problems in their relation to the question of further constitutional reforms'.[47] In 1926 Lajpat Rai and Madan Mohan Malaviya, among others, split from the Congress Swaraj Party and established an Independent Congress Party to contest the triennial elections to the central and provincial legislatures against those nationalists who, in their view, paid insufficient attention to 'Hindu' interests.[48]

There were other, younger nationalist leaders, nowhere identified with the older Hindu nationalist camp, who were moved by new government policies and the Hindu-Muslim strife of the later 1920s to speak of the need for 'Hindu' unity and the defence of 'Hindu' interests. Ganesh Shankar Vidyarthi serves as a striking illustration of this point, in view of his unceasing struggle against the politics of communalism down to the day when he lost his life at the hands of some communalist fanatic while seeking to assuage Hindu and Muslim tempers in the course of the Hindu-Muslim riots of March 1931 in Kanpur.[49]

I have quoted earlier some of Vidyarthi's writings from the mid-1920s regarding the need to oppose religious bigotry and to confine religion to the domestic sphere; and also Mahatma Gandhi's statement that the playing of music ('at any time') was no essential part of the Hindu dharma. The same militant nationalist and admittedly non-communal Vidyarthi responded to a Bengal government order of June 1926, banning the playing of music outside mosques in Calcutta at the time of the *namaz* (public prayers), by declaring that the right to play music had now become a matter of *dharma*, i.e. of duty or religion in the larger sense. In this context, Vidyarthi stressed the need for Hindu organization

[47] Nagar, *Lala Lajpat Rai*, p. 271.

[48] Motilal Nehru, among others, responded during the 1926 election campaign with the argument that he was 'as good a Hindu' as Malaviya and the rest; Pandey, *Ascendancy of the Congress*, pp. 119–24 and 142ff.

[49] Chitra Joshi notes that 'the only person about whose secular credentials there were no two views' when the different Enquiry Committees began their investigations after the riots of March 1931 was Ganesh Shankar Vidyarthi; 'Bonds of Community, Ties of Religion', p. 247n.

(*sangathan*) and reform, and urged the Hindu Mahasabha to convene a special session of its general body in Calcutta and to direct the Hindus of the city *en masse* to oppose the government's order.[50] Three months later, some Hindu activists of Patuakhali in the Barisal district of Bengal initiated a satyagraha against the government's directive that Hindus should cease to play music outside mosques anywhere in the district. Vidyarthi, like many other secular nationalists, read this act of the government as an attack upon civic rights, and applauded the satyagrahis of Patuakhali. These youths would keep alive the shining name of the Hindu organization, Vidyarthi wrote in an article entitled 'Patuakhali ke Vir'.[51]

These actions of government, which came in for criticism and opposition from Vidyarthi and other Congress leaders in 1926, were certainly open to the interpretation that they represented an encroachment on the people's—in this case, the Hindus'—rights. However, given the history of Hindu-Muslim antagonism and strife in the years immediately preceding 1926 (including a major riot in Calcutta in that year, which was the immediate reason for the government's new policy of strictly regulating the playing of music in the vicinity of mosques), Vidyarthi's appeal to uphold the shining name of the Hindu organization and the entire exchange between the government and the nationalists could also be taken as an indication of the 'Hindu' character of the Congress. That is how most Muslim politicians are likely to have seen it.

The example of Lajpat Rai and Madan Mohan Malaviya on the one hand, and Ganesh Shankar Vidyarthi on the other, should suffice to show that many of the concerns that were characteristic of early Indian nationalism—the need to build up 'Hindu' unity and 'Muslim' unity, to protect the rights and interests of the 'Hindus' and 'Muslims' respectively, and to build a national movement that would harmoniously accommodate both—survived into the 1920s and 1930s. If this was true of a Ganesh Shankar Vidyarthi and a Lajpat Rai, it was even more evidently true of a large number of those nationalists who happened to be

---

[50] *Kranti ka Udghosh*, II, pp. 914–15; cf. p. 920.
[51] Ibid., p. 953.

Muslims (or Sikhs, for example), because of the uncertain position of their 'communities' in a rapidly changing political situation and because of the very history of Indian nationalism. It is notable that the continued concern for Community and Country should have given rise to the category of the Nationalist Muslim—a term used by the whole gamut of nationalist writers and publicists, Hindu as well as Muslim, inside and outside the Congress, in the 1920s, 1930s and 1940s.[52] That there was no equivalent term for the Hindus speaks eloquently of the paradoxical position of the Muslims in the discourse of even the more advanced nationalists.

It is perhaps appropriate to conclude this statement on the making of nationalism and communalism in India with the dissenting note of a Nationalist Muslim. Maulana Zafar-ul-Mulk, who was a member of the Congress Kanpur Riots Enquiry Committee of 1931, expressed his disagreement with many parts of the final report. Some of the grounds on which he did so are of more than passing interest. Although he went along with 'a good many' of the remedies suggested in the report as an answer to growing Hindu-Muslim differences, Zafar-ul-Mulk felt unable

to give [his] wholehearted support to the introductory note, at least, so far as it deals with the idea of the fusion of the Hindu-Muslim cultures.... As for the Musalmans, there can be very little doubt that the idea of keeping their general features distinctively separate from those of other nations and communities is as old as Islam itself.[53]

He wrote, further on, that he could not join in the appeal to his co-religionists to join the banking and insurance business. On the contrary, he would urge not only the Muslims but 'my Hindu brethren' as well to refrain from 'such immoral undertakings' which not only 'retard their moral and spiritual progress but tend to nourish capitalism, which is the source of incalculable mischief to humanity'.[54]

Zafar's own alternative remedies were simple. His language was at times Gandhian and his inspiration perhaps not altogether

[52] Cf. Barbara D. Metcalf, 'Nationalist Muslims in British India. The Case of Hakim Ajmal Khan', *MAS*, 19, 1 (1985)

[53] *Roots of Communal Politics*, p. 467.

[54] Ibid., p. 97.

different from Gandhi's, as the quotation in the previous paragraph will have suggested. 'Real unity can only be achieved by a change of heart', he said, in a phrase that was used time and again by the Mahatma. What was needed was 'spiritualism' which was another name for 'godliness' and 'purity of life'. What Indians had to do was to 'give up all cravings for Western ideals and habits and turn back to the old days of Vedas and Quran'. Along any other path lay 'ruin' of the kind that 'European Nations' had brought upon themselves by their own creation—'the Western Civilization'.[55]

This was evidently not part of the discourse of modernity from which the secular nationalists of the 1920s and 1930s derived their language. In this instance, the Nationalist Muslim delegate made his own distance from his 'secular' colleagues abundantly clear when he commented on the section in the Historical Retrospect that spoke of a medieval synthesis represented by the Sufi saints, Hindu *bhaktas, gurus* and *pirs*, and of course Akbar: 'I do not subscribe either to the cult of Kabir and Akbar [*sic.*] or to all that has been written here about them.'[56] At another place the report made a most curious 'Suggestion for the Future' in the form of a plan to rejuvenate the caste system as 'a system of real social organisation' (*sic.*) by returning to the four-fold division of 'men of knowledge', of action, of (economic) acquisitiveness, and of labour. Zafar-ul-Mulk felt the need to dissociate himself from this suggestion, too, arguing, with some justice, that it represented 'a purely Hindu viewpoint which cannot be shared by a humble believer in Islam like myself'.[57] Indian nationalism would not so easily be rid of its history.

Forty years after Partition and Independence, questions of the defence of custom, of established religious institutions (including buildings), of the rights of (religious) communities have again assumed an overwhelming importance in the politics of India. On all sides, Indian politics today is marked by renewed and exaggerated claims along these lines; and we face an increasingly strident demand for

[55] Ibid., pp. 474, 476–7.
[56] *Congress Kanpur Riots Enquiry*, p. 103n.
[57] Ibid., p. 42n.

recognition of what is called the essentially Hindu character of India, Indian civilization and Indian nationalism. At this juncture, it is necessary to reiterate that no such thing as India, Indian civilization or Indian nationalism was given from the start, from the dawn of history as it were. All of these were constructed through the manifold exertions of millions of men and women, and constructed (reconstructed?) to a large extent during the colonial period and in the struggle against colonialism.

The cry of Hindu nationalism in this particular form—of India as essentially the land of the Hindus—is part of the discourse of communalism that came to the fore in the 1920s. Before that, Indian nationalists had sought to emphasize the fact that India was more than only, or primarily, Hindu. As that leading proponent of Hinduism and Hindu culture, Madan Mohan Malaviya, put it,

हिन्दुस्तान में अब केवल हिन्दू ही नहीं बसते हैं—हिन्दुस्तान अब केवल उन्हीं का देश नहीं है । हिन्दुस्तान जैसे हिन्दुओं का प्यारा जन्म-स्थान है, वैसे ही मुसलमानों का भी है । ये दोनों जातियाँ अब यहाँ बसती हैं और सदा बसी रहेंगी . . .

Or again, as Lajpat Rai declared in 1920, 'The Indian nation, such as it is or such as we intend to build [it], neither is nor will be exclusively Hindu, Muslim, Sikh or Christian. It will be each and all.'[58] These were minimal propositions which any Indian nationalism worth the name would have to accept, whatever its understanding of the interests of the nation and the most appropriate means of achieving them.

The emergence during the 1920s of a powerful new strand in nationalism that aimed to go beyond the existing religious communities marked something of a break from this vision: but it was far from being opposed to the basic impulses of this composite nationalism. Building on earlier perceptions of the new solidarities that needed to be established in the country, it proposed to sidestep the religious communities, to confine religion to the private sphere, and to ground itself firmly in the common interests of the people (the millions of individuals who constituted India) rather than of any given communities.

From the 1920s, then, as this last chapter has tried to show, there arose a new contest between two different conceptions of

[58] See footnotes 25 and 27 of chapter 6.

nationalism—one that recognized the givenness of 'pre-existing' communities which were to form the basis of the new India, and another that challenged this view of history, past and present. Alongside these there developed yet another kind of 'nationalism'/ 'communalism' that sought to establish a hierarchy of cultures among the cultures of India (and, indeed, particular regions of India) and to assign to one or another a primary place in the future of the society.[59] It is possible also that the need felt by the new, 'secular' nationalism to forge a different kind of ('secular') historical tradition for the Indian citizen—a past with a lighter burden of 'community consciousness', and greater emphasis on tolerance, integration and on loyalty that tied the individual less to parochial groupings (caste, community, village, etc.), more to the larger whole (India, the Indian state or the Indian spirit)—contributed substantially to the counter-construction of the Indian past in more dogmatrically community (specifically, *religious* community) terms. The contest between these alternative views of nationalism, and these alternative readings of history, was not settled in the 1920s or 1930s or 1940s, and it has not been settled conclusively to this day.

What the student of Indian nationalism cannot disregard is that the nation was, and continues to be, the outcome of many different visions and the struggle between them. And that the rights of the individual—of the poorest and longest oppressed in the land—were as much a part of those visions as the rights of the (pre-existing?) community. Between those different conceptions of nationhood, those contending bases for the political community of the future, the struggle must still be waged—and new resolutions sought.

[59] This last led on, of course, to the politics of 'separatism', to exclusive demands for particular religious communities and even to the demand for nationhood on that basis (which has surfaced periodically from the 1920s to today). I should make it clear that I am not suggesting the existence of any hard and fast division between the advocates of these different kinds of nationalism. It is evident that the boundaries between the latter were more than a little blurred, and many of the same people spoke now in favour of one and now in favour of another.

Afterword
Communalism after Communalism

In the fifteen years that have passed since the publication of this work, the Babari Masjid, which is alluded to (though not by name) at the end of the book,[1] has been destroyed, an anti-Muslim pogrom in Gujarat in 2002 has carried state-sponsored violence against the minorities to another level, and there is much new evidence to show how the world of nationalist politics—linked for much of the twentieth century with the anti-imperialist struggle in Asia and Africa—has been transformed. In this altered context, the category of communalism is hardly as central to Indian (and, more widely South Asian) political discourse as it was even a couple of decades ago.

How do we write a history of so-called religious or sectarian violence and politics at a time when the term 'communalism' does not quite so readily apply as it once did? This is a question that needs to be asked in view of the major transformations that have taken place in our apprehension of political relations and activities, 'communal' and 'non-communal', over the past couple of decades.

I observed in the preface to the first edition that we would probably have to continue to use the term 'communalism' even after we have acknowledged that it is narrow, overdetermined by Western colonial perceptions of the East, and not always helpful in our efforts to understand the force, the politics, and the history that it seeks to describe. The persistence of this usage is dictated by the very availability of the term as part of the language of common political discussion, as well as by intellectual inertia. Nevertheless, a whole range of new terms and concepts has now come to inhabit the space of historiographical and political commentary alongside the vocabulary of communalism.

[1] See p. 259.

Political assertion and political commentary now speaks as commonly about majoritarianism, minorityism, and the appeasement of minorities as it does about communalism. There is widespread talk of fascism, fundamentalism, genocide, ethnic cleansing, and terrorism. Critics have noted too that much of the violent fallout of today's sectarian politics takes the form of pogroms and not communal riots, even if the term 'communal riots' continues to be used. The awareness of the inadequacy of existing terms of description, and the search for an alternative vocabulary, tells us a great deal about the changing conditions of contemporary politics, and of our engagement with it.

I have deliberately given this Afterword a provocative title, for there is an uncertainty and fluidity about our political world that we need to try and grasp anew. Referring in my 1990 introduction to Christopher Bayly's widely cited essay on 'the pre-history of communalism',[2] I pointed out that the search for eighteenth century precursors of communal conflict in the nineteenth and twentieth centuries was anachronistic. This was not simply for the reason that the term was not present in the earlier period. More to the point, it was because the context, the discursive space, and the social-political arrangements for the emergence of the category simply did not exist.[3] By the same token, I think it is possible today to speak of a condition of *post*-communalism, in which the context and the discursive space that made for what was characterized as communalism no longer endures.

The antagonisms, the suspicion and hatred, and the bloodletting between organized groups claiming to speak for different religious communities have hardly disappeared. On the contrary, they appear to have taken on more vicious and undisguised forms. However, the easy categorization of these politics as communalism—the other, and (truth to tell) the *subsidiary* other, of nationalism—is not quite so comfortably done: and the search is on for an alternative and perhaps more adequate conceptualization of these tendencies and occurrences. The reasons for unease perhaps lie in the erosion of the neat ideals

[2] C.A. Bayly, 'The Pre-History of 'Communalism'? Religious Conflict in India, 1700–1860', *Modern Asian Studies*, 19, 2 (April 1985).

[3] See above, pp. 15–16.

of nationalism and communalism, progress and reaction that we have long lived with. It is these we might examine a little more closely.

II

Communalism in its peculiar South Asian usage referred, as I noted in this book, and as other scholars have noted before and since, to political movements and activities based on the proclaimed common interests (economic, cultural, political) of members of a religious community, in opposition to the politics and activities of members of another religious community (or communities), and to the real or imagined threat from these. It referred also to the condition of suspicion, fear, and hostility between people belonging to different religious denominations that commonly accompanies or follows from these politics. Yet the significance of the concept was hardly exhausted by such definitions. What gave to the term 'communalism' its particular resonance and force was a certain relation to ideas of nationhood and nationalism, to the notion of community, and to the position of the state. Let me try to separate these out—even though they are not easily separable—and deal with each of them in turn, beginning with a reiteration of some of the points I made about the adjacency of communalism and nationalism.

There are two ways in which the connection between communalism and nationalism may be seen to operate. First, the politics of communalism and those of nationalism arose in tandem, in a relation one might say of interdependency. Communalism, communalist parties, and communalist politics were implicated centrally in a debate about nationhood—the character of the claimed political community, the emphasis to be placed on its different parts, the safeguards or special support that needed to be provided to particular segments of the population, and so on. Secondly, communalism sought to approximate nationalism. It appeared in a similar guise. On the face of it communalist politicians had little choice in this matter. For since the triumph of nationalism in nineteenth century Europe, and the emergence of the nation-state as the sole legitimate form for the political existence of people in the twentieth, all political movements that have claimed the rights of historical communities have had to cast themselves in the likeness of national movements. This helps to explain why communalist movements of this kind have gone on, in many cases, to demand the creation of separate provinces and states; and why no communalist or communalist party ever describes itself as communalist. On the contrary, one party's communalism commonly appears as another's nationalism.

I have argued that 'communalism' was a category of colonialist knowledge.[4] The irony of the situation was that anti-colonial commentators and publicists, fighting for the establishment of an Indian nation-state, did more than anyone else to propagate it. The category of communalism appeared in colonial discourse as a means of dealing with the political needs and aspirations of the subject population, and of making sense of the new kinds of plural societies that colonial rulers encountered in the colonies. In many of these, major world religions continued to exist side by side, and religion remained a major presence in daily life as well as public affairs: and while the latter was not entirely dissimilar to the situation in Europe and North America, the former opened up a whole new world and new possibilities of explication—often leading to curious propositions about a hierarchy of religions, as well as about the otherness and the lack of 'development', not to say primitive character, of many of these societies.

Anti-colonial nationalists, in their turn—schooled as they were in the virtues of European style nationalism, and in European histories that presented rosy accounts of the total separation of church from state in their countries—used the category of communalism to portray a certain position in debates on the political future of these same societies. They appropriated the term and exploited it as a weapon with which to tar the politics of those who made diverse claims on behalf of different religious, ethnic or caste communities.

In India, the politics of religion (as it was sometimes called) came to be labelled communalism from the 1920s, and communalism came to be represented as the chief obstacle to nationalism. Sectional demands for a share in public affairs and state power, based on the alleged interests of people of particular

---

[4] p. 6 above and *passim*.

religious denominations, began to be branded 'anti-national'. Nationalism was declared to be modern and progressive, reflecting the spirit of the age. Communalism was its opposite—reactionary and backward-looking, even a relic of ages past. The snag, as I have already indicated, was that what was communalism to some was nationalism to others. This was after all the claim that Jinnah and the Muslim League made on behalf of the subcontinent's Muslims in the 1930s and 1940s. Moreover, one might argue, it was the nationalist claim, rather than a communalist one, that the establishment of the independent state of Pakistan in 1947 seemed to uphold. The same sort of claim has been made by the right-wing Hindu parties that have recently gained ascendancy in India: and it is notable that a wide array of commentators now describe these parties in the terms that they themselves favour, as Hindu nationalists.

For all their violent and unfortunate consequences—and these were not trifling—communalisms, no less than nationalisms, had their life in the context of a vigorous debate about political futures—Indian, Nigerian, Malaysian, Sri Lankan, or other. What was called communalism acquired its meaning in a contest over the nature of an imagined, national community. What was the character of that political community to be? Should it be unitary or federal; what power should the federating units have; what was to be the basis of elections and the delimitation of constituencies? What should be the language (or languages) of the nation, its history, its culture, its flag and its anthem? What its civil code, its marriage and property laws, and the character of the economic development that it would seek? Should there be special safeguards for minorities and marginalized communities—in education, in public service, in the electoral arena, in the matter of religious and cultural practices?

Recall that, in the subcontinent, the term communalism was commonly applied in colonial times to describe the conflict between Brahmans and non-Brahmans and the emergence of a powerful non-Brahman movement in southern India. Likewise, the debate on the communal question at the Round Table Conferences of 1930–2 and the Communal Award that followed was concerned with the political weightage to be granted not only to religious minorities and the Anglo-Indians, but also to the so-called Untouchables (the Scheduled Castes and Tribes of the Government of India Act of 1935 and the Indian constitution of 1950). What was at issue in this politics of communalism was the place that would be found for diverse social-political communities in the affairs of the larger political community, itself claiming the status of nation-statehood.

Today, that relation to nationalism has disappeared. For one thing, nationalism no longer inhabits the same kind of *imaginative* moment. In large part, this is because nation-states, even pretend nation-states (if I may make such a distinction, since one might argue that the matter of pretence, in terms of whom they claim to speak for, applies more or less to all existing nations and states) are well entrenched—as states. In our times, therefore, different versions of communalism have either become nationalisms in their own right, or else, they have had to function in a far more subordinate and defensive capacity than before, in the shadow of a dominant nationalism. The Indian example is as pertinent as any.

All nation-states announce their birth with the unfurling of national flags, the singing of national anthems, and the visual representation of the national territory. Along with that, there is the gradual, and sometimes not so gradual, unveiling of an officially sanctioned account of the national past, the national culture, the national good, and the national interest. Disseminated in the press and on the platform, on TV and in textbooks, these often turn out to be only a little less sacred and unchallengeable than national flags, anthems, and maps.

With the establishment of the independent state of India, the boundaries of the new national community were clearly established, and marked and described in official maps. Its origins were now portrayed as being already *known*: at the dawn of history; in the achievements of the Mauryas, the Guptas and the Mughals; in the beautiful languages and poetry of early modern 'saints'; in the glorious anti-imperialist struggle of the nineteenth and twentieth centuries. Its exceptional culture was celebrated: 'unity in diversity'; the coexistence of Hinduism and Islam and other world religions; the spirit of accommodation (as if this were unique to this land, and as if there wasn't a great deal of counter-evidence); even the existence of 'secularism' from long, long ago. Its constitution was held up as an extraordinary achievement, as it certainly was in many important respects, and was represented as the infallible foundation of its democracy and its secularism.

Steadily, and almost unwittingly, we have seen in India a considerable consensus develop over many of these propositions among circles that have had a major influence over the regulation of public life: political parties, the national media, leaders of industry, commerce, and intellect. Numerous issues, relating to the nature of the national political community, and the rights and obligations of its constituent communities, continue to be debated, but the debate takes place largely within the confines of this 'national' consensus: this *is* a Hindu country, even if only by virtue of numbers; it *is* secular—and has always been; Kashmir and the Northeast *are* an integral part of the nation—and have always been; the constitution provides foolproof guarantees against any injustice to minorities; and so forth.

The vocabulary of communalism, communal movements, communal riots, etc., has not altogether disappeared, of course.[5] But wherever it is employed, it conveys a sense of being increasingly tired. Its use continues in part because earlier debates and conflicts (relating to the place of different 'minority' communities in the political arrangements of the nation) still go on; in part because of intellectual inertia—because this is a language that is understood and apparently evokes at least some understanding. At the same time, communalist (or shall we say sectional) demands that appear as a threat to the position and politics of those in power are now much more easily and unhesitatingly condemned as 'anti-national', 'secessionist' (which they may or may not be), and more recently 'terrorist'. I shall return to some of the more recent examples of change in the state's political vocabulary, and to their significance for contemporary politics.

[5] While this is true for some South Asian countries like India and Bangladesh, in others like Sri Lanka, a different vocabulary of 'ethnicity' and 'ethnic conflict' emerged fairly early as American social science took a new hold from the 1960s.

Before that, however, we need to dwell a little on the character of the communities that were (and sometimes still are) supposed to be the agents of communalism.

III

The notion of the community, which was crucially linked to the concept of communalism, requires some unpacking. It is important to note straightaway that the communities we speak of, as participants in a debate about the character of public life, must already be politicized in order to appear as communities. Whether these be religious, regional, caste-based, or indeed national, they are the politicized communities of the colonial and postcolonial periods. For, until that is their condition, the so-called 'communities'—of religion, caste, language, whatever— would appear to be rather too differentiated and unorganized to enter into the kind of dialogue or conversation in the legal-constitutional domain of the state that we have referred to above. What marked out all such communities in the era of anti-colonial struggle was an aspiration to citizenship and democratic rights. What marked some of them more than others was an anxiety about the conditions of this future citizenship, leading them to organize and agitate to turn those conditions into the most favourable ones possible. It is this that gave force to what was called communalism and communalist demands.

The situation has since changed. While the ideals and images, policies and practices of the nation and its state continue to be contested, the nation-state now exists as a powerful and tangible material, intellectual and spiritual force. It lays down the terms of debate in a way that sets out very differently what is acceptable and unacceptable, moral and immoral, legal and illegal. What emerges in this context is a notion of 'good' and 'bad' community. The nation of course becomes the supreme example of the good.[6] People may still belong to sundry communities, apart from the nation, but permission to belong and to proclaim such

---

[6] Cf. the important discussion of this theme in Partha Chatterjee, *The Nation and its Fragments: Colonial and Postcolonial Histories* (Princeton, N.J., 1994), ch. 11.

belonging depends to a large extent on the 'lesser' community's conformity or lack of conformity with the current state of the national project or, to put it more bluntly, on whether it is seen as threatening to the nation(al) community or not.

Members of marginal, subordinated or politically disadvantaged communities, who were and often continue to be the proponents of 'communalist' (again, read sectional) standpoints and the makers of 'communalist' demands, are now formally citizens. At the same time, they are seen as belonging to pre-constituted, and sometimes constitutionally recognized, 'minority communities'. These communities continue to be participants in political affairs, but in conditions that are very different from those that obtained before. They come to be treated as fixed entities, and become the object of governmentality in quite novel—and naked—ways.

In moments of heightened political tension or agitation, the citizenship of men and women belonging to these communities may easily become suspect. Which particular groups are affected depends of course on the issues involved. The case of the Muslims of India is paradigmatic: for, given the partition of the subcontinent, they have lived almost continuously since 1947 under the shadow of a suspicion—the suspicion of harbouring loyalties to Pakistan.[7] At these times of tension, the members of minority communities are always in danger of losing their rights as citizens, and of emerging as 'populations' to be managed by the government. Curfews, imposed neutrally over particular territories, towns, and villages, affect these suspect citizens more than any others;[8] surveillance procedures apply primarily to them.

The point about 'citizens' and 'populations', as bodies of people that are differently treated, requires some clarification, and it will help for this purpose to say a word or two about the relationship of modern states, colonial and postcolonial, to the populations they have governed. The colonial state everywhere worked with a sharp distinction between 'subjects' and 'citizens'. The former, who comprised the vast majority of colonial

---

[7] For an elaboration of this point, see my *Remembering Partition. Violence, Nationalism and History in India* (Cambridge, 2001).

[8] See the powerful testimony of the Indian police official Vibhuti Narain Rai in his fictionalized *Shahar Mein Curfew* (Delhi, 1987).

populations and indeed of the population of the world until the middle of the twentieth century, were in the colonial dispensation supposedly being trained for the conferral of citizenship—presumably in the rather distant future. They were, in Foucauldian terms, populations to be disciplined, educated, fashioned so that they might be infused with increased productive capacity and a greater respect for law and order.

The early nationalist states of the postcolonial era announced their arrival by the granting of citizenship rights to all who inhabited their territories, with just the occasional question mark over the status of marginal individuals or groups. These were professedly developmental states, under which the national population was to be made fit (and equal) in a modern world. The focus was supposed to be on education and all round economic growth as a means to establishing the necessary underpinnings of democracy and modernity.

The neo-liberal regime of our own time appears to have reverted to a colonial conception of productive 'citizens' on the one hand, who provide the elements of enterprise and modernity in our societies, and 'populations' on the other, who are lacking in resources, education and initiative and to that extent unworthy of the privileges accorded to proper citizens.[9] This is not a developmental state any more, even theoretically. Indeed, terms like 'development' and 'welfare' are at a discount, and 'poverty', 'the poor' and 'economic democracy' (or economic and social justice) have largely disappeared from ruling class discourse.

'The rights of ... the poorest and longest oppressed in the land'[10] are no longer proclaimed as being quite so critical as they once were. The political rhetoric of the day, and the practice of nations and states that follows from it, suggests on the contrary

[9] However, there is no escape from these populations—unwelcome, and sometimes illegal or barely legal, immigrants; slum dwellers; vagrant children and youth; and so on. They cannot easily be moved out. All that the state can do is to try and discipline them in such a way as to maintain, and if possible improve, conditions for the rapid economic advance of the country and its citizens (that is to say, of its more prosperous and privileged classes. Cf. Partha Chatterjee, *The Politics of the Governed: Reflections on Popular Politics in Most of the World* (Delhi, 2004) for an extended discussion of these issues.

[10] See p. 261 above.

that the 'rights of the individual' (poor or otherwise) hardly have the same value, in every class and every society, of every continent. It is as if one cannot even compare the Western world and the world of Islam, the Israelis and the Arabs, Hindus and Muslims. These are effectively different worlds, with different kinds of inhabitants, in which the practice of governance must necessarily function in somewhat different ways.

The point is illustrated very well indeed by the manner in which suffering and loss is reported in the context of natural disasters or political violence in different parts of the globe. Consider the official response to the lives lost in the attacks on New York and Washington on 11 September 2001. One aspect of this response that I found especially moving was the refusal for a good length of time to provide any estimate of the total number of people killed. 'Whatever the final number turns out to be,' the mayor of New York, Rudolph Giuliani declared, 'it will be too much to bear.' There was in this refusal to hurriedly name a figure an important sign of respect for the dead, and for the very large number of people who had lost loved ones. For those in the position of the latter, it goes without saying, even one death is always 'too much to bear'. It may help to stay with this sensitive suggestion to reflect upon how governments and publicists have represented and understood situations of brutal violence in other parts of the world.

In the Western press and Western writings more generally, a clear distinction emerges in reporting of this kind between 'our' casualties and 'theirs', between the carefully counted number of Americans reported lost in the 'war on terrorism' in Afghanistan and Iraq, and the 'uncounted' natives; between the 'hundreds' of Palestinians killed in the most recent *intifada* and the 2 (or 10, or 16, or 32) Israelis. In 1996, Madeleine Albright, then the US Secretary of State, was asked in a television interview what she thought about the allegation that 500,000 Iraqi children had died as a result of US economic sanctions. While it was 'a very hard choice', she said, 'all things considered, we think the price is worth it.' Three years ago, US officials made an argument of a similar kind on the question of civilian casualties or 'collateral damage' in the 'action' in Afghanistan. Pentagon spokespersons sought to clear themselves of responsibility by saying that they did not keep track of civilian casualties in that country. At the same time, the commander of the US forces there said that he did not wish to prejudge the results of an investigation ordered, apparently on the intervention of Hamid Karzai (then the leader of the interim government in Afghanistan), into a raid that killed at least 15 Afghans. 'The thing I don't think we'll do is be quick to rush to a judgement that takes as truth *information* that may be *provided by sources who do not share the same value of human life that we share in this country.*'[11]

This is a distinction—between 'us' and 'them', the 'civilized' and the 'uncivilized', mere 'bodies' as opposed to 'human beings'— that human beings had long lived with. It is a distinction that is made, consciously or unconsciously, in the visual representation of the war in Afghanistan, or Palestine, Rwanda, Congo or Sudan—where the 'madness', the collective horror, the dirt, and the utter hopelessness of the 'other' is regularly counterposed to the individuality, the identifiable wounds, the pain, and the suffering of survivors among 'us'. Think of the number of occasions on which we are faced with pictures of mourning relatives and bystanders, of surviving toddlers participating in a funeral; or, to take a different example, the long series of moving obituaries published by the *New York Times* of those who lost their lives in the attacks on the World Trade Center—an extraordinary number of them (as one colleague pointed out with fascination) apparently sports-men and women, all of them, in their different ways, brimming with life and hope and desire and laughter, and bringing these qualities to the lives of others. These are portraits of people who live on: alive even when they are dead. Compare this with pictures of captured Taliban prisoners, or the victims of atrocities perpetrated by state-sponsored militias in the Sudan— pictures of faceless hordes, lifeless, wild, and indistinguishable (even when photographed alone): dead even when they are technically alive.

The assumption is clear: 'our' losses, our suffering, our individuality, our history, are narratable—and must be narrated.

[11] *New York Times*, 8 February 2002, p. A14 (emphasis added).

'Theirs' belong to a world that is frankly incomprehensible, that is in a sense simply *like that*. This is a world that evidently has no history; there is nothing here that we can recognize as politics, and individuality counts for little if anything. This applies to 'populations' within nation-states—the Muslims of Gujarat are only one of India's most recent examples—as much as it applies to 'populations' seen from afar, in distant countries. Witness, one can almost hear the 'expert' right-wing commentators say in India as in the United States, the identical *burqas* of all those Muslim women, and the identical beards of all those Muslim men.

Groups like these were once given the status of 'communities', which were allowed their say in debates about political futures. The state now returns to them with a vengeance—to destroy them as moral/ethical communities and networks of sustenance— because they are collectivities with 'different' (not to say, abnormal) values, customs, and practices; people with a peculiar (and obviously unwarranted) sense of independence and pride. It seeks to 'discipline' these collectivities in the midst of much rhetorical talk of richness and variety, the co-existence of cultures and multiculturalism. These are populations that come to be viewed (once more?)—both at home and abroad—as people who are utterly unlike us, modern individuals: bodies of people that are not used to the practice of reason, and that cannot control their passions or their primitive beliefs. This is not altogether removed from the condemnation of 'communalists' and 'communalist politics' found in high nationalist discourse in the era of anti- colonial agitations, but this representation of difference, and of different political perspectives, now has other names and other political consequences.

IV

The point about other names and other consequences may be clarified by turning to the last facet of the communalist (and post-communalist) world that I want to consider—the resources and position of the state. Implicit in much of what I have said above is a recognition of the significantly altered situation of the state in recent times. Two aspects of this altered situation should perhaps be underlined. First, there is clear evidence of the increased and increasing power and reach of the centralized state and its various arms—the military, the police, bureaucracy, and intelligence. Even as the sovereignty of numerous states has been eroded in the context of globalization, their ability to maintain discipline in terms increasingly dictated by a new international order, but willingly accepted by diverse national elites, is in many instances greatly enhanced. National governments and ruling classes continue to specify the rules and conditions of political activity and debate within their borders. However, except in the case of so-called 'failed states', a significant number of them in Africa or the post-Soviet polities of Central Asia and eastern Europe, many of these regimes operate more and more openly in concert with what might be called an international ruling class. The anti-imperialist content of twentieth century nationalisms has largely disappeared, even from the ex-colonial countries of Asia and Africa. The nation-states of what used to be called the First, the Second, and the Third Worlds are now called upon to work together to keep up production for the international economic order, to hold labour costs down, and to prevent major threats to (national and international) security and property.

The second general point to note about the contemporary state is that this state and its several arms appear far less neutral, or at any rate, far less cautious about adopting a partisan position in relation to differences and conflicts *within* the countries that they govern. It bears reiteration that the modern state made its appearance as a more or less self-consciously 'neutral' force—that stood *above* society, abstracted from it. For a long period in the nineteenth and twentieth centuries, the state's claim to neutrality formed a large part of the argument for the perpetuation of colonial government in Asia and Africa. It is a claim that many postcolonial regimes put forward with even greater insistence, and for a while in democracies like India and Sri Lanka, perhaps with somewhat greater success. Here once the republic was in place, elected representatives and governments were meant—in classical republican terms—to speak not for specific constituencies, but for the nation as a whole. They were supposed to represent the abstract will of the republic, rising above the fray of sectional interests, including the interests of class, community, and region. So the theory went.

In fact, as subsequent events in both India and Sri Lanka have shown, history has taken a rather different path, and it has been difficult to sustain the myth of an abstract national will or a universally agreed national interest. Electoral imperatives, the need for rapid accumulation of wealth and power (whenever opportunity has arisen), the aim of making good quickly and at any cost, all of this has led over time to the consolidation of ruling class power through the whipping up of a diehard majoritarianism. Since the 1980s, in India, and somewhat earlier in Sri Lanka, arguments have been advanced about how the Hindu majority and the Sinhala majority respectively must unite to avoid being overwhelmed by the minority, how the minority (tied to international forces of various kinds) must not be allowed to hold the nation to ransom, and how it must most certainly no longer be appeased.

In India, the immediate context for this was provided by the collapse of earlier constituencies (most notably, perhaps, the alliance between the highest castes and the lowest, along with the Muslims, that had brought the Congress back to power in several elections), and by a new politics of coalitions, black money and muscle power. In this situation, Hindu right-wing forces—but not these forces alone, for the entire political spectrum has shifted to the right, in India as in other parts of the world—were able to generate a heightened rhetoric of 'natural' national unity, based now not on a political vision and programme for the future, but on religious symbols described as the nation's fundamental heritage. (Consider the mandatory lighting of lamps in more and more state-funded and civil society functions, or the *tilak* that visiting foreign dignitaries regularly get daubed on their foreheads, or the elaborate *puja* that has become a natural part of the inauguration of new public buildings.) The new commercialization and the much more evident flattening of cultures that came with liberalism contributed to this. An increasingly influential group of non-resident Indians, seeking identity and self-definition, now became ardent, long-distance nationalists—fervent supporters of the battle for new Sikh,

Muslim, and Hindu homelands and the destruction of a disused (but beautiful) sixteenth century mosque in Ayodhya—not on the basis of any historical debate or political struggle, but rather of the most ready-to-hand and reduced symbols of nation, community, and religion.[12]

Given such support, and the backing of well entrenched and well-trained police and para-military forces, on the one hand, and of major international states on the other, and faced by widely scattered, poor, and very largely unarmed minorities, right-wing Hindu parties in India have more or less successfully re-invented the nation-state in a chauvinist Hindu image and successfully cowed down the minorities—except in the border regions of Kashmir and the Northeast. Along with Trade Unions, secessionist movements, and other disruptive opposition moves (all equally disliked by the new globalizing and liberalizing international order), minority groups are very quickly condemned as anti-national for any 'deviation' from the so-called national mainstream, be this in a dispute over the site of the temple/mosque in Ayodhya or over the results of an India-Pakistan cricket match. Muslims in India, and increasingly the very small community of Christians too, come under suspicion because of their link to 'foreign' (anti-national) religions, hence 'foreign' (anti-national) forces, and more recently in the case of the Muslims to what is widely proclaimed as a worldwide network of terrorism. All of this has substantially altered the world of communalism.

After the 1980s, in India as in Sri Lanka, the state became a much more active (and openly one-sided) party to inter-community conflicts that, once upon a time, it was supposed to have mediated. Although there are some signs in both countries now of political forces attempting to pull back from the brink, the more fundamental change in the acknowledged capacity of the state to take partisan positions needs to be noted. If communalism refers to a condition of conflict and negotiation between two or more politicized religious communities, the Indian and Sri Lankan

[12] For the recent Gujarat case, see Upendra Baxi's comments on 'cosmopolitan' versions of Gujarati *asmita*, 'The Second Gujarat Catastrophe', *Economic and Political Weekly* (24 August 2002), p. 3523 and *passim*.

states—or, at least, important parts of these states—have in recent years acted rather like politicized religious communities themselves. And the 'communal riot', once thought of as the quintessential expression (and upshot) of communalist politics, has given place to a very different kind of violence.

On the question of partisanship, let me cite the testimony of a senior officer of the Indian Police Service. 'Since 1960, in almost all [communal] riots that have occurred,' he writes, 'the same picture has been painted in the same colours, a picture of a helpless and often inactive police force that allowed wailing members of the minority community to be looted and killed in its presence, that remained a mute witness to some of their members being burnt alive.' 'For an average policeman,' he goes on to say, 'collection of intelligence is limited to gathering information about the activities of communal Muslim organizations. It is not easy to make him realize that the activities of Hindu communal organizations also come under the purview of anti-national activities.... Similarly, preventive arrests, even in riot situations in which Muslims are the worst sufferers, are restricted to members of the minority community.'[13]

As to 'communal riots', it is enough to say that the worst examples of violence against minority religious communities, over the last two decades and more, fail to fit the description in any commonly understood sense of the term. It is unnecessary to recount details of the carnage that occurred in Delhi in 1984, in Bombay and other places in 1992–3, or in Gujarat in 2002. Suffice it to recall that, in these as in other instances, hundreds if not thousands of people from the majority community congregated at will for days (sometimes weeks) on end, to attack and loot the persons, property, and wealth of the targeted community. The habitations, houses and shops, vehicles and machines, fields and hand-pumps, that belonged to members of the minority community were identified and marked out in advance, with the assistance of electoral registers, tax rolls, census data, and local informants. The attacks themselves took place

[13] Vibhuti Narain Rai, 'An Open Letter to my Fellow Police Officers', reprinted in Siddharth Varadarajan, ed., *Gujarat: The Making of a Tragedy*, (New Delhi, 2002), pp. 211–2.

with the acquiescence (if not the active encouragement) of the police, the political leadership and even leading ministers in the government, and with almost no fear of counter-attack or loss of life (since the police is ready at hand to ward off and shoot any counter-attackers), or indeed of punishment (since the police and the existing political leadership is on their side, and even the judiciary seems to be mindful of the views of the political leadership, if not in agreement with them). These were certainly not 'riots'. They were organized political massacres, feeding on and fanning the hatred and prejudices of a growing segment of the majority community; pogroms; and examples of a new brand of state terrorism.

The worldwide 'war on terrorism' that has followed the attacks on New York and Washington on 11 September 2001, has provided a fresh justification for this kind of violence. Gujarat provides the most brazen example. Not surprisingly, there has been little discussion of 'communalism' in this instance, even if the term surfaces periodically in the writings and in oral commentary on the Gujarat violence. Far more sinister has been the widespread talk of 'terrorism'—in relation of course to Muslims alone. A press note issued by the state government after the attack at Godhra on 27 February 2002, described the torching of the train and the killing of passengers as a 'pre-planned inhuman collective violent act of terrorism'. Chief Minister Modi spoke of Pakistan's proxy war and its 'clandestine role ... behind the Godhra genocide', and referred to the latter as 'the pre-planned collective terrorism against Gujarat'. In his turn, one might add, Mr Modi has been hailed as 'the Sardar opposed to terrorism'.[14] Six months later, following what might much more reasonably be described as a terrorist attack on a Hindu temple in Gandhinagar, the then Prime Minister, Atal Behari Vajpayee, declared from the Indian Ocean island of Male where he was attending a SAARC meeting that terrorism was 'on its last legs', the Taliban and Al-Qaeda were finished, and there was a global war against terrorism in which India was fully playing its part.[15]

The rhetoric of Bush, Cheney, and Rumsfeld has clearly

[14] *Editors Guild Fact Finding Mission Report,* 13.
[15] *The Hindu,* 25 September 2002.

captured the imagination of interested parties in many places. Since September 2001, the 'war against terrorism' has become an instrument in the hands of numerous powerful groups and states in different parts of the world, India, Israel, and Russia among them, to settle old scores and make easy (financial and political) gains. There was for a while large-scale international public opposition to the war against Iraq. However, opposition to the longer term strategies adopted by governments far and wide in their efforts to combat 'terror' has been muted at best; and there has been far too little by way of a challenge to the nationalist, and even 'humanitarian', arguments advanced in justification of their actions.

Governments and bureaucracies have in any case over time accumulated increasing power to do as they want, largely unchecked—because of their invisibility, their access to information, and an easy recourse to arguments about the sanctity of national interests, above all, the interest of national security. Over the last few years, this exercise of bureaucratic, state power has been particularly arbitrary and unquestioned. This is surely the case in India today, as it is in that other 'great democracy', the USA. In both countries opposition, especially from the most important mainstream political parties, is often restricted to condemnations of Government for its poor timing or its failure to follow 'nationalist' policies (such as anti-terrorist measures, the exercise of a military option, or nuclearization!) vigorously enough. Large sections of the population have lived in a kind of 'security state' even in these leading democracies, with increasing restrictions on what official policies may be debated, let alone combated.

Anyone or any group that mounts a challenge to the proclaimed national interest may be denounced as an 'enemy' now. Very commonly, the charge is laid on members of 'minority' communities who are accused of having 'foreign', hence 'enemy', links. No particular argument is required to demonstrate their enemy status. It comes from their very being, and is 'proved' by their 'foreign' religions or languages, the mosques they congregate in, their links with people (sometimes relatives) in other countries, and the simple fact of loud, and repeated, assertion. These are enemies and terrorists almost by definition, wreckers of peace in the nation ('in every country they inhabit', it is commonly said in India about Muslims), wreckers of the nation. It is up to them—as it was up to Saddam Hussein—to prove that they no longer harbour weapons and drugs, that they have given up criminal intentions, and that they will now begin to live like 'us'.[16]

V

In the plural societies of large parts of Asia and Africa, where neither absolutist nor conquest state had emerged in the early modern period to homogenize religious traditions and cultural practices, the politics of communalism—or what has been called communalism—arose in the colonial period to become a major factor in political debates. Such a politics was often seen, justifiably, as disruptive of emerging struggles for nationhood and independence, especially since there was always a danger that communalist campaigns would sprout separate national movements of their own. But movements of this kind were also a part of emerging political contests in these complex, multi-layered, plural societies—one element in the negotiation of political futures, the outcome of which was hardly predictable in advance.

The increasingly centralized nationalist states that have arisen all over the world since then have altered the political equation almost beyond recognition. The statist chauvinisms that have often followed the establishment of these nation-states have refused to enter into any dialogue with the kinds of sectional, sectarian, or cultural movements that were once labelled 'communalist'. In addition, the 'collapse of socialism', as it is called, the emergence of a unipolar world, and the onset of an aggressive globalization, has eroded the grounds of contestatory democracy even further.

'Not so very long ago,' Jean Paul Sartre wrote in his preface to Frantz Fanon's *Les Damnes de la Terre* in 1961, 'the earth numbered two thousand million inhabitants: five hundred

[16] See in this connection, Mahmood Mamdani, *Good Muslim, Bad Muslim: America, the Cold War, and the Roots of Terror* (New York, 2004).

million men, and one thousand five hundred million natives.'[17] A half-century later, the distinction between 'human beings' and 'natives', or what we might call 'citizens' and 'populations', has begun to reappear in insidious ways, almost as sharply as it did during the European conquest and colonization of large parts of the globe. With the rapid advance of the kinds of arguments mentioned above, about threats to our nations, frequently portrayed as threats to civilization, the space for the imagination of alternative futures, and for the very recognition of difference, appears to be shrinking once again.

Yet, for all the talk of a globalized and 'smaller' world, our planet is perhaps a more contradictory and fragmented place than it was a hundred or even fifty years ago. There are many more sovereign nation-states, or at least nominally sovereign states; the vast majority of people are recognized as citizens of one state or another (even if there is, once more, a growing number of refugees and migrants without any surety of this); and there is increased talk, in many countries, of multiculturalism, of the contributions of privileged migrants and diasporic communities, as well as of the fundamental rights of all men and women in all parts of the globe. It is in the rhetoric of sovereignty and human rights, in the disorder of our political world, and in the messiness of our search for new intellectual/political ends, that we will still find grounds for struggle.

[17] Preface to Frantz Fanon, *The Wretched of the Earth* (New York, 1963), p. 7.

Appendix I

Patias circulating in Shahabad in the course of Hindu attacks upon Muslims in the district at the Baqr Id of 1917

Patia No. 1

"पतिया चला गौ लोक से । हिन्दू भाई के पास मिनती [विनती] है के गौ के धरम जाता है । सो का कसूर करता है के दूसरे के हाथ से मरता है । इसमें हिन्दू भाई निवेदन किया जाता है के गाँव-गाँव घर-घर गौ के खबरदारी रखें । अगर नहीं तो गाँव से गौ हाय मारके चल[I] जायेगा । मुसलमान के छन [संग?] गौ देखे तो ले लेने का धरम है । पाँच पतिया लिख भेजने का धरम है । न भेजे तो गौ मारे का हत्या हो । अगर भेजे तो पाँच गौ दान का धरम है ।"

['This *patia* comes from the world of the cow. It brings an entreaty to brother Hindus. The religion of the cow is being destroyed. What crime has she committed that she should be killed by non-believers [literally, 'others']. Hindu brothers are entreated to watch over the cow in every village and every house. If they do not, the cow will sadly breathe its last and disappear from the village(s). If you see a Musalman with a cow, it is your duty ['religion'—the word *dharma* stands for both] to take it from him. It is also your duty ['religion'] to write and send on five *patias*. If you do not, you bear the sin of cow-slaughter. If you do, it is equivalent to the gift of five cows.']

Patia No. 2

"बहुत मुश्किल के बात है के हिंदू और मुसलमान से गाय के बारे में तकरार पड़ल है । जे हिन्दू है जो [?] सो अपने बस्ती से मदद देवे, न तो हिंदू के धुतकार है । ये घड़ी दौदनगर में बड़ा बलवा है । हिंदू के लाजिम है के गौ के बारे में मदद दे । अगर अपना अपना हथियार लेके दौदनगर में ना आये, से मुसलमान का जाना [जना?] होये । और यह पत्री पावे सो पाँच पाँच पत्री लिख कर दूसरे दूसरे बस्ती में भेज देवे, ना तो हिन्दू को तिलक है ।"

['It is a matter of great difficulty that Hindus and Muslims are quarrelling about the cow. Every Hindu must come forward with support from wherever he lives, otherwise it is a snub to the Hindus. At this moment, there is fierce rioting in Daudnagar. It is incumbent upon Hindus to help in the matter of the cow. If they do not come with their weapons to

Daudnagar, then may they be born of Musalmans. Write and send five copies each of this *patia* (*patri*) to other habitations, otherwise it is a curse upon the Hindus'].

Patia No. 3

"हिंदू भाई के नमस्कार होइ । हिन्दू भाई के हम लिखते हैं कि हिंदू भाई मुसलमान के मदद देते हैं । ओ हिंदू भाई मुसलमान को छिपा रखते हैं । वह लोग अमझर दौदनगर अरवल में । हिंदू भाई बेटी के धिक्कार वो [व, और?] तिलक है, बल्कि अपना बेटी के सेज पर । वो अपना हथियार लेकर के लोग आओ । पतिया पाँच गाँव हिंदू भाई भेज दो ।"

['Salutations to Hindu brothers. We are informing [all] Hindu brothers that [some] Hindu brothers are helping the Musalmans, and providing them a hiding-place [in their houses]. There are such people in Amjhar, Daudnagar, Arwal. Fie upon such Hindu brothers' daughters[?] and a curse upon them: indeed they will sleep with their daughters. All of you must turn out with your weapons. Hindu brothers, send copies of this *patia* to five villages.']

Patia No. 4

"रामजी"

"हिंदू को लाज़िम है । आगे आप लोग को बिदित है के हिंदू और मुसलमान से बैर है कुरबानी के वास्ते । सो आप लोग खूब जानते हैं कि हिन्दू के बाँधकर दरख्त टाँग दिया है और कुरबानी गाँव में घुमाकर कुरबानी कर दिया । इस से हिंदू को बड़ा भारी लजाया है के जीना धिक्कार है । इस से मुसलमान का घर लूट लेवें और मुसलमान को मार दें और पतिया पाँच गो देहात में फैल[।] देवें । न पतिया फैलावें और न लूट मार के [करें?], तो बेटी पर चढ़ें, जोरू के मूत पियें, व भगनी पर चढ़ें । इस से बेहतर है के मातारी के मुसलमान से ब्याह कर दें । थोर [थोड़ा] लिखना बहुत समझना चाहिये । अगर ज्यादा मुसलमान तुम लोग से पिटाने काबिल न हो, तो डुम्राओं के महाराज के यहाँ खबर देओ, तुरंत बन्दूक समेत पल्टन आवेगा ।

"जर्मन के बादशाह, बंगाली, हिंदू छत्री बहुत मदद देता है और कहता है के लड़ो हम तुरंत आवेंगे ।"

'RAMJI'

['Those who are Hindus have no choice. You know that there is a quarrel [enmity] between Hindus and Muslims on the question of *qurbani*. And you know well that a Hindu has [or Hindus have—the local dialect leaves it unclear] been tied up and hanged from a tree, and in *qurbani* villages [villages where *qurbani* customarily took place] the cow has been paraded about and then *qurbani* has been performed. This has brought such shame upon the Hindus that being alive is a curse. Therefore, you must loot the houses of the Musalmans and kill the Musalmans, and circulate five *patias* each in the countryside. If you do not circulate the *patia* and do not loot and kill (the Muslims), then you do mount on your daughter, drink your wife's piss, and mount on your sister's daughter. It would be better indeed to marry your mother to a Musalman. A few words (from us) should be enough to indicate what needs to be done. If there are too many Musalmans for you to handle [literally, 'beat'], send a message to the Dumraon Raj: an armed force will come at once. The German King, the Bengalis, the Hindus, the Chhattris [?, the original has: 'Hindu Chhattri'] are giving great help and they say, 'Fight, we shall be with you immediately'.']

Patia No. 5

"सिरी सोस्ति [श्री स्वस्ति?] मौज़े गोंडपुर काली सिंह जी को लिखी जगदेव सिंह साकिन मौज़े आरा का सलान। आगे हमलोग हिंदू को मिलाप करने चाहिये के जिसमें गौ माता को रच्छा होना चाहिये। के कोई आदमी केराय पेठिया [बाज़ार] गौ बेचने को नहीं जाये। अगर साहेद [शायद?] ले जाने को मुस्तैद कोई आदमी हेठिया [पेठिया] गौ ले जाने को लाज़िम होये, बस्ती में कुल आदमी ताकीद कर दे के पेठिया पर गौ बेचने को नहीं जाये। इस पतिया सुनकर बारह पत्ती बारह गाँव भेज दे। अगर नहीं लिखकर भेजेगा तो पाँच गौ बध करने का पाप होगा। ज़रूर पत्ती भेज दो इत्ती अर्ज़।"

['(Benediction). Jagdev Singh, resident of *mauza* Arrah sends salutations to Kali Singh ji of *mauza* Gondpura. First, it is necessary for all of us Hindus to unite so that Mother Cow may be protected. So that no man may go to the market to sell a cow. If, by chance, someone is willing or coerced into taking a cow to the market, all the residents of the place must warn him that cows are not to be taken for sale in the market. On hearing [*sic.*] this *patia*, you must send twelve copies of it to twelve villages. If you do not write and send them, then you bear the sin of killing five cows. You must certainly send these *patias*, this is our supplication.]

Patia No. 6

"राम"

"आगे आप लोगों को बिदित हो के हिन्दू और मुसलमान से कुरबानी के वास्ते बहुत लड़ाई है। अगर हिन्दू होए तो गौ को उबर ले। इसलिये ताक़ीद किया जाता है के जहाँ मुसलमान को पकड़ो वहाँ जान मार डालो, गाँव लूट लेयो। पतिया पच्चीस गो लिख के अपने देहात में भेज देयो। ना लिखे और ना भेजे से बेटी पर चढ़े, जोरू के मूत पिये, बहिन का दूध पिये, माय को मुसलमान ब्याह

कर दे । हम लोगों को डर नहीं है । जर्मन बादशाह बहुत मदद देता है । वायबर जान मुसलमान ज़िंदा बीज नहीं रहे । जमतगर मुसलमान हो तो डुम्राओं महाराज के हाँ खबर देओ, तुरंत पलटन हर्बे-हथियार से तैयार पहुँचेगा भाई बन्दूक समेत ।"

'RAM'

['First you should all know that there is a great conflict between Hindus and Muslims on the question of *qurbani*. If you are a Hindu, you must liberate the cow. That is why, you are instructed that wherever you catch a Musalman, you must kill him and loot his village. Write out twenty-five copies of this *patia* and spread it in the countryside. He who does not write and send [these copies] will mount on his daughter, drink his wife's urine and his sister's milk, and marry his mother to a Musalman. We are not afraid. The German King is providing great support. Remember that not even the roots [literally, seed] of the Musalmans should survive. If Musalmans are assembled in strength, send word to the Maharaja of Dumraon: an armed force will immediately arrive ready with [sufficient] guns and troops.']

Patia No. 7

'To Hindu brotherhood from Mother Cow, with benediction. Be it known that in Bikramganj Cow is lying bound for being killed. Hindus come to help to save the life of Cow on Kuar 3rd dark fortnight Wednesday. Those reading the letter should issue 5 letters—Oath'

Patia No. 8

'Enmity has taken place between Hindus and Mussalmans. Oh Hindu brothers, help us. The Mussalmans kill cow for *kurbani* on 28–29th September. Those who are Hindus should assemble for cow protection and should write and make over 5 *chitthis* to others. Failing which he will be sinful of killing 5 cows. Place—Birahimpur [Ibrahimpur]'

Patia No. 9

'This *patia* is written on behalf of Barhamdeo Rai and Dharamdeo Rai of Taraon. Pauni Babus★ are informed that on Friday, Mauna will be looted. All on having assembled at Taraon shall have to go to Mauna. Whatever Hindu, on seeing this *patia*, will not come, shall incur the guilt of killing 7 cows.'

(★ The landowners or the dominant family of the village of Pauni. The colonial record notes that a copy of this *patia* was given by Ramjanam

Rai of Taraon to Ramyad Singh, *jeth raiyat* (literally, 'elder cultivator')
of Pauni.)

[*Source*: (IOR) L/P&J/6/1507, *patias* appended with letter no. 168/1-C,
H. McPherson, Chief Secretary, Govt. of Bihar & Orissa to Secretary, Home
Dept., Govt. of India, Patna 11 March 1918, and contained in Judgements
on Trial no. 1 of 1917, 'Emperor *v.* Balmukund Ahir, etc.' and Trial no. 5 of
1917, 'Emperor *v.* Akhaj Ahir, etc.'

Translations are mine, except in the case of the last three *patias* which are
found in the records only in translation. In these, I have retained the spellings
and capital letters of the official translation.]

Appendix II

भारतवर्ष की उन्नति कैसे हो सकती है?

(नवम्बर १८८४ में बलिया के ददरी मेले में आर्य देशोपकारिणी सभा में दिया गया, भारतेन्दु हरिश्चन्द्र का भाषण)

आज बड़े ही आनन्द का दिन है कि इस छोटे से नगर बलिया में हम इतने मनुष्यों को बड़े उत्साह से एक स्थान पर देखते हैं। इस अभागे आलसी देश में जो कुछ हो जाये वही बहुत कुछ है। बनारस ऐसे ऐसे बड़े नगरों में जब कुछ नहीं होता तो यह हम क्यों न कहेंगे कि बलिया में जो कुछ हमने देखा वह बहुत ही प्रशंसा के योग्य है। इस उत्साह का मूल कारण जो हमने खोजा तो प्रगट हो गया कि इस देश के भाग्य से आजकल यहाँ सारा समाज ही ऐसा एकत्र है। जहाँ राबर्ट्स साहब बहादुर ऐसे कलेक्टर हों वहाँ क्यों न ऐसा समाज हो। जिस देश और काल में ईश्वर ने अकबर को उत्पन्न किया था उसी में अबुलफजल, बीरबल, टोडरमल को भी उत्पन्न किया। यहाँ राबर्ट्स साहब अकबर हैं तो मुंशी चतुर्भुज सहाय, मुंशी बिहारीलाल साहब आदि अबुलफजल और टोडरमल हैं। हमारे हिन्दुस्तानी लोग तो रेल की गाड़ी हैं। यद्यपि फर्स्ट क्लास, सेकेंड क्लास आदि गाड़ी बहुत अच्छी-अच्छी और बड़े बड़े महसूल की इस ट्रेन में लगी हैं पर बिना इंजिन ये सब नहीं चल सकतीं, वैसे ही हिन्दुस्तानी लोगों को कोई चलानेवाला हो तो ये क्या नहीं कर सकते। इनसे इतना कह दीजिए "का चुप साधि रहा बलवाना", फिर देखिए हुनमानजी को अपना बल कैसा याद आ जाता है। सो बल कौन दिलावै। या हिंदुस्तानी राजे महाराजे नवाब रईस या हाकिम। राजे-महाराजों को अपनी पूजा भोजन झूठी गप से छुट्टी नहीं। हाकिमों को कुछ तो सरकारी काम घेरे रहता है, कुछ बॉल, घुड़दौड़, थिएटर, अखबार में समय गया। कुछ बचा भी तो उनको क्या गरज है कि हम गरीब गंदे काले आदमियों से मिलकर अपना अनमोल समय खोवैं। बस वही मसल हुई—'तुमें गैरों से कब फुरसत हम अपने गम से कब खाली। चलो बस हो चुका मिलना न हम खाली न तुम खाली।' तीन मेंढक एक के ऊपर एक बैठे थे। ऊपर वाले ने कहा 'जौक शौक', बीचवाला बोला 'गुम सुम', सब के नीचे वाला पुकारा 'गए हम'। सो हिन्दुस्तान की साधारण प्रजा की दशा यही है, गए हम।

पहले भी जब आर्य लोग हिन्दुस्तान में आकर बसे थे, राजा और ब्राह्मणों ही के जिम्मे यह काम था कि देश में नाना प्रकार की विद्या और नीति फैलावें और अब भी ये लोग चाहें तो हिंदुस्तान प्रतिदिन कौन कहे प्रतिछिन बढ़ै। पर इन्हीं लोगों को सारे संसार के निकम्मेपन ने घेर रखा है। "बोद्धारो मत्सरग्रस्ता प्रभवः स्मरदूषिताः।" हम नहीं समझते कि इनको लाज भी क्यों नहीं आती

कि उस समय में जब इनके पुरुषों के पास कोई भी सामान नहीं था तब उन लोगों ने जंगल में पत्ते और मिट्टी की कुटियों में बैठ करके बाँस की नलियों से जो तारा ग्रह आदि वेध करके उनकी गति लिखी है वह ऐसी ठीक है कि सोलह लाख रुपये की लागत की विलायत में जो दूरबीनें बनी हैं उनसे उन ग्रहों को वेध करने में भी वही गति ठीक आती है और जब आज इस काल में हम लोगों को अंगरेजी विद्या की और जगत् की उन्नति की कृपा से लाखों पुस्तकें और हजारों यंत्र तैयार हैं तब हम लोग निरी चुंगी की कतवार फेंकने की गाड़ी बन रहे हैं। यह समय ऐसा है कि आदि तुरकी ताजी सब सरपट्ट दौड़े जाते हैं। सबके जी में यही है पाला हमीं पहले छू लें। इस समय हिंदू काठियावाड़ी खाली खड़े खड़े टाप से मिट्टी खोदते हैं। इनको औरों को जाने दीजिए, जापानी टट्टुओं को हाँफते हुए दौड़ते देखकर भी लाज नहीं आती। यह समय ऐसा है कि जो पीछे रह जायगा फिर कोटि उपाय किए भी आगे न बढ़ सकेगा। इस लूट में, इस बरसात् में भी जिसके सिर पर कमबख्ती का छाता और आँखों में मूर्खता की पट्टी बंधी रहे उन पर ईश्वर का कोप ही कहना चाहिए।

मुझको मेरे मित्रों ने कहा था कि तुम इस विषय पर आज कुछ कहो कि हिन्दुस्तान की कैसे उन्नति हो सकती है। भला इस विषय पर मैं और क्या कहूँ। भागवत में एक श्लोक है ''नृदेहमाद्यं सुलभं सुदुर्लभं प्लवं सुकल्पं गुरु कर्णधारं। मयानुकूलेन नमः खतेरितु पुमान् भविाब्धि न तरेत् स आत्महा।'' भगवान कहते हैं कि पहले तो मनुष्य जनम ही बड़ा दुर्लभ है, सो मिला और उसपर गुरु की कृपा और मेरी अनुकूलता। इतना सामान पाकर भी जो मनुष्य इस संसार-सागर के पार न जाय उसको आत्म हत्यारा कहना चाहिए। वही दशा इस समय हिंदुस्तान की है। अंगरेजों के राज्य में सब प्रकार का सामान पाकर अवसर पाकर भी हम लोग जो इस समय पर उन्नति न करें तो हमारा केवल अभाग्य और परमेश्वर का कोप ही है। सास के अनुमोदन से एकांत रात में सूने रंगमहल में जाकर भी बहुत दिन से जिस प्रान से प्यारे परदेसी पति से मिलकर छाती ठंडी करने की इच्छा थी, उसका लाज से मुँह भी न देखे और बोलै भी न, तो उसका अभाग्य ही है। वह तो कल फिर परदेश चला जायगा। वैसे ही अंगरेजों के राज्य में भी हम कूँए के मेंढक, काठ के उल्लू, पिंजड़े के गंगाराम ही रहैं तो हमारी कमबख्त कमबख्ती फिर कमबख्ती है।

बुहत लोग यह कहैंगे कि हमको पेट के धंधे के मारे छुट्टी ही नहीं रहती बाबा, हम क्या उन्नति करें? तुम्हारा पेट भरा है तुमको दून की सूझती है। यह कहना उनकी बहुत भूल है। इंगलैंड का पेट भी कभी यों ही खाली था। उसने एक हाथ से अपना पेट भरा, दूसरे हाथ से उन्नति की राह के काँटों को साफ किया। क्या इंगलैंड में किसान, खेतवाले, गाड़ीवान, मज़दूर, कोचवान आदि नहीं हैं? किसी देश में भी सभी पेट भरे हुए नहीं होते। किंतु वे लोग जहाँ खेत जोतते बोते हैं वहीं उसके साथ यह भी सोचते हैं कि ऐसी और कौन नई कल या मसाला बनावैं जिसमें इस खेती में आगे से दूना अन्न उपजै। विलायत में गाड़ी के कोचवान भी अखबार पढ़ते हैं। जब मालिक उतर कर किसी दोस्त के यहाँ गया उसी समय कोचवान ने गद्दी के नीचे से अखबार निकाला। यहाँ उतनी देर कोचवान हुक्का पीएगा या गप्प करेगा। सो गप्प भी निकम्मी। वहाँ के लोग गप्प ही में देश के प्रबंध छांटतेहैं। सिद्धांत यह कि वहाँ के लोगों का यह सिद्धांत है कि एक छन भी व्यर्थ न जाय। उसके बदले यहाँ के लोगों को जितना निकम्मापन हो उतना ही बड़ा अमीर समझा जाता है। आलस यहाँ इतनी बढ़ गई कि मलूकदास ने दोहा ही बना डाला ''अजगर करै न चाकरी, पंछी करै न काम। दास

मलूका कहि गए, सबके दाता राम।'' चारों ओर आँख उठाकर देखिए तो बिना काम करने वालों की ही चारों ओर संख्या बढ़ती है। रोजगार कहीं कुछ भी नहीं है। अमीरों की मुसाहबी, दलाली या अमीरों के नौजवान लड़कों को खराब करना या किसी की जमा मार लेना, इनके सिवा बतलाइए और कौन रोजगार है जिससे कुछ रुपया मिले। चारों ओर दरिद्रता की आग लगी हुई है। किसी ने बहुत ठीक कहा है कि दरिद्र कुटुंब इसी तरह अपनी इज्जत को बचाता फिरता है जैसे लाजवती कुल की बहू फटे कपड़ों में अपने अंग को छिपाए जाती है। वही दशा हिंदुस्तान की है।

मर्दुमशुमारी की रिपोर्ट देखने से स्पष्ट होता है कि मनुष्य दिन दिन यहाँ बढ़ते जाते हैं और रुपया दिन दिन कमती होता जाता है। तो अब बिना ऐसा उपाय किए काम नहीं चलेगा कि रुपया भी बढ़े, और वह रुपया बिना बुद्धि न बढ़ेगा। भाइयो, राजा महाराजों का मुँह मत देखो, मत यह आशा रक्खो कि पंडितजी कथा में कोई ऐसा उपाय भी बतलावैंगे कि देश का रुपया और बुद्धि बड़े। तुम आप ही कमर कसो, आलस छोड़ो। कबतक अपने को जंगली, हूस, मूर्ख, बोदे डरपोक पुकरवाओगे। दौड़ो इस घोड़दौड़ में जो पीछे पड़े तो फिर कहीं ठिकाना नहीं है। ''फिर कब राम जनकपुर ऐहैं।'। अबकी जो पीछे पड़े तो फिर रसातल ही पहुँचोगे। जब पृथ्वीराज को कैद करके गोर ले गए तो शहाबुद्दीन के भाई गियासुद्दीन से किसी ने कहा कि वह शब्दभेदी बाण बहुत अच्छा मारता है। एक दिन सभा नियत हुई और सात लोहे के तावे बाण से फोड़ने को रखे गए। पृथ्वीराज को लोगों ने पहले ही से अंधा कर दिया था। संकेत यह हुआ कि जब गियासुद्दीन हूँ करे तब वह तावों पर बाण मारे, चंद कवि भी उसके साथ कैदी था। यह सामान देखकर उसने यह दोहा पढ़ा। ''अबकी चढ़ी कमान, को जानै फिर कब चढ़ै। जिनि चुक्कै चौहान, इक्के मारय इक्क सर।।''
उसका संकेत समझकर जब गियासुद्दीन ने हूँ किया तो पृथ्वीराज ने उसी को बाण से मार दिया। वही बात अब है। अबकी चढ़ी इस समय में सरकार का राज्य पाकर और उन्नति का इतना समय भी तुम लोग अपने को न सुधारो तो तुम्ही रहो। और वह सुधारना भी ऐसा होना चाहिए कि सब बात में उन्नति हो। धर्म में, घर के काम में, बाहर के काम में, रोजगार में, शिष्टाचार में, चाल चलन में, शरीर के बल में, मन के बल में, समाज में, बालक में, युवा में, वृद्ध में, स्त्री में, पुरुष में, अमीर में, गरीब में, भारतवर्ष की सव अवस्था, सब जाति सब देश में उन्नति करो। सब ऐसी बातों को छोड़ो जो तुम्हारे इस पथ के कंटक हों, चाहे तुम्हें लोग निकम्मा कहैं या नंगा कहैं, कृस्तान कहैं या भ्रष्ट कहैं। तुम केवल अपने देश की दीनदशा को देखो और उनकी बात मत सुनो।

अपमान पुरस्कृत्य मान कृत्वा तु पृष्ठतः।
स्वकार्य्य साधयेत् श्रीमान् कार्य्यध्वंसो हि मूर्खता।।

जो लोग अपने को देशहितैषी लगाते हों वह अपने सुख को होम करके, अपने धन और मान का बलिदान करके कमर कस के उठो। देखादेखी थोड़े दिन में सब हो जायगा। अपनी खराबियों के मूल कारणों को खोजो। कोई धर्म की आड़ में, कोई देश की चाल की आड़ में, कोई सुख की आड़ में छिपे हैं। उन चारों को वहाँ वहाँ से पकड़ कर लाओ। उनको बाँध कर कैद करो। हम इससे बढ़कर क्या कहें कि जैसे तुम्हारे घर में कोई पुरुष व्यभिचार करने आवै तो जिस क्रोध से उसको पकड़कर मारोगे और जहाँ तक तुम्हारे में शक्ति होगी उसका सत्यानाश करोगे। उसी तरह इस समय

जो जो बातैं तुम्हारे उन्नति पथ में काँटा हों उनकी जड़ खोद कर फेंक दो । कुछ मत डरो । जब तक सौ दो सौ मनुष्य बदनाम न होंगे, जात से बाहर न निकाले जायेंगे, दरिद्र न हो जायेंगे, कैद न होंगे वरंच जान से न मारे जायेंगे तब तक कोई देश भी न सुधरेगा ।

अब यह प्रश्न होगा कि भाई हम तो जानते ही नहीं कि उन्नति और सुधारना किस चिड़िया का नाम है । किसको अच्छा समझें? क्या लें, क्या छोड़ें? तो कुछ बातैं जो इस शीघ्रता में मेरे ध्यान में आती हैं उनको मैं कहता हूं । सुनो—

सब उन्नतियों का मूल धर्म है । इससे सबके पहले धर्म की ही उन्नति करनी उचित है । देखो, अँगरेजों की धर्मनीति और राजनीति परस्पर मिली है, इससे उनकी दिन दिन कैसी उन्नति है । उनको जाने दो, अपने ही यहाँ देखो! तुम्हारे यहाँ धर्म की आड़ में नाना प्रकार की नीति, समाज-गठन, वैद्यक आदि भरे हुए हैं । दो एक मिसाल सुनो । यही तुम्हारा बलिया का मेला और यहाँ स्नान क्यों बनाया गया है? जिसमें जो लोग कभी आपस में नहीं मिलते, दस दस पाँच-पाँच कोस से वे लोग साल में एक जगह एकत्र होकर आपस में मिलें । एक दूसरे का दुःख सुख जानें । गृहस्थी के काम की वह चीजैं जो गाँव में नहीं मिलती, यहाँ से ले जायें । एकादशी का व्रत क्यों रखा है? जिसमें महीने में दो एक उपवास से शरीर शुद्ध हो जाय । गंगा जी नहाने जाते हो तो पहिले पानी सिर पर चढ़ा कर तब पैर डालने का विधान क्यों है? जिसमें तलुए से गरमी सिर में चढ़कर विकार न उत्पन्न करे । दीवाली इसी हेतु है कि इसी बहाने साल भर में एक बेर तो सफाई हो जाय । यही तिहवार ही तुम्हारी मानो म्युनिसिपालिटी है । ऐसे ही सब पर्व सब तीर्थ व्रत आदि में कोई हिकमत है । उन लोगों ने धर्मनीति और समाजनीति को दूध पानी की भाँति मिला दिया है । खराबी जो बीच में भई है वह यह है कि उन लोगों ने ये धर्म क्यों मानन लिखे थे, इसका लोगों ने मतलब नहीं समझा और इन बातों को वास्तविक धर्म मान लिया । भाइयो, वास्तविक धर्म तो केवल परमेश्वर के चरणकमल का भजन है । ये सब तो समाजधर्म है जो देशकाल के अनुसार शोधे और बदले जा सकते हैं । दूसरी खराबी यह हुई कि उन्हीं महात्मा बुद्धिमान ऋषियों के वंश के लोगों ने अपने बाप दादों का मतलब न समझकर बहुत से नए नए धर्म बनाकर शास्त्र में घर दिए । बस सभी तिथि व्रत और सभी स्थान तीर्थ हो गए । सो इन बातों को अब एक बेर आँख खोलकर देख और समझ लीजिए कि फलानी बात उन बुद्धिमान ऋषियों ने क्यों बनाई और उनमें देश और काल के जो अनुकूल और उपकारी हो उसको ग्रहण किजिए । बहुत सी बातें जो समाज विरुद्ध मानी हैं किंतु धर्मशास्त्रों में जिनका विधान है उनको चलाइए । जैसे जहाज का सफर, विधवा विवाह आदि । लड़कों कों छोटेपन ही में ब्याह करके उनका बल, वीर्य, आयुष्य सब मत घटाइए । आप उनके माँ बाप हैं या उनके शत्रु हैं । वीर्य उनके शरीर में पुष्ट होने दीजिए, विद्या कुछ पढ़ लेने दीजिए, नोन, तेल, लकड़ी की फिक्र करने की बुद्धि सीख लेने दीजिए, तब उनका पैर काठ में डालिए । कुलीन प्रथा, बहुविवाह को दूर कीजिए । लड़कियों को भी पढ़ाइए, किंतु उस चाल से नहीं जैसे आजकल पढ़ाई जाती हैं जिससे उपकार के बदले बुराई होती है । ऐसी चाल से उनको शिक्षा दीजिए कि वह अपना देश और कुलधर्म सीखें, पति की भक्ति करें, और लड़कोंको सहज में शिक्षा दें । वैष्णव शक्ति इत्यादि नाना प्रकार के मत के लोग आपस में वैर छोड़ दें । यह समय इन झगड़ों का नहीं । हिंदू, जैन, मुसलमान सब आपस में मिलिए । जाति में कोई चाहे ऊँचा हो चाहे नीचा हो सबका आदर कीजिए, जो जिस

योग्य हो उसको वैसा मानिए । छोटी जाति के लोगों को तिरस्कार करके उनका जी मत तोड़िए । सब लोग आपस में मिलिए ।

मुसलमान भाइयों को भी उचित है कि इस हिन्दुस्तान में बस कर वे लोग हिंदुओं को नीचा समझना छोड़ दें । ठीक भाइयों की भाँति हिंदुओं से बरताव करें । ऐसी बात, जो हिन्दुओं का जी दुखाने वाली हो, न करें । घर में आग लगै तब जिठानी-दौरानी को आपस में डाह छोड़कर एक साथ वह आग बुझानी चाहिए । जो बात हिन्दुओं को नहीं मयस्सर है वह धर्म के प्रभाव से मुसलमानों को सहज प्राप्त हैं । उनमें जाति नहीं, खाने, पीने में चौका चूल्हा नहीं, विलायत जाने में रोक टोक नहीं । फिर भी बड़े ही सोच की बात है मुसलमानों ने अभी तक अपनी दशा कुछ नहीं सुधारी । अभी तक बहुतों को यही ज्ञान है कि दिल्ली लखनऊ की बादशाहत कायम है । यारो! वे दिन गए । अब आलस हठधर्मी यह सब छोड़ो । चलो हिंदुओं के साथ तुम भी दौड़ो, एकाएक दो होंगे । पुरानी बातें दूर करो । मीरहसन की मसनवी और इंदरसभा पढ़ाकर छोटेपन ही से लड़कों को सत्यानाश मत करो । होश सम्हाला नहीं कि पट्टी पार ली, चुस्त कपड़ा पहना और गजल गुनगुनाए । ''शौक तिफ्ली से मुझे गुल की जो दीदार का था । न किया हमने गुलिस्ताँ का सबक याद कभी'' । भला सोचो कि इस हालत में बड़े होने पर वे लड़के क्यों न बिगड़ेंगे । अपने लड़कों को ऐसी किताबें छूने भी मत दो । अच्छी से अच्छी उनको तालीम दो । पिनशिन और वजीफा या नौकरी का भरोसा छोड़ो । लड़कों को रोजगार सिखलाओ । विलायत भेजो । छोटेपन से मिहनत करने की आदत दिलाओ । सौ सौ महलों के लाड़ प्यार दुनिया से बेखबर रहने की राह मत दिखलाओ ।

भाई हिंदुओ! तुम भी मतमतांतर का आग्रह छोड़ो । आपस में प्रेम बढ़ाओ । इस महामंत्र का जप करो । जो हिंदुस्तान में रहे, चाहे किसी रंग किसी जाति का क्यों न हो, वह हिंदू । हिंदू की सहायता करो । बंगाली, मरट्टा, पंजाबी, मदरासी, वैदिक, जैन, ब्राह्मो, मुसलमान सब एक का हाथ एक पकड़ो । कारीगरी जिसमें तुम्हारे यहाँ बढ़ै, तुम्हारा रूपया तुम्हारे ही देश में रहे वह करो । देखो, जैसे हजार धारा होकर गांगा समुद्र में मिली है, वैसे ही तुम्हारी लक्ष्मी हजार तरह से इंग्लैंड फरासीस, जर्मनी, अमेरिका को जाती है । दीआसलाई ऐसी तुच्छ वस्तु भी वहीं से आती है । जरा अपने ही को देखो । तुम जिस मारकीन की धोती पहने हो वह अमेरिका की बनी है । जिस लकिलाट का तुम्हारा अंगा है वह इंग्लैंड का है । फरासीस की बनी कंघी से तुम सिर झारते हो और वह जर्मनी की बनी चरबी की बत्ती तुम्हारे सामने जल रही है । यह तो वही मसल हुई कि एक बेफिकरे मँगनी का कपड़ा पहिनकर किसी महफिल में गए । कपड़े की पहिचान कर एक ने कहा, 'अजी यह अंगा फलाने का है' । दूसरा बोला, 'अजी टोपी भी फलाने की है ।' तो उन्होंने हँसकर जवाब दिया कि 'घर की तो मूछैं ही मूछैं हैं ।' हाय अफसोस, तुम ऐसे हो गए कि अपने निज के काम की वस्तु भी नहीं बना सकते । भाइयो, अब तो नींद से चौंको, अपने देश की सब प्रकार उन्नति करो । जिसमें तुम्हारी भलाई हो वैसी ही किताब पढ़ौ, वैसे ही खेल खेलो, वैसी ही बातचीत करो । परदेशी वस्तु और परदेशी भाषा का भरोसा मत रखो । अपने देश में अपनी भाषा में उन्नति करो ।

*(Translation: Bharatendu Harischandra's lecture, delivered at a meeting orga-
nized by the Arya Deshopkarni Sabha at the Dadri mela in Ballia, in
November 1884).*

It is a day of great happiness today as we see so many enthusiastic people
gathered at a single place in this small town of Ballia. Even a small achievement is a great one for this luckless, lazy land. When nothing happens
even in great cities like Banaras, it is only fair to say that what we see in
Ballia today is highly praiseworthy. When I thought about the basic
reason for today's enthusiasm, I realized that all sections of society are
gathered here because of the country's [present] good fortune. Where
there is a Collector like Mr Roberts, why should there not be a gathering
like this? The country and the age that produced Akbar also produced Abul
Fazl, Birbal and Todar Mal. If Mr Roberts is Akbar here, Munish Chatur-
bhuj Sahai, Munshi Biharilal and so on are Abul Fazl and Todar Mal.
The people of Hindustan are like a train. Even if there are many fine and
expensive First Class and Second Class coaches in a train, it cannot run
without an engine: in the same way, the people of Hindustan are capable
of great achievements if they can find someone to move them.

You have but to say to them [as people said to Hanuman], 'Why are
you standing by silently, O Brave One?': then observe how quickly
Hanuman remembers his strength. But who will give them (remind
them of) that strength? Either the Rajas, Maharajas, Nawabs and notables
of Hindustan, or the Government officials. The Rajas and Maharajas
cannot take the time off from their worship, their eating and their useless
gossip. The officials are tied down to some extent by government work,
and to some extent by balls, horse-racing, theatres and newspapers. Even
if they have any time left, what need do they have to waste it in meeting
us poor, dirty, black people. It is like the old saying:

'When will you be free of others? When will I be free of sorrow?
Let us recognize the end (of our relationship), for neither of us is free'.

There were three frogs sitting one on top of another. The one on top said
'Wow!, the middle one said 'Oh!', the one at the bottom said 'Ow!' (I'm
finished!)'. The condition of the common people of Hindustan is like
that of the last one—'I'm finished.'

Earlier, when the Aryan people came and settled in Hindustan, it was
the duty of the kings and Brahmans to spread knowledge and morality
among the people. If these people so desire, Hindustan can still advance
not only day by day but minute by minute. But these very people have

been overtaken by (every kind of) idleness. 'The learned ones are stricken with jealousy and filled with malice' [and therefore able to do nothing]. I cannot understand why they are not ashamed: their ancestors who had no resources could, sitting in the jungle in makeshift dwellings and using bamboo pipes, work out the same results as are obtained today through the use of telescopes made in England at a cost of sixteen lakh [i.e. sixteen hundred thousand] rupees; and today, when thanks to English education and world progress we have lakhs of books and thousands of instruments, all we are becoming is a (municipal) dump-truck. This is an age in which the old and the young are all rushing forward. Everyone is determined to try and reach the goal first. At this time these Hindu puppets are standing idly by, digging the ground with their toes. Let alone others, (the Hindus) are not ashamed to see that even the midget Japanese have joined the race, (and are) panting as they run. The times are such that whoever is left behind now will, try as he might, never be able to catch up again. It can only be called God's wrath if one continues to be ridden by ill-luck and ignorance in this season of plenty.

My friends have asked me to say something today about how India can progress. What else can I say on this subject? There is a verse in the *Bhagavat (Purana)** . . . God says that, first of all, to be born a human being is itself great good fortune: in addition you have your *guru's* blessings and my favour. If with all this, a person can still not attain liberation, he can only be called a murderer of the self. That is precisely the condition of India today. If even under British rule, when we are given every kind of resource and opportunity, we do not progress, it can only be because of our (bad) fate and the wrath of God. When, with the permission of her mother-in-law, the bride goes into the inner chambers, at dead of night, to see the beloved (who has) returned after an age and to satisfy her longing, but is unable out of shyness to look at him or speak a word, that can only be called her misfortune. For he will go away again on the morrow. So also, if under British rule, we remain trapped like frogs in a well, an owl on its branch, or a bird in a cage, then we deserve all that we suffer.

Many people will say that they are never finished with the problem of earning their daily bread, how can they think of Progress? They whose hunger is satisfied, they can think of other things. But this kind of thinking is wrong. England too was hungry once. She fed herself with one hand, and cleared the path of progress with the other. Do you think there are no peasants, farmers, hackney-and cab-drivers, or labourers in England? There is no country in the world where everyone is well fed. But those

(*Bharatendu quotes the Sanskrit verse and then gives its sense in Hindi. I have only translated the Hindi here.)

people (of England) think, even as they farm, of new machines and fertilizers that will enable them to double their productivity. Even coach-drivers read newspapers in England. As soon as the master gets off to enter a friend's house, the driver takes out his newspaper from under his seat. Here, the coach-driver will smoke a hukka [pipe] or gossip during that time. That gossip [conversation] too is idle. People in England discuss the affairs of the country even in their small talk. The underlying principle is this, that not a second should be wasted. On the contrary, in India idleness is considered a sign of high status. Laziness became so rooted here that Malukdas put it into verse:

'The snake does nothing to earn its living, the bird neither:
Malukdas says: (Fear not,) Ram will take care of everyone.'

Wherever one looks, one only sees a growing number of people who have no work. There is no trade [or employment] for anyone. What lucrative employment can one find except to be the flunkeys or agents of the rich, or spoil their youthful sons or get hold of someone's savings. Poverty is enveloping all of us. Someone has rightly said that the poor family seeks to save its honour in exactly the same way as the daughter-in-law of a modest household tries to cover her body in ragged clothes. That is the condition of India today.

The census reports show clearly that the population of India is continually increasing and its wealth continually declining. Consequently, it is essential now to find ways of increasing our wealth: and that cannot be done without intelligence. Brothers, do not look to the Rajas and Maharajas [to deliver you], don't expect the Pandit to come up with some *mantra* [charm] that will increase the country's wealth and its intelligence. Pull up your socks yourselves. Stop being lazy. How long do you wish to be called primitive, uncivilized, ignorant and lazy? Move: whosoever falls behind in this (horse-)race is lost forever. 'When will Ram come to Janakpur again.' [When will another such opportunity arise?] If you fall back this time, you can only reach the nether-world. When Prithviraj [Chauhan] was captured by the Ghors people from the north-west, of a region near Kandhar], then someone told Shahabuddin's brother, Ghiyasuddin, that he [Prithviraj] was accomplished at aiming arrows at a sound. A gathering was called one day, and seven iron shields placed in position to be broken by arrows. Prithviraj had already been blinded. Prithviraj was told that at Ghiyasuddin's command, he should shoot at the shields [which would be sounded]. The poet, Chand, was also a prisoner along with Prithviraj. Seeing the preparations, he recited this verse: 'The arrow that is strung now, may be the last you string: Let the Chauhan not err: one arrow, one target.' Prithviraj understood the poet's words, and when Ghiyasuddin gave the signal by a sound, Prithviraj shot Ghiyasuddin with his arrow.

It is the same situation today. If you cannot reform yourselves even under the government of the (British) Sarkar and in this time of progress, then stay as you are. That reform, too, should be such that it leads to progress in every area. In religion, in domestic work, in work outside the home, in one's profession, in etiquette, in behaviour, in bodily strength, in intellectual energy, in society, in the child, in youths, in the old, in women, in men, in rich and in poor, in every aspect of society, in every caste, in all the country, let there be improvement. Discard all those practices that may prove to be obstacles in this path, even if people call you a wastrel or uncultured, a Christian or corrupt (for so doing). Consider only the fallen state of your country; pay no heed to such taunts.

'Accept the insults, disregard honour:
Dear Sir, one should achieve one's goal; to turn away from one's, endeavour—that is foolishness.'

Those who call themselves well wishers of the country should forget their personal happiness, sacrifice their wealth and (notions of) honour, and come forward (to work for the country). Their example will transform everything in a short while. Search for the roots of the evils in our society. Some are hidden behind a screen of religion, some in the ways of our country, some are lost in pleasure-seeking. Bring all these people out of their corners, arrest and tie them up. If anyone enters your house with adulterous intentions, would your anger not lead you to catch and beat him and, with all your strength, destroy him? In the same way, you must uproot and throw out anything that is an obstacle in the path of progress. Do not be afraid. No country can possibly be reformed without a hundred or two hundred people being dishonoured, thrown out of caste, impoverished, arrested or killed.

The argument will then be put forward that we are people who do not know what Progress and Reform mean: how can we judge what is right, what we should adopt, what discard? In response, let me say a few things that immediately come to mind. Listen:

Dharma [religion, a religious life] is the source of all progress. Hence it is *dharma* that must be first improved [elevated]. See how closely the religion and politics of the English are tied together, and how this leads to continuous advance. Or leave them aside, look at your own land. Your country is full of different kinds of morality, social organization, medicinal systems, etc., all of which assume the guise of religion. Let me give you one or two examples. What is the reason for this very *mela* of yours in Ballia, and this bathing festival. So that those who would never meet otherwise people from a distance of five or ten *kos* [ten or twenty miles] may meet at one place once a year, share each other's joys and sorrows, and buy those things that are needed for the home but unavailable in the village. Why does one have the fast of Ekadashi [the eleventh day of each fortnight of the lunar month]? So that the body is cleansed by fasting once or twice in the month. When one bathes in the Ganga, why does one put some water on one's head before putting one's feet in the river. So that the heat in the sole [of one's foot] does not rise to the head and produce a disorder. Diwali [the festival of lights] is celebrated so that, by this means, houses may be cleaned at least once a year. These festivals are like a municipality to you. In this way, every auspicious occasion, every pilgrimage is a contrivance [for some 'rational' end]. The needs of religion and the needs of society have been mixed up here like milk and water. The distortion that has since arisen is that people have forgotten the reasons why these rituals [practices] were introduced, and they have come to look upon these things as true religion. Brothers, true religion is nothing but worship at the feet of God. The rest is social religion which may be sought out and changed according to the changing needs and circumstances of the country. The other distortion that has occurred is this, that the descendants of those Mahatmas, wise men and *rishis* [who introduced many of these practices] have failed to comprehend what their ancestors were aiming at, and have made up numerous new rituals [practices] and written them into the Shastras. Therefore, you must understand once and for all why a particular practice was introduced by those wise *rishis*. You must accept those rituals [practices] that are consistent with the needs of the country and the times. There are many practices that are considered to be against social order, but that are sanctioned [under certain conditions] by the Dharmashastras: they must be allowed. Examples are voyages overseas, widow marriage, etc. Do not reduce the strength, potency and age of your boys by marrying them off at an early age. Are you their parents or their enemies? Let their virility grow, let them study a little, let them learn to fend for themselves before putting their feet in the stocks. End the practice of multiple marriages among [men of] respectable families. Educate the girls too, but not in the way they are educated today which leads to their fall rather than their improvement. Educate them with intelligence so that they may learn their duties to their country and their family, worship their husbands, and naturally [with ease] teach their sons. Vaishnavas, Shaktas and other groups and sects should end their mutual bickering. This is not the time for such quarrels. Hindus, Jains, Musalmans must all get together. Respect everyone, whether of high caste or low, and treat people according to their abilities. Do not look down upon and demoralize people of low caste. Everyone must unite.

It is meet for Muslim brothers, too, who have now settled in Hindustan, that they should stop thinking of the Hindus as inferior, and instead relate to them exactly as brothers do. They should give up all practices that hurt the feelings of the Hindus. When a house catches fire the elder and younger daughter-in-law have to forget their mutual jealousy and co-operate to put out the fire. Certain things that Hindus are unable to have, the Muslims obtain easily because of their religion. They have no caste divisions, no [wide-ranging] restrictions on cooking and eating, no restrictions on travelling abroad. It is remarkable that they have, even so, not yet reformed themselves. Many of them still think that the thrones of Delhi and Lucknow continue to exist. Friends! Those days are gone. It is time to bid farewell to laziness and intransigence. Come, join the Hindus [in the race for progress]; for two are stronger than one. Do not ruin boys in their childhood by reading them Mir Hasan's *masnawi* and *Indra-sabha* [poems and tales of desire and romance]. The consequence is that these boys have scarcely learned to think independently when they fashion their hair, wear tight clothes and begin humming love-poetry—'Since infancy I have longed for the flower. I failed to remember the lesson taught by the garden.'

Can one legitimately expect that, with this kind of training, those boys will not go wrong when they grow up? Don't let your boys even see such books. Give them the best possible education. Give up your faith in pensions and stipends and government service. Train your boys in some profession [trade]. Send them to England [for study and training]. Train them to work hard from childhood. Do not show them the path of pleasure-seeking in secluded mansions, which blinds them to the condition of the world.

Brother Hindus! You too must give up your insistence on minute details of [religious] belief and practice. Promote fellowship among all [who live here], and recite the following *mahamantra*. Whoever lives in Hindustan, whatever his colour or caste, is a Hindu. Help the Hindus. Bengalis, Marathas, Panjabis, Madrasis [*sic*], Vaidiks, Jains, Brahmos, Musalmans should all join hands. Do those things which will increase the country's industry and help to keep its wealth within the land. Just as the Ganga spreads out into a thousand estuaries before joining the sea, so your wealth flows to England, France, Germany, America by a thousand routes. Even an object as trifling as a match-stick is imported from there. Just look at yourselves. The *dhoti* [loin-cloth] that you wear is made of *markin* [thick, unbleached cloth] made in America. The upper-garment that you wear is made of long-cloth made in England. You comb your hair with a comb made in France, and that candle (made of fat) that is burning before you is made in Germany. It is like the story of the happy-go-lucky man who went to a cultural gathering in borrowed clothes. Recognizing the clothes, someone said, 'I say, that upper-garment belongs to so-and-so'? Another remarked, 'The cap is so-and-so's'? Our protagonist laughed and responded, 'It's only my moustaches that are my own?' Alas! you have come to this that you cannot make for yourselves even the [little] things required for your personal needs. Brothers! Now at least, you must awaken, and do all you can for the progress of the country. Read only those books, play only those games, have only those conversations that advance your interests [i.e. the interests of your country]. Give up the use of foreign goods and a foreign language. Work for the progress of your country through your own language.'

[*Source*: Hemant Sharma, ed., *Bharatendu Samagra* (Varanasi, 1987), pp. 1010–13. Translation mine. I owe thanks to Dr Asha Pandey for help in translating the Sanskrit phrases and verses contained in the speech.]

Bibliography

The sources for any study such as this are likely to be numerous and wide-ranging. I list below those documents and works that I have drawn from most heavily.

Manuscript Sources: Official

India Office Library and Records, London
    Bengal Criminal Judicial Proceedings
    Bengal Revenue Board of Commissioners (Customs)
    Board's Collections (early nineteenth century)
    Government of India. Home Proceedings (Confidential)
    Home Miscellaneous Records
    Public and Judicial Proceedings
    Revenue and Agriculture Dept. Famine Proceedings

National Archives of India, New Delhi
    Government of India, Home Dept (Political) Proceedings
    Report on Native Newspapers (also called Selections from the
        the Vernacular Newspapers) for Bengal, Bihar, North-
        Western Provinces and Oudh, and Punjab

West Bengal State Archives, Calcutta
    Board of Trade (Commercial) Proceedings

Bihar State Archives, Patna
    Government of Bihar and Orissa, Political (Special) Depart-
        ment files. Freedom Movement Papers

Uttar Pradesh Regional Archives, Allahabad
    Records of the Commissioner of Gorakhpur
    Records of the Commissioner of Varanasi
    Records of the Magistrate of Gorakhpur
    (especially, Judicial and Revenue departments)

Gorakhpur Commissioner's Record Room, Gorakhpur
Files in Judicial (Criminal), Administration, Revenue and
General Departments
Azamgarh Collectorate, Azamgarh
Files in Judicial, Revenue and General departments
Police Office, Azamgarh
Local Intelligence Unit records relating to selected towns and
villages

Manuscript Sources: Unofficial

Abdul Majid's 'Diary'/'Notes' (Courtesy, Sheikh Wazir Ahmad
of Muhalla Pura Sofi, Mubarakpur, Azamgarh)
Arzi ba Adalat Gorakhpur, ba silsila-i-jang Mubarakpur
(17 April 1813; courtesy, Qazi Atahar, Muhalla Haidarabad,
Mubarakpur, Azamgarh)
Macdonnell, A. P., papers (Ms. Eng. Hist. d. 235, Bodleian
Library, Oxford)
Malaviya, Madan Mohan, papers, selections from (courtesy, late
Pandit Padmakant Malaviya, Allahabad)
Oldham, C. E. A. W., papers (Mss. Eur. D. 1167, India Office
Library and Records, London)
'Petition of the Hindu Inhabitants of Mhow to Secretary of State
for India in Council' with numerous Appendices (n.d., 1893?;
courtesy, D. N. Pandey, Mau, Azamgarh)
Rajendra Prasad, papers (National Archives of India, New Delhi)
Waqeat-o-Hadesat: Qasba Mubarakpur
(1880s) (courtesy, Qazi Atahar, Mubarakpur, Azamgarh)

Printed Sources: Official Publications

Census of India. Reports and tables for North-Western Provinces
and Oudh, and Bengal, Bihar and Orissa, 1881–1921
District Gazetteers, UP and Bihar (various dates: late nineteenth
and early twentieth centuries)
Papers connected with the Industrial Conference held at Naini Tal (1907)
*Parliamentary Papers. House of Commons. Accounts and Papers vol. 44,
pt. 3.* (1857–58)

Report on the Railway-Borne Traffic of the North-Western Provinces and Oudh (annual; later nineteenth century)

Selections of Papers from the Records of the East India House relative to Revenue, Police, Civil and Criminal Justice under the Company's Government in India (London, 1820)

Selections from the Records of the Government of India, Home, Revenue and Agriculture Dept. no. CLXXX. Papers relating to the Crime of Cattle-Poisoning (Calcutta, 1881)

Selections from the Records of Government, North-Western Provinces. Part XL (Allahabad, 1864)

Settlement Reports for various districts of UP and Bihar (nineteenth and early twentieth century)

Statistical, Descriptive and Historical Account of various districts in UP and Bihar

Trial of Basantpur Riot Case in The Court of the Sessions Judge of Saran, 1893 (Calcutta, 1894)

Committee Reports

All Parties Conference 1928. Report of the Committee appointed to determine the Principles of the Constitution for India (Allahabad, 1928)

A History of the Hindu-Muslim Problem in India. From the Earliest contacts up to its present phase with suggestions for its solution. Being the report of the Committee appointed by the Indian National Congress (Karachi Session 1931) to enquire into the Cawnpore Riots of March 1931 (Allahabad, 1933); reprinted with some deletions in N. G. Barrier, ed., *Roots of Communal Politics* (Delhi, 1976)

Indian Statutory Commission. Report and Evidence. vols. I-IV (London, 1930).

Reforms Enquiry Committee 1924. Report. (Calcutta, 1925)

Newspapers

Abhyudaya
Aaj
Leader
Pioneer

Printed Documents (containing writings and
speeches of prominent individuals)

Banerjea, S. N., *Speeches and Writings of Hon. Surendra Nath Banerjea
Selected by Himself* (G. A. Natesan and Co., Madras, n.d.)
Bharatendu Granthavali, ed. Brajratna Das (Kashi, 2010 Vikram)
Bharatendu ke Nibandh, ed. Kesari Narayan Shukla (Varanasi, 1952)
Bharatendu Samagra, ed. Hemant Sharma (Varanasi, 1987)
Congress Presidential Addresses, ed. A. M. Zaidi, vol. II (Delhi, 1986)
Dar, B. N., *Pandit Bishan Narain Dar's Speeches and Writings*, ed.
H. L. Chatterji, vol. I (Lucknow, 1921)
Gandhi, M. K., *Collected Works of Mahatma Gandhi* (Ahmedabad,
various dates)
Lala Lajpat Rai: Writings and Speeches, ed. V. C. Joshi (Delhi, 1966)
Malaviya, Madan Mohan, *Malaviyaji ke Lekh*, ed. Padmakant
Malaviya (Delhi, 1962)
———— *Speeches and Writings of Pandit Madan Mohan Malaviya*
(G. A. Natesan and Co., Madras, n.d.)
Mohammad Ali, *Select Writings and Speeches of Maulana Mohammad
Ali*, ed. Afzal Iqbal, vol. I (Lahore, 1944; second edn. 1969)
———— *Selections from Moulana Mohammad Ali's Comrade*, ed.
R. A. Jafri (Lahore, 1965)
Nehru, Jawaharlal, *A Bunch of Old Letters* (Bombay, 1958)
———— *Selected Works of Jawaharlal Nehru* (Delhi, various dates)
Patel, Vallabhbhai, *Sardar Patel's Correspondence*, ed. Durga Das,
vol. 3 (Ahmedabad, 1972)
Pratapnarain Granthavali, ed. Vijayshankar Mall (Kashi, 1958)
Syed Ahmad Khan, *Writings and Speeches of Sir Syed Ahmad Khan*,
ed. Shan Mohammad (Bombay, 1972)
Vidyarthi, Ganesh Shankar, *Kranti ka Udghosh. Ganesh Shankar
Vidyarthi ki kalam se*, ed. Radhakrishna Awasthi, two vols.
(Kanpur, 1978)

Other Contemporary Publications, including Early Histories

Ambedkar, B. R., *What Congress and Gandhi have done to the Untouch-
ables* (Bombay, 1946)
Beni Prasad, *The Hindu-Muslim Question* (Allahabad, 1941)
Buyers, W., *Recollections of Northern India* (London, 1848)

Cape, Rev. C.P., *Benaras, The Stronghold of Hinduism* (London, n.d.)

Chatterji, A. C., *Notes on the Industries of the United Provinces* (Allahabad, 1908)

Crooke, W., *The North-Western Provinces of India* (1897; Karachi, 1972)

———— *The Tribes and Castes of the North-Western Provinces and Oudh*, 4 vols. (1896)

———— *Religion and Folklore of Northern India* (Oxford, 1926)

Cummings, J. (ed.), *Political India* (London, 1932)

Dar, B. N., *An Appeal to the English Public on Behalf of the Hindus of the North-Western Provinces and Oudh, with an Appendix containing a full and detailed account of the Cow-killing riots in the United Provinces and All Public Documents on the same.* (Lucknow, 1893)

Dayanand Saraswati, Swami, *Satyarth Prakash* (Delhi, 1969; English translation, 'Light of Truth'; Allahabad, n.d).

———— *Swami Dayanand* (Arya Samaj Publication, Calicut, 1924)

Dutt, R. C., *A History of Civilisation in Ancient India based on Sanskrit Literature*, two vols. (Calcutta, 1899)

Elliot, H. M., *Memoirs on the History, Folklore and Distribution of the Races of the North-Western Provinces of India, vol. I* (London, 1869)

Ewen, J., *Benares: A Handbook for Visitors* (Calcutta, 1886).

Freedom Struggle in Uttar Pradesh, Source Material. vol. IV, ed. S. A. A. Rizvi (Lucknow, 1959)

Fremantle, S. H., *Report on the Supply of Labour in the United Provinces and in Bengal* (1906).

Forrest, G. W. (ed.), *Selections from the Minutes and other official writings of the Honourable Mountstuart Elphinstone, Governor of Bombay* (London, 1884)

Grierson, G. A., *Bihar Peasant Life* (1885; reprinted Delhi, 1975)

———— *Notes on the District of Gaya* (Calcutta, 1893)

Heber, R., *Narrative of a Journey through the Upper Provinces of India, from Calcutta to Bombay, 1824–25. vol. I* (London, 1828)

Hoey, W., *A Monograph on Trade and Manufactures in Northern India* (Lucknow, 1880)

Hunter, W. W., *The Indian Musalmans* (third edn, London, 1876; reprinted Delhi, 1969)

Ibbetson, D., *Punjab Castes* (1916; reprinted Delhi, 1974)

Irwin, H. C., *The Garden of India* (London, 1880)

Kabir, H., *The Indian Heritage* (1946; third edn 1955)

Kennedy, J., *Life and Work in Benares and Kumaon, 1839–1877* (London, 1884)

Malcolm, Sir John, *Political History of India from 1784–1823 in two volumes* (London, 1826)

Mill, James and Wilson H. H., *The History of British India (in ten volumes) vol. VII* (London, 1858)

Mookerji, Radhakumud, *The Fundamental Unity of India* (London, 1914)

Mufid-ul-Mominin by Irshad-ul-Mominin (pseud.) translated into Urdu from Persian by Maulvi Murtaza (Lucknow, n.d.)

Nehru, J., *Autobiography* (1936; London, 1947)

———— *Discovery of India* (London, 1951; Bombay, 1961)

———— *Glimpses of World History* (1934; second edn., Bombay, 1962)

Narendra Dev, Acharya, *Socialism and The National Revolution* (Bombay, 1946)

Prinsep, J., *Benares Illustrated* (three series of drawings) (London, 1831, 1832, 1834)

Reade, E. A., *Benares City* (Government Press, Agra, 1858)

Russell, R. V. and Hiralal, *Tribes and Castes of the Central Provinces of India* (London, 1916)

Sherring, M. A., *Benares. The Sacred City of the Hindus* (1868; reprinted Delhi, 1975)

———— *Hindu Tribes and Castes as represented in Benares* (1872; reprinted Delhi, 1974)

Silberrad, C. A., *A Monograph on cotton fabrics produced in the North-Western Provinces and Oudh* (Allahabad, 1898)

Sitaramayya, P., *The History of the Indian National Congress 1885–1935* (Madras, 1935)

Sleeman, W. H., *Journey Through the Kingdom of Oude, vol. II* (London, 1858)

Sundarnanda, Swami, *Hindustan and Untouchability* (1922; second ed. Delhi, 1945)

Tewari, Venkatesh Narain, *Musalmanon ki Dalit Jatiyan* (Lucknow, 2002 Vikram)

Yadav, D. S., *Ahir Itihas ki Jhalak* (Lucknow, 1915)

Younghusband, F., *Dawn in India* (London, 1930)

Secondary Works

Ahmed, Aziz, *Islamic Modernism In India and Pakistan, 1857–1964* (London, 1967)

Ahmed, Rafiuddin, *The Bengal Muslims 1871–1906. A Quest for Identity* (Delhi, 1981)

Alam, Muzaffar, *The Crisis of Empire in Mughal North India: Awadh and the Punjab 1707–48* (Delhi, 1986)

Altekar, A. S., *History of Benares from pre-historic times to the present* (Benares, 1937)

Anderson, B., *Imagined Communities. Reflections on the origin and spread of Nationalism* (London, 1983).

Archer, W.G., *The Vertical Man. A Study in Primitive Indian Sculpture* (London, 1947)

Ashraf, K. M., *Life and Conditions of the People of Hindustan* (second ed. Delhi, 1970)

Bagchi, A. K., 'De-industrialisation in Gangetic Bihar, 1809–1901' in B. De (ed.) *Essays in Honour of Professor S.C Sarkar.* (Delhi, 1978).

Barrier, N. G. (ed), *The Census in British India. New Perspectives* (Delhi, 1981)

Bayly, C. A., *The Local Roots of Indian Politics. Allahabad 1880–1920* (Oxford, 1975)

——— 'The Pre-history of "Communalism"? Religious Conflict in India, 1700–1860', *Modern Asian Studies*, 19, 2, (1985)

——— *Rulers, Townsmen and Bazars. North Indian Society in the Age of British Expansion, 1770–1870* (Cambridge, 1983)

Bose, Sugata, 'The Roots of Communal Violence in Rural Bengal. A Study of Kishoreganj Riots, 1930', *Modern Asian Studies*, 16, 3 (July, 1982)

Brass, Paul, *Language, Religion and Politics in North India* (Cambridge, 1974)

Chakrabarty, D., 'Communal Riots and Labour: Bengal's Jute Mill-Hands in the 1890s', *Past and Present*, no. 91 (May, 1981)

Chakravarti, U. and Haksar, N., *The Delhi Riots. Three Days in the Life of a Nation* (Delhi, 1987)

Chandra, Bipan, *Communalism in Modern India* (Delhi, 1984)

——— *Nationalism And Colonialism in Modern India* (Delhi, 1979)

Chandra, Sudhir, 'Communal Elements in Late Nineteenth

Century Hindi Literature', *Journal of Arts and Ideas*, no. 6 (1984)
—— 'The Cultural Component of Economic Nationalism: R. C. Dutt's "The Lake of Palms"', *Indian Historical Review*, XII, 1–2 (1985–86)

Chatterjee, Partha, *Nationalist Thought and the Colonial World: A Derivative Discourse?* (Delhi and London, 1986)

Chaturvedi, Sitaram, *Mahamana Pandit Madan Mohan Malaviya* (Varanasi, 1936)

Cohn, Bernard, *An Anthropologist among the Historians and other Essays* (Delhi, 1987)

Das, Veena (ed.), *Communities, Riots, Survivors. The South Asian Experience* (forthcoming)

Dasgupta, R., 'Factory Labour in Eastern India: Sources of Supply 1855–1946', *Indian Economic and Social History Review*, XIII, 3 (1976)

Dharampal, *Civil Disobedience and Indian Tradition. With Some Early nineteenth century documents* (Varanasi, 1971)

Dumont, L., *Religion/Politics and History in India* (Paris, 1970)

Engineer, A. A., *Communal Riots in Post-Independence India* (Hyderabad, 1984)

Fox, Richard, *Lions of the Punjab. Culture in the Making* (California, 1985)

Freitag, S., 'Religious Rites and Riots: From Community Identity to Communalism in North India, 1870–1940' (University of California, Berkeley, Ph.D. thesis 1980)
—— 'Sacred Symbol as Mobilising Ideology. The North Indian Search for a "Hindu" Community', *Comparative Studies in Society and History*, 22, 4 (October, 1980)

Gilmartin, D., *Empire and Islam. Punjab and the Making of Pakistan* (Delhi, 1989)

Gould, H. A., 'The Emergence of Modern Indian Politics: Political Development in Faizabad. Part I. 1884–1935', *Journal of Commonwealth and Comparative Politics*, XII, 1 (March, 1974)

Goyal, D. R., *Rashtriya Swayam Sevak Sangh* (Delhi, 1979)

Guha, R., *An Indian Historiography of India. A Nineteenth Century Agenda and its Implications* (Calcutta, 1988)
—— *Elementary Aspects of Peasant Insurgency in Colonial India* (Delhi, 1983)

——— (ed.), *Subaltern Studies*, vols. I–VI (Delhi, 1982–89)

Gulliver, P. H., (ed.), *Tradition and Transition in East Africa* (London, 1969)

Hardy, P., *Muslims of British India* (Cambridge, 1972)

Heitler, R., 'The Varanasi House-Tax Hartal of 1810–11', *Indian Economic and Social History Review*, IX, 3 (September, 1972)

Jha, Hetukar, 'Lower-Caste Peasants and Upper-Caste Zamindars in Bihar, 1921–25', *Indian Economic and Social History Review*, XIV, 4 (1977)

Jones, Kenneth W., *Arya Dharma. Hindu consciousness in Nineteenth Century Punjab* (California, 1976)

Jordens, J. T. F., *Dayanand Saraswati. His Life and Ideas* (Delhi, 1978)

Joshi, Chitra, 'Bonds of Community, Ties of Religion: Kanpur Textile Workers in the early twentieth century', *Indian Economic And Social History Review*, 22, 3 (1985)

Kaviraj, Sudipto, 'Imaginary History', Nehru Memorial Museum and Library 'Occasional Paper', second series, no. VII (September, 1988)

Kedourie, E., *Nationalism* (London, 1969)

Krishnamurthy, J., 'De-industrialisation in Gangetic Bihar during the nineteenth century. Another look at the evidence', *Indian Economic and Social History Review*, XXII, 4 (October–December, 1985)

Kumar, Nita, 'Popular culture in Urban India. The Artisans of Banaras 1884–1984' (Ph.D. thesis University of Chicago, 1984, since then published as a book by Princeton University Press)

Kumar, Ravinder, *Essays in the Social History of Modern India* (Calcutta, 1983)

Lelyveld, D., *Aligarh's First Generation. Muslim Solidarity in British India* (Princeton, 1978)

Lütt, J., *Hindu Nationalismus in Uttar Prades 1867–1900* (Stuttgart, 1970)

Macpherson, K., *The Muslim Microcosm; Calcutta 1918–35* (Wiesbaden, 1974)

Madan, T. N., 'Secularism in its place', *Journal of Asian Studies*, 46, 4 (1987)

Malik, Hafeez, *Sir Saiyyad Ahmad Khan and Muslim Modernisation in India and Pakistan* (New York, 1980)

Masoom Raza, Rahi, *Aadha Gaon* (Delhi, 1966)

McLane, John, *Indian Nationalism and the Early Congress* (Princeton, 1977)

Mehta, Deepak, 'A Sociological Study of Gandhian Institutions. Work, Weavers and the Khadi and Village Industries Commission'. (Ph.D. thesis, Sociology Department, Delhi University, 1990).

Meinecke, F., *Cosmopolitanism and the National State* (1907; translated, Princeton, 1963)

Melson, R. and Wolpe, H., eds., *Nigeria. Modernisation and the Politics of Communalism* (Michigan, 1971)

Metcalf, B., *Islamic Revival in British India. Deoband 1860–1900* (Princeton, 1982)

———— 'Nationalist Muslims in British India. The Case of Hakim Ajmal Khan', *Modern Asian Studies*, 19, 1 (1985)

Mujeeb, M., *The Indian Muslims* (London, 1967)

Nagar, P., *Lala Lajpat Rai. The Man and His Ideas* (Delhi, 1977)

Nandy, Ashis, 'An Anti-Secularist Manifesto', *Seminar*, no. 314

Page, D., *Prelude to Partition. All-India Muslim Politics, 1921–1932* (Delhi, 1981)

Pandey, G., *The Ascendancy of the Congress in Uttar Pradesh, 1926–34* (Delhi, 1978)

Rizvi, S. A. A., *Shah Wali-ullah and his times* (Canberra, 1980)

Robb, P., 'Officials and Non-Officials as Leaders in Popular Agitations. Shahabad 1917 and other conspiracies' in B. N. Pandey (ed.), *Leadership in South Asia* (Delhi, 1977)

Robinson, F., *Separatism Among Indian Muslims. The Politics of the United Provinces' Muslims, 1860–1923* (Cambridge, 1974)

Rowe, W. L., 'The New Chauhans. A Caste Mobility movement in North India', in J. Silverberg (ed.) *Social Mobility in the Caste System in India* (The Hague, 1968)

Saberwal, S., *India: The Roots of Crisis* (Delhi 1986)

Said, E., *Orientalism* (London, 1980)

Sangari, K. and Vaid, S., eds., *Recasting Women. Essays in Colonial History* (Delhi, 1989)

Sarda, Har Bilas., *Life of Dayanand Saraswati* (Ajmer, 1946)

Sarkar, Sumit, *The Swadeshi Movement in Bengal, 1903–8* (Delhi, 1973)

Sarkar, Tanika, 'Communal Riots in Bengal' in Mushirul Hasan (ed.) *Communal and Pan-Islamic Trends in Colonial India* (Delhi 1981)

Sen, Amiya, 'Hindu Revivalism in Action; The Age of Consent Bill Agitation in Bengal', *Indian Historical Review*, VII, 1–2 (July 1980 to January 1981)

Shukul, K. N., *Varanasi Down The Ages* (Patna, 1974)

Siddiqi, M. H., 'History and Society in a Popular Rebellion: Mewat, 1920–33', *Comparative Studies in Society And History*, 28, 3 (1986)

Singh, K., *History of the Sikhs vol. II. 1839–1964* (Princeton, 1966)

Smith, W. C., *Modern Islam in India* (London, 1946)

Srivastava, A. L., *The First Two Nawabs of Oudh* (Lucknow, 1967)

Stokes, E. T., *The English Utilitarians and India* (London, 1959)

Suntharalingam, R., *Politics and Nationalist Awakening in South India, 1852–91* (Arizona, 1974)

Tarachand, *Influence of Islam on Indian Culture* (Allahabad, 1963)

Thapar, R., et al., *Communalism and the Writing of Indian History* (Delhi, 1969)

Thompson, E. P., *The Making of the English Working Class* (Pelican, London, 1968)

Turner, V. (ed.)., *Colonialism in Africa, 1870–1960, vol. 3, Profiles of Change* (Cambridge, 1971)

White, Hayden., *The Content of the Form* (Baltimore, 1987)

Yang, A., 'Sacred Symbol and Sacred Space in Rural India. Community Mobilisation in the "Anti-cow killing" Riot of 1893', *Comparative Studies in Society and History*, 22, 4 (1980)

Index